Macrobiotics:
Yesterday & Today

Macrobiotics

Yesterday and Today

By Ronald E. Kotzsch, Ph.D.

Japan Publications, Inc.

Photography Credits:

Nippon C. I., photograph Nos. 1–17, 18–21, 24, 25, 40, 45–47, 54; Steven Baratz, 28; Mari Kennedy, 29–31, 41–44; Robert Schilling, 32; Alfred Lion, 33; Margaret Landsman, 35; Deborah A. Bowman, 36; George P. Karageorgos, 39.

Published by
JAPAN PUBLICATIONS, INC., Tokyo and New York

Distributors:
UNITED STATES: *Kodansha International/USA, Ltd., through Harper & Row, Publishers, Inc., 10 East 53rd Street, New York, N. Y. 10022.* SOUTH AMERICA: *Harper & Row, Publishers, Inc., International Department.* CANADA: *Fitzhenry & Whiteside Ltd., 195 Allstate Parkway, Markham, Ontario L3R 4T8.* MEXICO AND CENTRAL AMERICA: *HARLA S. A. de C. V. Apartado 30–546, Mexico 4, D. F.* BRITISH ISLES: *International Book Distributors Ltd., 66 Wood Lane End, Hemel Hempstead, Herts HP2 4RG.* EUROPEAN CONTINENT: *Fleetbooks, S. A., c/o Feffer and Simons (Nederland) B. V., Rijnkade 170, 1382 GT Weesp, The Netherlands.* AUSTRALIA AND NEW ZEALAND: *Bookwise International, 1 Jeanes Street, Beverley, South Australia 5007.* THE FAR EAST AND JAPAN: *Japan Publications Trading Co., Ltd., 1–2–1, Sarugaku-cho, Chiyoda-ku, Tokyo 101.*

First edition: September 1985

LCCC 84–081358
ISBN 0–87040–611–6

Printed in U.S.A.

For my Father,
Ernst Reinhold Kötzsch,
a lover of books.

Zeitz, Germany, 2 August 1900
Westbrook, Connecticut, 19 February 1985

Contents

Introduction   *9*

1. Ekken Kaibara: The Grandfather of Macrobiotics   15

2. Sagen Ishizuka: The Founder of Modern Macrobiotics   21

3. George Ohsawa: The Early Years (1893–1929)   37

4. George Ohsawa: The First Sojourn in the West (1929–1936)   51

5. George Ohsawa: Return to Japan in Crisis (1936–1939)   65

Photographic Interlude for *Macrobiotics Yesterday*   *81–88*

6. George Ohsawa: The War Years (1940–1945)   89

7. George Ohsawa: Hope for a New Japan and a New World
    (1945–1953)   103

8. George Ohsawa: The World Journey of the Penniless
    Samurai (1953–1966)   119

9. George Ohsawa: The Man and the Legacy   141

10. After the Master: PART ONE: America   163

Photographic Interlude for *Macrobiotics Today*   *193–208*

11. After the Master: PART TWO: Japan   209

8

12. After the Master: PART THREE: Europe and Elsewhere   219

13. The Gospel According to Kushi   235

14. Macrobiotics in Western Culture   251

15. Prospects for the Future   275

     Bibliography   *281*

     Index   *289*

Introduction

At a party in Boston in late 1966 I met a young man recently arrived from San Francisco. Sporting a ponytail and a Navajo headband, and with a glassy, faraway look in his eye, he was quite unlike anyone I had met during my just completed four years at Princeton. When he asked what I thought of "Mary Jane," I thought he was referring to the striking blonde in the corner. "I think she plays field hockey for Smith," I blithely replied.

This enigmatic retort inspired confidence, and shortly he was telling me about another California novelty, the "Zen Macrobiotic diet." In just ten days, he asserted, it would "clean out" my body. When he added that it consisted only of unpolished rice and soybean paste soup, I allowed that it indeed seemed likely to effect great changes. When we parted he slipped me a bagful of dried leaves, and told me to smoke them when I wanted to relax. I placed this on my spice shelf and forgot about it. I also forgot about the macrobiotic diet. I did not feel the need for a gastronomic roto-rooter.

A few months later I met a young couple who were actually on the diet. Vermont homesteaders and devotees of an Indian guru, they were also a bit outside the graduate school ambience in which I then lived. Still, they seemed healthy and intelligent enough, and when they told me that the diet involved a philosophy and a total way of life I was intrigued. Ever since learning as a teenager that "chocolate breeds zits," I had a vague sense that food and health were related. I had, a few months before, become a vegetarian for "ethical" reasons. When they told me macrobiotics had originated in Japan and was being taught in Boston by a Japanese man, I decided to see him. I was at the time in a doctoral program at Harvard studying Japanese language and religion.

Early in January 1967 I went with my Indian roommate and fellow vegetarian to the home of Michio Kushi [久司道夫] in Brookline. Homi, a native of Bombay and unused to New England weather, was wearing his British greatcoat. It was a massive garment, worn no doubt, by some colossal British general during the Crimean campaigns, and was known affectionately as "the bulletproof coat." As we entered the house, a modest frame residence on a quiet side street, he started to remove the coat, then refrained. The house was cold. It was also sparsely furnished, very clean, and pervaded by a churchlike and silent peacefulness. Mrs. Kushi, tiny, with long luxuriant black hair, and holding her youngest child, then two, directed us to the living room. Mr. Kushi, in stocking feet and wearing a somewhat shiny black suit, sat cross-legged in a tattered and outsized easy chair. To our hasty self introductions, he replied:

"Ah so, what can I do for you?"

10

"We're interested in finding out about macrobiotics," I said.

Very deliberately Kushi took out a cigarette, lit it, and holding it at a cocked angle took a deep puff. "Your general condition is all right," he said to me. "Your mother and father are very strong and you have avoided drugs."

"Oh," I said incisively before settling into long silence. Meanwhile, shivering in the seat beside me, Homi had discreetly donned his wool cap.

Kushi spoke with us for over an hour, presenting ideas which, though I had never heard them before, seemed strangely familiar, and eminently reasonable as well.

"It is natural for man to be healthy and happy, just as the animals in the forest and the birds in the air are without sickness and without cares. . . .

It is entirely up to us if we are healthy or sick, happy or sad. We are entirely responsible. By the way we live and especially by the way we eat and drink we are creating ourselves and our lives. If we become ill it is our own fault and the only real way to cure it is through our own will . . . .

There is an order in nature, and we should follow that, especially when we choose our food. Just as the animals eat the food which grows around them, we should eat the foods of our environment. If we eat foods that come from the tropics, like sugar or citrus fruits, we are violating this natural order. We become sick and are reminded of Nature's Order by our sickness. Sickness is our teacher . . . .

There is no disease which is incurable. We can reverse anything if we are able to change the way we eat and live and think."

By the time we left, my head was spinning with these and other new ideas. I knew I had come upon something that was for me of great importance. Homi was less impressed. "Bloody cold house!" he commented.

The next day I visited the macrobiotic food shop, Erewhon, a tiny subterranean storefront on Newbury Street in Boston. Its rough wood shelves were filled with bags of brown rice, whole wheat flour, sea vegetables and other exotica. I returned home with a supply of these foods and emptied my cupboards of the old. Soon I began to attend Kushi's twice-weekly lectures. Thus began my study and practice of macrobiotics, which has continued with varying levels of intensity and success for over eighteen years.

Early in 1967 the macrobiotic community in America was very small, with tiny groups in New York, California and Boston. The community which had grown up around the Kushis consisted of several dozen people, most of them young and on the periphery of polite society. Perhaps eight or ten would gather for Kushi's evening talks in a back room at the Arlington Street Church. Erewhon had a weekly gross sales of about two hundred dollars. The only literature available were several books published on the West Coast, including *Zen Macrobiotics* and *The Book of Judgment* by George Ohsawa [櫻沢如一] and a spiral bound cookbook called *Zen Cookery*. The diet was little known to the American public. To the extent that it was known, it had a negative image. Several unfortunate incidents had given it the nickname "the killer diet." In the medical and popular press it was attacked as leading to scurvy, rickets and general malnutrition.

Much has changed since then. The Boston macrobiotic community now consists of several thousand people and is the focus for a thriving national and international movement. The Kushi Institute trains lecturers, cooks, and counselors, and draws students from around the nation and the world. The East West Foundation organizes public programs and coordinates a growing network of East West Centers across North America, throughout Western Europe and in many other parts of the world. The *East West Journal* with a circulation of 60,000 is the largest of a number of macrobiotic magazines published here and in other countries. There are scores of books and pamphlets in many languages on the philosophy and practice of macrobiotics. Kushi has become internationally known as a lecturer and health consultant, whose worldwide seminars attract large audiences. Once maligned, the diet is now recognized by many medical authorities as healthful and perhaps therapeutic. Articles testifying to its ability to prevent and even cure serious illness have appeared in *Life* magazine and *The Reader's Digest*. Those who follow the diet include doctors and other professionals, movie stars, artists, as well as typical working men and women. In short, macrobiotics has grown greatly, has become respectable, and is slowly becoming part of the mainstream culture, here and abroad.

In the process, the principles and practice of macrobiotics have become better known and understood, even by much of the general public. However, the historical origins and development of the movement are at best vaguely known, even among long-time macrobiotic people. When and how did it begin? What role did George Ohsawa play? How has Kushi affected its direction? About questions like these there is little information. Instead there is a swelling body of legends and misinformation. Often I hear questions such as: Is it true Ohsawa was active in the Indian independence movement? Did he really steal his wife Lima away from her husband in the middle of the night? Is it true that Kushi is an extraterrestrial? (The answers incidentally are "No," "Kind of," and "Who cares," in that order.) The reason is simple. Until now there has been no systematic presentation of the origins and history of the macrobiotic movement. *Macrobiotics: Yesterday and Today* is an attempt to fill that void.

The research for this book began in December 1967, though I was scarcely aware of it at the time. I traveled to Japan with a vague plan to study Japanese culture and macrobiotics. The sojourn did not have a very auspicious beginning. I arrived in Tokyo and was met by the aunt of a Japanese friend. A lavish welcome feast had been prepared and was attended by several generations of family and friends. At that time pointy-nosed barbarians were in short supply in Japan and thus liable to receive unexpected honors.

As I walked into the banquet room I had my first minor setback. Unused to the fact that Japanese doors are made for Japanese, I went sailing in confidently at full height (five foot-eleven), with a smile of inane sophistication. Unfortunately, the doorway was only five-eight, and I finished my grand entrance hand to my head, ashen-faced, and listing heavily to port. I recovered quickly, but another poignant moment lay ahead.

A long, low table was spread with an array of rice, fish, sea vegetables and deep-fried vegetables, plus innumerable bottles of beer. The first and main course seemed to be beer, however, and soon I was seated happily amongst friends, chattering fluently (I thought) in Japanese. I was quite pleased with myself for sitting so long on my heels and for making such good use of my language study. After about two hours, I rose to pay a visit to the *o-te-arai* [お手洗], the "honorable place where one washes one's honorable hands." When I had stood to my full height and was towering like a Teutonic colossus over my hosts and the table, I made a rather sobering discovery. Two hours of *seiza* [正座] (correct sitting) had deadened every nerve below my navel. I stared terror-stricken at my insensate legs which could neither move nor support me. Chirping an apology I tried to sit down again, but before I could, I fell full length onto the table. Rice bowls, beer bottles, tea cups and chopsticks clattered and flew in all directions. There were titters from children, shrieks of terror from young ladies, knowing grunts from grandparents. I floundered like a beached whale before being hauled off and cleaned up.

In the weeks following I learned that in informal situations sitting seiza (for men at least) is an option, not a requirement. One can sit cross-legged or lean discreetly to one side. In formal situations, though, these more comfortable alternatives are a bit declassé. Realizing that twenty minutes of seiza paralyzed me, I was worried that the next year would be spent toppling onto unsuspecting university professors, *aikido* teachers, Zen masters and other hosts. I had a problem.

Fortunately, I discovered a book of Ekken Kaibara, [貝原益軒] a prominent philosopher of the 17th century and, it turned out, a forefather of macrobiotics. *Yōjōkun* [養生訓] or "The Classic for Nurturing Life," contains advice for maintaining health and achieving long life. It includes such valuable tidbits as:

"One should not sleep with one's mouth facing downward."

"It is not a good idea to drool while sleeping."

"People over forty should keep their eyes closed when they have nothing to do."

"One should not urinate or defecate in the direction of sun, moon, stars, towards the north pole or toward religious shrines or on sunlit or moonlit ground."[1]

It also contains a section entitled "So that the legs do not go to sleep." This reads:

"It sometimes happens that a person has difficulty standing up abruptly, and even falls over in an attempt because his legs have gone to sleep from sitting too long in a formal manner before a person of high rank and while attending his lord at a mansion. It behooves one therefore before attempting to stand up, to wiggle and flex the big toe vigorously and repeatedly. The feet will be prevented from going to sleep and one will not have to worry about falling down."[2] This advice proved to be helpful, if not foolproof, and I had a fairly successful visit in Japan.

The second stage of research began in 1976 when I resolved to finish my graduate studies. To receive a doctoral degree in History of Religions from Harvard I had only to write a dissertation. This was to be a substantial and original research project in Japanese religion. I brushed up my Japanese and flew to Japan early in 1977. I had a romantic notion of doing something on Japanese folk religion, of finding a remote village where the people spent their days digging happily in the fields and their nights by the hearth recounting Buddhist legends and ancient warrior epics. I traveled widely through the hinterlands of Japan, but found only that the "folk" were riding tractors and motorbikes and were wiling away the evenings eating ice cream in front of the TV.

It occurred to me finally that to discover the true spirit of Japan I might study macrobiotics and particularly the life and thought of its 20th century pioneer, George Ohsawa. My first researches corroborated this and I began a project which was to take four years. I began to collect materials relating to Ohsawa, about eighty volumes in all. I interviewed his wife Lima and many of his students and associates. I read enough of the materials to make a proposal to my professors back at Harvard. Receiving a tentative approval, I headed home after eighteen months with several boxes of books and papers.

I settled in Boston and for the next year and a half read and took notes on the books I had brought back. Ninety-five percent of them were in Japanese, of course, and probably had never been read before by a Westerner. Another eighteen months' organizing and writing resulted in a doctoral thesis titled "George Ohsawa and the Japanese Religious Tradition." This focused on Ohsawa's relation to traditional Japanese religion and, though not a biography, it included much biographical information. It also contained much about Ohsawa's teachers and predecessors. When the work was finished and approved I happily laid it aside, not expecting to have much to do with it again. In the two or three years following though, the several hundred requests I received for copies of the thesis showed that there was certainly interest in the history of macrobiotics.

In October 1983, Japan Publications, Inc. asked me to write a history of the movement. I agreed, and the third stage of research began. I visited macrobiotic centers on the West Coast, and then spent five weeks in Japan gathering information on Ohsawa and also on the movement there since his death in 1966. I spent six weeks in Europe touring the major macrobiotic centers there. I also pursued in depth a study which had long interested me: the occurrence of macrobiotic ideas in the philosophy and medicine of Western culture. And everywhere I went I talked with people about the future direction of the macrobiotic movement.

The result of all this is *Macrobiotics: Yesterday and Today*. There are four main sections containing a total of fifteen chapters. The first section (Chapters 1 and 2) covers the ancient and early modern roots of macrobiotics. The second (Chapters 3 through 9) follows the life and career of George Ohsawa, who dominated the movement until his death in 1966. This is to date the only detailed account in a language other than Japanese of Ohsawa's life and the development of his thought. It is an interesting story, full of adventure and drama, high hopes, bitter disappointments, success and failure.

The third section (Chapters 10 through 13) focuses on the development of macrobiotics since Ohsawa's death. It treats in detail the thought of Michio Kushi, who has emerged as Ohsawa's successor in the world macrobiotic movement. The fourth section (Chapter 14) looks at the philosophical and medical-nutritional traditions of the West for parallels to macrobiotics. A final brief chapter raises some issues regarding the future development of the movement.

This, then, is a history, but of a particular sort. It is written from within the movement and cannot claim that pure objectivity which is the ideal of academic study. My advantage is being able to write with a degree of understanding and sympathy. My disadvantage is being tempted to overlook shortcomings, failures and ambiguities. I have tried to cultivate the one and to avoid the other. Macrobiotics,

14

like everything in this world, has its Yin and Yang dimension, its front and back. I hope I have portrayed it in its fullness, complete with warts and moles as well as beauty marks.

This is also a general history, painted with broad rather than fine strokes. Since it covers a great deal, and since it is the first of its kind, it is not terribly detailed. Also, inevitably there will be some errors in fact. I apologize for both these failings and wish future historians well in correcting them. At the same time I hope I have not embarrassed my learned and kind mentors at Harvard who directed me through so much of this work. To them—Dr. Wilfred Cantwell Smith, Prof. Masatoshi Nagatomi, Dr. John Carman, and Dr. Jane I. Smith—I am very thankful. I am deeply grateful as well to Lima Ohsawa, Dr. and Mrs. Hiroshi Maruyama, Alcan Yamaguchi, Shuzo Okada and Yuko Okada, Michio and Aveline Kushi, Herman and Cornellia Aihara, Masahiro Hashimoto, Jackson M. Smith, Shizuko Yamamoto, to my principal proofreaders—Stevan Golden, Linda Roszak Elliot and Mary Colson—and their numerous helpers; and above all, to my parents and family (Anita, Edward, Christine and Ronny) who tolerated with love and patience my long presences as well as absences.

Each of these persons, along with countless friends in the international macrobiotic community, contributed by kindnesses great and small to the completion of this work.

RONALD E. KOTZSCH
The New North Church
Hingham, Massachusetts
18 March 1985

---

[1] Kaibara, Ekken, *Yōjōkun: Japanese Secrets of Good Health*, Tokuma Shoten Publishing Company, Tokyo, 1974
[2] Ibid.

1.

Ekken Kaibara:
The Grandfather
of Macrobiotics

As any history, that of macrobiotics begins best at the beginning. And as with any history, the beginning is very hard to find. Behind the obvious pioneers of the near past are lines of influence that stretch into the distant past and to the very dawn of history. So to choose a starting point for any narrative is by necessity somewhat arbitrary.

George Ohsawa (1893–1966) is generally regarded as the founder of macrobiotics. While he gave his distinctive imprint to the movement and did much to introduce it to the world, he was not its originator. Ohsawa himself often cites Sagen Ishizuka [石塚左玄] (1850–1910), a Japanese physician, as his inspiration and teacher. And though Ishizuka formulated many of the concepts which are the basis of modern macrobiotics, much of his teaching as well was a gift of the past. From him the lines of transmission stretch back to the dawn of civilization in East Asia, to the time of the *I Ching* [易經] ("The Book of Changes") and the *Nei Ching* [内經], ("The Yellow Emperor's Classic of Internal Medicine").

Between these ancient days and the modern era there were various philosophers and men of medicine, both in Japan and China, who helped transmit the seeds of macrobiotic thought. However, I have chosen Ekken Kaibara (1630–1716), in part from personal gratitude, to begin our story.

Kaibara was born just eight years before Japan began its policy of seclusion. After a century of contact with the West, during which the introduction of Christianity and of firearms caused much disruption, the Japanese decided to end all but token intercourse with the outside world. Kaibara was attracted particularly to classical Chinese learning (already an integral part of Japanese culture), and became a leading figure in the Neo-Confucian School.

Originally, Confucianism was a social and political philosophy. It emphasized the need for harmony and stability in all human affairs and taught an ethic of gratitude, subservience and responsibility to achieve this. All relations in family, community and nation were seen as hierarchic. To those above one should give absolute obedience and respect. To those below one should show paternal kindness and concern. If each person acted according to his place and duty, harmony and peace would prevail.

To this original teaching the "new" Confucianists added Taoist ideas about how the universe began and how it operates. Referring to the *Tao Te Ching* [道德經] ("The

Way and Its Power"), they called the universal absolute the Tao. This primal One-ness expresses itself as two opposite but complementary energies, Male and Female, Yin and Yang. From their interaction all things are created, and according to their laws all things move and change.

Kaibara embraced both this social philosophy and metaphysics. In his book *Onna Daigaku* [女大学] ("The Great Teaching For Women") he explains the role and duties of the feminine sex according to Confucian ideas. As a woman is fickle and liable to get into trouble she should, from girlhood through old age, be subservient to some male relation. As a girl she should defer to her father, as a wife to her husband, and as an old woman to her son. She should cultivate the virtues of modesty, quietness, gentility and purity. Such is her natural place and duty in human society.[1]

Kaibara was also an avid observer of the natural and human world. He traveled widely and wrote pioneering works on botany, geography, herbal medicine, and on popular manners and morals. At the age of eighty-three, he retired from active life, and, free to sift through a lifetime of experience and learning, wrote the *Yōjōkun*. It has been translated into English under the title *Japanese Secrets of Good Health* and includes the old sage's views on health and longevity.

He begins by asserting that physical well-being and long life are the natural condition of mankind. In Chapter One he writes:

"... it is only natural that one who has learned health preservation and who applies it, will become strong in body, will shirk off all diseases, and live to the age Providence meant him to live to, and enjoy it too ... (!)"[2]

A bit later he says simply, "One who is continent about food, drink, sex and sleep, takes a walk in the morning and in the evening will not get sick."[3]

For Kaibara human life is meant not only to be long and healthy, it is meant to be enjoyable. He writes:

Saints always expound on the delights of living. A poor fool like me can hardly understand the mind of saints, but at least I know that delight is something that Heaven and Earth meant living things to have, and something that man is born possessed of.[4]

And sickness, like health, is something which humankind creates. Quoting the *Tao Te Ching*, Kaibara observes "One's life is in one's own hands." Sickness comes only when one has willfully abused oneself. "Illness never comes without reason."[5] Yet more pointedly he observes, quoting an ancient Chinese sage, that "Calamity arises from what we say and illness comes in through the mouth."[6]

With this basis Kaibara offers various suggestions about staying healthy. Control of the principal passions and desires is essential. Lack of self-control, and indulgence in food, sleep, talk, and sex lead to trouble. Moderation and self-discipline are the keys to health and long life.

Kaibara discourses at length on the subject of food—its choice, preparation, and manner of eating. Among the things he counsels:

Eat rice as a daily, staple food.

Eat fresh vegetables when they are in season.

Eat simple light meals of foods that are clean, freshly prepared, peaceful in quality and balanced in terms of the five tastes: sweet, sour, salty, bitter and pungent.

Avoid heavy, greasy, overcooked, raw or unripe foods.

Avoid hard and fatty meat. Some lean poultry and game may be eaten sparingly. They decrease the life span, however, and can be dispensed with entirely.

Fish should be eaten whole if possible and cooked with ginger and soy sauce in order to neutralize poisons.

Above all do not overeat. Eat only to 80 to 90 percent of capacity, until just before one feels full.

Before eating remember with gratitude the farmers and others who have produced the food, the parents and benefactors who have supplied it, and those who have cooked and served it. Remember too those who are without food, and one's unworthiness before such blessings.

Never eat while angry or worried.

Do not eat between meals or immediately before going to bed.

After eating take a short walk to stimulate circulation. Massage the stomach and the abdomen lightly to encourage digestion.

For Kaibara restraint of the other desires is also important. One should get enough sleep but not too much. Excess sleep causes the vitality *ki* [氣] or "life energy" to stagnate. One should observe regularity in waking and sleeping, rising early and retiring at mid-evening. One should also control the desire to talk unnecessarily. Endless, pointless conversation depletes the vital energy and leads to instability of temperament and restlessness of mind.

Kaibara's suggestions about sexual activity are yet more complex and strict. Citing another Chinese source of antiquity he says that for a person between twenty and thirty years of age sexual intercourse is permissible once every four days; for a person thirty to forty once every eight days; forty to fifty once every sixteen days; fifty to sixty once every twenty days; and thereafter once a month. It is very important to conserve sexual energy since it deeply affects the function of the kidneys, and the kidneys are the seat of vital energy for all the other organs.

In addition, one must observe rules of propriety regarding time and place. One should not engage in sex during solar and lunar eclipses, lightning storms, high winds, downpours, sweltering heat, biting cold, earthquakes or the appearance of rainbows. It is also forbidden ten days before and ten days after the winter solstice; when one is tired, hungry, or thirsty; when one has eaten or drunk a great deal; and when one is angry, sad, worried or surprised. Sex should not be enjoyed in sunlight, moonlight, starlight, or before a religious shrine.

One is tempted, of course, to ask Kaibara and his ancient Chinese killjoys exactly when and where one is allowed to have sex. If all the restrictions are observed one may indulge only on cloudless overcast evenings during the new moon in a thatched cave opening to the northwest. It should be noted with gratitude that while many of Kaibara's teachings on food have passed into modern macrobiotics, his "bedroom rules" have been largely ignored.

Kaibara offers other practical advice on maintaining health and vitality. Daily physical exercise is important, including, at the least, a walk after each meal. One should avoid sitting or lying down too much. The vital energy must move. Also, to activate this energy one can receive a daily finger-pressure massage, or practice *dō-in* [導引], a method of self-massage imported from China. This is an excellent way to begin the day. Kaibara also recommends a deep breathing exercise to be carried out twice a day. This, he says, replaces stale, dirty air in the body with clean and fresh air.

"The correct position one should assume is that of lying stretched out and face up, with legs extended, the eyes closed, the hands firmly clasped, and a distance of about five inches between the two feet and the same distance between each elbow and the torso . . . . One should breathe in through the nose a lot of air from the outside. Once a lot of air has been accumulated . . . one should exhale slowly through the mouth."[7]

Kaibara also recommends keeping one's immediate environment orderly and clean.

"If the outside environment is clean, the inside too is cleansed through contact with it. Improving the inside from the outside makes eminent sense. One should keep one's living quarters free from dust and dirt. Physical exercise and the cleansing of mind and heart thus gained are essential to health."[8]

In case of illness one should first try fasting or a very simple diet as a cure. If that fails, then acupuncture, moxibustion (burning pellets of plant fiber on the appropriate *tsubo*, [壺] key energy points) and herbal remedies may be tried as a last resort.

Thus Kaibara offers a wealth of practical advice to keep the body well and vital. Yet he was deeply aware too of the relationship between body and mind. For true health one must cultivate a healthy emotional and mental life. Just as the physical desires should be controlled, the emotional tendencies must also be disciplined. One must avoid an excess of any of the seven emotions: anger, worry, pensiveness, sadness, fear, surprise and joy. In excess, any of these can decrease the vital energy and lead to sickness.

An effective way of achieving this even temper and self-control is to concentrate one's energy in the *hara* [腹], a point three inches below the navel. This is the vital center of the body. By correct posture, by focusing one's energy there mentally, and by deep, abdominal breathing one can realize an unshakable calm and steadiness. Kaibara recommends this as a technique used by Zen monks and by *samurai* [武士].

One should also develop positive mental attitudes. Above all one must cultivate a sense of gratitude, a deep awareness of life as a wonderful gift which has been received from Heaven and Earth, from parents and ancestors.

And one should practice the simple pleasures of everyday life: gardening; playing music and singing songs; writing and reading poetry; appreciating the natural beauty of the heavens and the earth; enjoying sports such as archery and horsemanship; spending days of quiet solitude; and enjoying evenings of companionship with the drinking, though not to inebriation, of fine wine. One should live a virtuous life, fulfilling duty to family and society.

To further insure peace of mind, Kaibara counsels, do not expect too much of yourself. If you make a mistake, accept the blame. Don't dwell on it. Thereafter, accept what you have done and its result as the will of Heaven.

And do not expect too much of others. To want perfection of others as of oneself makes a burden on the heart. This attitude leads to anger and to reproach.

Be satisfied with a few simple, but functional possessions. Don't crave the finest and the most beautiful. This leads to a restless mind. Be satisfied with what meets your needs. As Ohsawa was to counsel three centuries later, "*Vivere parvo*—Live with poverty."

Behind Kaibara's somewhat serious and puritanical tone is an optimistic, even joyful (in moderation) view of the universe and man's place in it. The cosmos is an orderly, harmonious whole operating according to predictable laws. "The seasons come and go," he writes, "with perfect regularity, and all things in the universe go as they should because the positive and negative dual forces are in constant flux and never stagnate."[9]

Man, created by Providence through the working of Heaven and Earth, is an integral part of nature. Health and happiness are his birthright. He need only observe the order and rhythm in nature and live in harmony with it. If he is sick or unhappy it is his own fault, and he can cure the situation by returning to the way of nature. By exercising care and discipline in how he eats and lives and in how he thinks and feels, man can realize a long, robust life filled with simple joys. Old age, in fact, when the passions have cooled, is the most peaceful and satisfying time of life.

Happily, it seems Kaibara epitomized these teachings in his own life. He traveled widely in his earlier years, satisfying an intense curiosity about the world and the laws by which it operated. Until the age of 70 he was active as the head of his family clan. Then he retired to record the harvest of his years. He studied, wrote and taught. Even at age 83 he had as yet all his teeth and his eyes were good enough so he "could both read and write even the smallest characters." About then Kaibara's beloved wife of many years passed away. The sage died shortly thereafter, as much from a broken heart it seems, as from any specific malady.

The spirit and letter of Kaibara's teachings lived on, of course, and deeply influenced both Ishizuka and Ohsawa, the pioneers of macrobiotics in the modern period. Hence Kaibara can be called "the grandfather of macrobiotics."

---

[1] Kaibara, Ekken, *Onna Daigaku* ("The Greater Learning for Women") as appearing in Chamberlain, Basil Hall, *Japanese Things*, Charles E. Tuttle Co., Rutland, VT., 1971, p. 502 ff.

[2] Kaibara, Ekken, *Yōjōkun: Japanese Secrets of Good Health*, p. 1

[3] Ibid., p. 7

[4] Ibid., p. 39

[5] Ibid., p. 25

[6] Ibid., p. 53

[7] Ibid., p. 46

[8] Ibid., p. 47–48

[9] Ibid., p. 21

Sagen Ishizuka:
The Founder
of Modern Macrobiotics

Ekken Kaibara was active at a time when Japan was turning away from the outside world, isolating itself, and above all, seeking stability and freedom from change. Ishizuka Sagen, the next main figure in the history of macrobiotics, lived in a much different era. Born in 1850 in the twilight of the Edo Period (1600–1868), he was active during the first decades of Japan's modern history. It was a time when Japan pursued and achieved rapid and radical change, replacing many elements of its traditional culture with borrowings from the West. Ishizuka, feeling that in the fields of diet and medicine much of great value was being lost, revived these old ways and presented them in a modern, scientific form. In doing so he started the movement which came later to be called "macrobiotics." His teachings were the foundation on which Ohsawa and others were to build.

To understand Ishizuka and his thought, we must understand the era in 'which he lived. From Kaibara's day through the mid-19th century, Japan successfully cut itself off from the rest of the world. No one was allowed to go abroad, or to return if they had managed to leave the island nation. Foreigners entering Japan risked death, and even those shipwrecked on its shores were not tolerated. Only a handful of Dutch traders on a tiny island in Nagasaki harbor were allowed to carry on trade.

For the most part the dream of internal stability and peace was realized. A strong central government under a military leader (*shōgun* [將軍]), maintained strict control over a complex feudal system. The population was divided into four fixed social classes—samurai, farmer, craftsman and merchant—each with specific duties and rights. There was little or no social or political turmoil. The economy grew, but very slowly and within the limits of a feudal agricultural society. Several urban centers including Edo (now Tokyo) and Osaka developed, and within them a rich and artistic culture emerged. Literature, painting, theater and a host of crafts developed to a high level. The whole culture was characterized by an aesthetic and cultural refinement seldom matched in human history. Viewed from a 20th century perspective, Japan of the Edo or Tokugawa Period seems like an exotic paradise set in amber.

Thus in the mid-19th century, Japan was, compared to the West, a medieval culture, untouched by the Industrial Revolution and the age of science. Both the diet and medicine of the country reflected this. The diet had changed little over many centuries. Rice was the staple, so central in the life of the nation that it was the basis for economic exchange. The wealth of a feudal lord was measured by how many *koku* [石] of rice his domains produced annually. Rice was considered a gift of the gods, given to the divine ancestors of the nation by the sun goddess herself. A common proverb said "Rice is the Buddha." The grain was eaten in a partially polished form by the wealthy and as brown rice by the common people. The poor mixed rice with other cereals like barley and wheat, or saved it for holidays or emergencies. A saying among the peasants, "It has come to giving her rice," meant that a person's sickness was severe enough to warrant feeding her rice. The term for a meal of any kind was *go-han* [御飯], "honorable rice."

Soybeans were another important element, used as a fermented paste (*miso*) [味噌], fermented sauce (*shoyu*) [醬油] and curd (*tofu*) [豆腐]. A wide variety of vegetables were eaten, some in pickled form, such as the *daikon* or large radish which was made into *takuan* [澤庵]. Fish and sea vegetables were also widely used. Fruits were not a particularly important part of the diet, with only the persimmon and tangerine being actively cultivated.

Little meat was eaten, there being rules against it both in the native Shinto religion and in Buddhism, which had been imported around A.D. 400. Chicken and wild fowl were the bulk of what was used. Raising large animals for food was virtually unknown. Cattle were kept as draft animals, but the idea of drinking the milk or using it for butter or cheese was almost incomprehensible. In 1859 when American ambassador Townsend Harris asked for a cow to use for milk the Japanese diplomats were incredulous. Well into the modern period these attitudes persisted in some areas. In her autobiography, *Daughter of the Samurai*, Etsuko Sugimoto [杉本鉞子] describes her childhood in provincial Japan not long after Harris' arrival.[1] It was believed that using milk and milk products made one into a cow and that eating meat was an abomination. When her grandfather was advised for medical reasons to eat meat, the doors of the household shrine were closed so that the ancestral spirits would not be insulted.

The traditional medicine was based on ideas and practices that go back to the dawn of Chinese history. According to this tradition, human physiology and health must be understood in terms of ki (in Chinese, *ch'i*), the life energy which permeates the universe, and which gives life to the body. This ki flows through the body along specific pathways or meridians. There are two main meridians, one on the front and one on the back of the body, plus six on the arms and six on the legs. These twelve are each connected to an internal organ or function, and disorder in an organ shows up as an uneven, stagnant or excessive flow of ki on its meridian. Through the balancing, stimulation or calming of energy flow, the various medical arts treated illness. Acupuncture used fine needles of silver or gold inserted at key meridian points to regulate ki. Moxibustion used the strong stimulus given by burning moxa plant fibers. In *shiatsu* [指壓] the stimulation and balancing was done by fingertip massage. Herbal remedies were also used, operating internally on the organs. The aim of these various techniques was the same—to create a free and harmonious flow of ki through the entire body so that the "primal ki," *genki* [元氣] (the Sino-Japanese word for "health") would be regained.

Regulation of diet was also part of this medical tradition, used by some doctors as a primary treatment, but by most as a supplement to their more immediate measures. In the film "Akahige" ("Redbeard") director Akira Kurosawa recounts the career of a physician of the Tokugawa Period. Though devoted mainly to the care of the poor, Akahige answers the summons of a rich lord. The bloated, over-stuffed noble is barely able to support himself in an upright position. The physician eyes him coldly, charges an outrageous fee (to support his clinic) and then advises him to eat nothing but brown rice gruel for an indefinite period. The man's dis-believing and aghast response explains well why this was a minor rather than a major element in Japan's pre-modern medicine.

So it was into a placid and traditional culture that Commodore Richard Perry intruded when he sailed his American warships into Edo harbor. In a typically subtle gesture of military diplomacy, Perry demanded that Japan open itself to foreign intercourse and promised to return the following year with more ships to press the point. The Japanese, seeing that their swords and bows were no match for the American cannon, gave in to the demand. Thus began the nation's modern history.

From the outset the proud and patriotic Japanese were determined not to become a Western colony. After political power had been restored to the Imperial family (1868) and a strong central government established, they began a conscious, ener-getic, and very successful attempt to modernize. The Japanese knew that to remain independent they had to be strong, and to be strong they had to borrow from the West. Official missions were sent to Europe and America to observe, study and bring back the key elements of Western culture. Foreign scientists, engineers, sol-diers, lawyers, and other specialists were invited and paid high salaries to come to Japan to live and teach. Thus, relatively quickly Japan imported and adopted Western science and technology, Western military techniques, and Western eco-nomic and political patterns. Telegraph lines, railroads, and factories appeared in the once pristine Japanese landscape.

The nation held to two ideals or themes during this period. The first was *fukoku kyōhei* [富國強兵] "a rich nation and strong military." The second was *wakon yōsai* [和魂洋才] "the soul of Japan and the technology of the West." The Japanese did not want to become a pale carbon copy of the West. They wanted to retain their national character, that elusive but powerful blend of courtesy, discipline and spirituality which was the *Yamato-damashii* [大和魂], "the spirit of Japan." They were willing, even anxious, to have Western practical and scientific knowledge, but not "the spirit of the West."

This distinction, however, proved difficult to uphold. The Japanese quickly im-ported new ideas in the sciences, in technology and industry, in law and government. But they also adopted, with equal fervor, patterns in Western art, music, literature, dance, dress, religion, philosophy and morality. The elite of Tokyo wore waistcoats and top hats, bonnets and long gowns, and amused themselves at Western-style grand balls. They listened to Bach and Beethoven, practiced the violin and the piano, studied Kant and Jeremy Bentham, and flirted with Christianity. In nearly every area of life, the traditional and the Eastern were discarded and replaced by the modern and the Western. In the newly established "public schools" which had supplanted the old *terakoya* [寺小屋] or "temple schools," writing brushes gave way

24

to fountain pens and Western musical notation took the place of the Japanese way of writing down music. Buddhist statuary, colorful woodblock prints, and ancient scrolls were sold for a pittance to Western collectors. Centuries-old pagodas, products of pure architectural genius, were torn down and used for firewood.

This rejection of the old and familiar and the blind adoption of foreign ways occurred in nutrition and medicine as well. At the time, Western medicine was progressing rapidly, discovering new and remarkable means to treat disease. In the late 18th century William Jenner had discovered a vaccine against smallpox. By the 1850s Frenchman Louis Pasteur had published his "germ theory of disease." According to this view the primary cause of human illness is the invasion of the body by harmful, microscopic forms of life. From this basis allopathic medicine developed, aimed at curing disease by destroying the pathogens. The discovery of chloroform in this same period was making possible the improvement of surgical techniques.

In 1871 the first in a succession of German physicians arrived in Japan to practice medicine and to teach. By 1883 the national government decided to prohibit the practice of traditional medicine, and to establish Western allopathy as the official system. A medical college, staffed mostly by Germans, was set up as part of the fledgling imperial university in Tokyo. Suddenly the age-old treatments of acupuncture, moxa, massage and herbal medicine were declared obsolete, and those who practiced them were outside the law. These healers did not simply stop practicing of course. Most simply went underground to emerge later in a more auspicious time. From this point, though, Western medicine was officially sanctioned and the old therapies (and the theory of human physiology which lay behind them) were considered primitive and unscientific.

The scenario was similar in the field of nutrition. In Europe the modern science of nutrition had begun to develop in the mid-19th century. Mainly through the work of pioneering German biochemist Justus von Liebig (1803–1873) and his students, the various nutrients in food were isolated and identified. Animal experiments were done to discover what nutrients in what quantity were necessary to sustain life and growth. Nutrient analyses were done on various foods. This early research laid the basis for modern nutrition and its various theories. Protein was considered the most important nutrient, essential for growth and for the repair of tissue. Therefore meat, eggs, cheese and other animal foods were highly recommended. Carbohydrates were seen as the source of energy, and high carbohydrate foods such as potatoes and refined sugar were seen as desirable.

Here too the Japanese government took the initiative in promoting Western ideas and practices. Wanting to improve the physique, strength and vitality of the people it urged the citizenry to add meat and dairy foods to their diet. It also suggested replacing rice with the wheat bread eaten in the West. At the time, the average height of a Japanese man was about five feet four, that of a Japanese woman less than five feet. The key to the size and strength of the Westerners, even their technological development, was thought to lay in meat, wheat and milk.

Slowly, Western foods became part of the Japanese diet. On the breakfast tables of the urban sophisticates at least, buttered toast, sausage and milk vied with the familiar bowls of miso soup, rice and tea. Despite its great cost, meat, especially beef and pork, came into great demand and beef-specialty restaurants sprang up in the cities. White sugar became an important part of Japanese cuisine. Most likely through the efforts of the sugar industry, the saying "sugar in cooking is a barometer of culture and refinement" entered the popular wisdom. In the preparation of even rice and vegetables as well as of candies and desserts, it became a fixture in the Japanese diet. Potatoes were introduced and their cultivation was encouraged, especially after 1888.

Of course the Japanese diet did not completely change overnight. Even today, a century later, rice, miso, sea vegetables, pickled vegetables, etc. are staples of daily life. For one thing, ancient customs do not die so easily. For another, it is impossible in Japan to produce much meat and animal food. Japan is a small, crowded country, four-fifths of which is steep mountains. The limited agricultural land is needed for high-yield crops like rice, beans and vegetables. To graze cows or sheep on the rest would require animals having two short (uphill) and two long (downhill) legs. At best, a farming family might manage a cow, a few pigs and chickens. Thus meat was, and remains, almost prohibitively expensive. Nevertheless, there were changes in the Japanese way of eating and as the Meiji Period (1868–1912) progressed, these continued.

Sagen Ishizuka was born just as Japan was about to enter this period of change. His family were samurai retainers in a remote domain facing the Japan Sea. His formal schooling ended when he was eighteen but he continued studying on his own, being especially attracted to foreign languages and to Western science. According to a biography, written by Ohsawa in 1928, Ishizuka mastered French, German, Dutch and English and used these to pursue his scientific studies.[2] He copied by hand an entire volume in Dutch on astronomy.

Especially drawn to medicine, Ishizuka worked in a hospital in his native Fukui Prefecture where he was exposed to traditional methods. Just as Western medicine was being introduced he moved to Tokyo, and began to work and study in a hospital there. He continued his study of Western medicine and science and in time acquired the status and title of a medical doctor. At twenty-eight he became a physician in the Japanese Army.

From childhood Ishizuka had a chronic kidney condition that caused a serious skin inflammation. Early in his military career this condition became severe and threatened to incapacitate him. Unable to get relief from the allopathic medicine he was practicing, Ishizuka began to look again at the traditions of Oriental medicine. He was most struck by the Yellow Emperor's Classic. It stimulated him to pursue a line of study and treatment totally at odds with the current of the day.

Written probably around 500 B.C., "The Yellow Emperor's Classic of Internal Medicine" is a compilation of the medical wisdom of ancient China. It is a textbook dealing with human anatomy, the types and causes of disease, the methods of diagnosis, and types of treatment. Its presentation is based on the Five-Element or Five-Energy theory, according to which there are five transformations of the ch'i or primal life-energy. These are earth, water, wood, metal and fire. Organs, diseases, symptoms and treatments (in fact, all phenomena) can be classified according to these five "phases," which are all dynamically interrelated. Most of the Classic is clinical and technical but it deals also with basic principles of human health and disease.

For example, the Classic maintains that there is a basic relationship between food, health and illness. According to the Five-Energy theory there are five tastes: sweet, sour, bitter, salty and spicy, each of which corresponds to certain bodily organs. Eating too much food with a certain taste will weaken the corresponding organ or function. Diet then can be a major cause of illness.

The text also asserts that food is an important means for treating disease. It says that in "medieval days" the sages treated illness first by diet, usually prescribing a regime of rice gruel for ten days.[3] If this treatment was not successful, then the roots and leaves of medicinal plants were used to harmonize the energies. Acupuncture and moxibustion were employed only as a last resort. If the emotions and the will of the patient are stable, says the Classic, then cereals alone can effect a cure.[4] Grains have a special importance and power as human food. Water and grains are the root of life and "death comes only when they are exhausted."[5] In particular, rice is mentioned as a vital and harmonious food. Methods of preparation and even the ideal fuel for cooking it (rice straw) are discussed.[6]

Underlying the Classic is the idea that by nature man is healthy and sickness is an anomaly. To maintain or regain health one need only live in harmony with the environment. The "true sage" lives according to the laws of Yin and Yang which control all phenomena. He drinks and eats moderately and regulates his life according to the cycles of the sun, the moon and the four seasons. Thus he is able to enjoy a long and happy life. He is not concerned with the cure of disease but with its prevention.

Another important influence on Ishizuka at this point was the work of Nanboku Mizuno [水野南北]. Nanboku was active in the late 1700s. He was a pioneer in physiognomy, the study of the relationship between bodily characteristics and human personality. To pursue this study, Nanboku spent years working first as a barber, then as an attendant in a public bath, and finally as a helper in a crematorium. He was thus able to observe countless individuals and to correlate body types and marks with personality and destiny. In 1788 the first five volumes of his *Nanboku Sōhō* [南北相法] ("The Nanboku Method of Physiognomy") appeared, and in 1805 the second five volumes.

Nanboku was concerned mainly with telling a person's character and past and future fortunes through close observation of physical appearance. His books contain long sections on the meaning of various types of noses, eyes, ears, mouths, head shapes and unusual marks. For example, widely-flared nostrils indicate a very energetic, perhaps aggressive person, and a mole high on the left cheek a very talkative one. Nanboku held that while our physiognomy (and hence personality and destiny) are largely inherited, our appearance, character and fate can be radically influenced by diet and way of living. This view, plus the idea that physiology is intimately tied to psychology, behavior and even spiritual condition, had a marked influence on Ishizuka.

Although he does not specifically mention it, Ishizuka certainly was also inspired by Kaibara's work. Study of the *Yōjōkun* was without doubt part of his early education, and in his own later writing he virtually quotes whole passages from it. Perhaps it seemed too obvious to mention. Perhaps the "Sage of Fukuoka" was considered too antique and unscientific at the time to mention in works with a scientific purpose. In any case, Kaibara must be counted among Ishizuka's mentors.

Stimulated by these several sources, the young doctor began to experiment with his diet. He gave up meat and milk and began eating unpolished rice as his main food. His illness subsided. By 1880 Ishizuka had, according to Ohsawa, formulated his basic theory. He wrote nothing down about it, however, until ten years later. In the meantime he continued his studies and research, accumulating corroborative data. He was above all a scientist in an age infatuated with science. He wanted to thoroughly test and validate his theories and to present them in a convincing manner. Otherwise he and his work would be greeted with derision and skepticism.

Over the next decade Ishizuka continued his experiments on himself. Once he lived for a month on sweet potatoes alone to determine their effect as a food. Also, as a doctor in the cavalry he was in charge of soldiers recuperating from wounds and illness. He tried various diets on the men to see which fostered recovery best. He was in charge of animals as well. One time there was an unruly horse in the camp. Ishizuka removed its feed of oats and salt (a human diet, he said) and allowed it to graze on wild grasses. The animal became docile and easy to manage.

Ishizuka also carried on anthropological research. Some was second-hand. He read widely about traditional peoples all over the world, of Eskimos, Mongolians, of the natives of Kamchatka, noting especially their diets, physiognomy and dominant characteristics. In the military he saw soldiers from many parts of Japan and China. He kept careful, systematic records of racial and physical type, diet and behavior.

Ishizuka also conducted chemical research, which was imaginative, if to our contemporary eye somewhat primitive. To compare the digestibility of egg yolk and egg white, for example, he designed a laboratory experiment with miso. The active bacteria in this fermented soybean paste are similar to those which activate digestion in the human intestines. So in separate plates Ishizuka mixed miso with raw egg yolk and egg white. The yolk decomposed more quickly and was thus deemed more easy to digest. In another experiment Ishizuka tested the effect of sodium on oxidation. He soaked a string in salt water, dried it, then measured its combustibility. It burned more slowly than an untreated string, so he concluded that an excess of sodium in the body inhibits oxidation. In addition, he read Western scientific journals.

Ishizuka also read on the history of food and on traditional wisdom about food, especially in the Orient. His study of Buddhism convinced him that the Buddha had forbidden his monks to eat meat not only to avoid taking life, but to avoid the adverse effects of meat-eating on spiritual development. The Buddha, he asserts, held that health is the natural state of the human body and that grains are a purifying food. The Chinese sages, Confucius and Mencius, had also advised against meat-eating and against the use of rich foods in general.[7] Ishizuka found that during the Han Period (207 B.C.–A.D. 220), a cultural high point in Chinese civilization, the staple food of the Chinese had been unpolished brown rice, roasted and then steamed.[8] Looking into Japan's past he learned that the Emperor Temmu [天武天皇] (reigned 673–686) had issued an edict against the eating of domesticated animals, and that in the samurai house laws of Kiyomasa Katō [加藤清正] (15th century) the polishing of rice was prohibited.[9] And he found that until the modern era the national custom had been to take only two meals a day, a practice which persisted in modern times in certain areas such as Niigata prefecture.

In 1895, while occupying a high post in the Army (he was, ironically enough, head of the Pharmaceutical Department) Ishizuka resigned. He started a private medical practice in Tokyo and began to prepare his work for publication. Just at that time there was a conservative and nationalist reaction in Japan. Western values, especially in morality and social relations, were being questioned. There was much emphasis on traditional Japanese culture and on retaining the Yamato-damashii. Perhaps Ishizuka was encouraged by this change in the temper of the times to present his views to the public.

In any case, in 1897 Ishizuka published his magnum opus, *Kagakuteki Shoku-Yō Chōjuron* [化学的食養長壽論] ("A Chemical Nutritional Theory of Long Life"). This is a compendious, 500-page tome containing the results of all his study and research. On page one he states his purpose: "to formulate a practical food discipline based on scientific laws."[10] He is true to it. His broad theory of human physiology, food, health, sickness and medicine is all based on the relationship between the elements sodium (Na) and potassium (K). Ishizuka describes the characteristics of the two and explains how their salts control the functioning of the entire human organism. He gives tables analyzing the sodium and potassium contents of various foods, and geographical charts showing their distribution. He cites countless experiments of his own and of others to support these conclusions. He presents so much scientific data that the practical import of his work is almost lost.

While Ishizuka does mention traditional practices and popular wisdom, he makes it clear that this is only corroborative evidence. His theory rests on modern "chemical" and "scientific" bases. Also, he does not use traditional terms. Ohsawa, who was to inject Yin/Yang thinking into the movement, claims that the sodium-potassium theory was derived from this ancient classification of phenomena. While Ishizuka probably was influenced by this way of thinking, ingrained deep in Japanese life, he gives no indication that there had been a direct influence. He mentions the terms once or twice, very much in passing, and keeps his approach and vocabulary admirably modern and scientific. Here again, writing in an age of science, Ishizuka did not risk diluting his message with categories and concepts considered outdated and superstitious.

In 1898 a second book appeared, *Shokumotsu Yōjōhō: Ichimei Kagakuteki Shoku-Yō Tai Shin Ron* [食物養生法化学的食養体心論] ("A Method for Nourishing Life Through Food: A Unique Chemical Food-Nourishment Theory of Body and Mind"). Ishizuka meant this as a daily reference of practical knowledge for the general public, a means for all to achieve "better health, good memory, mental development and spiritual refreshment."[11] Written in simple, direct language, and omitting most of the technical data, it focuses on practical ways to realize health and long life. Ishizuka does mention some of his experiments and does cite historical and anthropological evidence, but in the main refers his readers to his earlier book for more details. While clearly indicating that his work is based on rigorous scientific research, he focuses on its implications for daily life. Unlike the *Chōjuron* [長寿

論], which had but a single printing, the second book had wide distribution, going through twenty-three editions.

Ishizuka's theory is based on several simple concepts. First, he maintains that human health and longevity are dependent on a proper balance in the body between the salts of sodium and potassium. While Western nutrition (then as now) was emphasizing protein and carbohydrates, Ishizuka maintains that minerals, especially potassium and sodium, are most crucial. The ratio between them determines the body's ability to absorb and utilize the other nutrients. The healthy functioning of the entire human organism depends on their being in proper balance.

A second principle is that food is the most important factor in determining this critical balance. Other factors such as geography and climate and the amount of physical activity play a role as well. Living by the sea or in the mountains, in a dry or a moist climate, being sedentary or hard working all have an effect. But it is what a person ingests through the mouth that is the main determinant of the Na/K ratio in the body.

Hence, thirdly, human health and sickness depend on diet above all. The basis for physical well-being is daily food that provides a proper balance of minerals. Such a diet will give one a long life, free from disease. On the other hand, all sickness begins with an imbalance of Na/K caused by poor diet.[12] Both contagious and degenerative diseases, Ishizuka asserted, originate in food. Bacteria and viruses afflict only those who are weak and susceptible because of their Na/K imbalance.[13] A truly healthy person, even coming into contact with such pathogens, will not become sick. Thus allopathic medicine, seeking only to destroy disease-causing microorganisms rather than strengthening the person against them, is based on a total misconception.

Having established that health and long life are based on food, Ishizuka addresses the question of what is the proper diet for humankind. What should one eat in order to maintain the optimal balance between the mineral salts? In answering this, Ishizuka reasons from human physiology, ecology and history.

In choosing food, man first should consider his physical structure. Human dentition and the human digestive system both indicate that by nature man is a "grain-arian" or eater of cereal grains.[14] There are thirty-two teeth in the mouth. Of these, four are pointed canine teeth, well-suited to tearing foods such as meat. Eight are incisors, good for biting into crisp vegetables and fruits. The remaining teeth, five-eighths of the total, are best adapted to chewing grains. Man's dental structure indicates roughly what percentage of his diet each type of food should comprise. Also, man has a small stomach and a long, convoluted intestinal tract, rather than the large stomach and short intestines of a carnivore. Thus his body is especially suited to the digestion of vegetable-quality foods, the most compact and nutritious of which are cereal grains.

Man's environment and the foods it offers him must also be considered. For Ishizuka, man is above all a product of his natural environment. It provides those foods which allow him to function healthily and happily in that particular place and climate. Man should eat, then, those foods which occur naturally and abundantly where he lives.[15] These will supply the proper balance of nutrients, including the right proportion of Na and K. According to Ishizuka, except in arctic and tropical areas, the most plentiful and easily cultivated food is cereal grains. The type may vary from region to region, but generally in a temperate climate cereals should be the principal food. They have roughly a 3 : 7 ratio of sodium to potassium, which is ideal for human health. Unpolished grains which retain the natural proportions of minerals and other nutrients should comprise 60–70 percent of the daily food.

Ishizuka also argues for a cereal-based diet from the point of view of history. Every major civilization has had some grain as its main food. In Japan and south China it has been rice, in north China millet and wheat, in the Americas corn, in northern Europe barley and rye. Usually, the people's sense of dependence upon their staple food was such that the particular grain was deified and worshipped.

Ishizuka maintains, then, that man is by nature a cereal eater, and that for people living in temperate climates grains are the ideal principal food. Beans, vegetables, seeds, nuts, sea vegetables, fish, game and other indigenous products should supplement the grain base. As much as possible these should be eaten fresh and in season. Nature provides those foods for man at the time he needs them. Thus in the warm months he should eat the vegetables and fruits that are in season. In the winter he should rely on foods which keep long and easily (beans, sea vegetables, fish) and on dried fruits and vegetables. The daikon radish, pickled in salt and bran, while out of season, helps one adapt to cold weather.

Thus for Ishizuka, proper choice of food is the basis of good health. Preparation is also crucial. The use of heat, water, salt and spices in cooking, and the combination of various foods all affect the Na/K balance of a dish and hence the condition of those who eat it.[16] Even "good food" improperly prepared can lead to illness. And "unbalanced foods" such as meat (Na excess) and eggplant (K excess) can be made healthful by wise preparation. He points out that traditional recipes such as meat cooked with ginger and onions and eggplant cooked with miso reflect an awareness of this principle.[17]

The idea that food is the primary cause of illness suggests that it can also be a cure. If diet leads to the imbalance of minerals that presages sickness, it can also redress that imbalance. And indeed Ishizuka maintains that food must be the basis of any true cure. With food and cooking carefully tailored to the patient's condition, virtually any illness can be cured.

Ishizuka does not rely entirely on diet, however. He recognizes exercise and the use of baths as effective aids in medicine. Physical exercise to the point of perspiration discharges excess salts and improves circulation and digestion. Hot baths have a similar effect, removing minerals and creating balance.[18] Both his books include extensive discussions of the various types of baths (steam, hot stone, Turkish, etc.) and prescriptions for their use in different ailments.

With the success of his second book Ishizuka's fame grew. He was besieged from early morning, and the patients who arrived at dawn at his door received numbered chits. He had to limit himself to one hundred consultations a day. The humble and unpretentious Ishizuka, who persisted in writing his prescriptions on bits of scrap paper, became known throughout Japan. He was famous as the "Anti-Doctor," able to cure through food even those deemed hopeless by the conventional medicine of the day. And in fact he did shun all usual medications and surgical techniques. Ishizuka recommended instead a diet based on brown or whole grain rice, though for people with weak digestion he might recommend partially-polished rice. For a particular person he would advise specific side dishes, including daikon, burdock root, tangerines, etc., to restore their mineral balance. And he prescribed certain foods for certain maladies. To a person with poor digestion, for example, he would recommend *azuki* [小豆] beans, sea vegetables and bamboo shoots.[19] To someone with excessive sweating he would suggest *hijiki* sea vegetable.

Ishizuka's fame spread to the extent that letters addressed to "Dr. Daikon" or "Dr. Miso Soup, Tokyo" would reach him. Among his patients were the rich and powerful; high-ranking members of the aristocracy, government and military; as well as poor and common folk. In 1908 a group of these supporters decided to form an organization to promote Ishizuka's teachings. On the day of the Autumn Festival of the New Rice in that year, they founded the *Shoku-Yō Kai* [食養會] or the "Food-Cure Society," with the doctor as advisor. This was, in effect, the first macrobiotic organization. A center was established in Tokyo. Monthly meetings were held there and a monthly magazine called the *Shoku-Yō Shimbun* [食養新聞] began to be published. On its front page an English subscript read: "A journal dedicated to the encouragement of a new chemical science of cerealism introduced by Mr. Ishizuka Sagen."

Ishizuka continued to be very busy writing, lecturing, traveling, as well as giving consultations in Tokyo and elsewhere. The Shoku-Yō Kai grew and branches were opened in other cities, including Osaka, Shizuoka and Sendai. In 1910, however, Ishizuka developed a stomach catarrh, which, according to Ohsawa, was caused by overwork. He kept on his taxing schedule though, and on the day of the Harvest Festival, exactly two years after the founding of the Shoku-Yō Kai he passed away. Thousands joined his funeral cortege in Tokyo.

Ishizuka's work as a physician was based on the importance of food in human health and illness. But he saw it as the key factor in every aspect of life. Not only one's immediate physical condition, but physical characteristics, personality traits, psychological patterns, and even spiritual condition are determined by the interplay of certain mineral salts and thus by diet. Ishizuka in effect propounds a comprehensive theory of human development and behavior based on food. For him the diet of an individual and of a society was the critical factor in its moral, social, political, and religious as well as its physical life. His own sense of mission and his hopes for the Shoku-Yō Kai went far beyond just the treatment of physical, individual ills.

In the "*Chōjuron*" for example, Ishizuka observes that in coastal areas the inhabitants tend to be short, stocky and with round faces. This is due, he asserts, to the relative abundance of sodium in the soil, air, water, and thus in the food. On the continental plains, far from the sea and high in the mountains, potassium dominates in the environment and hence in the food (and people). The inhabitants tend to be taller, more slender, and with more oval faces. They lack the physical strength of the Na-dominant people, but they have more endurance and physical flexibility.

The Na/K balance directly controls much more than just physical type. In a chart in the "*Yōjōhō*," Ishizuka lists the following characteristics as also determined by this ratio of minerals:

Height, weight, rate of maturation, rate of development, length of life, type of voice, type of inflection in speaking, temper, memory, quickness of judgment, emotional responsiveness, business sense, ability to keep a secret, morality, quietness and strength of spirit, and good-heartedness.[20]

Ishizuka's description of Na-dominant and K-dominant types of persons is very thorough and specific. The former tend to be physically active, aggressive and loud. They are materialistic, worldly and ambitious. Their thinking is dualistic, in that they see opposite or distinct phenomena such as man and nature, good and evil, matter and spirit as absolutely separate and mutually exclusive. Extreme Na imbalance, as might be caused by a diet rich in meat and animal food, results in violent aggressiveness, greed, cruelty and a tendency to demean others.[21]

Potassium-dominant types (i.e., people who live on total or near-total vegetarian diets) are more quiet, sensitive and introspective. Their orientation to life is more spiritual than materialistic, and their thinking is monistic.[22] They see apparent opposites as part of a harmonious whole, and perceive contradictions and conflicts as apparent only, and not indeed real. While the sexual desire in Na-dominant people tends to be sporadic, intense and short-lived, that of K-dominant people is constant, gentle and active throughout life. While a sodium-rich diet develops *sai* [才] ("worldly cleverness"),[23] a potassium-rich one nurtures *chie* [知恵] ("spiritual wisdom").[24]

According to Ishizuka, even development to the highest levels of spirituality is controlled by food. The great sages and saints, he maintains, all lived on whole grains and vegetables cooked in salt. The effect of food is so powerful and subtle that the various grains produce different types of spiritual development. Pure spirituality at the highest level comes to those who eat rice as their main food.[25] A saint who eats wheat or mixed grains will realize a spirituality tinged with "worldliness," less pure but enabling him to deal with mundane affairs.

Thus man's whole being, life and destiny lies in his choice and preparation of daily food. If he chooses a diet that is appropriate to the natural environment, one with a harmonious balance of sodium and potassium, he will live a long and healthy life. He will develop a happy and loving mentality, will be naturally polite and moral, and will be able to rejoice in the joy of others. He will have a good memory and a lofty spirit. On the other hand, if he chooses food that violates the natural order he will become an animal in body, mind and spirit. Man can make himself into a "hungry ghost" (*gaki*) [餓鬼], enslaved by his desires,[26] or into a "bodhisattva" (*bosatsu*) [菩薩], the embodiment of selfless love and compassion.[27] The key is his daily food. Thus Shoku-Yō is a discipline of life crucial for the mind and spirit, as well as for the body. It seeks to cure and perfect the whole person, not merely to eliminate the symptoms of disease.

Ishizuka was concerned not only with individuals. Eating patterns determine how families and societies function as well. Shoku-Yō, then, can be a powerful medicine for the family, community and nation as well as the individual.

From this point of view Ishizuka analyzes developments in Japan after the Meiji Restoration. He states that since the introduction of Western culture there has been a decline in the physical and the moral-spiritual condition of the Japanese people.[28] The dominant physical-biological type has changed, with people becoming shorter and heavier, and maturing more early. There has been a decline in public health. Internal diseases such as tuberculosis and beriberi have been increasing steadily. In earlier times, *zukan sokunetsu* [頭寒足熱] ("a cool head and warm feet") was considered an indication of good health and was the common pattern among the people. By the mid-Meiji Period, the condition of most Japanese is just the opposite —"a hot head and cold feet"—an indication of general physical weakness and degeneration.[29]

Values and behavior also have changed. The people have become intellectually dull, morally confused and lacking in direction. Previously, Japan had been characterized by spiritual values, what Ishizuka calls *kokoro* [心] ("heart" or "mind"), and by *ōrishugi* [横利主義] ("horizontalism" or "altruism"), an ethic of gratitude, respect, humility and self-sacrifice.[30] Since 1868 these values have been steadily replaced by *jūrishugi* [縦利主義] ("verticalism" or "egoism"), an ethic of materialism, vanity and hedonism; of a lack of consideration for others; and of a lack of respect for society.[31] *Seidō* [正道], the "path of righteousness" is being replaced by *gon-dō* [権道], "the path of expediency and convenience." This egotism and commercialism, Ishizuka maintains, is rapidly spreading over all the world.[32]

Not surprisingly, Ishizuka sees the cause of this physical and moral decline in the changing food habits of the nation. Since the beginning of the modern era Japan has begun to use foods such as meat, dairy products, potatoes, eggs, white bread and refined sugar. These generally Na-dominant foods are suitable perhaps for someone living in the cold, dry climate of northern Europe, but they are not appropriate at all for the Japanese. In the warm and moist environment of the island nation the proper diet is rice, vegetables and sea products. To imitate Western diet, to import foods from abroad or to produce exotic crops at home, goes against the order of nature. The judgment visited on the nation is the loss of physical, psychological and spiritual vitality and harmony.

The solution, then, to Japan's crisis lies in Shoku-Yō, in the conscious and systematic return to traditional eating patterns. The nation should return to its traditional diet, with unpolished rice as its base and native foods as supplements. These foods should be cultivated according to natural methods using organic fertilizers. Chemical fertilizers, developed in Europe and beginning to come to Japan, destroy the natural mineral balance in soil and plants, Ishizuka warned. Japan should also recover and practice its tradition of therapeutic bathing, which had declined in the modern period. Through these measures Japan would regain its physical, moral and spiritual vitality.

Ishizuka's sense of mission went beyond the borders of his homeland. On the inside cover of the *Yōjōhō* he had the following inscription printed:

The foundation of the world is the nation.
The foundation of the nation is the home.
The foundation of the home is the body.
The foundation of the body is the spirit.
The foundation of the spirit is food.[33]

Thus he envisioned the relevance of Shoku-Yō to the health and well-being of

34

all peoples and nations. And he saw it as the secret key of a stable and peaceful world order. Healthy and happy individuals make up a stable household. In the same way, healthy and harmonious nations could comprise a stable and peaceful international community.

Sagen Ishizuka had a remarkable career. Even one who rejects his premises and conclusions must recognize the scope and noble vision of his work.

- He challenged the assumptions of modern nutritional theory, and presented instead an ecological nutrition based on a view of man as part of the natural environment and dependent on it.
- He challenged the assumptions of modern allopathic medicine, and presented instead a system of treatment based on simple food and on the body's natural inclination toward health.
- He presented both his nutritional and medical views in "chemical" and scientific terms, supported by a mass of empirical data—experimental, historical and anthropological.
- He developed a comprehensive theory of human development and behavior based on diet and on the idea that the human being is a pyscho-physical whole.
- He viewed the problems of his era from this perspective and offered a remedy that would apply to Japan and to all nations.
- Behind all this, he nurtured a dream for world peace.

Perhaps, as George Ohsawa asserts, Ishizuka was one of the great seminal thinkers of the modern world, and the publication of his books was indeed an event more significant than Columbus's discovery of America. And perhaps someday this will be widely recognized. For the moment, though, he is unknown and unheralded, even in Japan. His writings, until recently reissued by Nippon C.I., the macrobiotic organization in Tokyo, had long been out of print. Even in macrobiotic circles in Japan and around the world he is remembered only as an important but indistinct figure from the past. The true father of modern "macrobiotics" has yet to be fully appreciated even by those most affected by his legacy.

[1] Sugimoto, Etsuko, *Daughter of the Samurai*, Doubleday, Garden City, 1934
[2] Ohsawa, George (Sakurazawa Yukikazu), *Ishizuka Sagen* originally published 1928; reprinted by Nippon C.I., Shibuya, Tokyo, 1974
[3] Lu, Henry C., *A Complete Translation of the Yellow Emperor's Classic of Internal Medicine and the Difficult Classic*, Academy of Oriental Heritage, Vancouver, B.C. 1978, p. 84
[4] Ibid., p. 86
[5] Ibid., p. 86
[6] Ibid., p. 120
[7] Ishizuka, Sagen, *Kagakuteki Shoku-Yō Chōjuron*, 1897 Reissued by Nippon C.I. Kyōkai, Tokyo, 1975, p. 133
[8] Ishizuka, Sagen, *Shokumotsu Yōjōhō*, 1899, Reissued by Nippon C.I., Tokyo, 1975, p. 46
[9] Ibid., p. 25
[10] Ishizuka, Sagen, *Kagakuteki Shoku-Yō Chōjuron*, p. 1
[11] Ishizuka, Sagen, *Shokumotsu Yōjōhō*, p. 3
[12] Ibid., *Hanrei*, p. 1

[13] Ishizuka, Sagen, *Kagakuteki Shoku-Yō Chōjuron*, p. 330

[14] Ishizuka, Sagen, *Shokumotsu Yōjōhō*, p. 5

[15] Ibid., *Hanrei*, p. 2

[16] Ishizuka, Sagen, *Kagakuteki Shoku-Yō Chōjuron*, p. 266

[17] Ibid., p. 48

[18] Ibid., p. 106

[19] Ishizuka, Sagen, *Shokumotsu Yōjōhō*, p. 74

[20] Ibid., p. 157 ff.

[21] Ibid., p. 26

[22] Ibid., p. 27

[23] Ibid., p. 35

[24] Ibid., p. 35

[25] Ibid., p. 33

[26] Ibid., p. 86

[27] Ibid., p. 86

[28] Ibid., p. 55

[29] Ibid., p. 84

[30] Ibid., p. 76

[31] Ibid., p. 78 (ca.)

[32] Ibid., p. 91 (ca.)

[33] Ibid., On inside cover of book.

3.

George Ohsawa:
The Early Years (1893–1929)

Several years after the founding of the Shoku-Yō Kai, a student in Kyoto came across a work of Ishizuka, probably in one of the second-hand bookshops he loved to haunt. The young man, Yukikazu Sakurazawa [櫻澤如一], later known as George Ohsawa, was to become the next central figure in the Shoku-Yō movement. A gifted and original thinker, he greatly extended the intellectual scope of the movement. A tireless writer, lecturer and social activist, he did much to spread Shoku-Yō in Japan and to the world beyond. It was Ohsawa who brought it, under the name macrobiotics, to Europe and America. The story of the Shoku-Yō movement from about 1923 to 1966, the year of Ohsawa's death, is basically the story of his life and work.

On a fine spring day in about 1890, Magotaro Sakurazawa, a young man of the samurai class, was boating on a river near his home in Wakayama Prefecture, south of Osaka. He lost control of his craft and was caught in the swift, if shallow, current. A young woman passing on a nearby bridge saw his distress, and unwinding her long *kimono* [着物] belt, or *obi* [帯], let down one end of it so that the man could regain the shore. Her name was Setsuko and she also was of warrior lineage. This was her first meeting with the man who was to become her husband.[1]

Soon after the marriage Setsuko became pregnant and the couple decided to move to Kyoto, Japan's capital until 1868. Magotaro had been educated in the traditional arts of the samurai, including swordsmanship and archery. But the warrior class had lost its special status and privileges in the Meiji era, and it was necessary to earn a living through more mundane activities. This was more easily done in the bustling and growing city.

Their first child, Yukikazu, was born in a western suburb of Kyoto on October 18, 1893. Another boy, Kenji, was born two years later and a girl, who died in infancy, several years after that. The family's fortunes did not prosper. Magotaro, possessing an overmeasure of samurai pride and stubbornness, and an impatience with workaday life, found adjustment to the mercantile urban life difficult. He taught *kendō* [剣道] or swordsmanship, for a while and also worked as a policeman but could not hold a job for long. Much of the little money he brought in he spent on his own evening amusements.

Still, the family tried to uphold the samurai values of self-reliance and stoicism and to pass these on to their sons. When Yukikazu was a toddler, he was playing one day throwing pieces of coal into a rain puddle. The water splashed and dirtied the side of the neighbor's house. This act violated the cardinal virtue of consideration for others (*meiwaku o kakenai* [迷惑をかけない], "causing no trouble"), and

38

his mother struck Yukikazu so hard that blood ran freely from nose. She then tied him up with cord until his father came home to repeat the beating. When it came time to teach the young Ohsawa to swim, Setsuko took him to a bridge overlooking the Kamo River which flows through the heart of the city. She pushed the little boy into the shallow but turbulent waters. Yukikazu thrashed around for a bit and just before he was ready to go down she went in and pulled him out. They went up onto the bridge again, and the process was repeated until the boy had begun to improvise a few elementary strokes.

When Yukikazu was six, his father exercised a right, then still current, in patriarchal Japan. He summarily divorced his wife and took another woman, leaving Setsuko to fend for herself and the two boys. The family finances were desperate, with only the mother's spinning of thread for kimono belts as a source of income. Even after Setsuko became a nurse and midwife they were in dire straits. Yukikazu and his brother often had to go without shoes and socks, and in midwinter lacked overcoats.

When Yukikazu was about twelve his mother contracted pulmonary tuberculosis, at that time a common and usually fatal disease in Japan. For months she was bedridden, nursed largely by the boys. Each morning she went out to the garden to bury the blood and phlegm discharged during the night so that the children would not be infected. Near the fatal end of her illness, the young Ohsawa, for the first time, burst into tears at her bedside. Setsuko, true to the samurai ideal of self-control, of never openly expressing emotion, scolded him for being a *yowamushi* [弱虫] (literally, a "weak insect"), the Japanese equivalent of "crybaby."

The two boys were taken into Magotaro's new household, but apparently it was an unhappy arrangement. According to Ohsawa's recollection, his father's wife fulfilled the stock role of the cruel stepmother. She made him clean the wooden lattice work on the house front with cold water every day, even in winter. Soon the boy was put under the care of priests at a Buddhist temple in the city, where he was the gatekeeper and errand runner. Then he was taken in by the family of a school-friend. They were tea merchants, kindly people who treated the boy as one of the family. Already a bibliophile, he would sequester himself in the bath with a lamp to read late into the night.

Ohsawa's measure of youthful sorrow was not yet full, however. By the time he graduated from middle school at the age of sixteen he was a budding romantic, very fond of poetry and literature. He wanted desperately to attend Tokyo's Waseda University, a mecca for writers and critics. His father opposed this choice, maintaining that his son should pursue a more practical and lucrative line of study. Bitterly disappointed, Ohsawa enrolled in a commercial high school in Kyoto, where he studied business for the next four years. His father lent him just enough money for the tuition. Ohsawa, too poor to buy books, had to borrow texts from classmates, copy them by hand or read them during vacation period.

Despite these difficulties, Ohsawa seemed to thrive. He was a successful student and became head of the debating society. Though commercial subjects dominated the curriculum, he studied Japanese and Western literature as much as he could. He began to study English on his own and organized groups of students to go to the theater for productions of European works.

When Ohsawa was eighteen his brother died, also of tuberculosis. Shortly there-after, Ohsawa himself began to cough up blood. Doctors diagnosed a severe case of intestinal and pulmonary tuberculosis and gave him little chance of survival. It was then that he chanced upon one of Ishizuka's books, however, and learned about Shoku-Yō medicine. He tried the recommended diet of unpolished rice, vegetables, salt and oil. The symptoms disappeared.

Ohsawa continued to follow the Shoku-Yō regime, but did not get involved in the formal activities of the Shoku-Yō Kai. Young, energetic, ambitious, his main desire was to see the world. When he graduated from school in 1913 he moved to Kobe, a port city about twenty-five miles southeast of Kyoto. Then, as now, it was a bus-tling international center, with many trading firms, Japanese and foreign, a sizable foreign community, and a palpable Western ambience. It was the ideal place for a young man attracted to the glittering, if distant, culture of America and Europe, and possessed of a strong wanderlust.

Ohsawa first got a position in a Japanese trading firm as an office boy. Meanwhile he began to take classes in a French language school run by the French consul. The foreigner was impressed by the young man and helped get him a job on a merchant vessel transporting war materiel to Britain. The First World War had broken out and Japan, technically neutral, had become a major supplier to Great Britain. The freighter was chartered by a British firm, and Ohsawa's interest in foreign lan-guages served him well for the first time. Over the next year Ohsawa took several trips to Europe, stopping en route in Southeast Asia, India, and Egypt. It was his first direct exposure to the large and fascinating world outside his native Japan. His boyhood experiences in the Buddhist temple proved useful. Whenever there was a death at sea he was called to recite a Buddhist funeral sutra for the deceased before the body was consigned to the deep.

Returning to Kobe in 1915, Ohsawa became the office manager of a trading com-pany. A restless young man eager for as much varied experience and responsibility as was available, he changed jobs several more times. Finally in 1917 he became the head of the Kobe branch of a Tokyo firm that specialized in the export of silk. This was still a major export item for Japan and for the six years Ohsawa remained with the firm he traveled widely. He went to Southeast Asia many times, returned to Europe and may even have visited the United States.

During this period Ohsawa lived a double life. On one hand he was a world trav-eler, and a Western-oriented urban sophisticate. After a first marriage arranged by his father had ended in fiasco after a few weeks, Ohsawa married an American-born Japanese girl. She was a "liberated woman" and they had a very unusual relation-ship. Most of the time they lived separately. On his European business trips Ohsawa reveled in the Western fashions and fads of the day. He returned from London once with a wardrobe of the finest formal attire. A photo shows him in a Saville Row morning suit, smiling broadly beneath his bowler hat! From France he brought back a mandolin, learned to strum it a bit, and despite an admittedly meager singing talent regaled his friends and guests with the latest European hits.

Ohsawa was also cultivating a deep interest in French poetry, especially that which spoke to his romantic nature. In 1921 he published a Japanese translation, probably the first, of Charles Baudelaire's *Les Fleurs du Mal* ("The Flowers of Evil"). The following year he translated a collection of verse by the Frenchman Gustave Rodenbach and published it as *Te no Suji* [手の筋し] ("The Lines of the Hand").[2]

Ohsawa also got involved in bringing the latest European technology to Japan. From a 1920 trip he returned with some of the first radio transmitters and receivers brought to Japan. Obtaining distribution rights from a French parent company, he began to import new low- and high-speed cameras, as well as parabolic lenses for them. He even developed and patented a movie projector that used half-size film. In both the artistic and technical areas, Ohsawa was beginning to cultivate one of the roles he was to take seriously throughout his life, that of a cultural broker between East and West. At this early stage of his life he concentrated on explaining and introducing bits of Western culture to his fellow Japanese. Soon he was to begin the equally large and crucial task of introducing Japanese culture to the West.

While a student and a devotee of European culture, Ohsawa also was a patriot, deeply conscious of the unique genius of Japan. Even while reading and translating French poetry, Ohsawa was immersed in the classics of his own Japanese and Oriental tradition. He studied the great philosophers of the East, including Confucius and Lao Tzu, and the important texts of Japanese and Chinese medicine. With a few close friends he led evening study sessions in his home. The texts most often used were the *Manyōshū* [萬葉集], the *Tannishō* [歎異鈔], and the *I Ching*. The *Manyōshū* ("The Collection of Ten Thousand Leaves") is the first collection of native Japanese poetry and dates back to the 8th century. Its simple and elegant poems reflect the Yamato-damashii, or "spirit of Japan" prior to Chinese influence. They are filled with a joyful appreciation of nature and of the simple pleasures of human life. The *Tannishō* ("Regrets Concerning Heretical Teachings") by the 12th century Buddhist saint Shinran also reflects an aspect of the unique Japanese awareness. Despite man's weakness and sin, he is absolutely and always part of the cosmic Buddha or divine universe. The *I Ching* or "Book of Changes" is a Chinese work which dates to around 1000 B.C. It is a book of divination which is based on the interaction between Yin and Yang, the two cosmic energies by which all things are created. In these and similar classics of his culture Ohsawa found inspiration and direction as his own world view was developing. And when he wished to express his romantic and poetic spirit, he turned to the 31-syllable form of the traditional Japanese *waka* [和歌]. These he collected in 1924 under the title *Nippon Shishū: Kotoba no Hanataba* [日本詩集＝言葉の花束] ("A Collection of Poems of Japan: A Bouquet of Words").[3]

Despite his fits of Western dandyism and his dabbling in European musical fads, Ohsawa was deeply aware of himself as a scion of the samurai class. He, like his ancestors, was the special embodiment and guardian of the Yamato-damashii. One of his young employees of the Kobe period, a Mr. Fukashi Ishiko [石河浚], relates that when he first met Ohsawa in 1917, the older man remarked that they were both of samurai stock, and thus were both destined to have that combination of courage and obstinacy which characterizes the class.[4]

Ohsawa's attraction to traditional and Japanese values was evident as well in his involvement in the Shoku-Yō Kai. While focusing on diet, the organization also defended the native culture and morality against Western intrusions. In 1916 Ohsawa officially joined the group. He used his office in Kobe to distribute Shoku-Yō food, and organized meetings and lectures. He also began to contribute articles to the Shoku-Yō monthly magazine.

The first of these had to do with the plight of the aboriginal Ainu people of Hokkaido, Japan's northernmost island. Ohsawa pointed out that their traditional culture had been based on hunting, fishing and the gathering of wild plants. Of late, the Japanese government, imitating the colonial policies of Western nations, had been imposing a rice and dairy farming economy on the Ainu. This is out of harmony with the natural environment, Ohsawa asserts. This new food economy and diet will lead to the biological and cultural destruction of the race.

Ohsawa's second major piece concerned the relation between mental telepathy and diet. He recounts how the manager of his office had gone to Viet Nam on business, leaving Ohsawa in Kobe to oversee matters. Ohsawa took his responsibilities seriously, working late into the night, eating very little and taking catnaps at his desk. One night he dreamed of his superior, seeing him stand on a foggy railway platform, then walk into an open freight car and be driven away. The next day Ohsawa received a telegram saying that the man had died. Rushing by boat to Saigon, Ohsawa learned that he had died just at the time of the dream. While in Viet Nam he had another dream encounter with the deceased. Ohsawa was convinced of the validity of these experiences. His strict practice of the Shoku-Yō diet had so refined his body and mind that such experiences occurred spontaneously, he believed. Ohsawa concluded that in a traditional, pure society, spiritual communication is a matter of course. Such must have been the case, he reasoned, in ancient Japan during the Manyōshū era.

This division in Ohsawa's personality was not his alone. It was shared by many of the young people of his generation and by the nation as a whole. Within the Japanese soul wrestled these same two inclinations: one toward the traditions of the past and one toward Western modernism.

Japan's love affair with Western culture had continued in the first decades of the 20th century. Besides Western science and technology, the latest trends in art, literature, social and political thought, and popular culture quickly made their way from Paris, London, New York and Berlin to Tokyo, Osaka and Kyoto. Abstract art, atonal music, Dadaism, free love, baseball, the cinema, socialism, Marxist-Leninism, etc., were embraced, appreciated, retained in part, discarded in part.

At the same time there was a growing appreciation of Japanese cultural traditions. This too had its roots before the turn of the century, in the revival of the nationalistic ideology called *Nippon-shugi* [日本主義]. This "ideology of Japan," whose roots as a self-conscious movement go back to the 12th century, is based on the mythologies recorded in the *Kojiki* [古事記] ("Record of Ancient Things") and the *Nihon Shoki* [日本書紀] ("Annals of Japan"), both written down in the 8th century. In the 1880s, after more than a decade of Japan's total blind infatuation with the West, this ideology re-emerged as a conservative backlash. Citing the ancient scriptures as proof, the movement asserted several basic ideas. These included:

• The Japanese imperial line and the nation as a whole is descended from divine, celestial beings. The first emperor was the great-great-grandson of the sun goddess Amaterasu, and all later emperors also have been lineal descendants.

42

- Japanese culture is likewise of divine origin. Its language, arts, crafts, foods, social patterns, etc., are all creations of the gods.
- The Japanese nation and culture, then, are unique and superior among the world's nations.
- Wherever possible Japan should return to and nurture its traditional cultural patterns, in morality and social relations, in literature and art, in political institutions.

The advocates of Nippon-shugi looked aghast at Western values and morals in particular. They saw Western culture as materialistic, hedonistic, individualistic and egalitarian. Western man, focused only on the material realm, is preoccupied with the physical world and with accumulating wealth and power. He considers himself above all an independent individual, and seeks his own selfish benefit and welfare. He is addicted to the gross physical pleasures. And Western society sees each person as having equal rights and responsibilities. These patterns directly opposed those of pre-modern Japan. These ancient ideals the nationalists described as spiritual, collectivist, self-sacrificing and hierarchic. Japan must return to these values, they urged.

From the mid-1880s various groups formed to advance the tenets of Nippon-shugi, trying to preserve the "national essence" of the Yamato-damashii, and to oppose Western influence. Some focused on education and propaganda. Some used threats, intimidation, bribery and violence to accomplish their aims. While these groups fought Western influence in almost every area of life, they continued to embrace it in technology and science, including medicine and nutrition. Industry was needed to make the nation strong materially and militarily. Western medicine and diet was needed to strengthen it physically. Ishizuka and the Shoku-Yō Kai were in a broad sense part of the Nippon-shugi movement. Their voice was one of the few, however, which challenged the modern "scientific" medicine and nutrition.

For Ohsawa, however, by 1923 the balance of loyalties had shifted definitely to the Japanese, traditionalist side. He was prompted to action by the great earthquake and fire in Tokyo in 1923. This destroyed his company's home office and cost him his job. Seeking a new start, he decided to devote himself full-time to the Shoku-Yō movement. He moved to Tokyo, opened a rice shop, and soon obtained a position on the staff of the organization. In the process he divorced his modish wife and married a more typical and conservative Japanese woman. Ohsawa quickly became a leading figure and spokesman of the group, lecturing, writing, and traveling on its behalf. Within two years he was the supervisor of the Shoku-Yō Kai and the editor of its magazine. Over the next several years all traces of infatuation with Western culture are absent from Ohsawa's writing. There is instead a strong nationalistic and anti-Western tone.

It is not surprising that within Ohsawa the Japanese samurai and patriot won out over the Western-oriented dilettante. From an early age he had been exposed to strong nationalistic influences, first in his home life and later in school. During and after the Russo-Japanese War of 1904–05, the imperial government emphasized military and patriotic virtues in all grades. A class in morals (*shūshin*) [修身] was part of the general curriculum. In it were taught the unique origins and character of the Japanese nation, and the need to work and to sacrifice for the Emperor and for the national welfare. Ohsawa, already keenly aware of his samurai heritage, was then an impressionable middle-school student of eleven or twelve. He was a sensitive boy, made more impressionable no doubt by the breakup of his family and the death of his mother. While he later transcended the narrowness of these teachings, they nevertheless left a deep imprint upon him.

A decade later, as a young man, Ohsawa was shocked and disillusioned by the fratricidal carnage of the "Great War" in Europe. For him and for countless others in East and West, the myth of Western progress and the assumption of European superiority had been destroyed in the bloody trenches between France and Germany. Ohsawa himself visited the military cemetery at Verdun after the war and later recalled the deep and dark impression made upon him by the endless rows of white crosses.

Also, in Tokyo, Ohsawa could see first hand the excesses of the hedonistic subculture which had developed under Western influence. Bars, cabarets, movies and dance halls were frequented by young men and women who flaunted traditional morality. It was a pleasure-hungry and morally ungrounded world, not unlike that of Paris, New York and Berlin around the same time. It was a subculture dedicated to *ero* [エロ], *guro* [グロ], and *nansensu* [ナンセンス], "the erotic, grotesque, and nonsensical," and dominated by the thrills of the three "S's," sports, sex, and screen.[5] The moralistic impulses of a stern son of a samurai were probably repulsed by this.

Within the Tokyo Shoku-Yō Kai Ohsawa met many influential men. Members of the court nobility, of the military elite, and of conservative business and political factions, they tended to be supporters of Nippon-shugi. They saw Shoku-Yō as the expression of the ideology of Japan in medicine and nutrition. They took seriously Ishizuka's idea that the first step to regaining the "national essence" must be a return to a traditional diet. Working, studying and teaching within this milieu certainly influenced Ohsawa as well.

In any case, by the mid-1920s Ohsawa was firmly within the Shoku-Yō-nationalist camp. In charge of publications for the organization, he wrote widely on Shoku-Yō topics. A number of these articles from the magazine were collected and published in 1927 as *Nihon Seishin no Seirigaku* [日本精神の生理学] ("The Physiology of the Japanese Spirit"). The following year his eulogistic biography of Ishizuka was published. Also in 1928, the five volumes of his *Shoku-Yō Kōgi Roku* [食養講義録] ("The Shoku-Yō Lectures") appeared. This work included an explanation of Shoku-Yō philosophy, as well as detailed practical instruction on food preparation, on the cure of specific illnesses through diet, and on the use of external treatments.

For the most part, Ohsawa draws from his predecessors, particularly Ishizuka. He echoes the Shoku-Yō founder's ideas about the crucial role of food in human life. It determines, he writes, man's health or sickness, sadness or happiness. It determines too his physical appearance, behavior, and moral and spiritual sensitivity. Through a diet of grains and vegetables man can achieve physical and spiritual well-being. Meat, dairy, refined foods, and products from different climates upset the physiological balance of sodium and potassium and result in sickness and unhappiness. Man is a ghost of his food. And, as food controls the destiny of individuals, it controls also the rise and fall of societies and nations.

There is also a strong influence from Kaibara, especially in moral principles. Affirming a general neo-Confucian viewpoint (which was also part of Nippon-shugi), Ohsawa often borrows phrases and sentences directly from the 17th century sage. Gratitude, filial piety (respect and obedience in relation to one's parents) and control of the desires are the essentials of the moral life. We must think of our life, Ohsawa writes, as a gift from nature and from our parents. We must feel endless gratitude for it. This is the key to happiness. There is no person more unhappy than he who knows no gratitude to his parents. To be happy one must feel grateful every day for food and for the very miracle of life. Human nature is basically good, but man inclines to overindulgence in the physical appetites. Physical and mental health depend on moderating our eating. Quoting Kaibara, Ohsawa advises eating only to four-fifths capacity.

Ohsawa also borrows, and here too with grateful acknowledgment, from a Dr. Manabu Nishihata [西端学]. Nishihata had become active in the Shoku-Yō Kai in 1913, and from 1919 was the director. He had helped the organization become more socially active, leading its sponsorship of a bill in Parliament that would have prohibited the mixing of sugar with rice, a common practice of the day. Nishihata also refined the thought of Ishizuka and, in "The Physiology of the Japanese Spirit," Ohsawa presents these refinements.

Apparently it was Nishihata who first used the phrase (in the Shoku-Yō context at least) of *shin-do-fu-ji* [身土不二], as an expression of the movement's world view. Borrowed perhaps from a Buddhist text, it means literally "body earth not two." In a broad sense, it means that man and his natural environment are deeply related. Man is an animate and cultural expression of the world around him, a transformation of soil, air, water, climate and vegetation. The statement is both descriptive and prescriptive. As a creation of the natural environment, man must live in harmony with that environment in order to be happy and healthy. Shoku-Yō is the practical application of this principle. *Shoku* [食] or "food" refers to the obvious nourishment taken through the mouth, but it means air, light, moisture and cultural influences as well. *Yō* [養] or "nourishment" is the proper way to take these various "foods" to insure health and happiness.

Nishihata had done extensive research on various cultures and on the relation between daily life and natural environment. While Ishizuka had emphasized choosing food that is in harmony with one's surroundings, Nishihata saw that human dress and housing must also express this unity. Man's food, but also his clothing and shelter, are crucial in protecting his body, in regulating its temperature and proper functioning. Thus they too have a key role in maintaining human health. In a tropical climate, then, the inhabitants can and should live on fruits and tubers, go about barefoot and almost naked, and live in houses made of grass. In a rigorous temperate climate such as that of northern Europe, the natives should eat grains and animal foods, wear woolen and leather garments, and live in cave-like houses. Arctic dwellers conform best to their environment by eating mostly fish and meat, dressing in animal skins, and living in ice shelters. In the mild temperate zone of a country like Japan, for example, with four distinct seasons, the proper diet is based on grains and vegetables. Clothing should be of vegetable fibers such as cotton and flax, or occasionally silk, and shelters should be made of wood.

Ohsawa also was influenced by the Nippon-shugi ideology of the day. This is evident in his handling of Western culture, especially its science and medicine, of Japanese culture and history, and of the contemporary situation in Japan. In these areas he develops themes which Ishizuka, in a broad and gentle manner, had outlined. Ohsawa is much more strident and harsh. There is an urgency and zeal in his presentation. Ishizuka was first of all a man of science. His crusading on broad social and cultural issues was secondary and done with a tone of reserve. Ohsawa was a crusader and a zealous advocate, even a propagandist, more than anything else. The Japanist themes and the urgency with which they are presented remained part of his work for many years.

Japan is a nation founded by the gods, Ohsawa maintains, reciting the central tenet of Nippon-shugi. Its imperial line extends back to this divine origin and distinguishes Japan from other nations of the world. Its climate is ideal for human habitation, with each season clearly defined and possessing its unique beauty. The divine ancestors taught how to live in harmony with this natural environment, weaving their wisdom into the daily life of the people. Through this the Yamato-damashii or spirit of Japan was biologically nourished and maintained, principally by the simple diet of rice and vegetables. It is a spirit and a way of life that is quiet, elegant and simple; that seeks to live in harmony with nature; that possesses gratitude, humility and a willingness to sacrifice oneself for the common good. It is a spirit which is uniquely sensitive to the world of invisible realities. Also very flexible and accepting, it can embrace, absorb and perfect foreign ideas and practices.

Again, pursuing a Nippon-shugi theme, mentioned in passing by Ishizuka, Ohsawa romanticizes earlier periods of Japanese history. The era of the *Manyōshū*, he writes, was a time when the soul of Japan was purely manifested, and when the nation was a peaceful and idyllic community, every person being a poet and a mystic. The Tokugawa Period, shattered by the intrusion of the West, had been a "paradise on earth." During this period the samurai had exemplified Japan's unique moral and spiritual genius. Strong, brave and selfless, the warrior was willing to die for his lord and for the cause of justice. Yet he was also an artist, a master of the tea ceremony, and a seeker after ultimate truth. As a poet, he composed verses as he marched into battle, and later, if mortally wounded, would trade a poem with his vanquisher before the *coup de grâce*.

Against this background Ohsawa describes the culture of the West, of the meat and dairy food eaters, who had violated this Garden of Eden. Again Ishizuka's themes are repeated, but in an extreme and demagogic way. Ohsawa describes Westerners as short-tempered, short-lived, violent, greedy, exploitative, lazy, fault-finding, and lacking in gratitude and humility. They are subject to sexual perversions, and need cosmetics and perfumes to hide their bad smell. Western sports are merely the biologically necessary attempts to discharge the excess energy that comes from meat-eating. Western law, medicine, and insurance are just symptoms of the fear and mental illness that permeate the entire culture. Western life in general, Ohsawa asserts, is based on the exploitation of *Ten* [天] and *Chi* [地] ("Heaven" and "Earth"), the world of nature. The crass destruction of the environment reflects a materialistic view of the world, a quest for selfish pleasure, a belief that man is the center of all things (anthropocentrism), and a blindness to the world of the spirit.

Ohsawa singles out Western science and medicine for special analysis and criticism. Contrasting them with parallel but basically different Eastern disciplines, he derides and belittles them. This was a task he would pursue throughout his life.

Western scientific method, Ohsawa writes, is nothing more than the accumulation, classification and recording of everyday experience. The knowledge it gains is superficial, lacking real insight into the nature of the universe and the meaning of life. Its practical application in technology produces conveniences and creature comforts only. In terms of true human happiness and health, these are worthless. Ultimately, they lead only to the opposite, enslaving man and weakening him, physically and spiritually.

Ohsawa contrasts Western science (*kagaku*) [科学] with Oriental science or *gakumon* [学問]. The first is less than three centuries old and only observes, measures and analyzes nature. It focuses on the small and isolated phenomenon, forgetting the whole. It seeks to understand only to subjugate and exploit. The other dates from the dawn of human civilization. It is intuitive in method, and tries to immerse man in direct and ecstatic union with nature. Its aim is human health and happiness and the highest fulfillment of the human spirit. Ohsawa writes: "Kagaku makes a genius into a fool. Gakumon makes a fool into a genius. Kagaku is a tool of specialization. Gakumon makes one understand all things through the study and mastery of one art."[6]

While Eastern "science" seeks mystic union with nature, it is also capable of great discoveries and marvelous technologies. Ohsawa cites the navigational techniques of the ancient Chinese, the unmatched metallurgical skill of the medieval Japanese swordmakers, as well as Ishizuka's discovery of Shoku-Yō as examples. The Japanese should not be ashamed of the absence of a Western-style science and industry in their pre-modern culture. Their gakumon has perfected a means to human happiness, a goal which has eluded Western civilization.

Ohsawa also uses his critical rapier on Western medicine. It is skilled in diagnosing and naming disease, but at little else. It does not know the real cause of disease, so it cannot really cure. Its treatments are only symptomatic and palliative, removing a symptom from one part of the body while harming another. Surgery is a mutilation rather than a cure. Also, Western medicine deals with sickness only when it has developed. It has no technique for the prevention of disease, and none for maintaining a positive level of health and vitality. Ultimately, it is a failure. There are still many diseases which resist all efforts for even symptomatic treatment, that are "incurable."

And not surprisingly, Ohsawa rhapsodizes over Eastern medicine. It is based on a clear grasp of man's nature and of his relationship to the natural environment. It sees that health depends on a harmony with nature, especially through proper food. Thus it can prevent disease through sound diet and a prudent way of life. It treats disease with the most fundamental medicine, proper food. Its supplemental treatments, such as acupuncture, moxibustion and herbs, recognize the sensitivity and inter-relatedness of the organism, and have no harmful side-effects. The highest medicine of the East, i.e., Shoku-Yō, aims at the cure of the whole man, not just of his symptoms and disease. It tries to give the means to a positive and vibrant state of health.

Ohsawa's view of modern Japan follows from this contrast between Eastern and Western culture. Since its opening to the West, Japan's physical and mental health and its unique spirituality have been undermined by the importation of Western culture. Western food, medicine, and Western values (materialism, hedonism, individualism, etc.) are undermining the nation. The battle is almost lost. In physical health and in manners and morals, the people have degenerated. Simplicity has given way to garishness, respect to insolence, gratitude to egotism, and hierarchy to anarchy. Except in a few isolated farming communities and among a few practitioners of the ancient arts and crafts, the old ways and values are lost. The first decades of the 20th century represent the greatest disgrace and crisis in the three-thousand-year history of the nation. And it is the intellectuals who are the chief culprits, the scientists, physicians and scholars who slavishly defer to the ways of the West and who promote them among the people. These men, who ignore and attack the traditions of Japan's ancient culture, are traitors and criminals who are destroying the nation.

In this critical and somber situation, Shoku-Yō looms as the last great hope of the nation. It is, Ohsawa writes, "the single clear path which has nourished the Japanese people for centuries."[7] Now it is the only means to save Japan from the "monsters" in the guise of "culture," i.e., Western medicine, science, education, and so on. On it depends the physical, moral and spiritual health of the nation, its very destiny. The Shoku-Yō movement is a holy crusade to preserve and maintain the Yamato-damashii in the 20th century. Its founder, Ishizuka, is a "saint of the Meiji Period" who gave Japan a means to protect itself from the hedonism of the West.[8]

Ohsawa develops one other theme upon which Ishizuka had dwelt but briefly, that of spiritual development. Ohsawa does this by introducing the concept of the "Tao." Central to East Asian culture, it can have one of several meanings. It can refer to the impersonal cosmic absolute from which all phenomena derive, or the manner or rhythm by which the ultimate operates in the world. Meaning originally "road" or "path," it can refer also to a spiritual path or discipline, that is, any study or practice which aims at the union of the individual with the absolute. In Japanese "Tao" is read *dō* [道], and hence *cha-dō* [茶道] (the Way of Tea), *ka-dō* [華道] (The Way of Flower Arrangement), *judō* [柔道] (the Way of Gentleness) and the other arts, crafts, and martial disciplines must be understood in this light. They are paths of spiritual development leading from the human to the transcendent realm.

Ishizuka, of course, had mentioned "spiritual refreshment" as one of the benefits of Shoku-Yō practice. Ohsawa takes this much further. Apparently drawing from Buddhist and Hindu sources, he outlines, in "The Shoku-Yō Lectures," a religious view of the world and human life. The phenomenal world around us, he asserts, is illusory and unreal. It can never satisfy the longings of the human spirit. The true aim of human life is to return to the ultimate source of life, the eternal and transcendent Self. This cosmic soul lies also within each person. It, rather than the petty ego of selfish wants and desires, is the true Self of man. True happiness and fulfillment come only when one can hear the voice of this inner Self, which is also the voice at the center of creation.[9]

Ohsawa then asserts that this experience of one's higher Self is the true aim of Shoku-Yō. In fact, the more appropriate term is *Shoku-Yō-Dō* or "the Tao of Food

48

Nourishment." By controlling appetite, by eating small amounts of grains and
vegetables, by chewing very well, one may advance on the spiritual path. Powers of
clairvoyance and foreknowledge will develop and one will see that life and mystery
fill the universe. Ultimately, one will see beyond time and space and will experience
one's identity with the universe.[10]

Also, during this time, Ohsawa began to apply Yin-Yang [陰陽] concepts and
terminology to Shoku-Yō ideas. As we have seen, Ishizuka shied from using this
ancient Chinese philosophy, but Ohsawa had no such compunction. It fitted too
well with the poles of Na-dominance and K-dominance in foods, people and illnesses. He began to refer to the former as "Yang" and to the latter as "Yin." The
full development was to come a few years later, but here was the start. Ohsawa also
began to toy with Taoist cosmogonies, or theories of the origin and structure of the
universe. He explains in the "Lectures," quite in passing, that the creation of the
universe occurs in evolutionary stages. This process begins with the absolute or Tao,
leads then to Yin and Yang, and thence to the various spiritual and material realms.
The culmination is man.[11] Ohsawa observes that all phenomena including man are
produced by the interaction of the energy of the earth (Yin) with the energy of the
heavens (Yang).[12]

Thus by 1928, his thirty-fifth year, Ohsawa had a comprehensive and integrated
world view: a vision of the universe and of human nature, of the true aims of human
life and of the contemporary crisis. Most of this he had inherited from Ishizuka,
Kaibara, and the champions of Nippon-shugi. But he was beginning to develop his
own ideas and method of expression, to expand the boundaries of this Weltanschauung. He was a man fully mature and ready to step out on his own.

And step out on his own was precisely what he did. In early 1929 Ohsawa resigned
his posts at the Shoku-Yō Kai and made arrangements for the care of his depend-
ents. He was going, he announced to startled friends and associates, to leave Japan
and to live in the West. It was the grandiose, courageous and impulsive decision of
a restless spirit who thrived on adventure. It was not the last such decision made by
Ohsawa.

---

[1] A primary source for biographical data contained in this chapter and in the following chapters
on Ohsawa is: Matsumoto, Ichiro: *Shoku Seikatsu no Kakumeiji: Sakurazawa Yukikazu no
Shisō to Shōgai* ("The Food Life Revolutionary: The Life and Thought of Sakurazawa Yukikazu"), Chisan Shuppan, Tokyo, 1976

   This is a biography of Ohsawa which was commissioned by followers in Japan. It contains
a great deal of valuable information. The balance of the biographical data in this and other
chapters is culled from recollections and reminiscences in Ohsawa's writings, and from con-
versations with Lima Ohsawa and disciples and friends of Ohsawa.

[2] Neither of these books is in print or currently available, but they are listed in the bibliography of the *George Ohsawa Album* issued by Nippon C.I. in 1976

[3] This book is also in the *Album* bibliography and is also unavailable. Ohsawa refers to it and
describes it in his other writings, however.

[4] These reminiscences are part of a privately published article by a Mr. Ishiko Fukashi "*Wakaki
Hi no Sakurazawa Yukikazu Shi*" ("A History of the Younger Days of Sakurazawa Yukikazu")
It is in the possession of Mr. M. Hashimoto, Nippon C.I.

[5] This description is taken from Reishauer, E.O., *East Asia: The Great Transformation*, Vol. 2,
p. 522 (Houghton Mifflin, Boston, 1965)

[6] Sakurazawa, Yukikazu, *Nihon Seishin no Seirigaku*, Nihon Shoku-Yō Kenkyujo, Tokyo, 1929, p. 98

[7] Sakurazawa, Yukikazu, *Shoku-Yō Kōgi Roku*, 1928, reprinted by Nippon C.I., 1977, p. 41

[8] Sakurazawa, Y., *Ishitzuka Sagen*, p. 38

[9] Sakurazawa, *Shoku-Yō Kōgi Roku*, pp. 86 ff. and p. 92

[10] Ibid., p. 86

[11] Sakurazawa, Y., *Nihon Seishin no Seirigaku*, p. 75

[12] Sakurazawa, Y., *Seirigaku Shoku-Yō Kōgi Roku*, p. 13

4.

George Ohsawa:
The First Sojourn in the West (1929–1936)

At the time George Ohsawa resolved to go to Europe, his life in Tokyo was a busy one, full of responsibilities. He was a high official and leading figure in the Shoku-Yō Kai, active as a writer, lecturer and medical consultant. His third marriage had just ended in divorce. There were children from this union as well as from his second marriage. Ohsawa was also responsible for the support of his aging father.

His prospects in Europe were at best uncertain. He had few if any contacts in Paris, and his language ability was very limited. He would have to struggle to earn a living while trying to realize his avowed purpose in going: to introduce Japanese culture, and particularly Shoku-Yō, to the West.

Ohsawa's decision, ill-advised as it may seem, gives insight into his character. He was above all a dreamer of great dreams. But he was not only a dreamer. Ohsawa was a man of energy, confidence, and action, willing to pursue his ambitions however grand they might seem. Within him too, was an element of impetuosity and willfulness. Also, he was, and was to remain throughout his life, totally committed to Shoku-Yō philosophy and practice, and willing to do almost anything to help spread it. And he was, despite his attitude toward Western civilization, a Francophile, a lover of France and its culture of elegance, *joie de vivre* and wit.

Ohsawa settled his affairs and packed several crates of books to be sent ahead by ship. Then on a sunny spring day in 1929, he departed Tokyo Central Railway Station with a few personal belongings. It was a day when his fellow Tokyoites were taking their families to enjoy the annual beauty of the cherry blossoms. Ohsawa traveled by train to the southern part of Japan, took a boat to Korea, then another train to the eastern terminus of the Trans-Siberian railway. There he began a fourteen-day trip, on cushionless benches, across the vastness of Asia and Europe.[1]

Ohsawa had decided to turn the trip into a dietary experiment and had brought as his main food, *musubi* [むすび] or "rice balls." He wanted to see how he would fare living on these alone. The musubi is a traditional and still popular Japanese picnic and travel food. It consists of a ball of rice, with a pickled plum or *umeboshi* [梅干] pressed into the center (to slow spoiling), and an outer wrapping of sheet sea vegetable called *nori* [海苔]. They are round, black and reasonably firm. At the Russian border, the Soviet guard suspected these were bombs and detained Ohsawa until convinced otherwise (perhaps by Ohsawa eating one!).

Ohsawa deeply enjoyed the long trip, sitting at the window and watching the boundless forests and plains of Siberia flow past. Two or three times a day he would slowly eat one of the musubi, still contemplating the snow-covered landscape. After several days, though, they had begun to go bad, developing a green mold on the outside and a sour taste within. With the unflagging enthusiasm of a true optimist, Ohsawa mused how sweet the rice seemed and how much it reminded him of *amazake* [甘酒・淡酒] or "sweet sake," a mild fermented drink used especially on festive occasions. When the musubi were gone, Ohsawa ate roasted brown rice which he mixed with boiling water in an army canteen. For the most part, the food experiment was a success. He felt hale and hearty as the journey progressed, except for a slight case of constipation. This he treated by eating some fruit borrowed from a fellow Japanese traveler.

Finally the train arrived in the Gar du Nord in Paris. Ohsawa was exultant, filled with enthusiasm for his new adventure. He was also quite poor, having only about 200 francs, enough money for a few weeks' living expenses. He rented an attic room in a French home. There were no windows in his quarters, only a skylight overhead. He set up the shipping crates used for his books as a desk and table. Upon this he placed a photograph of his mother, who was for him a strong source of inspiration. Even late in his life he would recall her deathbed advice. "Study all things. Never become a narrow specialist. Devote yourself to the welfare of the nation and of all humanity." Perhaps in these new and lonely surroundings Ohsawa was in particular need of this memory. He nicknamed his room *hamaguri* [蛤] (Japanese for "the clam") to describe the sudden lighting and darkening that occurred through the skylight at dawn and at dusk.

Having set up house, Ohsawa considered how best to pursue his aims. He had come to teach but also to study. He wanted to confront Western science, medicine and nutrition, and to demonstrate the superiority of the Oriental approach represented by Shoku-Yō. More generally, he wanted to introduce the essence of Japanese culture, the Yamato-damashii and the various arts and disciplines which it had produced. But also he wanted to study the West deeply. He wanted to truly grasp Western science, philosophy and religion, and to see how Western man experienced the world.

Ohsawa's choice of Paris for this enterprise was a wise one. The city was then the cultural capital of the Western world. In art and literature, in science and medicine, the "City of Light" nurtured its native geniuses and attracted leading figures from other lands. Frenchmen like Paul Valéry, André Malraux and expatriates like Ernest Hemingway, Gertrude Stein and James Joyce made it a Mecca for writers and poets. Great scientific minds gathered as well, and through work done at such places as the Pasteur Institute, Paris was a center for scientific and medical research. And the city was still a nexus of political power. It was the hub of a far-flung, still vital world empire, with colonies in Southeast Asia and throughout Africa.

Besides, Paris was a center for the study of Asian history and culture by Western intellectuals and artists. Serious scholarly study had been going on for some time, with Indian and Chinese texts having been available for over a century. In particular, the languages and scriptures of Buddhism, the literature and science of China, and since its opening, the art and culture of Japan, had come under close and systematic scrutiny. Japanese aesthetics had even had a strong impact on the development of modern art in France. Back in the 1880s, the first wave of woodblock prints imported from Japan had inspired the *cloisonné* style of Vincent van Gogh. In this manner of painting solid blocks of striking and contrasting colors are the basic structural element. And in the 1920s Japanese painting and other art work was still very much in vogue. Paris, then, was an ideal place for Ohsawa to present Oriental culture in his own terms, and to gain a deeper understanding of the West.

The first months were difficult ones for Ohsawa. He wrote articles on Japanese culture and, walking the length and breadth of the city (in order to save the carfare), presented them to magazine editors. But there were no buyers. Very short of funds, Ohsawa could afford as food only a mixture of millet and broken grains sold as birdseed in the petshops. This he supplemented by picking wild herbs in the public parks. On Sundays Ohsawa would go to the suburbs with his fellow Parisians to pick wild vegetables, and especially to hunt snails, considered a delicacy by the French. He cooked these things on a single gas burner he had installed in the "hamaguri."

One evening while returning to his room, Ohsawa passed behind a vegetable market and noticed in the street a pile of broken and bruised produce that had been swept out as rubbish. There were broken carrots, beet greens, the outer leaves of cabbages, etc. He bent down and slipped some of these into his briefcase. Returning home, he cooked some for dinner and hung others on a line in his room to dry. The market back door became a regular stop on his homeward journeys. One day a group of Paris street urchins also appeared and began to fill a cart with food for their pet rabbits. They were a bit taken aback by a distinguished Oriental gentleman stuffing his briefcase with radish leaves. "How many rabbits do you have at home?" they asked. An embarrassed Ohsawa replied "Oh, just one, but it is a big black one." Their curiosity aroused, the boys insisted that Ohsawa take them home to see this rare marvel, and he had a hard time discouraging them.

To support himself that first summer, Ohsawa took a job as a cook at an international student camping jamboree outside Paris. He began to lecture there informally about food and health. One of the woman students was suffering from an inflammation of the joints and Ohsawa, by changing her diet and by treating her with external compresses, cured the painful condition. He was promoted to the role of regular lecturer.

Returning to Paris, Ohsawa enrolled as a special student at the Sorbonne and began to attend lectures at the Pasteur Institute. He was especially interested in studying chemistry and the other natural sciences from a Western point of view. He also continued trying to express in articles in French what he considered essential in his own Japanese and Oriental tradition. The next years were poor but carefree, pleasant, and intellectually stimulating for Ohsawa. He eventually moved to more comfortable quarters, taking a room with the family of a French doctor. Years later he reminisced nostalgically how delightful it was to rise early, to breakfast on croissants and coffee with the lady of the house, and then to spend the morning sitting in the sunlit courtyard reading a French novel.

During this period Ohsawa befriended a young Frenchman studying law. He was suffering from nervous exhaustion, though, and was unable to prepare for the examinations. Ohsawa prescribed a Shoku-Yō regimen of grains and vegetables, which the

54

desperate young man was willing to try. He recovered, and successfully completed his studies. However, when Ohsawa tried to explain the world view and the principles which lay behind the diet, the Frenchman was unable to understand.

This experience, and others like it, forced Ohsawa to consider how to present Eastern ideas and culture so that Western people would understand them. The Western mind is rational and inductive. It seeks truth by observing many separate phenomena, analyzing them and formulating a general law. The Eastern mind is intuitive and deductive. It begins with the direct apprehension of a universal law and then applies it to the particular. Ohsawa decided to communicate with the West on its own terms. He would present the philosophy of Yin and Yang as the foundation of the Oriental world view and culture. But he would explain it in an analytical and detailed fashion, and he would demonstrate then that it applies to all areas of natural science. The result was his first book in French, *Le Principe Unique de la Philosophie et de la Science d'Extrême Orient* ("The Unique Principle of the Philosophy and the Science of the Far East"), published in 1931 by Vrin, a highly respected publisher of philosophical titles.

This slim volume, still in print half a century later, is a remarkable work. In it Ohsawa covers the whole range of Eastern philosophy and culture, tying together philosophy, metaphysics, religion, art, diet, medicine and the natural sciences. It is one of the first comprehensive attempts to explain Oriental life and thought in a Western language.

Ohsawa's focus is what he calls *L'Inyology* or *In-Yō-gaku* [陰陽学], the philosophy of Yin and Yang, without which, he says, it is impossible to understand the culture of the East. The source of all that exists is *Tai-Kyoku* [太極], "the Great Ultimate" or as it is known in Buddhist philosophy, *Shunyata*, "the infinite emptiness." From this absolute and primal oneness emerge the antagonistic yet complementary principles Yin and Yang. Yin is expansive, cold, dark—the feminine principle. Yang is contractive, hot, and active—the male principle. These two act and interact, creating all phenomena and their changes in the universe.

To explain the origins of L'Inyology, Ohsawa tells the story, based on Chinese legend, of the Emperor Fou Hi [伏羲]. He ruled the ancestors of the Chinese when they were still pastoral nomads living on the central Asian plateau. Ohsawa describes in rather fanciful detail how Fou Hi would emerge from his tent before dawn to observe the processes of nature, and how he would sit by the campfire for long hours, pondering what he had seen. And he relates how after years of observation and meditation, Fou Hi discovered the law which governs the universe. He saw that everything is always moving, always changing. And he saw that this constant flux comes from the attraction between two opposite forms of energy, which had originated in a cosmic unity. Thus Fou Hi gave to humanity the philosophy of Yin and Yang, a unique tool for understanding the universe.

According to Ohsawa, this universal law was passed from these ancient peoples to the three great civilizations of India, China and Japan. In each it was expressed somewhat differently, according to the particular genius of the people. In East Asia, where the terms Yin and Yang persisted, the philosophy, through many interpretations and reinterpetations, had become confused and imprecise. But Ohsawa asserts that it can be expressed in clear and precise terms which are understandable to modern man. And it can be used to advantage in every field of human inquiry and activity.

Thus, early in the book, Ohsawa lists for the first time the twelve principles of the Unique Principle.[2] Even as he does so he notes that the law of Yin and Yang can be truly grasped only by direct intuition, and that he is presenting it as a set of clear and separate laws for the benefit of the Western mind. Also, to make it more understandable, he presents it in a physical rather than a metaphysical way. In traditional Chinese thought all phenomena, beginning with Heaven and Earth, were classified according to their function. The heavens, in which all creation is begun, are Yang, while the earth is Yin. Ohsawa classified these according to structure, and thus the endless expanse of the heavens is Yin and the contracted solid earth is Yang. Thus while Ohsawa purports to present an ancient Oriental way of thinking, in practice his Inyology does not correspond to the classical Chinese system. Although he may have made it easier to understand for Westerners, he created between his own thinking and that of traditional Oriental medicine, a rift which has yet to be bridged.

This philosophy, Ohsawa asserts, can be applied to every field, to psychology, economics, history, and sociology, and also to biology, chemistry, physics and medicine. To prove this he ventures to explain various scientific problems in terms of Yin and Yang, professing meanwhile that he is a rank amateur in these Western disciplines.

Ohsawa begins by asserting that all chemical elements can be classified according to Yin and Yang. The recently developed science of spectroscopy had shown that when elements are heated they give off varying wavelengths of light and energy. Elements such as carbon, hydrogen and sodium emit wavelengths toward the red and orange end of the spectrum (6,500 Angstroms). These are more Yang, Ohsawa asserts, dominated by contractive or centripetal energy. Elements which give off light waves toward the violet end of the scale (4,300 Angstroms) are relatively Yin, expansive in nature. These include potassium, oxygen, calcium and iron.[3]

With this overview all chemical reactions can be understood. It is natural that hydrogen (Yang) and oxygen (Yin) should readily combine into the stable compound H_2O (water). It is obvious, too, why iron heated in water combines with the oxygen, while hydrogen is released as gas. This is because iron and oxygen, both being Yin, will combine only when there is a Yang factor present, namely heat. Hydrogen is repelled by the fire, and attracted instead to the Yin of the atmosphere.[4]

The law pertains too in the biological world, of course. The plant world (immobile, green, cool—hence Yin) breathes in carbon monoxide (Yang) and breathes out oxygen (Yin). Recently it had been discovered that some plants, such as buckwheat, do not grow when deprived of potassium. It is natural that this element, revealed by spectroscopy to be Yin, should control the function of growth, also Yin (expansive). Ohsawa cites research (*K et Na Chez Les Vegetaux* by M.D. Perietzeanu) which indicates that the shape, color, height and functioning of plants depends on the ratio between sodium and potassium. Again, since these elements are respectively strongly Yang and Yin, this is to be expected. In fact, Ishizuka had discovered this same principle half a century before.[5]

Ohsawa also ventures into the domain of physics, and using his Yin Yang theory proposes some radical ideas. The atom, he asserts, is not a stable structure of particles and energy. Actually, it is a spiral in which the peripheral (Yin) electrons are orbiting steadily inward toward the central (Yang) protons in the nucleus. There the two will combine to form a neutron. Yin attracts Yang, Yang attracts Yin. Everything is changing into its opposite on the atomic level, as on all levels of reality.

The principles can be used too to understand the true nature of gravity. Newton's theory of universal gravitation, upon which all Western understanding of the heavens is based, is, Ohsawa blithely maintains, incorrect. Gravity is not the attractive pull of a large mass acting upon a small one. Instead, it is the natural movement of energy from the periphery (Yin) of a system to the center (Yang). The earth is the midpoint of an immense spiral of energy, constantly coming in from the cosmos. It is this energy, not any attraction of the earth, which causes gravity. Objects are not pulled toward the earth, they are pushed down to it.[6]

Eventually, Ohsawa deals with medicine and nutrition, including his Shoku-Yō views about food and health as one application of the Unique Principle. Foods can be classified according to Yin and Yang, depending on their chemical composition. Illnesses are also Yin or Yang, and are caused by foods which have an excess of one or the other. The highest medicine cures simply and easily by using food to restore the Yin-Yang balance in the body. With this balance, all illness can be prevented. The whole person—his psychological, moral and spiritual functions, as well as the physical—can regain and maintain health.

After demonstrating Yin and Yang in the physical sciences, Ohsawa goes on to broader issues of human nature and destiny, of civilization and history. Here he reiterates many of the themes of his earlier writing. The visible universe is a geometric point in infinity, a small and "fragile ship of shadows" sailing in an endless sea. Human beings vainly seek happiness in this world but are endlessly disappointed. Everything is always changing, passing away. True joy and freedom can be found only by returning to the cosmic Self or *Tai-Kyoku* (*le grande Moi*), and by transcending the ego self or *le petite moi*. Then there is no space nor time. Everything is beautiful, and we realize that we are eternal and infinite. This awareness cannot be achieved by intellectual knowledge, only by intuition.

Ohsawa also deals at length with the nature of Asian culture. Each of its civilizations was nourished by the Yin-Yang philosophy of Fou Hi. But in each, the particular climate and diet led to a different expression and application. In India, the hot weather and a more Yin diet of vegetables, fruits and sweets resulted in a more complex, expanded philosophy, and a way of life which, tending to ignore the material realm, focused on the spiritual world. In China, the cooler, more rugged climate and the resulting diet of grains, animal food and vegetables led to a more practical culture. Yin and Yang was applied with particular insight to the material and social world. Physiology, mechanics, astronomy, government and social organization were areas in which the Chinese excelled.

In Japan, the moderate climate and the diet of grains and vegetables has led to a balance between the mystical and the practical. The Japanese have been concerned both with the spiritual and the material world. What emerged was a culture in which every aspect of daily life was formed according to the law of Yin and Yang and with an awareness of man's spiritual destiny. Thus diet, medicine, the various fine arts and crafts, and the martial arts are all based on the universal law and lead man back to *Tai-Kyoku*. They are all *dō*, spiritual paths. And since this perfect conscious-ness cannot be expressed in words (except perhaps suggestively as in a *haiku* [俳句] or 17 syllable poem), and since in fact the written or spoken word destroys it, Japan has been a culture of silence. Until the modern period it lacked an explicit meta-physics, morality or science.

Ohsawa also uses his earlier comparison of West and East, describing European culture as materialistic and scientific—so busy trying to analyze and control the world that it has forgotten the larger harmony of nature and man. But the Japanese have no cause for pride, Ohsawa says, however elevated and elegant their traditional culture. It is only an accident of geography and climate. These factors have made possible, even unavoidable, a diet of rice and vegetables. It is this diet which has produced the Japanese mentality and way of life. Likewise, Western civilization is an expression of the damp, dark and cold environment of northern Europe, and the foods of that region. There is no particular virtue or vice in either culture. "History is a translation of geography."[7]

Ohsawa includes two appendixes. Both are translations of classic Buddhist texts. One is the *Maha Prajna Paramita Hrdaya Sutra* [摩訶般若波羅蜜多心經] ("The Secret of the Perfection of the Great Wisdom"), known popularly as "The Heart Sutra." In it the Bodhisattva of compassion, Avalokiteshvara, explains how to transcend suffering in the world. This is through the "perfection of wisdom," the realization that everything in the world is unreal, is "empty" or *shunya*. All objects, possessions, sensations, desires and thoughts, pain, suffering, death, even life itself, are illusory. To attain this wisdom is to be free of all fear, desire and suffering, to enter into Nirvana or pure bliss. And, the text asserts, all creatures are destined to realize this.

> All arrive at the banks beyond,
> All gather together by the consciousness
> Perfect and adorable.[8]

The second appendix is of the *Tannishō* of Shinran [親鸞]. Shinran founded the *Jōdo Shinshū* [浄土眞宗] or the "True Pure Land Sect" of Buddhism, teaching that to achieve salvation in the celestial "western" paradise, one need only recite with sin-cerity the words *Namu Amida Butsu* [南無阿弥陀佛] ("Hail to the Amida Buddha"). According to Ohsawa, the Amida Buddha is naught else but *Shunyata*, Tai-Kyoku, the ultimate reality which creates and protects all beings and which brings all back to perfection and bliss.

Underlying Shinran's thought, then, is the idea that man is part of the absolute, and ever remains so. Even when lazy, ignorant and immoral a person is at one with the Buddha. In fact, in that state one is more likely to experience this unity than when one is moral and upright. The good are hindered by their self-righteousness and pride. It is the fallen and wretched who see their own smallness and frailty and who will experience the all-encompassing love of Amida. Suddenly they will know that they are accepted by the universe. Ohsawa writes:

As it is said, the *nembutsu* [念佛] is the totally spontaneous exclamation, like the one of a young child when it looks upon the face of its mother. We have no need to ask or to pray. We are right in the center of the happiness that Nature offers us. We have only to busy ourselves thanking her, to enjoy it completely. That surpasses thanksgiving. All that is necessary was prepared before man was created. We have only to make use of it. What kindness! Everything that happens is necessary, however sad and disagreeable it may be.[9]

Thus, according to Ohsawa, both texts are merely different expressions of his own Unique Principle. It is a bit curious, though, that he would include them and would go to such lengths to explain them. Their relation to his own presentation is scant, and they had played little role in his earlier writings. Ohsawa here is doing something that he often did later as well. He was associating something in vogue with his own theories, in order to get more attention and credibility. In France at the time, among the intellectuals at least, there was a strong interest in and respect for Buddhist philosophy. By connecting the Unique Principle and Shoku-Yō with this fashion of the day Ohsawa strengthened his own case. As he was to use Shinto in the late 1930s, Christianity in the late 1940s, and Zen Buddhism in the late 1950s, Ohsawa, with a conscious if well-intended cultural opportunism, used Mahayana Buddhism here.

Ohsawa's book was well-received and a few months later Vrin published a number of his pieces under the title *Le Livre du Fleurs* ("The Book of Flowers"). Ohsawa focuses on art, explaining the nature of the artist, the purpose of a work of art, and the role of art in Japanese culture.

The true artist, Ohsawa asserts, has a single purpose: to depict in palpable form the eternal and infinite Oneness which lies behind all existence. In the sounds and images of a poem, in the line and color of a flower arrangement, in the black flowing strokes of a calligraphic scroll, he seeks to depict the mystery of Tai-Kyoku. To do this the artist must be a mystic, a person who, through inner purity and discipline, is himself immersed in the hidden world of the spirit. If not, he can at best be a craftsman who copies material forms or expresses his own petty sentiments. If the true artist creates successfully, his work has a special power. For the hearer or viewer it is a means to be transported to that other world beyond time and space. True art reminds one of God and of one's spiritual origin in God. Thus the creation of art is religious, as is its appreciation.

Ohsawa then deals particularly with ka-dō, the Tao of Flower Arrangement, and its role in Japanese culture. The Japanese attitude to flowers reflects their attitude to nature as a whole. Nature is perfect, and everything in nature expresses this perfection, pointing to the absolute harmony of Tai-Kyoku. Flowers are pretty things, but more importantly they are fingers pointing to the Infinite. Besides, each flower, like all living things, has a spirit, and a specific personality. It must be treated with infinite care, love and compassion. The individual flower is an embodiment of the Buddha, of God, and must be regarded with appropriate respect. Inanimate things, such as a remarkably shaped stone, or a jutting mountain peak, also embody the divine. Thus, on the summit of most mountains in Japan, at countless waterfalls, rock formations, and other scenes of natural beauty, one finds a shrine honoring a holy presence.

Ohsawa also explains the concept of civilization from the Japanese point of view. The term *bunmei* [文明] literally means "culture of light." To be civilized is to live in the consciousness of the Infinite, to see everywhere in nature and in art the intimations of the Divine. It has nothing to do with material wealth or technological progress. Wealth and comfort actually distract one from the sacred and the infinite. Poverty and simplicity of life help one develop the gratitude and the spiritual sensitivity needed to perceive Oneness. A rich man may with effort realize perfect consciousness, but certainly wealth alone cannot bring happiness. True wealth, true "nobility," lies within. It is the mind of peace, which has transcended pain and which sees the reflection of God in all things. To give up wealth, status and learning, to detach one's self from the things of the world, is the surest way to true happiness and freedom.

Ohsawa's second book also was well received. He began to move in more elite intellectual circles and to meet some of the writers and scholars whose works he had been studying. From early in his stay Ohsawa read widely in French, keeping abreast of new intellectual developments. He was especially interested in scholars known as experts in Oriental or non-Western cultures, and in writers who might be open to his own point of view. Some, like the German scholars who researched Chinese herbal medicine, or de la Rey, the expert on Chinese science and technology, were to Ohsawa poor prospects. The former might isolate the active ingredient in a Chinese herbal remedy. The latter might discover that the Chinese were able to predict eclipses or to navigate on the open seas. But neither had much interest in, or the ability to grasp, the philosophy and world view which lay behind the medical and the technological achievements. They were trying to understand the culture of the Far East without grasping the laws of Yin and Yang on which it was built. Ohsawa's disappointment regarding these experts helped convince him to write *Le Principe Unique.*

Others, though, excited Ohsawa's interest and hope. Perhaps they were, as they seemed, kindred minds and spirits who would understand what he was saying. Ohsawa did meet the noted writers Paul Valéry and Romain Rolland, the anthropologist René Levy-Bruhl, and the eminent Japanologists Serge Eliséev and René Gruisset.

For the most part Ohsawa's hopes were not fulfilled. For example, he had been greatly impressed by the writings of Eliséev. The scholar appeared to have a genuine grasp of Japanese literature and culture. Yet in person he seemed to have only a narrow, intellectual understanding, not a deep empathy. In mind and spirit, he had remained totally a Westerner, untouched by the Yamato-damashii. Ohsawa was disappointed as well by his meeting with the novelist Rolland, also a noted pacifist. He had sensed that Rolland was one of the few European intellectuals capable of understanding that the world of matter and spirit were one, that the finite world lay always in the arms of the infinite. Hopefully he showed his translation of the *Tannishō* to the Frenchman. Rolland saw the obvious parallels to Christian thought, but not the more subtle metaphysics that lay behind.[10]

Levy-Bruhl was a pioneer in the study of the pre-literate or so-called "primitive" peoples. Ohsawa read his comprehensive survey called *Le Mentalité Primitive,* and was struck by the similarity between the world-view of the "primitive" and that of the Japanese. In both, the worlds of matter and spirit are deeply interwoven. Ohsawa was also struck by the scholar's care in amassing so much data on various cultures. On meeting and talking with him, though, Ohsawa sensed a man so completely rational that he could not make the intuitive leap to really comprehend the primitives or the Japanese. Ohsawa promised Levy-Bruhl that he would write a book on the primitive mentality from the perspective of a true primitive, namely himself. Though it took ten years to do it, and though he wrote the book in Japanese, Ohsawa finally kept his promise. Early in World War II, he published *Mikaijin no Seishin to Nihon Seishin* [未開人の精神と日本精神] ("The Spirit of the Primitive Man and the Japanese Spirit").

There were, however, some hopeful signs as well. One of these was the work of a Dr. René Aranji. Aranji was a Frenchman and the leader of a group of doctors who objected to the dominant medical theories and practices of the day. Challenging the germ theory of disease and the dependence on allopathic medicine, they favored what would today be called a "holistic" approach. Aranji maintained that human health is determined by the biological, emotional and psychological state of the person much more than by the kinds of microorganisms with which he comes in contact. A strong, well-balanced person will resist the bacteria and organisms that will make a weak and unhappy person ill. Medicine should concentrate on strengthening people and on improving their ability to deal with stress, rather than just on destroying pathogens. While emphasizing the role of psychological factors, Aranji recognized the important role of nutrition in the prevention of disease.

Ohsawa and Aranji met and became friends. Realizing the compatibility of their approaches, they began to support each other's work. Aranji introduced Ohsawa's ideas on food and health to his colleagues. Ohsawa carefully studied the Frenchman's book called *Les Idées Medicales* and planned to translate it into Japanese. He wanted to inform his fellow Japanese about this development in Western medicine.

Meanwhile, Ohsawa was also keeping an eye on developments in Japan. Through most of the 1920s Japan's domestic and external affairs had been fairly stable. The country was ruled by a coalition of party politicians, government bureaucrats and business leaders. There were few signs of discontent among the lower classes. A respected member of the League of Nations, Japan was apparently dedicated to international cooperation and peace.

Late in the decade, a powerful, ultra-nationalistic movement emerged. It consisted of conservative aristocrats and military leaders above, and hard-pressed farmers and tradesmen below. Espousing a Nippon-shugi point of view, it called for an end to Western influence, and a return to the Yamato-damashii and the traditions of the past. According to this group, political party rule should end, and real power should be restored to the Emperor and his advisors. Socialist and communist groups should be suppressed. Western manners and morals should be replaced by traditional Japanese patterns of behavior. The Western imperial presence throughout Asia should be destroyed and replaced by the benevolent rule of Imperial Japan. These groups resorted to intimidation and violence to further their ends. They began to exercise much influence, both in the government and in the society at large.

At the time, Japanese forces were stationed in Manchuria, a part of northern China, supposedly to protect Japanese business interests there. In September 1931 Japanese soldiers instigated a fight with the Chinese army. They quickly overran the region and set up a puppet government controlled by the Japanese military. At home the civilian voice in government waned and that of the nationalists and militarists increased.

Ohsawa watched these developments with severe misgivings. He shared, of course, many of the ideas about a return to the true "spirit of Japan." But he opposed the intolerance and violence of the movement at home and its military expansionism abroad. If Japan were to continue on this course, Ohsawa felt, it would get involved in a disastrous war with the Western powers. Not one to sit idly by when duty or adventure called, Ohsawa decided to take positive action.

Thus in 1932 he bought a fourth-class ticket on a ship to Japan, planning to spend a few months there, and to try to influence the course of events. After forty days in steerage Ohsawa disembarked in Japan. En route he had purchased some books in a Chinese port and soon resold them at a profit to pick up some cash. His financial situation had improved little during the first three years in Paris. Ohsawa immediately began to contact high military and government officials to arrange interviews. Through influential friends at the Shoku-Yō Kai, he was able to talk with various officers at the Army Ministry and at General Staff Headquarters. Also, he gave a series of lectures before the young men at an army officers' candidate school. Ohsawa's theme was everywhere the same. Japan's foreign policies are leading to conflict with the West, and in such a conflict Japan will fare poorly. An entirely new approach is needed in understanding and in dealing with the Western powers.

His lectures to the cadets were put in book form under the title *Hakushoku Jinshu o Teki to Shite—Tatakawaneba Naranu Riyū* [白色人種を敵として——戦わねばならぬ理由] ("With the White Race as Opponent: Why Japan Must Fight"). Published shortly after Ohsawa's return to France that same year, this work presents his full message to his fellow Japanese.

The main part of the book describes Western culture and then contrasts it with an idealized version of Japan. It is Ohsawa's first attempt to explain the West in a full and systematic way, and he cites his long experience in Europe as a qualification for the task. This book is largely a reiteration of Nippon-shugi concepts, with an occasional personal anecdote offered as support. Western man is afflicted with "spiritual myopia," Ohsawa writes, an inability to see or appreciate the invisible world. From this stem the materialism, hedonism, individualism, and egalitarianism which permeate Western life. These values are everywhere and always apparent: in the obsession of Western science with what can be seen and measured; in a tradition of painting that is purely pictorial; in a self-serving religious morality that seeks only rebirth in heaven; in language whose forms of address lack terms of respect; and even in the manner of addressing mail, with the name of the individual first.

With this, Ohsawa contrasts the "spiritual" culture of Japan. A deep awareness of the invisible world is its basis, and from this derive the spirituality, collectivism, self-sacrifice, humility, gratitude and respect which characterize Japanese life. The language is filled with subtle distinctions to show humility and respect. Its art is mystical in purpose and inspiration. Japanese addresses begin with the name of the country or province and end with that of the person.

Having shown this polar opposition, Ohsawa points out the cause of the current crisis. Japan and the West find it very hard to understand each other. They look at the world from contradictory points of view. Each judges the other according to its own perspective and is constantly shocked and bewildered. In foreign relations this chronic misunderstanding is leading to direct military conflict. Unless one or both change their way of thinking and acting, there will be a war. And, Ohsawa adds prophetically, in this war Japan will be defeated.

After centuries of separation, the East (Yin, spiritual, passive) and the West (Yang, materialistic, aggressive) are inevitably drawn together. Eventually they will become one, but the process of attraction and synthesis also contains a stage of conflict. It is up to Japan to see that the confrontation between herself and the West is a peaceful one. Thus Ohsawa's book, despite its combative title, is actually a plea for peace. Japan, he says, must abandon its militarism and aggressive expansionism. These are contrary to the "Japanese spirit." It should try to understand the West on its own terms. And it must try to make the West understand its own culture and point of view. It must begin an "ideological war," a dialogue to show the value and validity of the Japanese Way. In this manner much violence and destruction will be avoided. The two cultures will meet peacefully, will learn from each other, and will form a new, enriched world culture of East and West. Through such a policy of peace and cultural exchange, Japan will be true to the meaning of the Yamato-damashii and will emerge "the final victor."

Ohsawa's plea got a mixed response. His views on Japanese and Western culture pleased some of the nationalists. One advocate of Nippon-shugi, Tadanao Nakayama [中山忠直], became his host and patron during the visit. Nakayama was a physician, and a leader of an intellectual circle which promoted Japanist ideas. In his book *Nihonjin no Erasa no Kenkyū* [日本人の偉さの研究] ("The Superiority of the Japanese"), Nakayama claims that the Japanese overshadow the West in science and technology as well as in morality and art. It was, he argues, a Japanese who first developed an airplane. In the 17th century an Edo carpenter apparently had constructed a wooden frame with wings and had sailed down from a great height. If not exactly a Japanese Orville Wright, he was at least an accomplished hang-glider. Nakayama suggested to Ohsawa that he translate Aranji's book to earn money for the return passage, and later supervised its publication.

In other circles, Ohsawa's dire warnings about war with the West were less well received. Extreme right-wing elements were angered by this treasonous thought and planned to waylay Ohsawa after one of his speeches. A friend of Ohsawa, a high ranking military officer, heard of the plot and whisked the intended victim away in his automobile.

After several months Ohsawa returned to France by boat. On the long westward voyage he penned the following poem:

> Armed not with a sword
> But with this pen
> I go to defend
> The spirit of Japan.

As usual he saw his personal life in terms of larger movements and causes. His task now was to present the Yamato-damashii to the West, in the hope that through "ideological" exchange a military conflict would be averted and the synthesis between East and West would be accomplished.

Ohsawa spent most of the next three years in Paris although he did visit Japan again. When he returned to France this first time he brought with him a copy of Nakayama's book *Kanpō Shin Kenkyū* [漢方新研究] ("New Researches in Chinese Herbal Medicine"), which he duly translated into French. Nakayama had been working to revive Chinese herbalism as a respected form of medicine in Japan, and to lessen the domination of Western allopathy. Ohsawa saw his work as yet another part of Japanese culture of which Europe should be aware.

Ohsawa also met and befriended at this time a Dr. de Soulie Morant. He was a French physician who had spent many years in China. There he had been impressed by acupuncture and had begun to study it. The two began a productive collaboration and wrote together *L'Acupuncture et la Medicine Chinoise* ("Acupuncture and Chinese Medicine") which was published in 1935. This was one of the first attempts to explain the principles of acupuncture and moxibustion in a Western language. It is still considered a classic in the field, being cited as a seminal work, for example, by Ilza Veith in the introduction to her own pioneer translation of "The Yellow Emperor's Classic."

As a cultural broker between East and West, Ohsawa tried rendering Japanese literature into French. He translated the historic tale *Chūshingura* [忠臣蔵] ("The Treasury of Loyal Hearts"), known also as "The Tale of the Forty-Seven Rōnin." During the Edo Period two feudal lords or *daimyō* [大名] in attendance at the court of the shogun came into conflict. One of these, Lord Asano, was provoked into drawing his sword in the palace, a crime punishable by death. Asano was allowed to commit *hara-kiri* [腹切], a death more honorable than execution, but his family was stripped of its lands and his samurai retainers became *rōnin* [浪人] or masterless samurai, literally, "men of the waves." Some dispersed, but many took a pledge to avenge their lord. They knew that a vengeful attack upon Lord Kira, their own lord's enemy, was expected so they pretended to disperse and to fall into dissolute, wasteful lives. Meanwhile, they secretly plotted. After several years of planning and waiting, the rōnin seized their opportunity, and on a snowy evening attacked. They invaded the villa of Lord Kira, capturing and killing him. Then the surviving forty-seven warriors marched together to Asano's grave. After presenting the severed head of their enemy, they committed ritual suicide.

This story is a classic of Japanese historical literature. Told and retold countless times in prose, poetic, dramatic and cinematic form, it never fails to reduce a Japanese audience to tears. It epitomizes the values of duty, loyalty and self-sacrifice so close to the heart of Japanese culture. The spot in Tokyo where the forty-seven rōnin gave their lives is still a popular focus of pilgrimage. However, Ohsawa was unable to find a publisher for his French version of the story. He was told that it lacked any "romantic interest," and that the exact motivation of the samurai was difficult to understand. This was a perfect example of the gulf between Eastern and Western culture.

Meanwhile, the social and political situation in Japan was growing more critical. The right-wing groups were increasingly active and effective, discouraging opposition through intimidation, and inspiring support by their absolute dedication and self-sacrifice. Both public opinion and government policy were moving to the right. Repression at home and expansionism abroad increased. Ohsawa could no longer watch his country pursue this collision course with disaster. He resolved to return to Japan to see if he could help change the direction in which it was moving.

In the months prior to his departure from France Ohsawa had a liaison with an Armenian woman who was a political refugee and a teacher of mathematics. At the time of departure, unknown to Ohsawa, she was pregnant with his child. He returned to Japan clearly aware that he must help save his nation. He did not likely suspect, though, that he would never see this woman again, nor that he was leaving a child behind, nor that it would be twenty years before he would see his beloved Paris again. And he did not likely suspect that twenty years later in Paris, a young man would approach him after a lecture and introduce himself as his son.

Thus ended a productive and happy period in Ohsawa's life. He had learned much about Western culture and he had conveyed this through his visits and writings to his fellow Japanese. He had done much to promote understanding of Japanese culture in the West. And yet this was for him a relatively relaxed and carefree period, to which in later years he often referred with great fondness and nostalgia. As Ohsawa returned to his homeland, behind him lay the beauty of Paris, the "City of Light," and a life of freedom and exploration. Before him under an ominous cloud lay Japan, where he would experience years of toil and pleasure, frustration and exultation.

---

1 Here again the main sources of biographical data are Matsumoto's biography, Ohsawa's own reminiscences (in print), and the recollections of those who knew him.
2 Sakurazawa, Yukikazu, *Le Principe Unique de la Philosophie et de la Science d'Extrême Orient*, Vrin, Paris, 1931, current edition, 1978, p. 36
3 Ibid., p. 69
4 Ibid., p. 4
5 Ibid., p. 79
6 Ibid., p. 92
8 Ibid., p. 42 (ca.)
7 Ibid., Appendix
9 Ibid., p. 107
10 Sakurazawa, Yukikazu, *Haku Shoku Jinshu o Teki to Shite* ("With the White Race As Opponent), 1932, p. 29

George Ohsawa:
Return to Japan
in Crisis (1936–1939)

The four years between 1936 and 1939 were tumultuous ones for the Japanese nation. On Febuary 26, 1936, a group of young army officers staged a coup and for three days controlled the government offices in Tokyo. Though finally driven out and punished, they had captured the imagination of the public and had greatly advanced the cause of the militarists and ultra-nationalists. Soon these elements were in full control of the government. A conservative, nationalist ideology, based on Nippon-shugi became official policy. All dissenting views, liberal, socialist, or communist were suppressed. State Shinto, emphasizing reverence for the Emperor as the em-bodiment of the *Kokutai* [國体] or "mystic essence of the nation," and absolute obedience to the state became the offical religion. In manners and morals, economics, law and other areas, a return to traditional patterns was encouraged. Wherever possible, Western influences were ferreted out. Though the Japanese could not bring themselves to get rid of baseball, a terribly popular sport, they replaced terms like "strike," "base," "pitcher," etc., with Japanese equivalents. Medicine and nutrition were two areas where Western influence remained strong. In the national health programs designed to strengthen the nation, Western allopathy and ideas about diet dominated.

This "purification" at home was accompanied by expansion abroad. Efforts to settle thousands of Japanese in Manchuria and thus create "a new Japan" were pur-sued with great vigor. In July 1937 war began with the Chinese Nationalist govern-ment of Chiang Kai-Shek [蔣介石], and the Imperial armies swept over most of the northern and coastal areas. In November 1938 a program was announced to create a "Greater East Asia Co-Prosperity Sphere" [大東亜共栄圏]. This was a family of Asian nations, freed of all Western control and influence and under the paternal supervision of Japan. Obviously, an open conflict with the Western powers was in the offing. Actually, in the war with Chiang Kai-Shek, who was backed by the British and Americans, it had already begun.

The period was an intense one for Ohsawa as well. He arrived home determined to do all he could to save the nation from disaster. For these years (and beyond) he was incredibly active as a businessman, writer, administrator, lecturer, medical consultant, and translator. An ardent, tireless crusader, he wrote and spoke on a variety of issues from diet and cooking to international politics.

Ohsawa had brought with him from France the production rights for a tiny one-person airplane called *Le Poule* or "the flea." Gathering some capital, he arranged for an existing company to manufacture the plane for him. Six years in the Shoku-Yō Kai and six years as an expatriate intellectual had not dulled his entrepreneur's instinct. The project ended after about a year, but Ohsawa realized a large profit.

Also from the outset Ohsawa threw himself into the activities of the Shoku-Yō Kai. The organization was, he believed, the great hope for transforming Japan. At the time, the group was actively spreading Ishizuka's teachings, but on a modest scale. Admiral Hajime Sakamoto [坂本一], well into his eighties, was the director. Ohsawa wrote a number of articles for the organization's magazine as well as a slender volume called *Shin Do Fu Ji* [身土不二], outlining Shoku-Yō principles. Soon he assumed the responsibilities of chief-editor of publications and general superintendent of the group. He helped fund (with his profits from *Le Poule*) and supervise the construction of a three-story building as a new national headquarters. This center contained administrative and publishing offices, rooms for lectures and cooking classes, and food distribution facilities. On the top floor was the *Mizuho* [瑞穂] ("Grain of Rice") Clinic and Hospital which treated patients according to Shoku-Yō principles.

Ohsawa was involved in almost every sphere of activity. He wrote constantly and tirelessly. By 1939 he had published ten or more books and scores of articles. He took part in overall administration. In the clinic he was active as a consultant, diagnosing patients and prescribing diets and simple external treatments. Ohsawa honed his skill in diagnosis and physiognomy during this period. He learned to tell from a person's physical appearance their favorite foods and their diet of the previous days, as well as much about their personality and personal lives. Ohsawa also lectured a great deal in Tokyo and around Japan. He visited branches of the Shoku-Yō Kai, giving seminars and consultations. He went even beyond the home islands, visiting both Taiwan and Manchuria in 1938.

During this period, and especially after the outbreak of war with China, there was a rapid growth of membership. In 1938 the first National Congress of the Shoku-Yō Kai was held. Among those present were many influential members of the aristocracy and military establishment. Plans were made to establish a Shoku-Yō community in the countryside and for the group to take a more active role in society. Membership at the time was about 2,500. Ohsawa's level of activity during this period raises a question. How did he manage to fill so many roles in a busy and expanding organization? Where indeed did he get the energy and time? The answer is both interesting and important. It is interesting because it helps bring into focus a distinct personality. It tells us much about Ohsawa the man. It is important because the patterns so clear at this time were present to some degree earlier, and they continued to characterize Ohsawa through most of his life.

For one thing, Ohsawa was absolutely dedicated to the Shoku-Yō movement. He considered it a "sacred crusade" which would save Japan and all humanity. Everything else paled in significance beside it. Accordingly, Ohsawa seems to have eliminated from his daily life anything not directly related to the movement. He neglected his children. He had no discernible hobbies. He never took a vacation. He was a classic workaholic, careful that nothing interfere with his central mission in life.

Also, Ohsawa did not waste time. He slept as little as possible, three or four hours a night. His usual pattern was to retire around ten and be up by 2:00 A.M. He would write and read until the normal workday began. During the day he would catnap when possible, during a train or taxicab ride, for example. He tried to do everything quickly and efficiently, priding himself on not spending more time than necessary on any task. His casual walking pace was a half jog to most and he took stairs two and three at a time. He did much of his writing and reading at odd moments— waiting in a railway station for a connection, on a long train trip, or in hotel rooms before and after lectures. Sometimes he worked continuously for blocks of time, neither eating nor sleeping. In this way he wrote a 400-page book called *Shizen Igaku* [自然医学] ("Nature Medicine") in just five days, and translated Alexis Carrel's *L'Homme Inconnu* ("Man the Unknown") from French to Japanese in ten.

Part of the reason Ohsawa was able to maintain such a pace was his diet. From Ishizuka's time a simple vegetarian, but very salty, diet had been the Shoku-Yō standard. Even as a young man Ohsawa found that this suited him. Salty, well-cooked food (extremely Yang) helped balance his rather weak (Yin) native constitution. It helped him become strong, energetic and resistant to cold. Even in winter time he was able to go only with a light coat, and often without socks. Although in France he had eaten less strictly, once back in Japan he returned to his earlier pattern of eating: thick miso soup, rice cooked with salt, vegetables heavily seasoned with salt and soy sauce, and as a garnish, *gomashio* [胡麻塩], sesame seeds and salt mixed at a six to four ratio. Ohsawa estimated that he was taking about thirty grams (two or three teaspoons) of salt a day! On a trip to Taiwan in August 1938, he stood on the deck as the boat entered Taipei Harbor. Ohsawa was sweating in the tropical heat and drew his hand across his forehead. He felt something like grains of sand, which turned out to be crystals of salt. Even eating 150 bananas and pineapples (very Yin) during his brief stay did not slow him down.

There was an extra benefit to this diet besides the vibrant, if hyperactive, health it gave Ohsawa. He reports that his poor diet had made him weak during the sojourn in Paris, and he had not been able to enjoy tobacco and alcohol. Now, restored by Shoku-Yō eating, he was able to have these again. From this time on Ohsawa frequently enjoyed good quality Scotch, beer and wine. And till the end of his life he was a chronic smoker of pipes and cigarettes. The stimulation of nicotine certainly helped his long intellectual labors.

Devoted assistants and associates also made Ohsawa's schedule and output possible. During these years in the Shoku-Yō Kai he kept several secretaries busy. Two of these, Toshi Kawaguchi [川口トシ] and Michi Ogawa [小川みち] were absolutely devoted to Ohsawa. They worked tirelessly for him, seven days a week, with little or no compensation. Even when Kawaguchi's father died, she did not take time off to attend the funeral. These intelligent and well-educated young women (Kawaguchi had been a journalist in Manchuria before she met Ohsawa, and Ogawa a music and cooking teacher) greatly lightened Ohsawa's day-to-day burden. There was also a small group of associates within the Shoku-Yō Kai anxious to help. At about this time, Ohsawa met Hiroshi Maruyama [丸山博], a professor of nutrition at the national university in Osaka. The young academic became convinced of the validity of Shoku-Yō, and supported Ohsawa and the movement in many ways. At the summer camp in Manchuria, for example, he took over much of the lecturing.

Maruyama, Kawaguchi and Ogawa all remained loyal supporters of Ohsawa throughout his life and still are active in macrobiotics in Japan today

Support and sustenance of a more intimate kind entered Ohsawa's life during this period. In 1937 an attractive, though married, woman began to attend Ohsawa's lectures at the Shoku-Yō Kai. Her name was Sanae Tanaka [田中早苗] and she had been born into a samurai family in the mountains of Yamanashi Prefecture. At the age of eighteen she was introduced to a prospective husband chosen by her father and uncles. Sanae did not like the man at all, but in the patriarchal milieu of the day, her wishes were overruled. She married, but against her will. A few months later she returned home for a visit and refused to go back to her husband. Her family forced her to return. Later discovering she was pregnant, she resigned herself to the situation. Soon the marriage existed in name only, but Sanae persevered. In about 1936, very unhappy, fragile and sickly (she weighed only 65 pounds), Sanae sought help from a Professor Toshihiro Eguchi [江口俊博]. He practiced and taught a healing art called *te no hira* [手のひら] or "palm-healing." Sanae began to gain strength, and Eguchi suggested that she attend lectures given by his friend Ohsawa (still known as Sakurazawa at that time).

On her first visit to the Shoku-Yō Kai, Sanae was very surprised. The ideas expressed in the lecture astounded her. She had never heard before that sickness is both caused and cured by food, that each person is totally responsible for his own health and happiness. She was also surprised by the meal which followed. It consisted only of soup, rice and a piece of daikon pickle. Everyone ate slowly, chewing each mouthful a long time. There was scarcely any conversation. At the meal's end each person took tea in his rice bowl and scoured it with the bit of pickle so that not a trace of food would be wasted.

Nevertheless, Sanae began to change her diet, and returned for more lectures. Her husband was unsympathetic and finally Sanae resolved to leave him. Meanwhile Eguchi had introduced her to Ohsawa. Ohsawa was then living alone, responsible for several of his children, and he needed someone to care for them. He asked Sanae to join the household and she consented. From that time, Ohsawa and she lived as a common-law couple. Ohsawa renamed her Lima [里真] and they were officially married about ten years later. Sanae's family were scandalized and disowned her, refusing to have anything to do with her for many years.

Lima was and is still today (at an active, vibrant eighty-five years) a classic example of traditional Japanese femininity: elegant and gracious; deferential and self-effacing; on the surface, frail and gentle as a flower; but beneath remarkably strong and tenacious. She became Ohsawa's companion and helpmate. For the next thirty years she cooked his food, managed his household and arranged his personal finances. Ohsawa, free from most mundane tasks, was able to write, think and teach as he wished. When his adventuresome spirit landed him in difficulty Lima was there to extricate him and, if necessary, to nurse him back to health. It was not an easy role. Ohsawa could be a demanding taskmaster. It took several years before he allowed that Lima had become a passable cook. And he once wrote in half jest that he had married her to see if he could make a worthwhile human being out of a completely incompetent one. In truth, of course, there was an immeasurable love and respect, perhaps even a measure of dependence. Ohsawa's life and achievement from 1937 can be understood only by recognizing Lima's critical role.

These several factors then—Ohsawa's absolute dedication to his work, his diet and use of stimulants, his efficiency, and the support he received from Lima and others— helped him pursue his work for the Shoku-Yō Kai. There were, however, disadvantages involved. The tempo at which Ohsawa moved didn't allow him to do everything well. He was always in a rush and his work showed it. He himself confessed that he was frequently short and curt with patients in consulations. He was especially impatient with those who didn't understand him the first time through an explanation.

This haste is especially obvious in his writing. Some of his books are well done, but in this 1936–39 period, the majority are not. Ohsawa wrote at great speed, and often sent manuscripts to the printer with little editing or correcting. Most of his works are poorly organized, sloppily written, and hopelessly repetitious. Ohsawa jumps from theme to theme, pursues a tangent here, a dead end there, and always winds up at the same place—the Shoku-Yō philosophy and diet. To the discerning reader the books are often almost an insult. But of course Ohsawa was not writing for academic, literary purposes. He was responding to the crisis of the day, trying to change the way people thought, lived and ate. He wrote mostly for the layperson, often for women, who he thought were the key to the nation's fate. Sometimes he wrote expressly for the elite, as in his book on Manchuria, but even here the mark of haste is obvious. Ohsawa was a man in a big hurry.

Ohsawa's intensity, caused probably both by schedule and diet, occasionally led to his losing his temper. Even earlier, during his second marriage, he was not a man to be crossed. If his wife served his dinner late or cold, Ohsawa would place his hands under the low Japanese table and throw it and the meal into the air. In 1938 he writes that he had been outraged by two girls working in the Shoku-Yō Kai. Discovering that they had gone out and eaten ice cream, he fired the girls and sent them home in disgrace. And in many of his writings of this time, as we shall see, there is an edge of anger and intolerance. He tends to label those who disagree with him as dupes and traitors. This is somehow incongruous for one who professed to be teaching the Tao, the Way taught also by Lao Tzu and Confucius.

Finally, his zeal for promoting the Shoku-Yō movement did little for his children. Shunted from household to household, enjoying little contact with their busy father, several had a difficult and very unhappy adolescence. According to Ohsawa, two of his sons spent time in a reformatory.

Whatever the pros and cons of Ohsawa's life-style at this time, he pursued his purpose with a vengeance. And it was a straightforward aim: to spread Shoku-Yō throughout Japan. Only through the Way of Eating could the nation escape ruin. Japan was at a crossroads. One path, the current one, led to calamity. The other, that of Shoku-Yō, led to health, peace and prosperity. The nation's destiny was hanging in the balance and there was not a moment to lose.

Ohsawa's basic message is a familiar one. Food is the source of all phenomena. Produced by the forces of nature, it in turn creates, nourishes and determines human life. Man's health and well-being depend above all on his daily diet. If he eats the products of his environment he will be healthy and happy and feel joyfully at home in the universe. This is his birthright, the natural condition of human life. If he violates the natural order in his eating, sickness and trouble come, both as a just punishment and as a loving reminder from nature to follow her laws. All sickness can be cured by a simple, carefully prepared and gratefully eaten ecological diet. The Shoku-Yō regime is an inexpensive and easy path to health and happiness that can be practiced by anyone any time.

Japan, once a nation which lived according to Shoku-Yō principles, now has forgotten its traditions. Since the beginning of the Meiji Period it has copied Western diet, consuming more and more meat, dairy foods, potatoes, and so on. It has completely neglected the principle of shin do fu ji. Its fish comes from distant waters, its grains from Manchuria and Mexico. It polishes and bleaches its sacred rice, and consumes quantities of white sugar, tropical fruits and chemical additives. The result is a rapid decline in the nation's health. Child mortality rates are the highest in the world. Tuberculosis and other diseases are epidemic and still on the rise. Forty percent of all military draftees fail the medical examination. And the Western allopathic medicine on which Japan now depends does not know the real cause of disease and thus cannot cure anything.

Japan must return to its traditional diet of native foods. Through the national application of the principle of shin do fu ji the health of every individual will be realized, and order and well-being will be reflected throughout the society. Japan will become an example and inspiration to all the peoples of the world. It is in fact Japan's responsibility to spread this wisdom so that all humanity may live in health and peace.

Ohsawa was convinced this was possible, even imminent. On the occasion of the Shoku-Yō Kai's first National Congress he prepared a little book called *Kenkō Techō* [健康手帖] ("Notebook for Health"). This work included an easy-to-follow explanation of the theory and practice of the Shoku-Yō way plus a diary section to record one's change in diet and progress in health. Ohsawa describes real health as having six essential aspects: good sleep, boundless energy, good appetite, personal orderliness, good humor, and a sense of humility and gratitude. Shoku-Yō is the only way to truly achieve this. Ohsawa's hope and plan was to distribute a copy of this notebook to everyone in the nation, to give the means to health to each Japanese man, woman and child. This was the first and necessary step in a national transformation. And Ohsawa, aware of the growing momentum of the movement and optimistic at heart, felt that this renewal was indeed about to occur.

In aspiring to make the Shoku-Yō Kai the center of a broad-based national movement, Ohsawa was adding a new dimension to its activities. In practice, anyway, the organization had been quite content to be rather low-key, focusing on medical and individual applications of the diet. And Ohsawa added ideas in several other areas, further unsettling a comfortable status quo.

One of Ohsawa's first publications on returning to Japan was *Konpon Musō Genri* [根本無双原理] ("The Basic Unique Principle"). This was a rewritten version of *Le Principe Unique*, presenting the Yin-Yang theory he had developed in France. The twelve principles which he lists are, Ohsawa asserts, a universal law. Man can understand all phenomena by it and should order every aspect of his life according to its principles. It is applicable to every domain of inquiry and activity: biology, chemistry, physics, agriculture, diet, medicine, economics, etc. Shin do fu ji and Shoku-Yō teachings on food and health are, in fact, only applications of the Musō Genri. It is interesting that Ohsawa edited out the strong Buddhist perspective of his French work. The government was promoting the native Shinto national faith, and Buddhism, as a foreign faith, was out of official and popular favor. Here again, Ohsawa was quite sensitive to the dominant popular and intellectual currents of the day.

In other writings of this period Ohsawa deals often with areas which earlier he had seldom touched on, if at all. One of these is national political policy. Ohsawa becomes a harsh, often truculent critic of the government, focusing on its policies related to food, health and medicine. He bitterly reviews the entire program of the Ministry of Welfare, which had been created to promote the health of the nation. All the new doctors graduated and all the new hospitals built, he rails, are an indication not of health but of the degree of sickness. Vaccinations lower the general level of health in the country and increase chronic sickness. Nutritional propaganda for vitamins, meat and cod liver oil is based on fallacy and is undermining the people's health.

And of course Ohsawa had a host of suggestions for the government. He visited the Ministry of Agriculture and pleaded that they prohibit the polishing of rice. This measure would increase food supplies and improve health he argued. (A year later, because of food shortages, the government did enforce half-milling.) In his writings Ohsawa urges that the government should encourage the consumption of local foods and should discourage by high taxes imported and luxury items such as sugar. Organic agricultural methods should be promoted and the use of chemical fertilizer and insecticides discouraged. Fruit orchards should be returned to rice cultivation. The government too, Ohsawa urged, should stop promoting Western medicine. It should instead develop preventive programs and therapies based on traditional diet, on acupuncture, herbalism, and massage.

Ohsawa comments also on the purges which had been carried out in the universities and government. Liberal and leftist professors and officials has been ousted. This is fine, Ohsawa says. Japan's political, legal, and intellectual life must be purified. But what about the Western-oriented doctors and nutritional scientists, he asks. By accepting and promoting Western diet and medicine, the government has undermined the nation. It, and the bureaucrats who carry out its programs, are the real traitors to the people's welfare.

Ohsawa's interest in government policy is seen clearly in his involvement with Manchuria. The attempt to resettle Japanese on the Asian mainland had been going poorly, due mainly to health problems among the emigrants. A diphtheria epidemic had hit the Japanese colonists hard but had mostly spared the native Manchurians. In September 1938 Ohsawa left for Manchuria, intending to visit supporters there and to investigate the situation. On the way he stopped in Kobe to meet with a Shoku-Yō group, and to look into reports that an impostor was claiming to be Ohsawa and was charging high consultation fees. Then he went on to Fukuoka and visited the grave of Ekken Kaibara whom he recognized as one of the founders of Shoku-Yō and a true defender of the Japanese spirit. Ohsawa went by boat to the

Korean port of Pusan. Delayed there in the railroad station, he gave an impromptu seminar in the waiting room, surrounded by Shoku-Yō friends and associates. Finally he reached the Manchurian capital, Harbin, by plane.

Ohsawa gave lectures and consultations for the small, branch group. Most of his time, though, was spent studying the life and diet of the native people. He toured the region for several weeks, visiting farms, homes, schools, restaurants, food shops and inns. The people were poor and by Japanese standards the conditions were dirty and unsanitary. Flies and dust were everywhere. Meals were presented on soiled plates and dirty pieces of cloth. The people seldom if ever bathed, and washed their clothes only once a year. Yet Ohsawa relished and rejoiced in his experiences, inspecting the lunches brought by children to school, sharing a humble meal with a family in a cardboard shack. He saw that there was much wisdom in their style of life, and that it had allowed them to survive in a very harsh environment.

In the capital, Ohsawa met and befriended a Mr. Toshio Tamura [田村敏雄] who was head of the Education Ministry. The two shared a vision of Manchuria as a broad, open frontier where a new step in human social evolution could be realized. They spent many hours together. Ohsawa explained the Shoku-Yō philosophy and diet. Tamura was receptive and promised to implement it in the school system. Ohsawa left Manchuria buoyed by the hope that this unspoiled land might become a showcase of Shoku-Yō ideas.

Returning to Japan, Ohsawa recorded his observations and experiences, analyzing the situation and giving suggestions to improve it. The material he published early in 1940 under the titles *Manshū Shokuyō Tokuhon* [滿州食養讀本] ("The Manchuria Shoku-Yō Reader") and *Manshūkoku no Kōsei Undō* [滿州国の厚生運動] ("The Public Welfare Movement in Manchuria") which he submitted to the government ministry in charge of the region. Ohsawa claims that the general good health of the natives is due to their diet, which is based on millet and local vegetables. The main problem is getting enough salt and other minerals in their inland environment. Thyroid goiter, caused by iodine deficiency, is a common ailment. The reluctance to bathe is an intuitive attempt to retain body minerals. Ohsawa's main suggestion is that more sea salt be used in food preparation and that cooking time be increased. This practice would prevent goiter and other ailments and also increase the people's level of energy and ambition.

Regarding the colonists, Ohsawa recommends simply that they imitate the diet of the natives. To live on white rice and canned foods imported from Japan is a blind and dangerous violation of shin do fu ji. It is natural that they should be demoralized and plagued by disease. For the colonists to thrive, they need only eat the foods of the area.

Religion is another area that Ohsawa dealt with extensively during this period. In 1936 he published *Shizen Igaku to shite no Shinto* [自然医学としての神道] ("Shinto as a Natural Medicine"). Shinto was of course a dominant force in Japanese life, having been revived and supported by the government. Here again we see Ohsawa, sensitive to public opinion, presenting his basic Shoku-Yō message in a form which would more likely attract public notice and approval.

Ohsawa uses the myths of the *Kojiki* and *Nihongi*, and the rules and prayers of the *Engi Shiki* [延喜式] or "Records of the Engi Period," a historical record also dating from the 8th century, as the base of his discussion. He asserts that in philosophy, Shinto corresponds to his Unique Principle, and in food practice to the Shoku-Yō diet.

According to the first of Ohsawa's twelve principles, Infinity or Tai-Kyoku, absolute, undifferentiated, infinite oneness, separates into two opposite but complementary forces, Yin and Yang. From these are created all phenomena of the visible and invisible worlds. The creation stories of ancient Japan, Ohsawa asserts, are simply mythological expressions of this same idea. According to the *Nihongi*, the original cosmic god is Ame-no-minaka-nushi [天御中主神] "The Lord God of the Center of Heaven." From this god are formed two other deities. From this contrasting pair are created four other pairs of gods and ultimately the god Izanagi [伊弉諾尊] and the goddess Izanami [伊弉冉尊]. These two join to create the world of nature and man. The correspondences to Tai-Kyoku and Yin and Yang are obvious, Ohsawa observes.

Also in the mythic histories, and especially in the *Engi Shiki*, Ohsawa finds evidence that teachings about food are at the heart of ancient Shinto. Early in its history Japan was a theocracy, based on *saisei itchi* [祭政一致] "the oneness of government and religion." The emperor and other priest-rulers understood well the importance of food in the health and welfare of the individual and the community. In the seasonal offerings and prayers, they preserved and transmitted this wisdom concerning diet. The hymns or *norito* [祝詞] are expressions of thanks and joy sung by a people at home in the universe. But they are also a practical guide for realizing a state of health and harmony. According to the norito only certain foods are holy and may be offered to the gods. These same foods should comprise the diet of man. The primary food offerings are rice, salt and vegetables of the area. Of fish, only two kinds are permitted; of meat, only wild fowl. The flesh of four-legged animals is prohibited. Thus the norito and the seasonal ceremonies they accompany teach and remind the community that grains are the primary food of man; and that salt, fish, and vegetables, but not red meat, are appropriate supplements.

Ohsawa also observes that in ancient times, of the grains rice was considered particularly sacred. The mythologies record that when Amaterasu, the sun goddess, sends her grandson from Takama-no-hara [高天原] ("the high field of heaven") to the earthly plane, she hands him sheaves of rice. This, she says, is the food of the gods in heaven, and should remain their food on earth. And Ohsawa points out that at Ise, the great national sanctuary, while the inner shrine or *Naiku* [内宮] is dedicated to Amaterasu, the outer shrine or *Geku* [外宮] is for Toyouke-no-ōkami [豊受大神]. This is the god of food, and particularly of rice. Rice is the *wakemitama* [分御魂], the "shadow" or "essence of the deity," in physical form. In a sense, it is the god himself. Thus from ancient times rice has been understood as the basis of the nation's life. Japan is a land of rice, and the body and soul of the people are merely transformations of the grain.

Thus, according to Ohsawa, true Shinto is identical with Shoku-Yō philosophy and practice. Its cosmology is a dualistic monism corresponding to the Unique Principle. Its daily practice is founded on eating grains as the main food, and on eating according to the natural environment. Real patriotism, real devotion to the Emperor and to Japan must be based on eating the native foods of the country.

Ohsawa mocks the Ise pilgrims who pray before Toyouke's shrine, and then return to their hotels to feast on beef, white bread, sugar and tropical fruits. Their worship is just empty words, with no true understanding or practice. Ohsawa bitterly attacks the Shinto priesthood as well. Even those at Ise have forgotten the practical basis of religious life. They no longer guard the purity of the food of the nation, forgetting even the importance of the central elements of rice, salt and water. They are responsible for the decline of true religion in the nation and for the loss of physical and spiritual health among the people.

During this period Ohsawa added a distinct religious tone to his own expression of Shoku-Yō thought and practice. He writes in other books that rice and other foods are indeed manifestations of the gods. To eat, therefore, is to receive divinity, to take the sacred in physical form and to transform it into one's body and life. Each meal is a sacrament. The traditional though often peremptory grace *itadaki-masu* is an expression of this. It means "I humbly receive."

To revive this sacred dimension, Ohsawa gives specific instructions for mealtime decorum. One should begin with a *gasshō* [合掌] or gesture of respect, in which the hands are held palms together before one's face. Then five minutes of silent meditation are followed by the reading of a prayer (or appropriate proclamation of the Emperor). The food should be eaten slowly, carefully and with deep gratitude. Each mouthful should be chewed 120 times and there should be a minimum of talk. No morsel of the sacred food dare be wasted, so tea is drunk from the scoured rice bowl. A closing grace and prayer concludes the meal. Ohsawa even wrote a book of mealtime prayers that would create a proper frame of mind for eating and would express the sanctity of the event. This was published in 1937 under the title *Yashinai Kusa* [やしなひくさ] ("Nourishing Grasses").

In addition to national politics and religion, Ohsawa addresses international affairs. He does so, however, from a surprising perspective, one of which his earlier writings, give no clue. He interprets the current world situation and the history leading up to it in terms of a "Zionist-conspiratorial" theory. In works such as *Ningen no Eiyōgaku oyobi Igaku* [人間の栄養学及び医学] ("Human Nutrition and Medicine"), he presents this at some length.

The roots of the theory which Ohsawa espouses go back to the mid-19th century. At that time, the Zionist movement was founded to establish a Jewish homeland in Palestine. Later in the century a Russian journalist charged that the real aims of Zionism were much different. He claimed he had discovered a secret document called "The Protocols of the Elders of Zion." Supposedly, the Zionist founders had drawn up a list of strategies designed to consolidate the already substantial power of the Jews in Europe and to extend it over the world. The Protocols outlined various means to infiltrate and to weaken a country so that it was susceptible to control by the international movement. Foment social and economic unrest, it recommended. Incite political revolution. Gain control of education and the media. Use these to undermine the morals and values of the people, especially the youth.

This theory of an international Jewish conspiracy spread quickly through the Western nations, being added to the old and ample litany of anti-Semitic ideas. By the early 20th century it made its way to Japan. Ohsawa writes, though, that he first heard of it in France. His eyes were opened there, he recalls, to the fact that Jews control life in the West, dominating intellectual, cultural, economic and political affairs, and spreading their influence throughout the world. He learned that there are secret fraternities of Jewish men which are part of the larger conspiracy. To talk of this publicly means certain death. Ohsawa doesn't mention what persons or groups had influenced him in France. He does write, though, that by the time he returned to Japan he had become something of an expert on "Jewish affairs."

Once back in Japan Ohsawa apparently began to associate with a group of right-wing intellectual and military figures doing research on Jewish influence in the world. This included Unosuke Wakamiya [若宮卯之助], a writer; Ohsawa's friend Dr. Nakayama; and an army general from Manchuria named Yasue. The group published a periodical called "Kokusai Himitsu Kyoku no Kenkyū" [國際秘密局の研究] ("Research into the Secret International Power"). The magazine tried to piece together evidence indicating the activities of the conspiracy. Not distributed publicly, it was sent only to certain sympathetic people. There is evidence that Ohsawa was quite active in the group and under a pseudonymn wrote pieces for the magazine. He mentions a pamphlet he had written on the topic, remarking that he would like to make it public, but all copies have disappeared. In *Kōfuku to Kenkō* [幸福と健康], however, he presents in some detail his views of the subject.

For three thousand years, Ohsawa asserts, the dream of the Jewish people has been to dominate the world. They have tried to gain political and economic power and to impose their ideology, based on materialism, hedonism and individualism, on other peoples. The Zionist conspiracy is only the most recent expression of this centuries-old campaign. Already America and most European nations have fallen prey to it. Jews and half-Jews rule directly (as in the case of Roosevelt and Chamberlain) or indirectly (as with the Astors and Rothschilds). The Russian revolution was financed by Jewish investors and orchestrated by Jewish agitators. Half of the present Politburo is Jewish. Culturally too, Ohsawa charges, the West has given in to Jewish influence. Modern science, philosophy, morals and popular culture are merely expressions of the Jewish ideology.

Through Western (i.e., Jewish) imperial expansion, much of Africa and Asia have fallen under this same influence. India, China and Southeast Asia have been taken. Japan is the last stronghold defending its independence and a true heritage. The rebirth of nationalism and traditional values in Japan is part of a resurgence of spiritual values. The war with China, Ohsawa observes, is the start of the last and violent stage of the struggle between materialism and spirituality. Chiang-Kai-Shek, a tool of Zionist elements in Britain and America, represents decadent Western and Jewish values. Upon Japan falls the responsibility to defend and revive the spirit of the Orient.

At this time, of course, the National Socialists were in power in Germany, and under Adolf Hitler's leadership were transforming that country's culture. Although we tend in retrospect to equate Nazism with military expansionism and Jewish genocide, it was a complex phenomenon. The National Socialists made radical changes in the medical, cultural and agricultural spheres. Some of these, viewed from a great distance with and through his Shoku-Yō perspective, were quite interesting and attractive to Ohsawa.

For example, the German medical system was completely reorganized. In 1937, a conference was held concerning the re-education of the healing professions. Medicine was defined as a public service rather than a professional business. Physicians were charged with protecting and promoting the health of the nation, not merely with curing illness after it had developed. The government promoted preventive medicine, sponsoring nationwide physical exams, teaching hygienics, and encouraging sport and physical labor for all citizens. Various forms of traditional and natural medicine were nurtured.

When Hitler rose to power in 1933 he named agronomist Walther Darré as Minister of Food and Agriculture. This man had attracted the attention of the Nazis with a book on the role of the German peasant as the "life source" of the Nordic race. It was based on the idea that a mystical bond exists between the soil of Germany and the body and spirit of the German race. Darré helped institute the national policy known as *Blut und Boden* ("Blood and Soil"). The German peasantry was given their land in perpetuity, and was charged with feeding the nation with indigenous products. An energetic attempt was made to achieve agricultural self-sufficiency.

The Nazis also tried to revive the consciousness and morality of a tribal past. They taught that the German people were a single organism, mystically bound by blood, soil, and history. In the welfare and development of the nation, rather than in personal gain, does the individual fulfill himself. As with the physicians and farmers, the Nazis emphasized dedication to the common good as the central motive in life. Communal pride and cooperation, service and self-sacrifice were the cardinal virtues. Simplicity in daily life, disdain for material gain, and delight in accepting physical and mental challenges completed the official ethic.

These developments in Germany struck a responsive cord in Ohsawa. The medical reforms reflect an attitude toward health and medicine much like that of Shoku-Yō. The *Blut und Boden* policy seems a Germanic version of the principle of shin do fu ji. Ohsawa wonders, in fact, if Darré had been influenced by any of his own writings in French. The revived awareness of the nation as a racial organism struck him as a version of the Japanese concept of *kokutai* or "mystic body of the nation." And the new (or old) morality seemed to parallel the traditional moral and spiritual values of his own culture.

Of course, the Nazis at the same time were conducting a vigorous campaign against Jews, making it harder and harder for them to live in Germany. The Nuremberg laws of 1935 forbid marriages between Jewish and "Aryan" Germans, and deprived Jewish citizens of many of their rights. There was a systematic attempt to remove Jews from positions of influence in the intellectual and cultural world. Though the horrors of the extermination camps lay yet in the future, it was clear that the Jews were being persecuted.

Ohsawa actually applauds these measures as well. Germany is in a death struggle against the force of international Zionism and its ideology of materialism and individualism, he maintains. In purging the Jews, the Nazis are trying to recover the original spiritual genius of the German people. Japan should follow her ally's lead and remove those who promote hedonistic and materialistic values. Soon, Ohsawa predicts, Japan and Germany will be matched against the rest of the world in a final devastating conflict. He says this with great sadness, since he had hoped there would be an "ideological" rather than a military war. He had worked hard to that end, but apparently to no avail.

Ohsawa, of course, was watching developments in other Western countries with equal care. As self-appointed broker between East and West, he wanted to be aware of any hopeful signs in the darkening gloom. In 1938 this watchfulness was rewarded. A book called *L'Homme Inconnu* ("Man, The Unknown") by Alexis Carrel came into his hands.

Carrel, a biologist, had been awarded the Nobel Prize for Medicine in 1923 for an experiment in which he kept the heart of a chicken alive in solution long after the bird had died. A long-time fellow at the Rockefeller Research Institute in New York City, the Frenchman had become interested in broader issues of science and civilization. In 1935 he published his book, severely criticizing Western science and technology and the modern civilization these have created.

Science, Carrel observes, is well-suited to the investigation of the physical material world. Dividing nature into small and manageable units, it has observed, measured and analyzed; discovering many facts and laws. Using this knowledge, Western man has developed a complex technology capable of controlling and exploiting nature. He has made himself rich in material goods, convenience and comfort. With little effort, modern man is able to satisfy his desires for food, physical ease and pleasure.

Yet, Carrel continues, science is not able to understand the human being. Its methods may apply to the study of a rock or a chemical reaction, but not to man. Man has an invisible, or spiritual, dimension which cannot be quantified or analyzed. Thus in spite of the advance of modern science man himself remains unknown. And in spite of technological benefits he remains unhappy and unfulfilled. Inner frustration and outward violence mark modern man's life, personal and collective.

Confronting this crisis, Carrel calls for the creation of a new "science of humanity." This would focus on man as man, that is, as a complex but unified living organism. It would study his body, mind, and spirit, and the deep relationships among these. It would seek a way to achieve true health and happiness, a harmonious perfection of body, mind and spirit. Carrel recommends that modern civilization make this "science of humanity" its highest priority, and that it be willing to change to suit the findings. He suggests many areas for research, including the effect of chemical agriculture on food, and the effect of food on human thought and behavior. Carrel looks ahead to the discovery of a single overarching principle that would unify man's understanding of himself and his life, and would be a reliable guide in all his affairs.

Ohsawa read the book and was enthralled. Immediately he wrote to Carrel for permission to translate it into Japanese. He was excited for two main reasons. Here was a distinguished scientist of the West echoing many of Ohsawa's own themes of the past decade: the limitations of science; the false happiness of material wealth and comfort; the degeneration of modern man; and the need for a totally new way of thinking and of ordering society.

Also, Carrel was aspiring to establish a "science of humanity" and to discover a universal principle. This was precisely what Ohsawa believed he himself had to offer. His "Unique Principle" was just this universal law, and Shoku-Yō and the other applications of this law were the "science of humanity." Perhaps the world was ready for his teaching after all. In any case, Ohsawa closeted himself with the book for ten days and the resulting translation was published in 1938 by Iwanami Shoten, a major Japanese publisher. It was one of the very few of Ohsawa's books during this or any other period, which he did not have to publish by himself or through the Shoku-Yō Kai. Ohsawa also began a correspondence with Carrel, hoping to explain his solution to the dilemmas of the age. This was soon interrupted, though, by the intensifying wartime situation. The faint glimmer of hope was lost in the dark reality of the Second World War.

These then were somber and tense years. War seemed to be approaching and in China and in Europe it arrived. The themes of Ohsawa's writings reflect the situation. Discussions of the physical and moral decline of the nation, of the stupidity and treachery of the priests and intelligentsia, of the ill-conceived government policies, and of the Zionist conspiracy run like dark threads through most of his books. The happy alternative of Shoku-Yō is always presented, but usually in a strident and desperate tone.

It would be wrong to conclude that this was an unhappy period for Ohsawa. He tended to vent emotion in his writing, and the bursts of anger and judgmental intolerance give a false impression of his usual mood. In fact, his friends and associates of the day affirm that he retained throughout a basic optimism, a *joie de vivre*, and even a sense of humor. Photos from the period show him youthful and self-confident, usually beaming from ear to ear. His account of his Manchurian visit contains a humorously self-demeaning incident. After one of his night-long sessions with Tamura, Ohsawa went back to his hotel only to find it locked up. Knocks and whistles drew no response. Ohsawa crawled into a vegetable seller's stand, wrapped himself in old newspapers, and settled down to sleep. The next morning the stand's owner was shocked to find he had had an overnight boarder.

In one book of this time, Ohsawa seems to forget about Japan's and the world's troubles. It is the *Shoku-Yō Jinsei Tokuhon* [食養人生讀本] ("The Shoku-Yō Human Life Reader"). Ohsawa deals with the origin and aim of human life, with marriage, child-rearing, education and various other issues, most of them day-to-day practical ones. His perspective is broad, his tone positive, and the bright and optimistic side of his personality and world view shine through clearly. It is no wonder that two decades later in America, Herman Aihara would choose this as the first of Ohsawa's Japanese works to render into English, publishing it as *The Macrobiotic Guidebook For Living*.

This universe is a paradise, Ohsawa begins, full of miracles and joy. It consists of two realms, apparently separate, but actually deeply interrelated. One is the material visible world, the other is the spiritual, invisible realm, infinite and eternal. From this we have come, and to it we ultimately shall return. Our aim in life is to play freely in both realms, to enjoy the pleasures of this world but also "to commune with the gods." The secret to this life of play is simple. We should eat humble food that is in harmony with our natural environment, and we should live for the benefit of others. This is the essence of Shoku-Yō, which is not a dietary discipline. Rather, it is a way of life according to the laws of nature and of the spirit. Through it one receives the natural birthright of health and well-being, and one is able to enter into the spiritual realm.

There is no unavoidable suffering in human life, Ohsawa asserts. Sickness and unhappiness come only from unwise, usually luxurious, eating and from living selfishly in pursuit of wealth and pleasure. Yet even when it occurs, suffering has a meaning and benefit. It is not a punishment. It is the gods' loving and compassionate way of calling us back to right ways of living. Even old age and death, which the Buddha saw as painful and inevitable, can be positive, happy experiences. In old age, when the passions are dimmed, it is easier to live simply, with loving concern for all persons and creatures, and in ecstatic harmony with the universe. At death one returns to one's origin and home in the world of the spirit. For the healthy and moral man, death is a joyful homecoming and a continuation of his life of amusement.

Against the backdrop of this happy Weltanschauung, Ohsawa discusses family life and especially the responsibilities of women. The family is the basic unit of the nation and the foundation of public welfare. Its well-being depends mainly on the understanding of food by the wife and mother. If she chooses the daily fare according to the order of nature, and prepares it with care and love, the family will thrive. Love between her and her husband will grow. He will become strong and brave and will work for the benefit of humanity. The children will be healthy, vital and responsible members of society.

Food, while of primary importance, is not the only factor. A mother's education of her children is important too. This begins before birth. During pregnancy, a woman should eat proper (i.e., Shoku-Yō) food, but also, she should be careful in how she thinks and lives. She should work hard physically, and read religious scriptures and other elevating books. She should live simply and cultivate a feeling of love and sympathy for all things. After the birth, she should nurse the infant, but be careful not to smother it with sentimental love. The infant should be exposed to fresh air, cold and hunger. It should not be cuddled or picked up without reason. There should be no toys. This approach will develop its physical hardiness, emotional independence, and imagination. The adolescent should be urged to work, to assume responsibility, and to experience the challenges of the world.

In formal education, Ohsawa recommends keeping boys and girls separate from the age of seven through their late teens. Thus their special masculine (Yang) and feminine (Yin) characteristics and energy will develop. The attraction between the two will become strong and later relationships will be stable and fulfilling.

Of greatest importance is acquaintance with the Order of the Universe, Yin and Yang, and with its application in diet. With this philosophical compass and simple practice children will grow strong and supple in body, and peaceful and grateful in mind. They will be able to overcome all difficulties, to cure all sickness and to solve all problems, of themselves and others. They will realize all hopes and ambitions. More and more they will experience God as the sum of life that fills the universe, and will realize that they are a part of that divine unity. Thus education is a first and crucial step in the individual's realizing his spiritual destiny.

Also in the *Shoku-Yō Jinsei Tokuhon*, Ohsawa introduces a theory to explain why food is such a crucial factor in the development of consciousness in the individual.

80

The human brain, he says, is like a radio receiver. It can pick up waves from the various levels of existence. The nature and clarity of its reception depend on the raw materials which make it up and on the energy which powers it. These are both determined by food. If one eats meat, sugar, chemicalized food, and so on, then the brain will pick up vibrations from the material world only and in a chaotic way. If one eats simple, whole vegetable foods then the receiver automatically receives the more subtle vibrations of the spiritual world. Properly nourished, it ultimately will receive Infinity itself. Thus through proper food one may become a citizen of the spiritual world.

Here Ohsawa expresses his deep faith in human nature and potential. The human infant is born healthy and good. If properly nurtured and educated he will grow up healthy and good. If he continues as an adult in a life of simplicity and virtue in eating and behavior, he will live totally in the awareness of the Infinite. This vision of Ohsawa's is a remarkable and inspiring one, next to which his darker moods and pronouncements of this period pale.

This section of Ohsawa's career ends in a surprising way. Late in 1938 and in 1939, despite (or perhaps because of) his many contributions to the Shoku-Yō Kai, opposition to Ohsawa began to grow within the organization. To some of the long-time members, he had strayed too far from the original teachings of Ishizuka. He had injected philosophy and religion, and domestic and international politics into what had been a straightforward health method based on diet. And some of his ideas were not only seemingly irrelevant, they were imprudent, even dangerous. Ohsawa's bitter denunciations of the Shinto clergy, of scientists, doctors and government officials, and his predictions of Japanese military defeat only invited trouble. In an increasingly totalitarian society where repression and violence were common, it was wise to keep a low profile. This Ohsawa seemed unwilling or unable to do. Also, energetic and rushed as he was, he ruled the organization with an autocratic and perhaps abrasive manner. He had risen very quickly to the top and perhaps neglected some of the nicer points of Japanese etiquette in dealing with more senior members. In any case, late in 1939 Ohsawa was asked to resign by the governing board.

So in November of that year Ohsawa inserted a *Sayonara* or "farewell" banner headline into the "Shoku-Yō Zasshi." He bid goodbye to the membership, saying that he was going to devote himself to social and policial reform, not just to curing illness. For four years Ohsawa had struggled mightily to prevent disaster for the nation. A figure at once courageous and pathetic, insightful and quixotic, he had tried to redirect the river of history. Deprived of even the modest resources of the Shoku-Yō Kai he resolved to continue.

1.   Ekken Kaibara (1630–1716).

2.   Sagen Ishizuka (1850–1910).

3.   Dr. Manabu Nishibata.

■ Yukikazu Sakurazawa (George Ohsawa)

4. Mother, Setsuko, 1906. Taken the year she died at age 32.

5. With parents and younger brother, 1901.

6. Ohsawa in Paris, 1920.

83

7. Ohsawa making macrobiotic "coffee" at the International Peace Congress in Cherreuse, outside Paris.

8. At a Shoku-Yō Kai meeting in Japan, 1940.

9. **Farewell party for Michio Kushi at Hiyoshi M. I., Yokohama, 1949. Kushi was departing for the U.S.**

10. **The study at M. I., Nishihara, Shibuya, Tokyo.**

11. Ohsawa and Lima say farewell at Kobe port, October, 1953. They are embarking on a world tour to teach macrobiotics. First stop, India.

12. Ohsawa introduces Master Masahiro Oki, Yogist, in Europe.

13.   George Ohsawa in Paris, 1957.

14.   With Lima in Los Angeles, 1960.

15.   Last birthday, October 18, 1965. Ohsawa was 73 years old.

16. Last of a series of lectures for future macrobiotic leaders, January, 1966. The location is the New East University or "No-No School" in Ebisu, Tokyo. Series began in October, 1965.

17. In front of Hiroshima's atomic bomb dome, during the First International Spiritual Olympics, 1966.

6

George Ohsawa:
The War Years (1940–1945)

So as the new decade dawned, Ohsawa, who had just turned forty-seven, found himself for the first time in twenty years not connected with the Shoku-Yō Kai. He had to continue his mission without the help of the group's established reputation, its publishing facilities, and its influential membership. A handful of devoted followers including Ogawa and Kawaguchi left with him, and he could count on the support of some men like Maruyama and Eguchi. But it certainly was a setback. Ironically, within a year the Shoku-Yō Kai closed down. Its building was sold and the proceeds were divided. No part went to Ohsawa who had helped finance it.

There was advantage to the break as well. Ohsawa now could budget his time and energy exactly as he wished. Even before he left Ohsawa had been trying to cut down on the time spent in medical consultation. In 1937 and 1938 he would often spend half a day with a single individual, diagnosing their condition, explaining the Shoku-Yō approach to its cure, and making careful dietary recommendations. He had had significant success in this, helping to cure a variety of illnesses, from tuberculosis and ulcers to chronic depression. By late 1939, Ohsawa had changed his *modus operandi*. The national situation had become critical. The war had spread from China to Indo-China, and rapidly worsening relations with the United States indicated greater crises to come. Wishing to be free for activities directed to the public he tried to economize on consultation time. He might spend an hour with a patient and then refer them to his writings. Then he began to charge very high fees to discourage people, and limited his advice to fifteen minutes. He refused to see anyone more than one time. The principles of the diet were simple and clear enough, he reasoned, that a person with strong motivation could learn to apply them on their own.

After leaving the Shoku-Yō Kai, Ohsawa carried this inclination to its logical conclusion. On April 3, 1940, he met with a small group of close associates. They decided to launch a national movement that would aim specifically at introducing the entire nation to the Shoku-Yō diet and way of life. It would present an integrated philosophy and practice which could solve the various problems of the nation. The curing of individual sickness was to be de-emphasized. Accordingly, Ohsawa stopped all individual consultation to devote himself entirely to the spread of what he called *Shin Seikatsu Hō* [真生活法] ("the True Way of Life").

Otherwise, Ohsawa's activities did not change much. He wrote prodigiously as usual. He continued the magazine *Musubi* [むすび] ("connecting or organizing principle"—a Shinto term). He had started this in 1937 as a supplement to the *Shoku-Yō*

Zasshi [食養雑誌]. He wrote and published over thirty books during the next five years, though hampered by paper shortages and increasingly strict censorship. Ohsawa lectured widely and organized conferences and seminars. He tried to influence people in the government and military. Ultimately, he was to become involved in direct political action.

Ohsawa pursued this course with his usual energy and intensity. Each moment is as valuable as a 10,000 Yen note, he writes. He shaved while standing on his tiptoes in order to get some exercise in the process. When receiving visitors in his office he would do other things at the same time, straightening out his desk or even talking on the phone. He was gruff and impatient with his associates, expecting of them a similar intensity. Ohsawa continued his spartan diet of rice and vegetables. He still took plenty of salt, as much as thirty grams a day, and wondered if his treatment of fellow workers would be more gentle if he didn't! He was, as ever, a man in a desperate hurry, convinced of the urgency and importance of his message to the nation and to the world.

In the early months of 1940 Ohsawa got his books on Manchuria into print. Then in June he published *Kome no Chishiki: Takikata to Tabekata* [米の知識—たき方とたべ方][2] ("An Understanding of Rice and How to Cook and Eat It"). In this book Ohsawa returns to the unchanging foundation of his teaching: the importance of food, and particularly of rice in human (especially Japanese) life. Rice has been the source of the Japanese people's body and spirit for centuries, he asserts. The national welfare depends directly on the quality of its rice. This, in turn, depends on how it is grown, harvested, processed and cooked. Ohsawa then gives detailed suggestions for each of these processes. Chemical fertilizers upset the balance of minerals and nutrients in the rice and thus undermine the strength of the people. While economically beneficial, their use is unwise. Rice, as the basis of life, cannot be treated as an economic commodity. And farming cannot be done as primarily a profit-oriented business. Upon agriculture and its products rests the very existence of the nation. Ohsawa also gives directions for the proper processing of rice. It should be harvested just before it is fully ripe and then allowed to dry slowly out of the sun. It should be left unhulled until shortly before it is eaten, and then hulled gently by water power or by hand. If possible, rice should be left totally unpolished, so that all nutrients are preserved. If a person has a problem eating brown rice, however, rice that has been twenty or fifty percent polished is permissible. In that case, one needs more vegetable side dishes. The rice must be cooked slowly and carefully, if possible over a fire of rice straw or wood. It should also be eaten slowly, each mouthful chewed over a hundred times. If the whole nation were to adopt these practices, Ohsawa maintains, a variety of problems, from the food shortage to low industrial production would be solved. If the root of national life, rice, is sound and whole, then each individual and the entire nation will reflect that strength and harmony. To impress this idea upon the government, Ohsawa suggests that all officials work daily in the fields or spend two months a year on a farm!

In the summer of 1940 Ohsawa organized a *Musō Genri Kaki Daigaku* [無双原理夏期大学] ("Unique Principle Summer University") for adults, and a *Kenkō Gakuen* [健康学園] ("The School for Health") for children. Both were held high in the mountains of Shiga Prefecture not far from Kyoto. Ohsawa was particularly fond of the children's camp. He spent much time preparing his talks about the Unique Principle and the Shoku-Yō diet for the young people. He walked with them in the mountains, enjoying the beauties of nature and collecting wild plants to add to meals. Ohsawa later wrote that during the camp, each of the children had transcended their usual ego-centered consciousness and lived happily and simply in the embrace of nature. This proved, he said, that by nature children are loving and good, and that they are spoiled by sentimental parents and rigid schooling. The biggest problem was the attempt by mothers to slip their darlings candies and other treats.

Ohsawa wrote a play for the children to perform, calling it *Mahō no Megane* [魔法の眼がね] ("The Magic Spectacles"). It is a light and playful piece even though it has a serious message. It shows Ohsawa's brighter side again, even in these somber days. In the play, a group of boys and girls are wandering in the mountains, searching for *Fushigi no Mikoto*, ("Lord of the Gods"). In order to find him the children begin to fast, and suddenly, after testing their courage with a thunderstorm, the god appears. He takes them above the clouds to the Land of Truth. He shows them the tree of life, and explains that it will nourish them without sickness for a hundred years. They drink from it, but the overweight boy in the group indulges in a second glass and becomes sick. Greed and self-indulgence, especially in food and drink, is the cause of sickness. Mikoto explains too the Formless Form, the Unchanging Change which is the source of all. Then he teaches the children about Yin and Yang, the right and left hand of this Oneness, which create all that is. And he urges them to live according to the laws of Yin and Yang so that they will be happy and healthy.

Ohsawa was deeply concerned about the proper rearing and education of children at this time. They are the nation's future and it is crucial that they be properly introduced to the Unique Principle and the Way of Eating. Ohsawa continued these summer camps for the next several years, always including a children's session. A book published the following year, called *Kenkō Gakuen*, was a practical guide to organizing such a camp. Ohsawa hoped that various Shoku-Yō groups around the country would also work among the children and youth of the nation.

In September 1940 Ohsawa moved from the Tokyo area to Ohtsu, a small city on Lake Biwa near Kyoto. He rented a former restaurant and established the *Musō Genri Kōkyūjo* [無双原理講究所] ("The Unique Principle Lecture and Research Center"). Meetings and lectures took place downstairs, while the family and guests lived and ate upstairs. Ohsawa arranged conferences and tried to bring in various teachers to augment his own point of view. Apparently he wanted to broaden the narrow food focus of the Shoku-Yō movement. Around this time, a young scientist, (named Keishi Amano [天野慶之] now president of the University of Forestries and Fisheries in Tokyo), visited Ohsawa in Ohtsu, and attended one of his camps there. Amano, recalls that among the other lecturers there were Tenkō Nishida [西田天香], founder of *Ittōen* [一燈園] ("The Garden of a Single Light"), a communal village near Kyoto; Ugen Mohara [茂原右眼], who developed a system of *Shizen Undō* [自然運動] ("natural movement") or spontaneous exercise to overcome disease and tension; Eguchi Toshihiro, who had developed a palm-healing technique and also methods of diagnosis and treatment that could be used without the patient being present; and a scholar named Shūzo Takada [高田集蔵], who was an expert in ancient languages.

Soon after the move to Ohtsu, Ohsawa experienced government harassment for the first time. Previously, his critiques of the military and bureaucracy had attracted the attention of right-wing groups, but his influential connections at the Shoku-Yō Kai had protected him. Without them now, he was targeted by the police and press. Ohsawa later hints that it might actually have been some enemies from the Shoku-Yō Kai who were behind the action. In any case, one day without warning several national newspapers carried stories describing Ohsawa's arrest as a medical fraud, swindler, and debaucher of young women. This was a bit premature, since Ohsawa was away on a lecture trip. Returning home by train he read the story with understandable surprise. Once back in Ohtsu, he was arrested along with several associates. Ohsawa spent the next ten days in jail and took the opportunity to fast. He was then summarily released. Never easily intimidated, Ohsawa demanded an apology from the police, but one was not forthcoming.

Ohsawa continued trying desperately to gain the support of the public and government for his program. In November he published *Shokumotsu no Rinri* [食物の倫理] ("The Ethic of Food"), warning that only a return to traditional food patterns could avert a national catastrophe. He traveled and lectured around Japan. Early in 1941 he had an opportunity to demonstrate the effectiveness of his dietary program in a hospital setting. For one month at a Tokyo military recuperation center, Ohsawa oversaw the application of Shoku-Yō treatment to a group of twenty-three sick and wounded soldiers. All medications were stopped and the men were fed brown rice and vegetables. Their wounds and infections were treated with salt water only. Each day Ohsawa visited to check on their condition, to give specific recommendations, and to lecture briefly. Later, in a short book called *Hitotsu no Hōkoku* [一つの報告] ("A Report"), he published the results. All the men had made significant progress both physically and in terms of morale. They were in much better condition than if they had received orthodox treatment. Ohsawa expressed the hope that such an experiment would attract the attention of medical and government authorities and that his methods would be adopted on a broad scale. He was disappointed though. There was little response to this pilot project as there was little response to his lectures and to other writings.

Ohsawa had to endure not only indifference from the government but active opposition as well. The harassment of late 1940 was followed by the banning of one of his books. In 1937 Ohsawa had reissued *Hakushoku Jinshu o Teki To Shite* under the title *Nihon o Horobosu Mono wa Tare Da* [日本を亡ぼすものはたれだ] ("Who are Those Who are Destroying Japan"). It was very well received at first. It was seen as a patriotic book, extolling the unique genius of Japan and explaining the mind and life of the enemy as well. The military ordered 100,000 copies to distribute to its officers. By the spring of 1941 the government had officially banned the book. Its prediction of Japan's defeat in the event of total war with the West was seen as dangerous and subversive.

Undeterred, Ohsawa continued to express his misgivings. He did this on the lecture platform and in new books. In June 1941 he published *Kenkō Sensen no Dai Issen ni Tachite* [健康戦線の第一線に立ちて] ("Standing on the First Line of the Health War"). Germany, he claims, had lost the First World War because of a decline in the physical health of the people. This decline was caused mainly by a food policy based on faulty Western nutritional theory. Diet determines the winning or losing of a war. Then he analyzes the health of the various nations in the current world conflict. The situation of each is bad, but that of Japan is the worst. The nation's poor health, combined with her smaller economic and military resources, will bring defeat. The only hope is for the nation to adopt an ecologically-based (i.e,. Shoku-Yō) dietary policy. Ohsawa calls on the rulers to open their eyes. He warns them, even mentioning Prime Minister Fumimaro Konoe [近衛文麿] by name, that they will be responsible for the nation's destruction and humiliation. And Ohsawa reminds them ominously that after the first great war, the inept leaders of France were executed as traitors. Apparently, Ohsawa's analysis of the situation and his prophecy of doom caught the imagination at least of the reading public. The book went through five or six printings and sold 100,000 copies.

In December of that year the Japanese attack on America's naval base at Pearl Harbor began the total conflict which had long seemed inevitable. A short time thereafter Ohsawa was contacted by two generals on the National Mobilization Board. This was an emergency wartime agency established to insure that Japan make maximum use of all its human and material resources. Ohsawa was asked to draft a set of proposals that could be made into a national policy.

Quickly, hopefully, Ohsawa responded with a five-hundred-page book called *Atarashii Eiyōgaku* [新しい栄養学] ("The New Science of Nutrition"). It is a relatively well organized presentation of Ohsawa's central themes. He recommends a tax on sugar, increased domestic rice cultivation, organic agricultural methods, a massive public education program about the importance of food, and a re-evaluation of the medical and public welfare system. This book was well circulated too, being reprinted about seventy times. It had little effect, however, on the policies of the Mobilization Board. Soon Ohsawa was commenting with some bitterness on how useless it is to meddle in politics. In the affairs and decisions of government it is, he complains, money, status and connections, not the correctness of one's ideas, that make the difference.

One curious and troubling issue emerges in *Atarashii Eiyōgaku*. It concerns Ohsawa's attitude toward the war. All through the pre-war years, and even after the conflict with China had begun, Ohsawa urged Japan to pursue its aims peacefully. To be true to the peaceful spirit of its past, Japan must wage an ideological, not a military war, he declares again and again. It should return to its traditional ways and show the world by example the correctness of the Yamato-damashii. Ohsawa was about as outspoken a pacifist as one could dare to be in a militaristic state.

In *Atarashii Eiyōgaku*, though, he suddenly repeats with enthusiasm the standard government propaganda about the righteousness of the conflict. It is a just and necessary battle to free the captive peoples of Asia from the yoke of Western capitalism. It is a holy fight to save Japan and her sister nations of the East from the spreading cancer of materialism, hedonism and individualism Besides, it is an opportunity to spread the beauty and wisdom of the Japanese way of life through Asia and around the world. The Imperial Armies are the great benefactors of civilization who will liberate Asia and create a harmonious family of nations based on Shoku-Yō. Had Ohsawa suddenly turned into a war-monger, or at least an active advocate of Japan's role in the conflict?

Given the circumstances of the moment, this is not impossible. The destruction of Pearl Harbor and of American bases in the Philippines had opened Southeast Asia to Japanese attack. In the first half of 1942 the Imperial Armies swept through the region swiftly and easily, scoring triumph after triumph. The Dutch East Indies, Singapore, Malaya, and the Philippines were absorbed into the "Greater East Asia Co-Prosperity Sphere," as the Japanese empire was euphemistically known. The dream of a united Asia under benevolent Japanese hegemony seemed within reach. A paroxysm of enthusiasm for the war swept the nation. Even sober intellectuals and religious leaders shared the public fervor.

It is possible that Ohsawa was caught up as well. He was a man of deep sentiment, with a deep love of Japan and its heritage. He had long espoused the Japanist ideology of Nippon-shugi, and agreed with the government's general aim of liberating Asia, and of spreading the principles of Japanese life. But he had always, until now, differed radically on the means to achieve the end.

Perhaps Ohsawa did sincerely support the war at this point. But to judge him fairly we must keep in mind other factors. The book was directed specifically at the generals on the mobilization board. Ohsawa was more likely to gain their attention and approval if his message contained some of the patriotic slogans of the moment. Ohsawa may once again have let his instincts as a salesman influence the expression of his basic ideas. Indeed, after the war was over, Ohsawa writes that his main concern at the time was to bring the war to as early a close as possible. He had masqueraded as an advocate of the war so that the government might adopt his policies. If it had done so, the war would have ended sooner, in Japan's favor, and the benefits of Shoku-Yō would have been spread throughout Asia. The fact that over the next several years Ohsawa was to risk and almost lose his life several times trying to hasten the war's end, gives weight to his claim that he was throughout an opponent of it.

The tide of war changed during the latter half of 1942. The United States had broken the Japanese Navy's secret code and was thus able to inflict large losses at the battles of Midway and the Coral Sea. Soon the Allied forces gained control of the shipping lanes in the Pacific, cutting off the main islands from the far-flung colonies. The flow of oil and raw materials into Japan, and the export of supplies and arms were greatly curtailed. By the end of the year the Americans were ready to begin their steady and bloody island-by-island advance toward the Japanese homeland.

By this time Ohsawa had begun to despair of his suggestions being adopted by the government. There had been no response to *Atarashii Eiyōgaku* or to any of his other impassioned writings. No one seemed ready to listen and to understand. In *Shokumotsu to Jinsei* [食物と人生] ("Food and Human Life"), published in July of 1943, he describes with bitter regret a seminar he gave at a national conference of Shinto priests. For three days he lectured about food and its role in the ancient teachings, and its relevance to the crisis of the moment. The priests listened politely. But, overfed and fat, lacking all sense of responsibility and self-criticism, even they did not at all understand. Japan seemed on a road to inevitable defeat and humiliation.

Ohsawa moved with Lima, his family, and a few close associates to a small village deep in the mountains of Yamanashi Prefecture. He devoted himself to writing, particularly to a project which he called the P.U. Library—the Principe Unique Library. This was to be a collection of 48 volumes, in four sets of twelve, which would explain the Unique Principle and then demonstrate its application in a variety of areas. Ohsawa had begun this in 1941. Unsure now of Japan's future or of his own fate, he rushed to complete it. The series would be a legacy which would outlive him and which might give guidance to the nation after the war.

Two years previous, Ohsawa had written *Uchū no Chitsujo* [宇宙の秩序] ("The Order of the Universe"), and *Ningen no Chitsujo* [人間の秩序] ("The Order of Man") as foundation volumes in the series. Ohsawa presents his cosmology or view of the structure of the universe. He describes the finite world as six concentric circles, each created by the next larger and each creating, in turn, the next smaller. From the infinite Oneness which surrounds and contains all comes the first of these, the level of Yin and Yang. Thereafter follow the worlds of energy or radiation; of atomic particles; of chemical elements; of plants; and of animals. The universe is an integrated, dynamic whole. All the levels are interrelated and each is constantly changing into another according to the laws of Yin and Yang. In the second book Ohsawa focuses on human nature and destiny. On the material level man consists simply of recycled elements. On the spiritual level he is infinite and eternal, identical with the universe itself. By living according to its laws he can realize this identity.

Although Ohsawa never finished all forty-eight planned volumes, he did write many of them. In each he tries to focus on a particular theme. Despite this good intention Ohsawa seldom stuck to one topic. The title of a typical book refers at best to a starting point. Ohsawa deals with this subject for a while but is usually soon off on a tangent, pursuing other favorite themes. He may start writing about medicine and in a few pages be onto issues of science, politics, biology and religion. Usually there are a few autobiographical notes and personal reminiscences thrown in for good measure. In the end he may or may not return to the original theme. The result is a comprehensive, if confusing, overview of his main ideas. It sometimes seems that Ohsawa wrote the same book over and over again, with a different point of departure and a title appropriate to it. Ohsawa was a man who loved to write, and enjoyed nothing more than the publication of a new book. Nevertheless, there emerge in this period new ideas, or at least new applications of old ideas. From his unique perspective Ohsawa deals with ethics, Chinese history, military strategy, and anthropology.

In his early writings Ohsawa expressed Ishizuka's idea that *kokoro* ("heart" or "mind") is the product of food. Thus if the food is correct then the person's mental attitude and behavior also will be correct. Ethical behavior, in other words, follows cure. However in 1940 in a book called *Shokumotsu no Rinri* ("The Ethics of Food"), Ohsawa deals with the role of mental attitude and behavior in treating disease. He points out that not only diet, but also loving service to others is an important part of a Shoku-Yō cure. Ohsawa emphasizes the importance of two ethical concepts, *hō-on* [報恩] and *hōshi-hōkō* [奉仕奉公]. The first literally means "repayment of debts (of gratitude)." According to this principle, each person should always be keenly aware of the endless gifts received from ancestors, parents, teachers, nature and society, and should work tirelessly to repay them. The spirit of *hōshi-hōkō* ("public service and public duty") springs from this sense of endless indebtedness. It is a life of service and self-sacrifice for the common good. These originally Confucian ideas had become part of the official morality in Japan during the Edo Period, and had been revived with fervor during the war years. Ohsawa remarks that they are the basis of a true morality. They are essential to the practice of Shoku-Yō, and only by practicing them can one realize true physical health and mental peace.

There is here a small but important shift in Ohsawa's thinking. He seems to go beyond the idea that a loving heart and a moral life come from food alone. He seems to allow that mental attitude and ethical choice, while connected to physical health, are not wholly determined by it. To become well one must consciously cultivate a grateful and generous outlook and act accordingly, as well as eat a harmonious diet. The shift is subtle but important. It may have resulted from Ohsawa's experience as a consultant with the Shoku-Yō Kai between 1937 and 1939. He had helped many people cure ailments or at least relieve symptoms through diet. But many, perhaps most, once well went back to their old patterns of eating and drinking and eventually became sick again. Food alone had not been able to change the selfishness and self-indulgence which had made them sick in the first place.

On a winter day in 1943 Ohsawa picked up a school textbook on Chinese history, one belonging to his eldest daughter Fujiko. He read and then used this text as the basis for a book on history titled *P.U. Chūgoku Yonsennen Shi* [PU中国四千年史] ("The 4,000 Year History of China According to the Unique Principle"). It was volume one and two of set III of the P.U. Library.

Ohsawa observes that human history, like all other phenomena, follows the laws of Yin and Yang. And in China the rise and fall of political dynasties had followed just such a pattern of growth and decay, consolidation and dispersion. In fact, from ancient times Chinese historians had analyzed their history in this way. But while they had discerned the pattern, they had not understood its underlying cause—namely, the changing biological and psychological condition of the people involved. And these changes are caused in turn by shifts in diet and life style. Food is the hidden mechanism of history.

Ohsawa points out that the founders of each dynasty were usually poor outsiders, often from outlying and northern districts. They were nurtured by and lived on sparse diets. Hardened by rigorous climate, outdoor life and simple food, they had become rugged, energetic and brave. Thus when they were attracted to the power, wealth, and comfort enjoyed by the ruling dynasty, they were able to challenge and overthrow it. For a generation or two the new dynasty expanded and thrived, reaching in perhaps a century the full flower of political power and cultural development. Thereafter, its culture began to degenerate and its borders became vulnerable. Finally, after two or three hundred years of rule, it too was overthrown by a new and virile group of challengers. The decline of a dynasty, Ohsawa maintains, is just the symptom of the loss of physical and mental vitality in its rulers and people. The root of this, in turn, is a life of ease and luxury and especially a diet of rich and delicate foods. He points out that the last ruler of a dynasty was usually noted as a gluttonous gourmet. Though an unrecognized factor, food determines the destiny of a culture.

Inevitably, Ohsawa applies this lesson to the crisis of the day. The Chinese well understood Yin and Yang. They had in fact discovered it in ancient times. And in many areas of life they had successfully applied it, creating a brilliant and relatively stable culture. However, in the most basic of activities, that of choosing, preparing and eating food, this principle had been forgotten. As a result, Chinese history has been marked by periodic upheavals. In Japan, though, wisdom concerning food has been preserved in the prayers and rituals of Shinto and in the popular food customs of annual holidays. Thus, since the dawn of Japanese history there has been a single continuous dynasty. Only in the period since 1853 has this hidden essence of the *Kannagara no Michi* [惟神道] or "The Way of the Gods" been neglected and forgotten. And, Ohsawa warns in conclusion, unless it is rediscovered and followed, Japan will suffer the same calamities as its continental neighbor.

While visiting Tokyo during this period, Ohsawa discovered in a used bookshop in Kanazawa a copy of the *Heihō-Shichisho* [兵法七書] ("The Seven Articles of War"). Written in the 8th century by the Chinese general Song Tzu, this is a text on military strategy. While professing himself an amateur in the field, Ohsawa in his *Heihō Shichisho no Shin Kenkyū* [兵法七書の新研究] ("A New Inquiry into the Seven Articles on War"), interprets the classic and applies it to Japan's situation.

One of Song Tzu's key principles is that the combatant (whether an individual or a nation) must be soft, flexible, even gentle on the outside, and strong, brave, and determined on the inside. According to Ohsawa though, he neglects to explain how one can develop this supple exterior and inner firmness. The key of course is diet. Whole cereal grains supplemented by local vegetables will create just such a balance of Yin and Yang elements in both body and mind.

In September 1943 Ohsawa finally expressed in writing some ideas which had concerned him for over a decade. He had not yet fulfilled his promise to Levy-Bruhl to write a book about the primitive mentality. Finally with *Mikaijin no Seishin to Nihon Seishin* ("The Spirit of Primitive Man and the Japanese Spirit"), he kept his word.

So-called "primitive man," Ohsawa observes, is very hard for Western academics to understand. The way he thinks and acts seems childish and irrational. This is because primitive life is based on a deep awareness of the invisible or spiritual world, a world to which modern man has become blind. For example, a native of the jungle may dream one night that his neighbor has stolen a cabbage from him. The next day he goes to the man, tells of the dream, and demands compensation. Apologetically the "dream thief" complies. To the Westerner, who thinks the dream world an illusion, this is absurd. But for the primitive this is reasonable. For him the world of dreams, ghosts and spirits is as real as the material reality of waking life. In sleep, a man's spirit journeys into that realm, and what occurs there has equal weight to what occurs during the day.

Another key idea in primitive culture is that the two realms are deeply interconnected, and that what happens in this world usually has a hidden cause in the invisible domain. For example, the primitives do not recognize that sexual intercourse between man and woman is the cause of pregnancy. For a *civilisé* the relation between the act and the result is an obvious biological cause and effect. For the primitive, though, while coitus may precede the start of life, it is not the real cause. The real agent is a soul in the spirit world deciding to take on human form in a particular time and place.

Accordingly, for the primitive man nothing happens by chance. Sicknesses, misfortunes, deaths, natural catastrophes, and happy events as well all originate in the spirit realm. If a tree falls in the forest and injures a man, this is no accident. Perhaps the spirit of a dead ancestor is angry with him. Perhaps a living enemy is using black magic to destroy him. A shaman or medicine man must discover the true cause before treatment and recovery can occur. Once the man finds out what is the hidden cause, he can act to rectify it. He can make proper offerings to his ancestor. He can go to his enemy and apologize for past wrongs.

Related to this is the idea that ultimately each person is responsible for what befalls him. The primitive then is very careful in all dealings with people and spirits, never wishing to offend or harm. In particular, he cares for and offers respect to the family and friends who have died and gone to the spirit realm. They are nourished by the offerings and prayers of the living, and have great power to affect life in the physical world.

Ohsawa then points out that Japanese culture also is based on a deep awareness of the spiritual dimension. From ancient times, the Japanese have recognized the reality of the dream-world. They have understood that sickness and accident can result from spiritual agents, that the souls of dead ancestors should be revered and nourished, and that humility and constant self-criticism are essential in human life.

While to modern man this mentality of the primitive and of the Japanese seems crude and superstitious, it actually reflects the nature of reality. And it is the basis for true human culture. Above all, civilization involves moral and spiritual development. It does not necessarily involve literacy, or technological control over nature. While Western man looks down on non-literate peoples and considers them "uncivilized," primitive man may be more "civilized" than a citizen of Paris or London.

Ohsawa concludes by advising his fellow Japanese to keep this in mind as they deal with the primitives in the newly-acquired territories in Southeast Asia and in the South Pacific. They should respect these people as their brothers and equals. In fact they should learn from these unspoiled peoples, and be reminded of their own rich tradition of spiritual life which has been obscured by modernization. Only then will the dream of a harmonious and peaceful community of nations in Asia be realized.

While Ohsawa kept mostly to his mountain fastness, he occasionally lectured outside. In 1943 he spoke at Kyoto University on "The Primitive Mind." In the audience was a student named Takuzō Yamaguchi [山口卓三]. Yamaguchi was a native of the southern island of Kyushu and was studying philosophy. He was deeply impressed when Ohsawa, after describing primitive customs and ways of thinking, and after asking his audience what they thought of this culture, himself exclaimed "*Subarashii desu ne!*" ("It is wonderful isn't it"). Yamaguchi was soon drafted into the army and sent to Manchuria. Eventually he became a student of Ohsawa and one of the leaders of the macrobiotic movement in Japan.

While Ohsawa claimed to know the solution to the nation's and the world's troubles, his own understanding of Shoku-Yō, even at a very basic level, continued to grow. Early in the war, Lima had given birth to a baby girl named Mariko. Oh-sawa, believing that salt gives stamina, strength, and immunity to disease, fed the infant a fairly salty diet after weaning. She fell sick, probably with influenza, and because of complications, related perhaps to excess salt, died. Ohsawa later wrote that this tragedy had taught him that children should be given very little salt.

Despite this personal sorrow and his despair over the national situation, Ohsawa even in this dark period retained his underlying optimism and joy in life. He reports that he delights in every moment of every day, and that, like a young child, he is fascinated by everything around him. Each morning is the start of a new life. He describes how pleasant it is to live simply in the mountains, and to learn how to roast carrots, burdock and dumplings over an open fire. He enjoys skiing and tells with relish of meeting an Austrian ski instructor near the village (Hi no Haru) [日野春]. The man travels over the world teaching and skiing, taking a childlike delight in his life. Ohsawa salutes him as a kindred spirit, whose work is his play, and who lives in freedom and happiness.

And despite the fact that Japan and the world seemed to be going up in flames around him, Ohsawa kept faith that all would be well, for the nation and for all humanity. In *Saigo ni soshite Eien ni Katsu mono* [最後にそして永遠に勝つ者] ("The Final and Eternal Victor"), published in April 1944, Ohsawa uses Rolland's biography of the Indian poet, Rabindranath Tagore, as a starting point for discussing the future. Despite the suffering of the present time, he writes, the world is moving inevitably toward a period of harmony and peace. Eventually men everywhere will grasp the order of the universe (the Unique Principle) and live according to it (practice Shoku-Yō). Each will become peaceful at heart and able to understand the common bond between all men and all cultures. The misunderstanding and fear which cause war will disappear. This may take hundreds of years, but eventually it will come. In the meantime, the eternal victor is the person who lives now according to the law of the universe and who works for its spread among all people. Though the world may be in tumult around him, he has already realized perfect happiness and peace within himself. Eventually, through his work the rest of humanity will have this same joy and well-being.

Even in the depths of the war Ohsawa kept his transcendent perspective. This ultimate optimism, however, did not keep him from becoming restless. The long months of relative isolation and inactivity weighed heavily upon him. From 1944 even the outlet of publishing was denied him. Strict government censorship, plus a shortage of paper, greatly limited what could be written and printed. Ohsawa did manage to publish a couple of books, including *Eien no Kodomo* [永遠の子供] ("Eternal Children") a study of the French pacifists, Romain Rolland and Anatole France. This was secretly printed, and distributed by hand among his followers. Around the same time Ohsawa sent a telegram to all his disciples stationed on the battlefronts of the war: *Oishi mono o tsutsushimi, saigo ni katsu mono tare* [オイシモノヲツツシミ, サイゴニカツモノタレ], it read. Literally it meant "Be prudent about delicious foods and become the victorious one." Its hidden message was "Come home safely at all costs." Ohsawa was convinced that in the aftermath of defeat he and his followers would be needed to lead the nation into a new life.

In the next months, Ohsawa brooded on what he could do to shorten the agonies of the war. Japan's defeat was imminent. It was only a matter of time, but meanwhile thousands of the innocent were perishing. By nature Ohsawa was no recluse or ivory tower intellectual. Throughout his life he had been a man of action, as a businessman, entrepreneur, and world traveler, and then as a crusader for Shoku-Yō. Besides, he was a son of the samurai, heir to the noble tradition of selfless service to the nation and to humanity. *Hōshi hōkō* was a living reality to him. In Japan's past even the most spiritual of teachers, men like the medieval Buddhist saints Hōnen [法然], Shinran [親鸞] and Nichiren [日蓮] had been involved in the political issues of their day and had risked their lives for the public good. Ohsawa's nature and the inspiration of this heritage would allow him to stand idly by no longer.

By late in the year Ohsawa had formed a daring (one is tempted to say foolhardy) plan to singlehandedly bring the war to an end. He would go to Manchuria and make his way on horseback across Mongolia to the Russian border. There he would present himself as an unofficial emissary from Japan and continue on to Moscow and to the Kremlin. Then he would confront Stalin and ask him to mediate between Japan and America to end the war. The Soviet Union was still technically neutral in the Asian conflict, and a potential middleman between the warring nations. It was an imaginative and bold plan. Though unlikely to succeed, it might indeed avert much unnecessary suffering.

In late December Ohsawa began to carry out the plan. That it called for him, who had little experience with horses, to travel by horseback across northern Asia in the dead of winter did not deter him. Ohsawa went by ship to the mainland and then by train to Harbin, the Manchurian capital. He arrived on Christmas night. The temperature was fifty degrees below zero!

The next morning he contacted his old friend Tamura, who was still with the Education Ministry. Tamura listened to Ohsawa's plan and tried to dissuade him. It was too dangerous, he argued plausibly, and had little chance of success. Ohsawa persisted though, and Tamura reluctantly arranged for food, clothing, and two ill-starred animals for the journey. Meanwhile a telegram had been received from the Interior Ministry in Japan. Ohsawa's scheme had been discovered. He was to be arrested immediately and executed. Tamura intercepted and destroyed the message.

Ohsawa then tried to get a permit to cross the border from a General Doi, who was commandant of the region. Doi refused, and placed a guard around Ohsawa's hotel so that he could not escape. Undaunted, he escaped through a secret door and went to the Russian embassy. He attempted to deliver a letter there, outlining his plan and asking for help. Russian guards took Ohsawa into custody, interrogated and beat him, and then let him out into the street. The Japanese secret police were waiting. By this time Doi was ready to execute Ohsawa by firing squad, but Tamura interceded on his behalf, and he was allowed to return to Japan.

Once back home Ohsawa learned that his old friend, a General Watanabe, had been promoted to command of the army in Mongolia. He decided to try another route to the Soviet border. On January 15, 1945, Ohsawa gathered some of his friends and students at Hi no Haru for a farewell dinner. As they sat together at the table, the house was surrounded by police. Ohsawa was arrested and all his books, manuscripts and letters were confiscated.

At first Ohsawa fasted in prison. The authorities, fearful that he would die in custody, summoned Lima and she began to bring food for him. Ohsawa was kept in a dark underground cell where the temperature hovered near freezing. He was interrogated for hours, with a bright light directly in front of his face, and not permitted to close his eyes. When Lima finally was permitted to see him she was dumbstruck by his haggard and emaciated condition.

By March, Ohsawa despaired of his life. One day before returning his lunchbox to Lima he wrote a message in French on the inside of the wrapping paper. It was in effect his last will. Addressed to his disciples, it read:

> I believe my life to be at an end. I leave the teaching of the Unique Principle to my disciples. Please see to it that Lima and my daughter Fujiko are sent to Paris.
> 「私の命はないものと思え．PU のことは弟子たちにまかせて，リマと娘の不二子は妙高を引き揚げてパリへ行き，下宿屋でもやって暮らしたらいい．」

The next day, gaunt, crippled and nearly 80 percent blind, Ohsawa was carried out of the prison and taken to another facility.

The new location was kept secret from Lima. Frantically she went to Tokyo and then to Osaka for help. She returned to Niigata, on the western coast of Japan, with Dr. Maruyama. Obeying a sudden impulse, Lima approached a guard at the local police station. "Excuse me," she said, "I have heard that my husband, Sakurazawa, is being kept here and I would like to see him." Her intuition was correct. Ohsawa was there, and Lima was allowed to see him. She took a room nearby, cooked and brought him meals. In this less harsh setting Ohsawa recovered a bit. He kept busy and fit by cleaning the bathrooms and his cell daily. Ohsawa became the unofficial prison doctor, giving health and diet advice to both inmates and police. He was able to cure one officer of anemia. He kept the pits of umeboshi or pickled plums, drying them on his cell windowsill, and used them as medicine for his fellow prisoners. After their release many sent him gifts of food, which he then passed on to Lima. This led the warden to remark that usually prisoners received gifts of food from their families rather than the reverse. Eventually, Ohsawa was so well-liked and trusted that if the guard had to go out on an errand Ohsawa the prisoner was left with the keys to the jail!

Suddenly on June 30, Ohsawa was released. His writings and activities had been reviewed and the authorities had decided that he was neither a subversive nor a traitor. Still, Ohsawa had to agree not to sue for any violation of civil rights, and to promise not to leave the country again. Throughout the long ordeal no official charges had been filed.

By this time Japan had been devastated by American bombing. In a single raid most of Tokyo had been destroyed by fire-bombs, and more people were killed than in the later atomic bombing in Hiroshima. Almost every major city in the country, with the exception of the ancient capital of Kyoto, was being subjected to similar attacks. Ohsawa immediately became involved in another plot to end the war. A long-time friend, Yuzuru Iimura [飯村穣], had been appointed supervisor of the Tokyo defense system. With his cooperation, the support of the local defense troops could be obtained. Then the capital area would be occupied and a new government, willing to end the war, would be installed. While the plot was taking shape Ohsawa was arrested once again. He was imprisoned in the town of Beppu, then transferred to another prison in the Japanese Alps. The day after he was moved from the town it was totally destroyed by American bombs. The kind and protective angel who watched over Ohsawa through these years was on duty until the war's close.

That summer, of course, the war finally ended. Early in August, Hiroshima and Nagasaki vanished in the awesome light and heat of the first atomic bombs. Those who wished the Japanese to fight to the bitter end were at last overruled. The Emperor capitulated to the Allies and an armistice and unconditional surrender was signed. For the first time in its long history Japan had been defeated by a foreign power. For the first time it would have to tolerate an army of occupation. The land was a smoldering ruin. Its people were exhausted, dazed, demoralized, and full of anxiety about the future.

Ohsawa remained in prison until mid-September, a month after the armistice. Yet even deprived of his freedom, and unsure if the war continued, he was dreaming of the future. In his prison cell Ohsawa began to write a plan for a new, revitalized Japan.

7

George Ohsawa:
Hope for a New Japan and a New World (1945–1953)

Japan's surrender, with the arrival soon thereafter of foreign troops, certainly was the most traumatic event in the history of the Japanese people. Never before conquered, invaded or occupied, Japan faced an uncertain future in the hands of a feared and hated enemy. But the seven years of American occupation turned out to be a not unpleasant period. The Allies, under the charismatic American, General Douglas MacArthur, exercised near total power, but did so in a generous and benevolent fashion. There were at first severe material hardships—shortages of food, housing and clothes—but no one starved (due to imports of food from America), and conditions improved rapidly. It was, though, a period of great change. In national ideology, in political structure, in social and moral values, and in popular culture, Japan was virtually transformed.

Much of this change was imposed or encouraged by the Americans. They wanted a democratic and peaceful ally in East Asia—a buffer against Soviet and communist expansion in the area—and set about remaking the Japanese in their own image. And the inheritors of the Yamato-damashii, with a long history of borrowing and adaptation of foreign culture, proved to be willing and facile students.

The Allies immediately took measures to destroy the nationalistic state ideology, seeing it as a key factor in Japan's aggressive militarism. The Emperor was forced to renounce his divinity. Shinto was abolished as a state religion. All patriotic organizations, public and private, were suppressed, and about 200,000 officials in government, business and the military, plus many writers and intellectuals, were censured as nationalists. They were barred from holding any public post. Leading figures in government and the military were tried as war criminals. Seven were executed and many were sent to prison. The war, and the view of Japan's uniqueness, superiority, and imperial mission were totally discredited.

A constitution, suggested by the Americans, was adopted by the Japanese. It established a British-style parliamentary democracy based on the freedom and dignity of the individual. It granted universal suffrage and complete religious and civil liberty to the people for the first time. The Emperor kept his title, but only as a powerless symbol of the "unity of the people." And in the constitution, Japan promised never to use force to settle a dispute with another nation. It became the world's first, and only, officially pacifist nation.

This new political direction was supported by reforms in education, initiated and supported by the occupation authorities. The shūshin or "moral education" courses which had taught the state ideology, and which had promoted the virtues of obedience, submission and self-sacrifice, were abolished in the schools. Instead, liberal, egalitarian values, such as the importance of the individual, and the validity of questioning authority, were promoted.

At the same time Western, and particularly American, popular culture swept into Japan like a tidal wave. American books, music, art, movies, fashion, manners and morals were snapped up by a public hungry for almost anything from the culture of the victors. The young and the urban middle class especially, followed every fad and fancy brought over by the American G.I.'s. Academics and intellectuals showed a similar passion for Western books and ideas, both classical and current. The GHQ (General Headquarters of the Allied Supreme Commander in Asia and the Pacific) worked hard to promote this interest in Western culture. There was meanwhile little interest in traditional native culture. The old crafts and arts were carried on by dedicated individuals, but the passion of the age was clearly for what was American and new. It was a time similar to the period of blind and furious borrowing of the 1870s and 1880s.

In the post-war years, then, Japan turned her back on the immediate past, and ignored or rejected much of her traditional culture. She looked to the West for new ideas and cultural forms. Ohsawa's life and thought in this period reflects this trend to a good degree. The Unique Principle remained the basis of his world view, and the Shoku-Yō diet the foundation of his practice. But his views on social and political organization, on history, on personal development and morals all shifted noticeably. There was a whole new vocabulary and tone in his thought as well, one which reflected a turning away from the past and from traditional Japan and toward the contemporary West.

Because of his imprisonment during the last stages of the war, Ohsawa was at best vaguely aware of the bombings of Hiroshima and Nagasaki, and of the August 15th surrender in Tokyo Harbor. Yet on August 20th he began writing a book called *Naze Nihon wa Yabureta Ka* [ナゼ日本は敗れたか] ("Why Was Japan Defeated?"). Finally released from prison on the 24th of September, Ohsawa was met by Lima and his eldest son, Chūichi, and taken to the mountain quiet of Hi no Haru to recover. He immediately sent a letter in French to General MacArthur giving suggestions for immediate action in governing Japan. These included dissolving the secret police and disestablishing state Shinto. Finishing the manuscript begun in prison, Ohsawa sent a copy to be delivered by hand to MacArthur's aides.

The book is both an analysis of Japan's defeat and a blueprint for its future. Not surprisingly, Ohsawa focuses on food and health in explaining the loss of the war. Since the start of the Meiji Era and the importation of Western diet and medicine, the Japanese people had declined physically and psychologically. People became sick, lazy, and weak. They lost their efficiency, courage, and sense of duty and responsibility. This ill health of body and mind is the root cause of Japan's defeat. It lay behind all the mistakes, inadequacies, and errors of judgment which lost the war.

The indirect cause, though, is the "slave mentality" of the Japanese people. For centuries the government has suppressed freedom of speech and thought. Thus, from

1868, the elite slavishly accepted Western views about diet and medicine (and many other things), and the public, in turn, meekly accepted the advice of these scholars and government experts. The traditional wisdom and practices were lost and the path to decline and defeat was taken.

In "Why Was Japan Defeated" and in a sequel published in May 1947, *Ningen Kakumei no Sho* [人間革命の書] ("Proposal for a Human Revolution"), Ohsawa presents a vision of Japan's future. Japan now has a chance to start anew, to correct the mistakes of the past, and to atone for the war. She should become a democracy, governed "of, by, and for the people." She should sift through her traditions and choose to keep what is valuable. Namely, she should rediscover the Unique Principle, the law of Yin and Yang, and apply it to all areas of life. Japan will realize a level of health and well-being that will inspire and guide the rest of the world.

The most important area of reform is that of food—its choice, production and preparation. Here Ohsawa reiterates many of his wartime suggestions. Japan should become self-sufficient, stopping all imports and concentrating on staples like grains, beans and vegetables. Cultivation of fruit, flowers, and tobacco should be stopped. There should be 1,000 percent tax on sugar. Traditional, natural methods of agriculture should be revived and the polishing of rice should be banned. There should be a national educational program to teach proper diet and cooking. The women of Japan should be the special focus of this program. They control the eating patterns and thus the well-being of the nation. Ohsawa suggests too, that the medical system be completely revamped to concentrate on the prevention of disease and on traditional therapies.

But Ohsawa does not talk only of food and medicine. He deals at length with political, social, and economic reforms for a new Japan. All decision-making should be democratic, at the local level by direct vote, and on the national level by indirect or represented vote. Every adult should have a full and equal share in the making of decisions, and leaders should be chosen without regard to sex or age.

In social organization, Ohsawa recommended a family-centered communalism. Each family would belong to a *tonari gumi* [隣組] or "neighborhood association." If possible, these would function as limited communes, with separate living quarters for each family group but with common kitchens, dining rooms, libraries, and so on.

In economic organization, agriculture should be viewed as the necessary substructure. Each family would be guaranteed an adequate amount of rice and other foods. Also, each would be given access to a farm plot of its own to supplement this supply. The currency would be based not on paper or gold but on specific units of rice or koku as in the Tokugawa Period. The central government would own and operate the major industries, though on a local level there would be free enterprise. Ohsawa suggests, though, that Japan not try to develop her manufacturing or mining at first, but concentrate on agriculture. Full-time farmers would receive three months a year paid vacation to develop themselves culturally, and all public officials would be required to spend a portion of each day or of each year doing agricultural labor.

Thus, with his familiar Shoku-Yō philosophy as a basis, and with elements of democracy, socialism and communalism, Ohsawa formed a new version of his *Shin Seikatsu Hō* [新生活法], or "new way of life." He hoped that in the post-war years the nation would choose to follow this path to secure the health and happiness of all its citizens. And he hoped that the world would be inspired by Japan's example and would follow accordingly. A world community of peace and harmony would follow. With his usual single-mindedness and energy, Ohsawa devoted himself to the realization of this vision in the coming years.

By December 1945, due to the careful and constant nursing of Lima, Ohsawa was well enough to teach actively again. At the invitation of a loyal associate, a Mr. Ruizō Kobayashi [小林類蔵], he came to Tokyo and in Kobayashi's home set up an educational center. It was called the *Shin Seikatsu Kyōdō Kumiai* [真生活協同組合] ("The True Way of Life Cooperative Center"). With the new year, Ohsawa began a series of lectures on democracy. He also began to publish a monthly magazine which he called *Konpa* [コンパ] ("Compass"), and opened a small natural food center.

In April Ohsawa moved to neighboring Kanagawa Prefecture and founded the *Joshi Rōdō Daigaku* [女子労働大学] or "Woman Worker's College." The school and its name reflected Ohsawa's view that the future of Japan, and of humanity, rested primarily on women, and particularly on those of the laboring classes, who until now had been suppressed. During the summer Ohsawa returned to Hi no Haru for a summer camp and lectured mainly on democracy. In October he moved the school to Yokohama, renaming it the *Yokohama Rōdō Daigaku* [横浜労働大学] ("Yokohama Worker's College"). Ohsawa founded at the same time the *Seishin Bunka Kagaku Kenkyū Kai* [精神文化科学研究会] ("The Spiritual, Cultural and Scientific Research Center"). Despite their grandiose names these institutions were very modest. Japan as a whole was devastated and struggling to survive. Ohsawa himself had little money or resources. The buildings were rickety and small, and the students involved were few in number.

Early in 1947 Ohsawa moved yet again, this time to the Myōrenji district of Yokohama where he rented a tiny house. He called this the Maison Ignoramus, "House of the Ignorant." These frequent transfers reflect the housing and economic difficulties of the time. Perhaps too, they reflect Ohsawa's restlessness, his search for a context in which he could express himself fully and organize his activities most effectively.

Later that year Ohsawa read in the *Reader's Digest* a condensed version of a book called *The Anatomy of Peace* by the American Emory Reeves. He was much impressed by its vision of a world political structure to prevent war. Shortly thereafter, Ohsawa came into contact with Japanese representatives of the World Federalist movement. This group had begun in the United States after the war, mainly through the work of intellectuals and public figures associated with the University of Chicago. It aimed to establish a world government, with all the elements of a national government: a parliament, president, even a "world army" to enforce the authority of the central government. It was hoped that an international rule of law would achieve world peace. Centers were set up in various countries, and efforts were made to draw up a satisfactory world constitution.

Ohsawa saw World Federalism as the perfect complement to his own Shin Seikatsu Hō. His vision of a peaceful world community began with individual biological regeneration. That of World Federalism began with a global organization based on law. Ohsawa joined the movement and quickly became one of the leaders of the nascent Japanese branch.

With this broad new perspective, Ohsawa tried to give his activities an international ambience. He adopted the term "macrobiotics" derived from Greek and meaning "great, all-embracing life." It is not clear where Ohsawa got the term. It may have come from the title of a book by an 18th century German physician named von Hufeland (see Chapter 15). Whatever its source, the term was more international than Shoku-Yō or Shin Seikatsu Hō. Ohsawa also changed his own name. He substituted an alternate reading of the "sakura" or "cherry tree" ideograms (ō), and came up with "Ohsawa." George came as a fanciful pronunciation of Jyoichi [如一], a possible reading of his first name characters. Hence he became George Ohsawa. Also he gave many of his students Western style P.U. (Principe Unique) names such as Augustine and Gertrude. A few managed to escape this scourge, though with some difficulty. Ohsawa felt he was training citizens of the world, international missionaries who would bring the gospel of biological revolution and world government to all nations.

In 1948 Ohsawa moved the Maison Ignoramus to the Hiyoshi district of Yokohama, where it was to remain for four years. He gave it a second name, "The World Government Center," and put a large sign with those words on the roof of the small house. He continued to teach about the importance of food in health, and published a magazine called *Sana* [サーナ] ("Health") to spread these views. He also began to publish a newspaper (every ten days) called *Sekai Seifu* [世界政府] ("World Government"). In it he addressed broader social, economic and political issues from his combined macrobiotic and world federalist perspective. Beginning in 1948 Ohsawa drafted a monthly letter to the leaders of the world, presenting his suggestions for solving current problems. The letter was rendered into fractured English, mimeographed, and then sent to 100 prominent political and cultural figures including Stalin, Truman and Einstein. The single reply was from Dr. Albert Schweitzer in Africa, and included an invitation to visit. Schweitzer probably never suspected that the unknown Japanese would someday actually arrive in Lambarené with his wife.

At the same time Ohsawa tried to inject his macrobiotic views about the role of food in human life into World Federalism. He wrote to the leaders of the movement, complimenting them on their draft of a world constitution but chiding them for ignoring the role of food in establishing world peace. A world of peace can be realized only by a world of healthy and happy individuals. And this can be accomplished only by sound diet in accordance with the law of nature. If the leaders and citizens of the world eat foods such as meat and sugar, which generate fear and hostility, there will never be peace, regardless of a world political structure. Ohsawa coined the phrase "biological theory of revolution," and argued that until now all attempts to improve the human condition have focused on changing social, political and economic forms. They have ignored the biological basis of human life—food. Hence they have failed. Only a revolution which keeps this idea in mind will be effective and lasting. The movement for world peace must understand diet and apply this understanding in its work. In the summer of 1949 Norman Cousins, one

108

of the American leaders of the World Federalist movement and founder of *The Saturday Review of Literature*, visited Hiyoshi. He stayed for a week, sharing the simple diet of miso soup and brown rice.

Ironically, as Ohsawa was adopting his "citizen of the world" stance, he was censured by the government as an ultranationalist. After the war the authorities surveyed all war-time writings to ferret out "dangerous persons." The 1937 version of *Hakushoku Jinshu o Teki to Shite* had been banned as seditious by the Imperial Government in 1941. Now that same book was judged dangerously patriotic, and Ohsawa was officially blacklisted. He was barred from holding public office, which he did not mind, and from traveling abroad, which he did indeed mind.

For the next four years Ohsawa, not knowing when he himself would be able to go abroad, devoted much time and energy to the training of the students at the Maison Ignoramus. They would be his proxies in spreading macrobiotics in Japan, and particularly in the world beyond. Very consciously and carefully he sought to train people to be missionaries to the world. A small dormitory was built in the garden, containing a men's and a women's section. With bunkbeds arranged three or four high it could accommodate about thirty people. It was usually full. Many of those who came were young idealists, sincerely attracted to Ohsawa and his mission. Others were interested more in the opportunity to go abroad. All were free to come and go as they pleased. The school was organized on the principle of "He who comes let him come, he who goes let him go." Of those who came and stayed, many were to remain active in the macrobiotic movement for years.

Ohsawa ran the school as a *dōjō* [道場], a place where a Tao or spiritual discipline is practiced. It was not a clinic or hospital. No sick people were allowed. Conditions were spartan, with no heaters, no radios, and no newspapers. Ohsawa, as *sensei* [先生], or "Master" was the absolute authority. The students or *deshi* [弟子] were there to train themselves physically, mentally and spiritually. They looked to him for guidance and obeyed him absolutely.

Each day followed a strict schedule. The students rose at 5:00 A.M. and went immediately to a nearby aikidō [合気道] dōjō for an hour and a half of martial arts training. Returning to the school, they performed *o-sōji* [お掃除], or the "honorable cleaning" of the dōjō buildings and grounds. The place was completely swept and then the straw mat floor, wooden pillars, and verandas were scrubbed down with cold water. Ohsawa, who usually had been up since two or three A.M. writing, would join the students in this task. Brandishing a duster in each hand, he would clean the walls with the speed of an ambidextrous swordsman. He would scrub the floor squatting on tiptoes, moving the rag vigorously with both hands. In all things he gave the students an example of efficiency, speed and concentration. Ohsawa would also sweep the street and clean the sewerage ditch that ran from the house to the station. One day the passing milkman had compassion on the poor fellow shoveling out the ditch and offered him a job. Ohsawa politely refused.

After a brief period of free time the three-hour morning lecture began. Ohsawa stood before a blackboard in the narrow main room. The students sat in stiff seiza, the formal seat-on-heels position, on the floor about him. He lectured on a wide variety of topics—current events, history, art, literature—surveying all from the perspective of the Unique Principle. He spoke very little about food and almost never about medical problems. Aveline Kushi, who was a student for two years at the Maison Ignoramus, recalls that Ohsawa barely mentioned diet in his lectures while she was there. It was assumed that everyone understood the importance of food, and would eat the simple fare offered at mealtime, but food was not a major focus. The emphasis was on the Unique Principle and on its many applications, particularly to the problem of world peace.

Morning lecture was followed by breakfast at between 11:00 and 12:00 A.M. Usually prepared by Lima with the assistance of some of the girls, it was most often simply miso soup, brown rice and a few vegetables and tea. An hour of free time following breakfast led into the afternoon work period. The students all had tasks around the school. Some were involved in maintenance and housekeeping. Some worked on the newspaper, writing and editing. Many went out each day with bundles of *Sekai Seifu*, hawking copies on street corners and railway stations. Within a year, circulation by this method had grown to 9000. The evening meal, also spartan, was served at around 5:30 P.M.

From 7:00 P.M. to around 10:00 P.M. there was an evening lecture by Ohsawa. Often it would take the *mon-dō* [問答] or "question and answer" form practiced in the Zen tradition. Ohsawa might begin by asking the students what they had learned that day. Surely everyone had learned something interesting and important. They had the magic key of the Unique Principle. They should be constantly learning, receiving new insights all the time. Then Ohsawa might pose a basic question and require of each student a concise and ready answer. "What is freedom?" Ohsawa would ask, pointing his finger directly at someone. His judgment on answers was immediate, usually harsh, but often humorous. "You have the mind of a dog," he might say, or "Your thinking is very sentimental. You must die soon." Often sixty to seventy people would jam into the small room, with commuting students joining the full-time residents.

While deeply and affectionately concerned about his students, Ohsawa often practiced direct and harsh criticism. It was a means to instill humility and to encourage the self-reflection necessary for growth. Alcan Yamaguchi remembers Ohsawa scolding a young man for a minor misdeed. "You must leave here," he said. "There is no way you can apologize to me with words. You must apologize with your whole life!" Occasionally this critical vein was made general and formal. The evening meeting would become a "*waruguchi konkoosu*" [悪口コンコース] or session of open and honest mutual criticism. Each person in turn became the focus of attention, and Ohsawa and the other students would make comments. The Sensei, too, took his turn. "You are arrogant." "You are too easily angered." "You have no sense of humor," the students would say and Ohsawa, smiling, would nod his head in assent.

Eventually some of the more promising students were sent abroad. The first actually to go was Michio Kushi. He had met Ohsawa in 1948 while studying law at prestigious Tokyo University. While interested in the issue of world peace and world government, he was at first mystified by Ohsawa's teachings about the crucial role of diet. Convinced in time, he commuted for several months to lectures at Hiyoshi. Ohsawa soon declared that Kushi had grasped the Unique Principle and had successfully graduated. With sponsorship from Norman Cousins, Kushi left for America in 1949. As he was to do again for other students, Ohsawa sold personal possessions, including books of his own and musical instruments belonging to Lima, to help finance Kushi's trip. In the years following, other students of the Maison Ignoramus went abroad. Not all actually ended up teaching macrobiotics, but some did, and soon there were young "missionaries" from the M.I. in France, Germany, the United States and Brazil.

During this time Ohsawa's intense involvement with young people and with their training caused him to focus on child-rearing, education and personal development. In lectures and writing he often addressed the questions: "What are the factors in early childhood which help create a healthy, happy and free person?" and "What can one do as an adult to become happy, healthy and free?"

In answering the first question, Ohsawa revived many of the ideas expressed in "The Shoku-Yō Human Life Reader" of 1938. He advises mothers to eat well during pregnancy and to feed their infants good food. This regime provides the necessary biological basis of physical and mental health. Beyond that he counsels: Do not feed them too much and to not feed them every time they cry for food. Expose them to cold and to hunger. Do not spoil them with toys, presents, money or too much open affection. Allow them to face their problems and difficulties on their own. Teach by example only, do not over-instruct. Let them discover how to do things for themselves. And in particular, exemplify in your own life humility, honesty, self-criticism, a sense of wonder at the world, and a love of adventure. This kind of child-rearing, Ohsawa promises, will produce a person strong in mind and body, one who will enjoy life and do good in the world. On the other hand, overfeeding, coddling, catering to every desire and appetite will create an egocentric, weak, and unhappy person.

Ohsawa realized, of course, that few receive the type of upbringing he recommended. To those not so blessed he offered a full curriculum of physical, mental and moral self-education. Its elements, which he tried to embody in the life and teachings at the M.I., include the following:

- Learn the law of Yin and Yang, the Order of the Universe. Practice seeing all phenomena in terms of it, and develop the ability to judge immediately if something is Yin or Yang. The Unique Principle is an "Alladdin's Lamp" which will illuminate all mysteries.
- Eat a simple macrobiotic diet of grains and vegetables. Eat good food in small quantities. This will make all other steps in self-development much easier.
- Seek out physical challenges and difficulties. Expose yourself to cold, hunger and the demands of physical work.
- *Vivere parvo*. Live simply, with a minimum of material goods and money. These things seem to give people happiness, but do not. They make us lazy and weak.
- Be grateful for everything, for the troubles of life as well as its joys. Be especially thankful for critics and enemies. They make us strong.
- Constantly practice self-criticism. Look for the virtues in others, and for the shortcomings in yourself. Remember that every misfortune or attack is our own fault. Reflect on vices and flaws, and correct them.
- Choose a great ambition and dedicate yourself to it. Human life is a drama in which each person is the writer, director and performer of his own script. We are

free to create exactly what we wish, so we should invent a drama that is exciting and grand. We should not hesitate to devote ourselves to a grand scheme. Only through this does one become a "free" person, who lives exactly as he wishes and is universally loved and respected.

For his students and followers Ohsawa added the observation that the greatest ambition imaginable is to distribute the secret of happiness and health to all humanity and thus create one peaceful world. In other words, teach macrobiotics. Since this was Ohsawa's own dream and task, he offered to do anything to help in its realization. He wished to be a stepping stone for those wanting to leap into the future with this dream.

During this time, as always, Ohsawa was very watchful for people in the West who might understand his philosophy and way of life. In 1948 he came upon a book called *The Meeting of East and West* by F.S.C. Northrop. Not since Carrel's *Man, The Unknown* had a book so impressed Ohsawa and filled him with hope that he might find a sympathetic ear in the West. Ohsawa was especially taken by the Yale professor's grasp of the different mentalities of the Orient and the Occident. He said that Northrop understood the Eastern mind and world view better than any Easterner understood the culture of the West. Obtaining translation rights, Ohsawa spent about a year working with associates to render the large and difficult book into clear Japanese.

Northrop contends that there are two contrasting, yet interrelated, realms of reality. Each is perceived by a different faculty in man. The "all embracing, undifferentiated ontic continuum" is grasped by the "aesthetic" or artistic-intuitive sense. It has been the focus of Oriental culture. The "determinate, differentiated" realm is understood through the "theoretic" faculty, which is analytical and rational. It has been the focus of European and American culture. The great task of the 20th century, he says, is the synthesizing of Eastern and Western culture, the enrichment of one by the theoretic sense, and of the other by the aesthetic sense.

Ohsawa was stunned by the correspondence to his own ideas. "The all-embracing ontic continuum" is simply "Tai-Kyoku," Infinity, the cosmic Oneness. The "determinate" realm is the phenomenal world of time and space, which arises within Infinity through the operation of Yin and Yang. And indeed while Eastern man has focused on the former, using his more developed intuition, Western man, using his powers of observation and analysis, has emphasized the latter.[1] And inevitably, humanity is moving toward a synthesis of the two. Ohsawa marveled at the profundity of Northrop's thought, and adopted some of the vocabulary and ideas in his own lectures and writings. Around the dinner table at Hiyoshi, references to the "ontic continuum" flew as fast as requests for the soy sauce.

Yet Ohsawa felt he had much to teach as well as to learn. He began an exchange of lengthy letters with Northrop, hoping to fill the gaps, as he saw them, in the American's theoretical and practical wisdom. He tried, in short, to explain macrobiotics and the Unique Principle to Northrop. The key to understanding the relationship between the "determinate" and the "undifferentiated" realm, he writes, is the "spiral of materialization." Within the ocean of infinite expansion (the "ontic continuum") arise spirals of centripedal energy. Thus Yin and Yang, the cosmic energies of expansion and contraction, are born. Their interaction creates the other levels of the phenomenal world: that of electromagnetic energy and light; of sub-atomic particles; of chemical elements; of the vegetable, and of the animal-human world. Each is a contracted form of the previous level. The whole forms a continuous, three-dimensional spiral. Every point in the material world is connected through this spiral to the Infinite. The phenomenal world exists as a geometric point within the infinite Oneness, from which it derives all its energy and to which it returns.

This may be Ohsawa's first written presentation of this "spiral of materialization." In "The Order of the Universe" of 1941 he described the same general structure but did not emphasize its spirallic nature or its continuity. To Northrop he explains that with this principle one can solve all the dualisms that befuddle modern man. The apparently unbridgeable antagonisms—between God and man, man and nature, body and spirit, good and evil—if understood in terms of the spiral and the law of Yin and Yang, can be seen as complementary. And, Ohsawa asserts almost as an aside, the application of Yin and Yang in the realm of diet and health is the key to human development and to world peace.

In his replies, Northrop confessed that he found Ohsawa's ideas hard to understand. Ohsawa invited him to come to Hiyoshi so they might converse directly and so that Northrop could experience "the Yoga of the dinner table" which was being practiced there. The American expressed the desire to visit but the meeting never occurred. Still, Ohsawa always recommended *The Meeting of East and West* as one of the most significant books of the 20th century.

Ohsawa's writings of these post-war years contrast with those of the earlier periods. There is a playfulness, exuberance and optimism, understandable now that the war is over. But there is a difference in content as well as tone. Ohsawa's basic ideas and themes had not appreciably changed. His confidence in the Unique Principle and in the importance of food is still the foundation of his thought. But on other issues, on Japanese history, and particularly on Western man—his character and personal values, his religion, art and literature—there is a significant change.

Previously, for example, Ohsawa had tended to idealize Japan's past. Now he does acknowledge that the ancient Japanese had discovered the Order of the Universe and had indeed fashioned a way of life, including a way of eating, which reflected it. But he asserts that for the past 1,000 years military government had enslaved the people and destroyed their mind and spirit.[2] The Tokugawa Period, which previously he had called "a heaven on earth," Ohsawa now portrays as a time when the farming and laboring classes were cruelly oppressed by the military rulers. The samurai class no longer represents the "soul of the nation," but is rather the self-seeking elite which led Japan down the road to self-destruction. Admiral Perry and his black ships are "liberators" of the people from centuries of stagnation and suppression.[3] The armies of the Emperor which sought to create an Empire are now "toilet tissue," according to Ohsawa, and men who gave their lives for this ill-begotten cause are "fools."[4]

There is a similar reversal in Ohsawa's treatment of the West. Gone are the tirades against Western materialism, hedonism, individualism and aggressiveness. Gone also are all traces of Ohsawa's concern about an international conspiracy, and of his view that the Jews embody the West's materialism and lust for power. Of course, given the political realities of the day, to evoke these themes would have been imprudent or impossible. But Ohsawa does not merely keep silent. He enthusiastically praises the West and its traditions. In his blueprint for a new Japan he proposes democracy and egalitarianism as the basis of society. He applauds the American spirit of independence and of determination in the face of difficulties.[5] He cites the British "Anglo-Saxon" tradition of justice, fair play, openness and honesty in times of disagreement.[6] The British, by trying to understand their colonial subjects, Ohsawa notes, had been able to maintain their Empire for centuries, while the Japanese had lost theirs after less than a decade.

This new attitude toward Western culture is especially clear in the three books in which Ohsawa focuses on education, child-rearing and personal development: *Clara Schumann* (1948); *Eien no Shōnen* [永遠の少年] ("Eternal Youth") (1953); and *Flippu Monogatari* [フリップ物語] ("The Story of Flip") (1949). Each is a commentary on a Western personality, and each shows a new and deep respect for Western values and culture.

In 1948 Ohsawa read a biography of the great German pianist, Clara Schumann, wife of composer Robert Schumann. The book had emphasized the strictness and apparent cruelty of Clara's father, Frederick Wieck. Wieck made Clara even as a small child practice many wearying hours. In her moments of greatest triumph as a young performer, he criticized her. And when she and the budding, if unstable, composer Robert Schumann wished to get married, he forbade it. Schumann would first have to demonstrate an ability to earn a living on his own, Wieck stipulated. When the two ran off anyway Wieck disowned Clara. While often portrayed as an unjust villain, Wieck, to Ohsawa, was Clara's great benefactor. A man who understood the laws of Yin and Yang, Wieck realized that only difficulties create strength and freedom; that discipline must precede creativity; that self-criticism is necessary for personal development; and that obstruction increases rather than destroys love. The education he gave Clara was the soil from which her great strength, talent and achievement sprang. Ohsawa notes sadly that following the break with her father, Clara lived a life of confusion and misery.

The Eternal Youth is a commentary on the life and thought of Benjamin Franklin as it is recorded in the American's *Autobiography*. Ohsawa describes the hardships of Franklin's younger years—the poverty, hunger, and harsh treatment—and notes their similarity to the difficulties of his own youth. Then he describes how Franklin, strengthened by these trials, triumphs over them to become one of the great men of the age, an inventor, social leader, diplomat, and philosopher. The American is for Ohsawa a model of the "free man" who through discipline, hard work, humility and self-criticism develops himself and achieves great things. Ohsawa offers the book as an inspiration to the young working men and women of Japan, and calls on them to become as great or greater than Franklin. Ohsawa distributed copies of the book free among working class young people.

The Story of Flip is a translation with commentary on a children's book by the American writer-illustrator Wesley Dennis. Flip is a young colt born on a spacious American farm. His mother's stall, Ohsawa laments, is larger than many a Japanese house. Flip is born full of energy and joy, and is soon romping through the world, wondering at its beauty. Suddenly he confronts an obstacle, a river running through the meadow. His mother blithely leaps across, leaving him behind. She ignores his pleas for help. Finally Flip tries to jump across. He fails and tries again. He fails once more and tries once again. Then, making a great effort, he leaps across the water. He is filled with joy at his new-found strength and ability.

From this story Ohsawa draws lessons for both child-rearing and for personal development. He cites Flip as an example of the American spirit of determination, of adventure and freedom. A mother who wishes to develop this in her child should emulate Flip's mother. She should not coddle or overprotect. She should allow the child to meet difficulties on his own. She should nurture rather than suppress his sense of wonder. Any person who wants to develop this spirit in himself must happily seek out challenges. He must try and fail until he succeeds and then seek out greater challenges. "Jump! Jump!" Ohsawa exhorts his youthful countrymen.

During this period Ohsawa also had words of praise for Western art, music, and religion, which for years he had ignored or had portrayed as inferior products of a materialistic, "spiritually myopic" culture. He was much impressed by the American painter Georgia O'Keeffe. Her "Abstraction No. 1" achieves, he maintains, the highest aim of art. It successfully portrays the unity of the material and the spiritual worlds. In *Clara Schumann*, Ohsawa notes that Western art, including music, has as its aim the elevation of the human spirit into the pure realm of the sacred. Wieck and the Schumanns, despite their conflicts and troubles, all shared this artistic ideal and were able to realize it.

From the time of his first stay in Paris, Ohsawa had described Christianity as a superstitious and primitive religion, lacking any real understanding of the universe or man. As he says in *Haku Shoku Jinshu o Teki to Shite* (1932), its worship is of material objects and symbols and its morality is a selfish one, seeking only rewards in an afterlife. Now Ohsawa writes that Jesus was teaching a world view identical to his own. The Unique Principle, he says with a note of deference, is only the "spirit of Christ" translated "into a modern principle for the purpose of human revolution."[7] Even Western languages earn a bit of praise. Previously, Ohsawa described them as crass and devoid of elegance, subtlety or sense of hierarchy. Now he recommends English as direct, clear and honest, and demeans Japanese as convoluted and filled with expressions of false modesty.

How can we interpret these new and apparently contradictory views of Ohsawa? Less than a decade before, in the heyday of Nippon-shugi, Shinto and the Yamato-damashii, he had espoused much different ones. Is he now just responding to the climate of opinion and again presenting his ideas in a context that would be attractive to the public? Is he a pure opportunist? Certainly Ohsawa was sensitive to the temper of the day and was willing to present his basic message accordingly. But at the same time, he maintained the integrity of his basic ideas. He did not compromise them. And in this period, his new ideas and attitudes were sincere responses to new experiences. While Ohsawa at times tried to use the popular milieu, he was also part of it.

Ohsawa's denunciation of military rule and its slave mentality is not so surprising. Throughout the pre-war and wartime period, he had consistently favored a conflict in ideology and opposed one in arms. And now, while he condemned Japan's militarism, he did not forget its unique spiritual tradition, including the Way of the Samurai.

In February 1951 Professor Jigorō Kanō [嘉納治五郎], the foremost master of judō, left for France. He planned to open a school and to introduce the "Tao of gentleness" to the West. To help the French understand this martial art, Ohsawa wrote a book called *Le Livre du Judo*. It was published in Paris the following year. Explaining judo as an embodiment of Japan's highest wisdom, Ohsawa uses the most elevated terms. It is not a sport or a form of physical exercise, he writes, but a physical and spiritual discipline which brings the individual into harmony with the universe. Judo creates a person who is full of courage, love and gratitude. Because he understands the universal law of change, this person can accomplish anything, can change an enemy into a friend through gentleness and silence. In critically judging Japan's past, Ohsawa did not intend to reject all aspects of it.

And yet Ohsawa's experiences had forced him to re-evaluate his earlier positions. In his imprisonment and torture, he had known the repression and cruelty of which a military regime, even in Japan, is capable. In the government's permitting Japan to be bombed to rubble, he had seen its stubbornness and pride. After the war there was a steady stream of evidence showing that Japan's empire in Asia had been as repressive and self-serving as any Western rule had been and that its people had detested the Japanese "liberators" as much as their earlier white rulers. Ohsawa, who like his fellow Japanese had had access only to state-controlled information, was surprised by this. In 1948 he read a book about the treatment of prisoners-of-war by the Japanese, and writes that he had been shocked and saddened by the meanness and insensitivity of the imperial soldiers.

In Ohsawa's appreciation of the West there were clear limits. Here, too, he maintained the integrity of his basic ideas. While he supported the World Federalist program for peace, he insisted that his own views on physiology and diet were absolutely necessary. And while Ohsawa praised democracy and Christianity, he did so on his own terms. He always retained the perspective of the Unique Principle and of the importance of food. While supporting the ideal of democratic rule, Ohsawa writes that in most cases it is only "the violence of the majority." In it, the selfishness and simple-minded hedonism of the masses is expressed. The leaders chosen are merely reflections of this low level of judgment. Real democracy can exist only when both candidates and electorate have achieved true physical and mental health. And this can happen only when they have adopted a diet that is in harmony with their natural environment. In other words, there can be no democracy without macrobiotics.

Ohsawa's interpretation of Christianity also is a rather free and personal one. He says that by the term "Heavenly Father" Jesus really meant "Infinite Expansion." Likewise, the Holy Ghost is just a simple phrase for the energy of the Infinite which creates and energizes man.[8] When Jesus says in Matt. 5:13 that "You shall be perfect even as your heavenly Father is perfect," he means that man is identical with the Infinite, and can realize perfect health and freedom on earth by living according to the Order of the Universe. And this life, says Ohsawa, must involve a vegetarian diet. The "Virgin Mary" really refers to the earth and its vegetation, which create, sustain and cleanse human life.[9] The plant world is the direct mother of humanity, and all human food should be taken directly from it. Besides, argues Ohsawa, if the spirit of Christ is love and non-injury, how can his followers take the lives of innocent animals? Christ's crucifixion is really the expiation for the bloody and senseless slaughter of countless defenseless creatures. Only vegetarians like Michelangelo and Albert Schweitzer have understood this "true spirit" of Christianity.

Still, there was definitely a new appreciation of the West, created and nurtured by new experiences and circumstances. For example, for the first time in his life Ohsawa had long contact with the Anglo-American part of Western culture. As a young man he had visited England and probably the United States as well. He spoke little English, though, and the stays were short. During the long sojourn later in Europe he was entirely in France and mostly in Paris. He associated with French academics and intellectuals. Ohsawa's view of the Western personality was based mainly on his experience of the French, which at best could give only a limited impression. After the war, however, he had a long and close view of the Anglo-American character. And like most Japanese he was pleasantly surprised by the liberal, even-handed nature of the occupation and the generally benevolent behavior of the American soldiers. Wartime propaganda had prepared the Japanese for hoards of pointy-nosed, red-bearded barbarians raping and pillaging. Instead the Allies arrived quietly, bringing candy, cigarettes and desperately-needed food, and thereafter helped to rebuild the country.

Ohsawa had a long and rewarding personal friendship with a young American lieutenant named George Martin. Ohsawa's son, Chūichi, was working at an American base and brought the officer home to meet his father. For the next several years, the two met often, frequently talking through the night, with Ohsawa in his limited English trying to explain his philosophy. After one intense five-day discussion, Ohsawa declared that Martin had indeed grasped the Unique Principle, theoretically and practically. In later writings he often mentioned Martin as one of the very few students who had fully understood his teachings.[10]

During this time too, Ohsawa learned much about Western thought and literature. Ohsawa was not a formally educated man. He did not have the broad liberal arts training that a regular university course might have given him. He was simply unfamiliar with much of Western, and especially Anglo-American, culture. An omnivorous reader, he had done much to educate himself. But his limitation of language and his personal tastes led him mostly to French literature and philosophy. This changed radically after 1945.

The GHQ was anxious to spread Western culture, and actively approved and distributed many American and British works, both classic and current. Ohsawa made good use of this resource. He discovered Franklin and "Flip" and the poet Walt Whitman. He reveled in the latter's *Leaves of Grass*, saying that the poems expressed not only the beauty and joy of the world, but also the mysterious Oneness which lay behind all phenomena. In Samuel Butler's utopian novel *Erewhon* he discovered a brilliant satire of modern civilization that seemed to reflect many of his own views. Butler, writing in Victorian England, describes a land where everyone is held responsible for his own health, and where the sick, as violators of the natural law, are sent to prison to live on bread and water. On the other hand, criminals, considered victims of poor education and social injustice, are sent to a hospital to recuperate and to be re-educated. Through Butler's work, Ohsawa became convinced of the "great genius of the British people."[11] Also, for the first time in his life, Ohsawa began to read the New Testament, a few chapters each day. This is a remarkable fact, considering he had been declaiming on Christianity and on Western spirituality (or the lack of it) for two decades.[12] Ohsawa's discovery of Northrop and his thought was part of this same process.

This period then was for Ohsawa one of real intellectual and personal growth. While his basic point of view did not change, Ohsawa was able to incorporate new information, experience and insights into his thought. He was in his late fifties during this time.

In 1952 Ohsawa received a letter informing him that his censured status had been lifted. He refused, however, to go to the government offices to receive the official notification. A legal summons finally required him to appear and explain himself. At the government office Ohsawa was confronted by an overweight bureaucrat smoking a foreign cigarette. "Why have you not come sooner" the man asked.

Ohsawa, musing on the irony of this official who had managed to grow fat during a time of food rationing and who was able to get contraband cigarettes, asking him such a question, replied: "The original judgment against me was incorrect and unjust. Thus there is no need to rescind it or to recognize its being rescinded."

Despite this pugnacious challenge, Ohsawa was exonerated and the travel ban lifted. Free at last to leave Japan, Ohsawa began to make arrangements to go to India. Some philanthropists in Calcutta had invited him to come to inspect their charity hospitals, which were using a naturopathic approach to medicine. Ohsawa also had the invitation from Dr. Schweitzer in Africa.

With only these assurances of hospitality, Ohsawa planned an open-ended journey. Declaring himself "a citizen of the world" and calling his trip "the world journey of the penniless samurai," Ohsawa vowed to spend the rest of his life traveling the world and spreading macrobiotics. On October 14, 1953, accompanied by Lima and sent off by a crowd of friends and students, Ohsawa boarded the steamer *Sadhana* in Kobe and sailed for India. A life that had been filled with adventure and drama was about to enter its not unworthy final stage.

[1] Sakurazawa, Y., *Heiwa to Jiyū no Genri* ("The Principle of Peace and Freedom"), 1949, reprinted by Nippon C.I. Kyokai, 1976, p. 220

[2] ———, *Naze Nihon wa Yabureta ka* ("Why Was Japan Defeated?") Musō Genri Kenkyūjo, Ohtsu City, 1947, p. 5

[3] Ibid., p. 107 ff

[4] ———, *Flippu Monogatari: Kaisetsu* ("The Story of Flip: An Interpretation"), March 1949, p. 54

[5] ———, *Konpa Bunko No. 4* (Konpa Magazine Collection 1/48–7/48) Reprinted 1960, Nippon C.I., Tokyo, p. 1

[6] ———, *Naze Nihon wa Yabureta ka*, p. 57

[7] ———, *Ningen Kakumei no Sho* ("A Proposal for Human Revolution"), 1948, Reprinted by Nippon C.I., 1976, p. 2

[8] ———, *Heiwa to Jiyū no Genri*, p. 66 & 208

[9] ———, *Clara Schumann*, Konpa Shuppan Sha, Tokyo 1948

118

10 ———, *Heiwa to Jiyū no Genri*, p. 24
11 ———, *Ningen Kakumei no Shō*, p. 31
12 Ibid., p. 29

8.

George Ohsawa:
The World Journey
of the Penniless Samurai
(1953–1966)

On October 14, 1953, Ohsawa stood with Lima on the deck of the *Sadhana* and watched the bowing and waving crowd on the dock disappear in the distance. He felt, he would later recall, like a young boy whose hands are filled with delicious cakes and who sits before a mountain of similar delights. He was a man with a message and a mission. The message was macrobiotics, a way to health and happiness, and the mission was to spread it around the world. The future lay before him full of adventure, and he exulted in it. Yet Japan lay behind him now, and he felt sadness at leaving his friends, students and beloved homeland. Tears welled in his eyes.

The voyage to Calcutta lasted four weeks and of course Ohsawa kept busy reading and writing. In fact, he wrote two books during the voyage. Ohsawa was not one to lounge restfully in the tropical sun, even after years of virtually ceaseless activity.

The first work was a sequel to the commentary on Franklin's life and was called *Zoku: Eien no Shōnen* [續永遠の少年] ("The Eternal Youth: Continued"). It focused on the life of Mahatma Gandhi, the Indian holy man and architect of national independence. Just before the Kobe departure Ohsawa was given a biography of Gandhi by Dr. Maruyama, and in the first part of the voyage, he scoured it for secrets to the man's greatness. Then he wrote the book as a letter of advice to a young man wishing to improve himself. It was meant primarily for the students whom he had left behind at the Maison Ignoramus. Ohsawa's concern for their development, and his sense of responsibility regarding them, continued despite their separation. Throughout the ensuing years of travel, he kept up a steady stream of books and letters to instruct, chide and encourage them. This commentary on Gandhi's life was a first installment.

According to Ohsawa, the first key to Gandhi's greatness lay in his humble and honest parents. His father was a deeply religious man and his mother had strength of will and a sense of order. If one lacks such parents, Ohsawa writes, he should not despair. Through self-discipline in eating and living, one can still become great like Gandhi.

One should follow a vegetarian diet, since real development is difficult without it. One should also practice strict moral discipline. Do not lie. Do not steal. Do not break promises. Do not criticize others. Criticize only yourself and never forget your own weakness and dishonesty. We are all thieves (even as Gandhi as a child was), we are always stealing from nature to nurture ourselves. Take care for even the small things of life. Anything that we touch we should render somehow more beautiful. Study the great religious scriptures and constantly consider such basic questions of life as: What is God? What is man? What is human destiny? Follow the principle of "one grain, ten thousand grains," that is, repay each gift of life ten-thousandfold. Have a great dream for the benefit of mankind and pursue it in the face of all difficulties for your entire life. Through such a path, one can become even greater than Gandhi.

At a stop in Rangoon, Burma, Ohsawa sent the manuscript back to Japan. Shortly thereafter, in the Straits of Malacca between Malaya and Sumatra, the ship's compass went awry, and for seven hours the *Sadhana* drifted aimlessly about. Ohsawa felt that the mishap had been caused by the spirits of the countless sailors and soldiers of both sides who had lost their lives so senselessly here during the war. To honor them Ohsawa and Lima fasted for a day. In their memory he wrote the following poem.

> Instead of the principle of an eye for an eye,
> A tooth for a tooth,
> One should follow
> The principle of
> "One grain, ten thousand grains."

Also on board ship Ohsawa wrote a commentary on an American book about embryology called *Biography of the Unborn*. Ohsawa begins by marveling at the ability of Westerners to observe and to analyze phenomena, including the development of a fetus. Yet from both a theoretical and practical standpoint, his own Oriental, macroscopic approach is perhaps more useful. The growth of the fetus through binary cell division is a perfect example of the operation of Yin and Yang. And the health of the fetus as it develops is dependent on the quality of food the mother eats. Certain foods at certain times have a particular effect. For example, if she eats too much fruit and sweets during the second month, when the heart is forming, then that organ will be weak. The physical characteristics of the infant, its internal organs, and even its sex, reflect the mother's food. If the pregnant woman's diet is balanced in terms of Yin and Yang, the child will be well-formed and healthy, and the labor will be easy. Birth defects, abnormalities and difficult deliveries are all caused by improper food. The food of the mother as she nurses is also crucial, setting a foundation for the infant's physiological and psychological destiny.

In the same pamphlet Ohsawa takes the opportunity to pose some difficult questions for his students. He wanted them to struggle with the answers and thereby raise their level of judgment. Why does the ten centimeter journey of the sperm take three days? Why do the egg and sperm unite? Use the Unique Principle, he encourages. All phenomena can be understood using it.

At last, on the 11th of November 1953 the *Sadhana*, after drifting with a broken rudder for several days outside Calcutta harbor, finally docked. Ohsawa was thrilled to be once again in the "Mother of Asia," in the "Homeland of the Buddha." It had been thirty-nine years since, as a young man of twenty-one, he had last stopped there while working on a freighter. Ohsawa came this time with a plan to restore India to her ancient ecological ways of eating, and thus to health. He thought that several weeks or a month would be necessary. He planned to contact government and political leaders, doctors, spiritual leaders, intellectuals and other members of the elite, and convince them of the truth of macrobiotics. India's biological transformation and cultural renaissance would be set in motion, and he would be free to continue his world journey. Ohsawa did not foresee much difficulty in accomplishing this. India's philosophical foundation, the *Vedanta*, was, as he saw it, simply another expression of the Unique Principle. Vegetarian India had long understood food's important role in human physical, psychological and spiritual life. It would be easy to remind men like Nehru (the new leader who succeeded Gandhi) and Vinoba Bhave (a leading social reformer) of this neglected wisdom.

Ohsawa and Lima were met by a Mr. Sarogi, who was head of the group of businessmen-philanthropists who had invited them and arranged for visas. Sarogi lodged them at his home and, impressed with the Japanese couple, tried to get Ohsawa to remain as administrator of the hospitals. Ohsawa did visit the hospitals, and gave his advice. But he was more interested in reaching the elite in order to spread macrobiotics most quickly. He visited government ministries, newspapers and medical centers. He was politely received, but hardly effected the immediate and massive changes he had hoped for. Mother India, it seemed, was not quite ready to respond to the wisdom of the fast-paced doctor from Japan. Discouraged, Ohsawa was tempted to move on immediately to Africa. However, he happened to meet another wealthy Calcuttan, a man named Chaitarangya. This man, much taken by Ohsawa, offered him an apartment in his huge marble mansion, the use of a car and driver, plus financial support. Ohsawa accepted, settled down somewhat, and started giving medical consultations. Perhaps the warm climate, the leisurely pace of life, and the delicious tropical fruits (very Yin, or expansive) were combining to slow Ohsawa down, or at least reduce his restlessness a bit. Ohsawa founded in Chaitarangya's home "The New School" and began to give lectures. The first had a single student—his host Chaitaranga. Soon, however, the effectiveness of his dietary advice began to attract attention. A steady stream of patients, mostly from the city's rich and privileged class, visited him at the mansion. According to Ohsawa's own account he was able to cure persons suffering with leprosy, epilepsy, Parkinson's disease and various tropical illnesses. They included government officials who promised to help implement Ohsawa's ideas about food and health into official policy. Somewhat buoyed by this success, Ohsawa delayed his departure. He began to toy with the idea of making India the center of international macrobiotics, and wrote to his students in Japan and the United States. The response was less than enthusiastic.

Meanwhile, Ohsawa became concerned with the situation back at the Maison Ignoramus. He had hoped that his students would continue to develop the work he had begun. He was sorely disappointed. Few bothered to write to him. Those who did told of grave difficulties. Discipline and order were breaking down in the house. Some students had left and some criticized Ohsawa severely. The overall work of the organization lagged. Before leaving, Ohsawa had organized the *Take no Ko Kai* [竹の子会], or "The Club of the Children of Bamboo," to help spread macrobiotics among men and women of the working class. Little had been done to promote this activity.

Virtually every day Ohsawa wrote letters to his followers in Japan. These were filled with his new ideas, discoveries and plans, and also with his stern, often caustic, advice and criticism. Some were quite long, running to many pages. One of these, *Sensanbyaku nen mae no ichi Jiyūjin* [千三百年前の一自由人] ("One Free Man of 1,300 years Ago") was published as a separate volume in 1959. Some others were collected and published in 1962 as *Byōki o Naosu Jutsu, Byōnin o Naosu Hō* [病気を治す術，病人を治す法] ("How to Cure Illness, How to Cure a Sick Person").

The first is another of Ohsawa's "inspirational biographies." Saichō was a Buddhist monk of the 9th century who imported the Tendai sect of Buddhism from China to Japan and established the great religious center of Hiei-zan on a mountain overlooking the capital of Kyoto. Ohsawa praises Saichō for his humility and honesty. He commends his ambition to help the nation and all humanity and his determination in the face of great difficulties. Then Ohsawa writes that he himself is on a similar venture. He is attempting to start a revolution in India and all over the world. It is biologically based and will eliminate all sickness, suffering and conflict. In India, though, it is a great challenge. The mentality of the people is dominated by egocentricity and arrogance. The caste system embodies this mentality and perpetuates it. Ohsawa urges his students to develop themselves quickly, to help him in the struggle for humanity. Those who want to hasten their evolution as strong and creative human beings should, like the monks and samurai of old, take a walking trip with no money.

In "How to Cure Illness, How to Cure a Sick Person" Ohsawa warns his followers that the only way to understand macrobiotics deeply is to practice it. They must follow the diet very carefully, and avoid backsliding into old and destructive eating habits. Many have been spoiled by an overindulgent, sentimental mother. They must overcome this handicap by continuously criticizing their own character and behavior. They must accept every attack on them as their own fault, and understand how they caused it. "Reply to my letters," he laments. "Carry on the work of the organization." He sounds like a distraught but loving father whose sons and daughters have gone astray in his absence. In effect, that is what he was.

Despite his inclination to continue on to Africa, Ohsawa remained in India. He and Lima were more or less at leisure. Ohsawa did help out a bit at the naturopathic hospitals and gave consultations. He lectured occasionally at the Theosophical Society in Calcutta. But he had much free time to relax and study, a luxury which he had not enjoyed for years. He also relaxed in his eating and experimented with various foods. While Lima supplied a basic diet of rice gruel, cucumbers and other vegetables, Ohsawa reveled in the strength which forty years of sound diet had given. He enjoyed freely the mangoes and other tropical fruits available, and even indulged in Indian sweets and whisky. When at the age of sixty-two Ohsawa began to have gray hairs for the first time, he ate a pound of black unrefined sugar each week to turn these black again. Among the little pleasures of this period he recalls doing his own laundry by hand.

Ohsawa read widely during these peaceful months, often in areas that were new to him. He read for the first time the *Ayurveda*, the classic text of Indian medicine. He became convinced that, just as Indian Vedantic philosophy corresponded to the Unique Principle, the Ayurvedic science of health and medicine corresponded to macrobiotic practice. He wrote to Dr. Maruyama in Japan suggesting that a research center be set up to study this ancient medical wisdom. Ohsawa also read widely in Western literature and philosophy, continuing the broadening of intellectual horizons which had begun after the war. He was particularly interested in Utopian writers such as Fournier and St. Simon. Comparing the plans of these men for the remaking of humanity and of human society with his own, Ohsawa was convinced of the superiority of the macrobiotic approach. The others focused on changing social and economic patterns, but forgot the crucial and largely hidden role of food in human society. An awareness of diet was the unique value of the macrobiotic approach.

After about a year Ohsawa inevitably began to get restless. It was clear that no large-scale movement was developing. India was not going to become a macrobiotic country overnight. And Ohsawa the optimist, the romantic, the adventurer, the man with a world mission, was anxious to be on the road again, pursuing his dream. Over the sad protests of his host and many Indian friends, "the penniless samurai" began to plan the next stage of his journey.

Before leaving India, though, Ohsawa and Lima spent one month, May of 1955, at Pondicherry in south India at the Auroville ashram. Founded by the Indian spiritual master Sri Aurobindo, the community included religious seekers from many nations. It was run by Aurobindo's widow, a Frenchwoman affectionately known as "the Mother." The Mother, a lover of Japanese culture, was especially impressed by Ohsawa and Lima. A "Japanese Studies" department was set up in the ashram, with Ohsawa lecturing on philosophy and medicine and Lima teaching cooking and flower arrangement. The Mother asked them to stay on permanently but Ohsawa refused. He was too much his own man to work completely within an organization not his own. Besides, greater adventures beckoned. Before he left India, though, Ohsawa summoned several of the young people from the Maison Ignoramus, including Fujiko Sugamoto [菅本フジ子] (Ellie) and Kaoru Yoshimi [吉見馨] (Clim) to carry on his work.

On July 28, 1955, Ohsawa and Lima departed Bombay on the passenger ship *The State of Bombay*. The generous Chaitarangya, though reluctant to see his Japanese friends go, had supplied them with first class tickets as well as a sizable sum of money. Again there were tears of sadness as the ship pulled away. Early in August, the ship arrived in Mombasa, the port city for Kenya. Ohsawa went directly with Lima to the inland capital of Nairobi. Expecting a jungle environment, he was pleasantly surprised to find a bustling modern city with daily weather of 72 degrees and sunny.

Ohsawa had a letter of introduction to the Japanese ambassador in Nairobi. At the time there were few Japanese traveling the world, and virtually none rambling through Africa, and the arrival of the pair was a happy event. The ambassador invited them to stay at the embassy as long as they liked. Soon word got out that a respected doctor from Japan was visiting and people began to call for appointments.

An article describing Ohsawa, his unorthodox methods and often "miraculous" cures, appeared in a local newspaper. There was a stream of visitors and patients, here again mostly from the rich and influential class. Again Ohsawa stayed longer than he originally had intended and again it required an act of will to continue the trip.

The next destination was Dr. Schweitzer's medical mission in Lambaréné on the Ogawe River in what was then French Equatorial Africa. This lay about 1,500 miles to the west, across the continent. In order to save money Ohsawa decided to go by boat and car directly westward. Just before leaving Kenya, Ohsawa visited a mansion, and in his bedroom happened to find a large bottle of pills. Curious, he dropped one into a glass of water. It started to bubble and the mixture, when Ohsawa drank it, tasted like champagne. Ohsawa happily finished off the bottle of "champagne" pills, discovering later that they were an anti-malarial medication. He became very sick, nauseated, and unable to eat. Yet the arrangements for the trip had already been completed, so off the two went in an open car piled with their baggage and driven by a black African driver. Ohsawa lay sick and exhausted on the back seat. Beside him sat Lima, prim and innocent as a schoolgirl, her hand wrapped with a white bandage covering a recent kitchen burn. Though she spoke little English and no French at the time, most of the practical arrangements of the journey fell perforce now to her. Unfortunately, there seems to be no photographic record of this epic journey, though in 1958 the two published an account called *Nihon Jōsei Saishō no Chūō Africa Ōdan Ki* [日本女性最初の中央アフリカ横断記] ("A Record of the First Crossing of Africa by a Japanese Woman").

After leaving Kenya in early August, Ohsawa and Lima stopped first at a plantation in Tanganyika owned by a Mr. Naranji. The wealthy Indian, whom Ohsawa describes as a "supermarket of diseases," had asked Ohsawa to visit and help him before going to the Congo. Lima and Ohsawa stayed three weeks, with Lima cooking for herself and Naranji, whose condition improved rapidly. Ohsawa remained sick and unable to eat. He theorized later that his condition was not caused by the pills taken in Kenya. Rather, after two years of strict vegetarian eating in India his body was going through a major readjustment. The chill weather of the high African plateau was acting as a catalyst, causing his body to discharge its past excess.

The journey continued even though Ohsawa was sick, helpless and still unable to take food. He was convinced throughout that he was going to die. It took four weeks to reach Leopoldville in the Belgian Congo. Along the way Ohsawa had what he refers to as his *satori* [悟り] or enlightenment experience. Perhaps because of the cleansing of his body, he experienced totally for the first time, according to his own description, a unity and harmony with the whole universe. He saw and felt that life and death, matter and spirit, good and evil were one. His earlier discussions of ultimate reality, and of the aim of human life as union with it, had been based on partial or second-hand experience. Now he knew totally for himself.

When Ohsawa's appetite returned it was at the large French hotel in Leopoldville. No doubt to Lima's horror, Ohsawa immediately gratified himself in the hotel dining room on the usual hotel fare. It was by now the end of September, and after a short rest the two journeyed upriver to Lambaréné to meet Schweitzer. The doctor had been born in 1875 in the Alsace region of Germany, the son of a Lutheran pastor. As a student he studied theology and soon became known for his scholarly work on the New Testament. His book, *The Quest for the Historical Jesus,* became a classic in the field. Schweitzer was also an organist and musical scholar, known for his interpretations of the work of Johann Sebastian Bach. In his early thirties Schweitzer astounded his family and friends by resolving to become a medical missionary. He saw this vocation as a way of expressing his Christian faith and the principle of "reverence for life." Laying aside his academic and musical careers, he began the study of medicine, and once graduated, had set out for Africa.

By the time Ohsawa arrived in Lambaréné in late 1955 Schweitzer had already been at work there for about forty years. There was a large clinic and hospital staffed by Schweitzer, other European doctors and nurses, and native helpers. Natives came from a wide area, often accompanied by their families, to seek medical treatment. By this time Schweitzer had become internationally famous for his philosophy of "Reverence for Life," according to which the Christian principle of love translates to non-injury to all creatures. A strict vegetarian, he lived with a menagerie of wild and domestic animals. Winner of the Nobel Peace Prize in 1952, he was considered the great sage and saint of the 20th century. Accordingly, Ohsawa had great hopes for his meeting with Schweitzer. He would talk with the doctor and convince him of the validity of the Unique Principle and of macrobiotic medicine. If Schweitzer, the single outstanding figure in the intellectual and spiritual world at the time, would adopt macrobiotics, it would have a great effect. A rapid and massive change in Western thinking would follow, as would perhaps a genuine world "biological revolution."

When Ohsawa and Lima finally got to the mission on October 29, Schweitzer was not there, being still on a visit to Europe. Undaunted, the two set up housekeeping in a small grass hut on stilts near the mission. Lima began to cook corn and manioc, the local staples, and to search the area for wild grasses to supplement this fare. Ohsawa, always more daring, decided to dine with the European staff in the main compound. He felt that it was more important for him to share their meals and to get to know them. Most of the food was imported from Europe and included canned meats and vegetables, crackers and sweets.

Meanwhile, Ohsawa was observing the natives and how they lived and ate. The real culprit causing their health problems, he soon concluded, was the food of the white man, especially white sugar and the various imported products, such as evaporated milk, which contained large quantities of it. He reasoned that the natives had only small amounts of meat in their diet and thus no strong Yang element (excess sodium and related minerals). They were consequently extremely susceptible to the harmful effects of the extremely Yin sugar. He began to offer dietary and medical advice to some of the natives. According to his own accounts he cured many, including some who were deemed "incurable" by the hospital doctors. Ohsawa writes that he cured the houseboy of leprosy. His method, of course, emphasized a simple diet of corn and manioc, with local vegetables, free of all foreign foods.

While awaiting Schweitzer's return, Ohsawa began to write a book which he titled *La Philosophie de la Medicine d'Extrême Orient* ("The Philosophy of the Medicine of the Far East"). He meant this work (published in English as *The Book of*

Judgment) as an introduction to his thought especially tailored to the Western mind. It was in effect an updated version of his 1932 work *Le Principe Unique*. Ohsawa tries to present macrobiotic philosophy and practice in a clear, simple and analytical fashion. He lists the principles and axioms of the Unifying or Unique Principle, then demonstrates their application to diet, medicine, education, science, religion and philosophy.

In his presentation Ohsawa makes much use of a sevenfold system of classification. He had used this previously in describing the different levels of the universe from the Infinite to the animal-human. Now he applies it to the stages of illness, levels of human judgment, levels of medicine and other things.

The stages of illness include for example:

1. Fatigue
2. Pain
3. Chronic symptoms
4. Malfunctions of the autonomic nervous system
5. Malfunctions of the structural organs themselves
6. Psychological disease
7. Spiritual disease—intolerance and arrogance[1]

They describe the progressive decline of the human organism.

The *Seven Levels of Judgment* are the stages of human awareness, each progressively broad and encompassing. They are:

1. Physical judgment, which is blind, mechanical, responding automatically to external stimuli.
2. Sensory or aesthetic judgment, responding to sensory stimulation and classifying according to pleasant and unpleasant, beautiful or ugly.
3. Sentimental or emotional judgment, responding to emotion and classifying according to love or hate, like or dislike.
4. Intellectual judgment, responding to ideas and concepts and judging them true or untrue.
5. Social judgment, responding to patterns of social behavior and organization and judging them beneficial or harmful to society.
6. Ideological judgment, responding to ideologies (social, political, economic, philosophical, etc.) and classifying them as just or unjust, valid or invalid.
7. Supreme judgment, which responds to everything with absolute and universal love and compassion and which sees harmony in all antagonisms.[2]

Ohsawa's central theme is that until now Western culture has been based on a false view of the world and on false logic. Its materialistic world view has ignored the invisible spiritual realm. Its logic is dualistic, based on the idea that things are either identical or not identical. It does not realize that opposite phenomena are complementary, and that because everything is changing, they are turning into each other. Thus the medicine, education, science, philosophy and religion of the West are all basically flawed. The West must now embrace the philosophy of complementary dualism, which comes from the Orient but which even there is almost forgotten. This view recognizes the complementary and dynamic nature of reality. All oppositions comprise a single harmony; everything is turning into its opposite. Ohsawa puts himself at the disposal of anyone who wishes to learn this philosophy and its countless applications, theoretical and practical. Then he vows to travel till the end of his life, helping his "Occidental brothers and sisters" grasp this wisdom and its benefits.

Just as Ohsawa was finishing the book he began to suffer from an illness called tropical ulcers. His body became covered with pustules, which when they broke left oozing sores about the size of a half dollar. Lima applied *dentie*, a black powder made of the ash of eggplant stems mixed with salt. The pain subsided and Ohsawa resumed his normal activities, trying to finish the manuscript by Schweitzer's birthday. He did so and presented it to the German doctor.

During his stay Ohsawa went about barefoot and bareheaded like the natives. The Europeans all wore jungle helmets, high boots and high socks impregnated with antiseptic. One day Ohsawa was clipping his toe nails and in order to lengthen the time between the next cutting clipped them very short. He happened to cut slightly into the quick of the nail on his large toe. Then he went to the trash area behind the hospital, where all the medical refuse was dumped, to sweep and clean. During this task filarial worms entered his body. These are microscopic parasites which cause cysts and attack the urinary tract.

Soon the ulcers began to worsen. Ohsawa, afflicted mainly on his back, had to sleep on his stomach. The sores were so sensitive that he could tolerate no covers. On January 30 the filarial infestation began to show. Hard bumps appeared on his neck and head, and his hair began to thin. On February 3, 1956 Schweitzer visited Ohsawa, who was now lodged at the Mission. He told him to go on immediately to Europe, that his only chance for survival lay there. In the jungle the mortality rate was virtually 100 percent.

Schweitzer, to Ohsawa's surprise and dismay, mentioned nothing about the manuscript. Rather than converting him, Ohsawa's presentation of Oriental philosophy and medicine may only have angered and alienated the doctor. After all, in his listing of the seven levels of medicine Ohsawa assigned allopathy, the type of treatment which Schweitzer had used for over four decades, to the lowest level. Ohsawa describes allopathy as a blind attempt to eliminate symptoms without understanding the true cause of disease. It relies on drug medicaments ("the devil's bullets") and the brutal knife of surgery. At the highest and seventh level he had put his own "Supreme Medicine" which is biological, physiological and educational. It helps a person discover the very structure and order of the universe. It cures all past and present illness and prevents all future sickness and misfortune. Ohsawa could hardly expect Schweitzer to be very impressed with the book. His life's work had been insulted by it even as the author lay before him wasting away with disease!

Schweitzer's secretary, Emma, who had befriended Ohsawa, urged him to follow the doctor's advice. Reverend Meyer, a church missionary whose daughter had been helped by Ohsawa's dietary advice, agreed. Ohsawa resolved instead to turn this misfortune into opportunity. He reasoned that if he could cure this usually fatal illness with macrobiotic medicine, then surely Schweitzer would be impressed, even converted. He fasted briefly and then began to eat simply and sparsely. A telegram had been sent to the Kushis, then in New York City, and soon a package with brown rice, miso, sea vegetables and other basic Japanese foods helpful in a therapeutic diet arrived. Ohsawa began to eat mainly brown rice with a lot of sea salt. To take as much salt as possible, he wrapped spoonfuls in sheets of *nori* sea vegetable and swallowed it whole. He drank little or nothing.

Ohsawa became so dehydrated through this treatment that he had to manually extract his feces. From the second day, though, the therapy began to have an effect. After six days there were massive discharges of blood, followed by rapid improvement. By the eighth day only one large ulcer remained. By the tenth day, when Schweitzer paid another visit, there were only healing scars. The doctor did not comment on Ohsawa's improvement, but only repeated his order that he continue on to Europe as soon as possible. Again there was no comment on the book or the philosophy which Ohsawa had presented in it.

Disappointed, Ohsawa decided finally that it was futile to try to change Schweitzer's mind. In the meantime, airplane tickets had arrived from New York. Aveline Kushi, while riding the subway, had seen an airline ad which suggested "Fly now, pay later." She and Michio, feeling that Ohsawa and Lima had better leave Africa soon, had used the offer and sent them tickets to Paris. Ohsawa and Lima gathered their modest baggage, went by boat to Leopoldville, and in a few days were flying over the Sahara on their way to France. Ohsawa, while he had failed in his objective, had learned much from his stay. He saw that there is nothing in the world to be afraid of. To the person following the Order of the Universe, no harm can come.

It was almost twenty years since Ohsawa had left Paris in the years before the war. Returning now, he was pleasantly surprised at the amount of interest there was in Oriental, and especially in Japanese culture. The early work he had done with de Soulie Morant had taken root and there were numerous acupuncture clinics in the city. There were also many dōjō where the various martial arts, including judō and aikidō were being taught, and schools for tea ceremony, flower arrangement and the gentler disciplines. There was much interest in Buddhism, particularly in the philosophy, psychology and art of Zen Buddhism. Daisetz Suzuki's writings on Zen and Japanese culture were coming into vogue around this time.

Ohsawa took this all as a promising sign. Perhaps now the Western world was ready to understand and accept his teachings. Macrobiotics was, after all, only the philosophical and biological basis of these various cultural forms. Ohsawa renewed some of his old contacts, made new ones, and soon set up an information and study center in Paris. A magazine was established called *Yin and Yang*, and from 1957 began to appear monthly. Though he definitely centered his activities in Paris, Ohsawa made trips to other European countries, visiting Belgium, Holland, Germany and Sweden. Here again he wished to attract the people of intellectual and social status and influence. Through these he could affect the rest of society. And indeed, among those who did come to Ohsawa in those first years in Europe were many serious-minded professionals, including doctors, lawyers and scientists.

In September, 1956 an interesting incident occurred. On a tour through the Black Forest of Germany Ohsawa and Lima stopped at an inn called the Sonnenhof ("Inn of the Sun") in the village of Belchem. Ohsawa had been directed to the place by his disciple Kiyozumi Kawano [河野清澄] (Augustine) who recently had successfully treated the daughter of the innkeepers. Ohsawa and Lima joined the luncheon crowd of about 25 persons and, though he spoke only a few words of German, Ohsawa soon engaged almost everyone in lively conversation. Afterward he asked the inn's owner, Helmut Finsterlin, if he and Lima could stay on for several weeks.[3]

The Finsterlins were members of the Anthroposophical movement, followers of the German philosopher and mystic Rudolph Steiner. Steiner, who died in 1925, had incorporated many ideas such as karma and reincarnation, usually regarded as "Oriental" ideas, into a new, Christ-centered synthesis. One evening at dinner Ohsawa happened to notice a portrait of Steiner hanging on the inn wall.

"Who is that?" he asked, rising from his seat and going to take a closer look. "This is a true Initiate (into higher spiritual wisdom)", he continued. "Who is he? Where does he live? Can one meet him?"

Finsterlin explained that Steiner was dead, that his work was being continued by the Anthroposophical Society, and that the group was centered in the town of Dornach, Switzerland. A few weeks later he drove Ohsawa, Lima, Kawano and another Japanese young man across the border to Dornach. A delay at the border crossing cut short their time for visiting but Ohsawa marveled at the architecture of the Goetheanum, the central building which had been designed by Steiner, and at the general ambience of the place.

On Ohsawa's last evening at the inn he gave a talk, saying,

> "Until now I did not believe that there was any true spiritual life in Europe. But now to my great surprise the Spirit does indeed have a dwelling place in Europe (the Goethenaum and the Anthroposophical Society). This moves me greatly and demands that I must reconsider many things. I must change all my plans."

These encouraging signs and discoveries, and Ohsawa's early successes in presenting his teachings in Paris and elsewhere, were accompanied by some disillusionment. On closer inspection, the interest in Japanese culture in France turned out to be superficial. Ohsawa visited a leading scholar of Zen and was disappointed to find the Frenchman's interest only in the philosophical and psychological aspects of the religion. He had no understanding of the biological basis which, according to Ohsawa, lay at the heart of Zen. He could not recognize the role of Buddhist vegetarian cooking, *shōjin ryōri* [精進料理] ("the cuisine for the advancement of the spirit") in Zen life. Also, a year or two of living again in the West convinced Ohsawa that Western urban life was fundamentally bestial and cruel.

In 1958 Ohsawa wrote a book called *Jack et Mitie dans la Jungle dite Civilisation* ("Jack and Mitie in the Jungle Called Civilization") expressing and documenting this disappointment. The book is a thinly disguised account of his and Lima's experiences and impressions in Paris. Jack and Mitie are visitors from a mythical country called "Erewhon." They are surprised and distressed at the savagery which lies just below the surface of life in the glittering Western metropolis.

"Monsieur Jack" in recounting the tale observes that while on the surface the city is civilized, it is really a jungle. He notes the sides of bloody meat hanging in the butcher shops, the bunches of cut and dead flowers set in household vases, and the battered crucifixes which adorn the altars of the grand cathedrals. Beneath the bloodied image the people desperately seek a moment's respite from the materialism in which they live. In their speech and behavior the people are loud and crude. "Why does everyone speak in such a loud voice?" Madame Mitie asks timorously. "Is everyone deaf?" The people are also ungrateful, failing to feel or to express any real gratitude for the teachings of Monsieur Jack. They come to him, are cured of their ailments and promise to study his philosophy and medicine. Too chained to their possessions and professions, though, they soon forget their promise. The culture of the West, Monsieur Jack concludes, is ruled by money, force and law. Even its intellectual and spiritual leaders have only a low level of judgment.

In contrast, the land of Erewhon, an idealized version of Japan, is portrayed as a place of elegance, peace and health. Its economy is based on *vivere parvo* ("living with little" in harmony with nature) and on the boundless generosity and gratitude of the people. The king rules not through force but through the mutual love and concern between himself and the citizens. He understands the law of the universe, and living simply and poorly, he rules according to this law for the benefit of all the people. Even the bell of the temple in Erewhon reveals the profound differences between the two cultures. While the bells of the Parisian cathedrals are little more than timepieces, those in Erewhon are sacred instruments reminding the people of their spiritual home and calling them to it.

Jack and Mitie is a surprising, if honest, book. It is a work in French for the French, yet seems intended only to alienate its readers. Its substance and tone reminds one of Ohsawa's anti-Western diatribes of the late 1930s. At best it is a highly critical, at worst an insulting work. Yet in it Ohsawa reveals an important aspect of his method of teaching. One of the important roles of the traditional Japanese Master or sensei is to shock the student into deep self-criticism. Thus he arouses the humility and desire for growth which are necessary to the student's development. Here, as in India, Ohsawa was seeking elite persons who could really perceive their own shortcomings and the shortcomings of their culture, and who could thus deeply study the philosophy and way of life which Ohsawa offered. The book was meant as a means to shock its readers into self-criticism and humility.

Ohsawa used a similar technique in his individual consultations and in his lectures. In Europe, as in Japan, he was harsh and critical with long-time students and with newcomers as well. "Madame, you are a walking garbage can!" he might comment to a bejeweled and fur-draped lady of Paris who had come for advice. "Your mentality is that of a cow," he might reply to a student who had answered poorly in lecture. This was done very consciously by Ohsawa, not from anger or cruelty but from a desire to help develop the student's judgment. The third of the "Seven Rules of Macrobiotic Education" which he set forth at this time is "Do not give compliments to the student. Rather give shame so they will know the depth of their ignorance."

Late in 1958, Ohsawa returned to Japan for a month to report on the first five years of his "samurai world journey." His teaching method notwithstanding, he was able to report substantial progress in Europe. And in spite of his disillusionment with European society, he spoke optimistically of the future. He reports on the confrontation between Eastern and Western ideas taking place during his trips, and says that the former are faring well indeed. Listing his accomplishments of the past five years, Ohsawa says he had:

1. published ten books in French.
2. founded an "Ignoramus" magazine.
3. set up a Unique Principle center in Paris which was very popular and strong financially.
4. helped establish macrobiotic restaurants and had introduced "Ohsawa" (macrobiotic) foods into the health food stores.
5. earned $10,000 in one year from lecture fees and publications.
6. received an award from the city of Paris as a noteworthy citizen.[4]

In this report, Ohsawa presents some of his statistics in a rather cavalier fashion. Due to his work, there is a 20 percent reduction in meat consumption in Paris, he says. And there are tens of thousands of Europeans eating brown rice, miso soup and tamari soy sauce. While he had by this time a substantial number of followers, many of whom were very devoted, it is unlikely that they numbered more than several thousand. Ohsawa's lectures in Paris and Brussels, the two main centers, attracted several hundred listeners at most.

Ohsawa also gave his plans for the future. He wanted:

- to establish study facilities for Japanese students in Paris.
- to set up dōjō in Paris and other cities for the study of judō, aikidō, kendō (The Way of the Sword), flower arrangement, and other Japanese arts and spiritual paths.
- to establish macrobiotic lecture and study centers throughout Europe.
- to set up a macrobiotic hospital.
- to found macrobiotic farms and companies producing pure miso, rice and naturally fermented bread.

Ohsawa, whose strongest support was in Paris and Brussels at this time, resolved to focus his activities in other European countries, in North America and elsewhere in the world. Henceforth, he would spend six months of each year in Europe and North America, he promised, and six months in Asia and Africa.

Over the next several years Ohsawa was able to realize several of his ambitions, on a modest scale at least. In Paris the macrobiotic community grew, and the Institut Tenryu became an active study center which also provided macrobiotic foods. In Belgium there was a study center, as well as a restaurant and food outlets. In addition to Brussels, St. Martin-Latem became a focus of activity. In this small town near Ghent a noted Belgian painter named Edgar Gevaert lived with his large family. Gevaert had been a soldier in the First World War and afterward bought a piece of sandy wasteland in the countryside. He made it into a near self-sufficient homestead, living there with his wife and eleven children and pursuing his art. He was active in the World Federalist movement and it was through this connection that he met Ohsawa. Gevaert adopted Ohsawa's macrobiotic outlook and did a great deal to help activities. In 1959, with the cooperation of his eldest son, he established the Lima food company at St. Martin-Latem. This was the first explicitly macrobiotic food company outside Japan. Yoshimi and Sugamoto came, at Ohsawa's request, from India to teach cooking, miso-making and other macrobiotic food techniques. Lima Products flourished, soon distributing food all over Europe and to the United States. It has remained to this day a leader in the production and distribution of macrobiotic quality food in Europe.

In the summer of 1959 Ohsawa and Lima were in France and taught at a camp at Ste. Marie-sur-Mer in Brittany. It was attended by 500 people from all over Europe. Many seriously ill people came and made remarkable improvements with Ohsawa's dietary suggestions and Lima's cooking. The camp was called "The Camp of Miracles."

Late in 1959 Ohsawa made his first trip to the United States. He went to New York City, where a number of his students, including Michio and Aveline Kushi and Herman and Cornellia Aihara, had settled. Some modest attempts had been made to present macrobiotics, but for the most part Kushi, Aihara, and the others were busy supporting their families in a still strange country. Early in 1960 Ohsawa gave a series of lectures at the Buddhist Academy on Manhattan's Upper East Side. Attended at first mostly by members of the Japanese community in New York, the talks soon attracted a cross section of New Yorkers. They included people suffering from cancer and other serious illnesses. Having been accused of practicing medicine without a license in France shortly before, Ohsawa was very circumspect about recommending a particular diet for any specific illness. Still, a number of these people improved. These personal successes, plus Ohsawa's personal charisma, caused a small community of macrobiotic people to develop in the city.

Meanwhile, Ohsawa rushed to write an introductory book in English. He literally "dashed off" a book which he chose to call *Zen Macrobiotics* and which was meant as a practical supplement to "The Philosophy of Oriental Medicine." In it Ohsawa explains his Yin-Yang thinking in simple, easy to understand terms, then introduces his approach to medicine by declaring that "all diseases can be cured in ten days." Ohsawa then focuses on practical techniques to accomplish this. He lists ten variations of the macrobiotic diet, each containing different percentages of grains, vegetables, beans, fruit, and so on. Diet Number Seven consists of 100 percent grains cooked with salt, and Ohsawa recommends this diet, especially with brown rice, as the most effective means to reverse an illness. He notes that there are specific foods especially helpful for certain conditions (squash and azuki beans for diabetes, for example) and also prescribes assorted plasters and compresses.

Ohsawa also deals with broader issues, stating that the "American Gold World Empire" is about to topple. It is a sick civilization based on a mechanical, microscopic and analytical view of the universe. Its formal logic is false, as is its scientific method. The West can be saved from chaos and suffering only by abandoning its dualistic way of thinking and embracing the complementary monism of Yin and Yang together with its practical applications, including macrobiotics. All this is presented in a terse, dogmatic style. Ohsawa makes his points boldly and presents explanations of them afterwards, if at all.

On reading the manuscript Kushi told Ohsawa he thought its tone too sharp and its eating recommendations too strict. (Ohsawa advises eating Diet Number Seven with as much salt and sesame-salt as possible.) Kushi recommended the book be revised or that at least an explanatory appendix be added. Ohsawa, as usual very much in a hurry, allowed only that Kushi might write an explanation for a later edition. The book was rushed into print, the first edition being a crude mimeographed version sold at the lectures. Ohsawa also refused the advice of Kushi and others concerning the book's name. The use of the term "Zen" was a conscious ploy to capitalize on the Zen fashion then current in America and fueled by the work of Suzuki, Alan Watts, and "beatnik" poets and writers. Ohsawa's inclination to present macrobiotics in terms of a current vogue had not disappeared.

Ohsawa's stubbornness on both these points was to bear bitter fruit later on. While *Zen Macrobiotics* introduced many people to the movement, its dogmatic and simplistic tone also repulsed many. The strictness of the diet it recommended also caused problems as enthusiastic converts tried to follow a regimen for which their bodies were not ready. Ohsawa's appropriation of the term "Zen" angered many people in the serious Zen movement in America and Europe, and for years macrobiotics was considered an insolent and opportunistic upstart.

In the summer of 1960 the first macrobiotic summer camp in North America was held at Southampton, Long Island. It was called "The New Alternative." Interest continued to grow and a second summer camp was planned for Mountaindale, New York, near Bear Mountain. When Ohsawa returned in May 1961, international tensions were very high. The building of the Berlin Wall by the Soviets had brought Russia and the United States to the verge of a nuclear confrontation. Ohsawa began to predict a nuclear conflict between the superpowers in the near future. A number of his followers in New York resolved to take some action. They decided to move from the city to an area which would be safer in the event of war. They learned that the Sacramento Valley in California, surrounded by mountains on all sides, would be relatively immune to the effects of wind-born radioactive fall-out. In August of 1961 thirteen families totalling thirty-six men, women and children, drove west in a caravan to find a new life. An advance group including Herman Aihara and one-time musician Bob Kennedy had decided on Chico, California, north of Sacramento, as a desirable spot. With much attention from the media, and with Ohsawa declaring it to be a modern parallel to the Israelite Exodus from Egypt under Moses, the group arrived in Chico. To establish a livelihood and to make good food available, they pooled resources and formed the Chico-San Company, the first macrobiotic food company in the United States.

Ohsawa and Lima stayed on in New York long enough to celebrate his sixty-eighth birthday. It was a gala affair at the Wellington Hotel in Manhattan, attended by about 200 people. Ohsawa, who wrote later that he was painfully shy before crowds of such size, entertained his well-wishers by singing some Japanese songs.

Thereafter, Ohsawa continued his whirlwind travels, dividing his time between Europe, America and Japan. He spent much of 1963 and 1964, however, in Tokyo working on a new and, for him, special project. Around 1961 Ohsawa had met in Paris a French scientist named Louis Kervran. The Frenchman had heard of Ohsawa's theory that one chemical element could be transmuted to another without the application of great amounts of energy, as in an atomic reactor. Kervran attended a lecture by Ohsawa and afterward the two men talked. Kervan told Ohsawa of his own research which showed, much to his surprise, that plants, animals and human beings were able to change one element into another under ordinary biological conditions. He added that because this was against the prevailing scientific dogma, he had not published his findings.

Greatly excited, Ohsawa encouraged Kervran to publish his work, and began to translate it himself for publication in Japanese. In December, 1962 *Seitai ni yoru Genshi Tenkan* [生体による原子転換] ("Atomic Transmutation in the Living Body") was indeed published in Tokyo. Ohsawa was enthusiastic because Kervran's experiments verified his own theory. Based on Yin and Yang and on the spiral of materialization this hypothesis until now had lacked supporting scientific evidence. According to Ohsawa, the creation of the "world of elements" begins with the formation, from invisible energy, of the single proton and the single electron of the hydrogen atom. The combination of hydrogen atoms results in the formation of elements such as helium and oxygen with low atomic numbers. These elements then combine to form the more complex and heavier elements of the periodic table. Since a molecule of iron (atomic weight—20) is composed, according to Ohsawa's theory, of two atoms of carbon (atomic weight—6) and one atom of oxygen (atomic weight—8) it can decompose into these elements. Also, theoretically, it can be fabricated from these elements. Chemical elements are constantly being formed and broken down in the normal organic processes of nature. Every living thing is a "micro-cyclotron" capable of synthesizing necessary but unavailable chemical elements out of simpler ones which are available.

Ohsawa invited Nevan Henaf, an Irish biochemist and a supporter of macrobiotics, to come to Japan to help him and several Japanese associates in research on "atomic transmutation." Ohsawa referred to this project as "the last great challenge of his life—the creation of a new alchemy." In a letter to Mme. Francoise Riviere, a devoted student and the proprietor of the Institut Tenryu in Paris, Ohsawa says that all through his life he has developed only through the great difficulties and challenges which came to him. This "last challenge" is the greatest and it will take him three years to overcome, he predicts.

Henaf left the project in April of 1964 and Ohsawa continued alone. A few months later he announced that he had changed sodium into potassium using only very low electrical energy, and that he had verified it using spectroscopic analysis. On August 28, 1964, he announced that he had produced iron from carbon and oxygen, again in a low heat, low energy apparatus. Moreover, Ohsawa maintained that he "theoretically" had discovered how to synthesize gold, mercury and platinum!

With typical panache, Ohsawa proclaimed the beginning of a "Third Industrial Revolution." The first had been marked by machine and steam power, and the second by polymer chemistry and nuclear energy. The next would be characterized by the transmutation of elements. He asserted that with the discovery of a way to synthesize potassium (a key element in agriculture and industry), iron, and other economically important elements, a principal reason for the competition among the world powers had been eliminated. While he had begun this research to show the validity of the Unique Principle and of macrobiotics to the world, its success would have a marvelous byproduct. World peace could now be more easily established.

Even in Japan, though, the response to Ohsawa's claims was not exactly over-whelming. He tried, without success, to have a demonstration in the Japanese Parliament. He contacted the research laboratories of several large Japanese cor-porations, such as Sony and Toshiba, but received no reply. An article on his work, supposed to appear in the large national daily, the *Asahi Shimbun*, was not printed.

Later, in the United States, Ohsawa visited the corporate headquarters of Union Carbide Corporation to talk with officials there. He was accompanied by Kushi and by Cecile Levin, his American secretary. He outlined his experiments to the com-pany representative. But as always Ohsawa withheld one secret element, fearing that if he revealed everything, no commitment would be made. The "missing ele-ment" was the Unique Principle, the law of Yin and Yang. The executive thanked Ohsawa and then, escorting the group to the door, explained, "If you knew how many crackpots come through here every day with all kinds of crazy schemes, you would understand why we can't deal with your work." Once outside, the three laughed.

Throughout these years Ohsawa continued to write, of course. He kept up the torrent of letters to Japan when he was abroad, encouraging and scolding his stu-dents. His caustic judgments on their faults and inactivity were so powerful that the arrival of each letter provoked fear and trembling in the more sensitive of his followers. Ohsawa also shared his new experiences and discoveries. He relates, for example, that the national magazine in France, *Noir et Blanc*, had done a story about macrobiotics and had referred to him as "the Japanese doctor who wants to cure France." He laments this immense misunderstanding and insult. For years the Europeans have insisted on calling him "Doctor," but all along he has tried to be something quite opposite. He has only been trying to teach humanity to cure its own diseases. All he teaches is how to eat; it is really a kind of humorous fraud. In a long letter entitled *Seigi* [正義] ("Justice"), Ohsawa reports that at the age of sixty-nine he has made a great discovery: the seventh condition of health. To his earlier list of good energy, good sleep, good appetite, etc. Ohsawa adds a seventh which is worth fifty-five out of a possible 100. Actually it includes several points: never lying to protect onself; being precise in all that one says and does; loving everyone; seeking difficulties and overcoming them; and becoming the happiest of persons by spread-ing the secret of macrobiotics. The key to attaining this "justice" or seventh con-dition is eating a macrobiotic diet, but in very modest amounts. In the years between 1953 and 1966 Ohsawa was to write over 5,000 letters back to Japan, all of which he numbered in sequence and many of which he made copies.

Ohsawa increasingly wrote in French and English, directing his major books of this period to his Western audience. In 1962, for example, he published *L'Ere Ato-mique et la Philosophie d'Extrême Orient* ("The Atomic Age and the Philosophy of the Far East"). Atomic war, Ohsawa asserts at the outset, is the most serious disease of modern man. Like all other diseases, it begins with low judgment and false think-ing. It can be cured only by the Unique Principle and its practical applications, including of course the macrobiotic diet. Ohsawa then gives his usual rather erratic and broad presentation of his views in various areas. He also cites new biological research in Japan which he says will cause a revolution in biology. A Dr. Keiichi

Morishita [森下敬一] has demonstrated that red blood cells are produced in the small intestines and that they are direct transformations of food chyme. A Dr. Kikuo Chishima [千島喜久男] has shown the relation between diet and various diseases, including cancer. The work of both men corroborates theories already held by Ohsawa.

In autumn of that same year the Cuban missile crisis occurred. President John F. Kennedy challenged the Soviet's basing of missiles in Cuba, and until Premier Khrushchev backed down, again the world teetered on the brink of war. Ohsawa responded to the crisis with an "Open Letter to Kennedy and Khrushchev." War, he writes, has four causes or necessary elements. The first is leadership which does not know the Order of the Universe. The second is a people also ignorant of this order. The third is fear and a tendency to violence which come from this ignorance. The fourth is the arms to express this fear and violence. Ohsawa then gives the two world leaders the following advice.[5]

1. Launch a total nuclear attack.
2. One hour later declare a peace.
3. a. Open up both nations to the free exchange of ideas and people (in effect, begin an "ideological war").
   b. Open up research institutes to investigate cooperatively the issues of war and peace, education, science, medicine and government.

Ohsawa made the first two suggestions with tongue in cheek, and mentions parenthetically that it would be better, if possible, to omit them. The other steps though, he asserts, will lead to world peace, especially if the world research institutes recognize and learn to apply the secret power of food in human life.

Ohsawa's last major book was *Le Cancer et la Philosophie d'Extrême Orient* ("Cancer and the Philosophy of the Far East"). He presents himself as "the last philosopher of the Orient" who has come to the West to introduce macrobiotics and the Unique Principle and thus free Western man from his physical and psychic suffering. Cancer, Ohsawa writes, is the natural result of a way of life ruled by egocentric pleasure seeking. It is thus a plague appropriate to 20th century Western life. Yet cancer is really modern man's greatest benefactor. It forces him to see that he has been living contrary to the law of nature. It will help him discover a way of life according to the Order of the Universe and find true health, happiness and freedom.[6]

This book reflects Ohsawa's confidence and optimism at the time. The macrobiotic movement, though very small, was growing both in Europe and in America. Ohsawa was in constant demand in those places as well as in Japan. The summer of 1965 was, as Ohsawa describes it, the happiest time of his life. It began with a trip to Viet Nam in May. Some years before, unbeknownst to him, his writing had inspired a small group there to begin a macrobiotic way of life. By 1965 there were some three hundred people involved, and they invited Ohsawa to visit and lecture. After his visit Ohsawa predicted that the United States would be defeated in the rapidly escalating war with the Viet Cong communist rebels. The reason: the Viet Cong were eating an essentially macrobiotic diet of rice and vegetables and thus would enjoy a distinct physical and mental advantage over the Western troops living on canned meats, sweets, and the like.

From Southeast Asia, Ohsawa and Lima went on to summer camps in Europe and America. At a camp in Port Maneche, France, Ohsawa mentioned that he still had the filarial parasites in his body. When he ate poorly, especially when he ate meat, they would activate and he would see signs of them on his toes. By the end of the summer Ohsawa and Lima had circumnavigated the globe, traveling 30,000 miles in 102 days. The "penniless samurai" was indeed realizing his dream of an endless world journey.

These years were not without shadows, however. Early in 1965 a young woman in New York named Beth Ann Simon had died while following what seemed a macrobiotic diet. She was taking birth control pills at the time and had begun a very strict Number Seven regime. The strain proved too much and she died from an apparent combination of malnutrition and dehydration. Ohsawa was out of the country but when he returned he was sued for medical malpractice. Ultimately he was exonerated but both he and the macrobiotic diet had received much adverse publicity. Besides, the woman's father was an influential lawyer and there was soon pressure felt from the Federal Food and Drug Administration (FDA). The Ohsawa Foundation in New York, run by Irma Paul, was raided late one night and found to be selling food, as well as books recommending the food as a cure for illness. Charged with "false advertising," the center was closed down. Activities in New York came to a halt, and, with the Kushis having moved to Boston, the focus began to shift to there.

Early in 1966 Ohsawa published a pamphlet called *Sekai Kōkyū Heiwa e no Michi* [世界恒久平和への道] ("A Proposal for Lasting World Peace"). In it he presents a plan for the reorganization and renewal of world society according to macrobiotic principles and practices. It is in effect an international version of his earlier vision for Japan written in 1946. First Ohsawa suggests the selection of some 40,000 "world leaders." These men and women, chosen from the biologically and psychologically elite of all nations, would study macrobiotic principles and techniques. They would have to apply these in their own lives to establish physical and mental health. Then they would be put in charge of their national governments and of the world government. In the reorganization of social, economic, political, agricultural and industrial life they would be free to apply the principles which they had learned. Special attention would be paid to improving the quality of food for all citizens. Through the increase of healthy individuals in the world society, a firm basis for world peace would be established.

As an initial step to realizing this vision, Ohsawa began to organize what he called the "First International Spiritual Olympics." He hoped to have one hundred visitors, mostly established macrobiotic people from Europe and America, come to Japan. There they would be brought together with one hundred Japanese people, including intellectual and cultural leaders, religious teachers and masters of traditional arts. For two months all would live, study and travel together, observing, meanwhile, a macrobiotic diet. Thus the foreigners would be given an in-depth view of the life and culture of the Orient, and the Japanese would have the rare experience of extended contact with Western people. A step toward mutual understanding and cooperation would be made.

To commemorate the "Olympics" Ohsawa wanted to introduce a "macrobiotic beer," a refreshing cool drink that didn't have any alcoholic or extreme Yin side effects. He began to experiment daily with mixtures of Oriental herbs, drinking with relish the various brews. Some, he commented happily to Lima, were very close to the taste of Guinness Stout, a rich dark Irish beer which he especially liked. Lima noticed, however, that some of the symptoms Ohsawa had experienced in Africa during his bout with tropical ulcers and filariasis were reappearing. Ohsawa's hair began to thin and there were lumps on the back of his neck. She urged her husband to stop his experiments, but Ohsawa did not heed her advice.

On April 23, 1966, Ohsawa delivered a lecture at the main Tokyo headquarters of *Seichō no Ie* [生長の家], a religious group which had begun after the war. The founder of this "House of New Life," Masaharu Taniguchi [谷口雅春], had realized that his and Ohsawa's aims and approach were very similar and had invited him to speak from time to time. In the late afternoon Lima and Ohsawa returned to their apartment. During the day there had been the usual visitors and companions, both Japanese and foreign. That evening, however, they were alone, an unusual circumstance. Lima served dinner around 5:30 P.M. and Ohsawa began to eat, glancing over a manuscript as he did so.

Suddenly Ohsawa stood up, put his hand over his heart, and fell to the floor. As Lima rushed to his side he complained of a sharp pain in the small of his back. She put her hand there to soothe him and asked if she should call a doctor. Ohsawa replied faintly, "*Moo ii'n desu yo*" ("No, it's all right."). Those were his last words. Within moments he lost consciousness. By the time Dr. Moriyasu Ushio [牛尾盛保], a medical doctor associated with the macrobiotic movement in Tokyo, arrived, Ohsawa was dead.

According to Ushio's *post mortem* examination, the immediate cause of death was a *shinzō mahi* [心臓麻痺], a "paralysis of the heart" or "heart attack." Ushio and Lima theorized that this had been caused by the filarial parasites Ohsawa had picked up in Lambaréné. As Ohsawa had himself observed, these had remained dormant in his body. They had been a good barometer of his overall physical condition, forming pustules around his toenails when he was lax in his eating. With the "beer" research, Ohsawa's condition apparently had declined. The parasites, becoming active again, may have gathered at his most active organ (the heart) and caused the seizure. Since no autopsy was performed, however, this exploration could not be verified. Lima has since mentioned that Ohsawa's long-time smoking habit (which she disliked) was also a contributing factor. The same opinion is held by some of Ohsawa's longest associates and fellow teachers of macrobiotics. Clim Yoshimi, who was with Ohsawa much during the years prior to 1966, points out that Ohsawa preferred an American brand known as Kools. This is a menthol cigarette which Yoshimi says has a particularly bad effect on the heart.

The news stunned the macrobiotic world community. Many simply refused to believe that it could be true. "He was so strong and full of life, I thought he would never die," recalls Mitsuhiro Matsuda [松田光弘] (Michel), at the time a student in Japan, and now an acupuncturist in Boston. It took several days before all of Ohsawa's disciples in Europe and America knew clearly what had happened and overcame their disbelief. In Paris hundreds of people filed past a funeral altar adorned with flowers and a picture of "le Maitre," set up at the Center on Rue

Lamartine. In America the small groups in New York, Boston and Chico also expressed their sorrow and gratitude.

Some of Ohsawa's students and associates, particularly the very devoted ones in France, believe that Ohsawa foresaw his death. Mme. Riviere says that he told her in 1963 that he had "only three more years," that his work would be done and that he would be free to move on. At the final camp at Port Manech in 1965, Ohsawa apologized to his French friends, saying that although he had criticized them in the past for being ungrateful they really were quite kind and appreciative. And during his last months in Japan Ohsawa made an unusual round of visits to long neglected friends and family members. He apologized to them, saying that he had been so busy for so many years that he had not visited enough or spent enough time with them. René Levy feels Ohsawa saw clearly that his work was done and was aware (and glad) that he was to go on.

Whatever the case, Ohsawa was gone. His body was cremated and the ashes placed in the Sakurazawa family grave in Kyōzo-in [教蔵院] of Honpō-ji [本法寺], a Buddhist temple in Kyoto.

---

[1] Ohsawa, George, *The Book of Judgment*, Ignoramus Press, The Ohsawa Foundation, Los Angeles, 1966, p. 122

[2] Ibid., p. 143

[3] These reminiscences appear in an article entitled "Ohsawa in Deutschland: Eine Ost/West Begegnung" ("Ohsawa in Germany: A Meeting of East and West"). It appeared in "Durchblick" a German-language periodical of the Anthroposophical movement in Europe. It should be available through the Goetheanum, Dornach, Switzerland. The article was published in about 1979.

[4] ———, *Heiwa to Jiyū no Genri*, p. 306

[5] ———, *Clara Schumann*, p. 37 ff

9

George Ohsawa:
The Man and the Legacy

In the past six chapters I have tried to give a straightforward and systematic account of Ohsawa's life, work and thought. To date this has not been done in a Western language. Over the years much misinformation and myth has grown up around Ohsawa, which while often interesting, does disservice to the man and his memory. I hope our story thus far has presented a clear if rudimentary picture of his career, writings and major ideas. I hope too that this will be a helpful basis for future and more thorough biographers.

In this account, of course, some image of Ohsawa the man has come through. From the events of his life and the development of his thought can be inferred his energy, courage and impetuosity. Before we move on to the history of macrobiotics after Ohsawa, it would be fitting to focus on him in a more systematic way. What Ohsawa was like as a person, as a thinker, as a teacher, will be our main concern in this chapter. It will conclude with an evaluation of his achievements and failures, and of his legacy, both positive and negative.

Ohsawa, following his inclination to analyze things in terms of sevens, said that there were seven areas in human life. In portraying the man himself we can utilize this seven-fold schema, and look successively at the physical, sensory, emotional, intellectual, social, ideological and "supreme" sides of Ohsawa the man.

Ohsawa was, by Japanese standards, a large man. At five-feet-nine he was several inches taller than the average Japanese male of his generation. He was slender but well built, and had the square jaw of a man of action and will. He wore eyeglasses, but only after 1945 when his eyes had been damaged by the tortures of his wartime imprisonment. His hair was black, of course, and remained so, so that even at the end of his life there was only a little graying at the temples. His voice was deep and sonorous. According to Cecile Levin, his body was so pure and strong that it acted as a resonator, and even if he spoke softly, Ohsawa's voice could be heard at a great distance.

Ohsawa was a person of great, almost boundless physical and mental energy. Even as a man of seventy he walked with a spring in his step and normally bounded up steps two or three at a time. When he walked in the streets, his fast pace would usually leave companions behind. With Lima he had developed a system of shrill whistles so they might locate each other when he had gone ahead. In his early life, and particularly during the wartime exile in Yamanashi, Ohsawa enjoyed skiing, but otherwise he did very little sport per se. He preferred exercise that was a part of ordinary life. Ohsawa took particular delight in cleaning, dusting and mopping with a vigor that gave him a good daily workout. As a result of this activity and his generally spartan diet of rice and vegetables, Ohsawa was lean and strong. Once he did a few sessions of judō at a dōjō. The teacher, impressed with his leg and lower body strength, asked him how long he had been practicing the martial arts. "Only since I have been coming here," was the reply. Ohsawa maintained this energy and strength while sleeping at most four hours a night, often only two. He also took catnaps when possible, during taxi rides or at an uninteresting movie. Even in later life his vitality seemed not to diminish. Combined with his relatively youthful appearance it made him seem much younger than he was. The anthroposophist Finsterlin, meeting Ohsawa when he was actually 63, had assumed he was in his late 40s or early 50s. And until the day of his death Ohsawa kept up the whirlwind schedule of a man in his prime, lecturing, writing, studying and traveling.

For the most part Ohsawa's eating habits seemed to follow his own teachings. Except for the period in France, he apparently followed a strict diet for most of the first half of his life. Then from 1937 on, most of his food was prepared with great care by Lima, who was with him almost constantly. Ohsawa admits, though, to being on occasion both a glutton and a master of *jashoku* [邪食] ("bad eating"), that is, bingeing on non-macrobiotic food. As a young man he had made himself sick by overeating and by eating poor quality food. He writes of going to a famous *soba* (buckwheat noodle) restaurant in Tokyo with some friends and eating twelve bowls at a single sitting.

Late in his life Ohsawa seemed to enjoy eating and drinking very freely. He taught that the aim of macrobiotics was to achieve the health and freedom to be able to eat exactly what one wants. And often he seems to have made use of that freedom. Michio Kushi tells of going to a coffee shop with Ohsawa following a lecture in Cambridge in 1965. Much to his surprise, Ohsawa ordered cheese-cake and Coca Cola. Kushi ordered the same and Ohsawa advised him to "chew very well." Around the same time, in New York City, Cecile Levin stopped into a diner on the way to visit Ohsawa, and found him there enjoying donuts and coffee. Again, he proclaimed his secret as being "very good chewing." Such incidents, though, were exceptions to the rule. Despite this adventuresome streak Ohsawa watched his diet carefully. Sometimes he would go for long periods eating very simply and modestly. When translating Northrop's book and when working on the transmutation experiments he ate little more than rice and miso soup.

On the sensory level Ohsawa was a lover of order and cleanliness. His enthusiasm for them became well-known among his followers. Whenever he stayed as a guest somewhere he would get up early and clean the whole house. While staying at Mme. Rivière's Paris apartment in 1961 and rendering *Zen Macrobiotics* into French, Ohsawa cleaned the bathroom, and especially a wooden toilet top, with such care, that his hostess thought it was a newly bought fixture. When in 1946 Ohsawa lodged at the Kobayashi house his aim, he said, was not only to maintain the place, but to leave it much improved.

Ohsawa was particularly insistent on cleanliness in the kitchen and at the dining table. Before each meal he made sure that the eating area was immaculate. This is a sacred place, where the sacrament of changing one form of life into another would take place.

Ohsawa's meticulousness was apparent in his personal clothing and appearance. While he was a fashionplate only in his early years, he always enjoyed fine clothes well taken care of. Except during the sojourns in India and Africa, Ohsawa generally wore a coat and tie. He kept his pants "ironed" by putting them under his *futon* or cotton mattress during the night, a habit he developed as a young man. When he returned to Japan from Europe in 1958 he came wearing fine Italian shoes. Yūkō Okada [岡田雄公], now a leader of the macrobiotic community in Osaka, was a young boy at the time. When Ohsawa stayed at the Okada home, the youngster was sent to polish his shoes. Okada still remembers marveling at the exotic shoes. In informal circumstances, however, even in wintertime, Ohsawa often wore just sandals without socks. This practice was very healthful, he said, helping one develop the condition of "warm feet and cool head." Ohsawa had learned it from a traveling Russian in Kyoto early in his life. Even in the casual and sometimes primitive condition of summer camps where he would often go barefoot, Ohsawa always appeared neat, orderly and cleanly-shaven, with his hair combed smartly back.

In regard to all things, even small and apparently unimportant ones, Ohsawa tried to exercise the same care. He treated everything he owned or with which he came into contact, with the greatest respect. He said it was a person's responsibility to nurture and beautify all he touched. Thus he was able to keep personal items for many years. Late in his life he remarks that he had been wearing one particular necktie for forty years, and that all his writings were written with a single, treasured Waterman pen bought in France when he was a young man.

Ohsawa never wasted anything. He was especially scrupulous in regard to food. He taught and practiced that after finishing a meal one should clean one's bowl of every grain of rice. One grain wasted is ten thousand grains wasted. At a summer camp in France someone working in the kitchen threw out some rice which had begun to sour. Ohsawa retrieved it from the trash and ate it at the next meal. Grain that has begun to "spoil," he asserted, is especially healthy. Since the decomposition has already begun the food is very easy to digest.

Ohsawa hated to waste anything—paper, string and time included. He always used both sides of a sheet of paper and would write notes on the blank back and inside surface of used envelopes. Sometimes manuscripts of books were sent to the printers written on what was essentially scrap paper. When Ohsawa did ask his secretaries to make copy of something, his tiny and barely legible handwriting on folded and often soiled paper made the task nearly impossible. When Aveline Kushi wrote a letter to Ohsawa introducing herself and expressing her desire to come to study with him, she wrote in large, classically beautiful writing on fine paper. When Ohsawa saw her for the first time, his initial greeting was "You are very uneconomical!" Even bits of cord were saved, tied together and used later for wrapping books and packages. Ohsawa said he did all this because everything we have and use is a gift of the universe and must be treated as sacred. He did it also to honor the memory of his mother and of all mothers who have had to raise their children in poverty.

Ohsawa, however, did not pose as a saint or ascetic. He openly and happily indulged in some of the popular "vices." He enjoyed good quality beer, particularly the dark and heavy Irish brew, Guinness Stout. He also relished a glass of good

Scotch whisky. Apparently he used these in moderation, an occasional garnish to his diet. Ohsawa was teaching, of course, that in food and drink one must keep both quality and quantity in mind. One can use a food or drink that is extremely Yang or Yin (such as Scotch), if a high quality version of it is used in small amounts.

In pursuing another indulgence, that of tobacco, Ohsawa did not observe this principle so carefully. Through the last three decades of his life he smoked heavily, a pipe earlier on and then cigarettes. In his latter years in Europe and America he preferred mentholated brands. Through most of this period smoking was looked upon as a rather benign habit. Only in the early 1960s, with the research linking it to lung cancer and other degenerative diseases, did it get a very negative image in the public eye. Ohsawa, never hesitant to get attention by taking a controversial stand, declared that smoking could actually be used as a cure for cancer. Tobacco smoke (Yang), he claimed is an excellent treatment for cancer (Yin).

Emotionally, Ohsawa seems on the surface to have been a typically non-demonstrative Japanese male for whom an open display of affection was rare. In fact sometimes he seemed almost cruelly indifferent. One evening at a lecture in Brussels he mentioned very casually that one of his close followers probably would die very soon. His absolute matter-of-fact tone shocked some in the audience. However, beneath this exterior, the legacy perhaps of samurai upbringing, lay very profound emotions. They surface sometimes in Ohsawa's more personal writings when he recalls with great anguish the suffering of one of his students or the death of his child. It is especially apparent in nearly every mention of his mother. Her suffering and death left a deep mark on him and he was, throughout his life, almost obsessed by her memory. He laments that he did not know about Shoku-Yō at the time of her illness. He might have saved her from an untimely death. He writes that his life's work had been the result of her deathbed advice to "study all things and to benefit humanity" and that he can still recall poignantly the memory of her fragile figure under a heavy bundle heading off to the city market to sell her new-spun thread.

Ohsawa's tears on leaving Japan in 1953 show the same sensitivity, but it was not limited to such major events. Kushi remembers going to a movie, a sad love story, with Ohsawa in Boston, and at the end turning to find him drying his eyes with a handkerchief. Cornellia Aihara, who spent years with Ohsawa both in Japan and in America, comments that though he seldom showed it openly Ohsawa was compassionately aware of discomfort or suffering around him. He himself, particularly in childhood, had suffered much.

In general, Ohsawa's nature was an intense one. When he decided on a goal he pursued it with absolute singleness of purpose, courage and determination. This is evident in his total commitment to macrobiotics for over four decades through many failures, defeats and frustrations. He went to Europe to introduce Shoku-Yō in 1929 and returned to Japan six years later having stirred but a ripple among the French intelligentsia. He tried to avert Japan's conflict with the West, then to stop it, and failed in both. He tried to have the nation adopt a macrobiotic, ecological way of life after the war, and watched it go in an opposite way. He spent a year and a half in India and five months in Africa with little to show for it. And while he attracted a following in France, Belgium and America in the last years of his life, it was hardly the mass social movement for which he had hoped. His "discoveries" in alchemy went unheralded. The pattern was not lost on Ohsawa. He once told his close French associate, René Levy, that "I have had a most interesting life. Everything I have ever tried has failed."

Through all this Ohsawa retained his vision and purpose and pursued it with optimism and a certain *joie de vivre*. After each setback he gathered himself together and set off with the energy and enthusiasm of a youthful adventurer on to the next challenge. When things failed to happen according to plan in India he went on to Africa. When Schweitzer did not accept his teachings he continued to Paris. And each time, Ohsawa went ahead hopeful, undismayed, with the zest and appetite of the urchin confronting the plate piled high with delicious cakes. The soul of a dreamer combined with the intestinal fortitude of a samurai. And when we consider that some of Ohsawa's longest journeys and greatest challenges were undertaken after his 60th year, they are all the more remarkable.

On the other hand, this intensity came out also as impetuosity, stubbornness, impatience, intolerance of those who did not see the world as he saw it, and as a quickness to anger. We see this in Ohsawa's early marriages, in his diatribes of the late 1930s, in his insistence on the early if flawed publication of *Zen Macrobiotics*. In his later years he mellowed quite a bit. He mused that his hope was to spend his last years writing romantic poems in Paris. Visiting the Kushis in New York in the early 1960s he spent much time playing with their little son Yoshio, something hard to imagine of him in earlier years. And what a beautiful miracle is a small child, he thought happily. The angry crusader of the '30s and '40s had been replaced by a more gentle, if equally determined, grandfather figure.

As an intellectual, Ohsawa must be understood primarily as a person of insight and intuition rather than of broad learning or systematic approach. He was not a well-educated man in the classic sense of the word. His formal education after middle school was a preparation for a business career, and it ended when he was twenty. Ohsawa read voraciously and widely, often devouring two and three books a day throughout his life. But as a youth he did not receive a broad-based education in the humanities, nor did he receive training in the deliberate and systematic approach of the natural sciences.

Ohsawa had, then, neither the encumbrances nor the advantages of formal higher education. On the one hand he was free to look at and to study the world without preconceptions, armed only with the Unique Principle and his own intuition and imagination. Many of his more interesting ideas bear the mark of this unencumbered approach: his view of the human mind as a radio receiver, of gravity as the result of centripetal cosmic energy, his biologicial interpretation of history. And apparently many of his ideas came indeed as sudden "insights" rather than as the result of long, systematic investigation. Ohsawa recalls that his vision of how the chemical elements were created from simple to complex and of how they could be expressed in a spirallic table came to him in a dream!

On the other hand, his lack of a broad base of knowledge helped lure him into the provincial and narrow-minded Nippon-shugi ideology. This nationalistic and xenophobic view was based in part on patriotism and love of Japan, but also on ignorance about the West. At the time he embraced it, Ohsawa knew very little of the history and culture of Western civilization. Despite his years in Paris,

Western music, religion and art were all *terra incognita* for him. He admits that he attended one concert in Paris in his early sojourn, but left without a clue of its meaning. He knew nothing of St. Augustine, Meister Eckhart, of Bach, Mozart, Rembrandt or Rubens. It was easy, then, to characterize Western culture as materialistic, hedonistic and spiritually blind. It was easy to fall prey to the temptation of comparing the most refined and idealized forms of Japanese tradition to the lowest and most debased aspects of Western culture. Of course cultural bigots in the West were doing the opposite with the same net result.

This lack of formal training is evident in Ohsawa's writings as well. On the one hand, his expression is usually powerful and direct, imbued with the spontaneity and conviction of one who has experienced the truths he is presenting. There is, however, a lack of organization and structure, which easily confuses and exasperates the reader. Also, Ohsawa has a tendency to make a bold point and to explain or defend it only afterward if at all. To those who already accept his general outlook this may be acceptable. But to the uninitiated, Ohsawa's declarations come across as dogmatic and baseless. For example, in *Zen Macrobiotics* Ohsawa writes that "Any disease, even an incurable one, can be cured in ten days." What he means is that since the blood is renewed completely every ten days, the beginning of the total physical transformation necessary for "cure" can occur in that time. To the average intelligent reader the statement is extreme, undocumented and even self-contradictory. Also, many of Ohsawa's "proofs" are in terms of Yin and Yang only. For example, his argument regarding smoking and cancer is based on the idea that tobacco, though it is a large-leafed and hence Yin plant, is made Yang by aging, drying, and then burning. Its smoke, thus made Yang, can cure cancer (Yin). While plausible to the macrobiotic mind, to a scientist or to a sophisticated, neutral layperson this is hardly a convincing explanation. This innocence about scientific rigor, combined with Ohsawa's impetuosity, caused him to proudly announce the "success" of his experiments in transmutation before he really had sound evidence.

In Ohsawa's defense it must be said that he was (as he noted himself) a deductive thinker who applied universal principles to particular phenomena. He decried the microscopic, analytical, empirical method of the scientific approach, saying it led to an incomplete view of reality. Though Ohsawa operated by deduction and intuition, he was deeply concerned that his discoveries be accepted by people who held the scientific method as the standard of truth. While a book like *Zen Macrobiotics* certainly turned many people toward the path of macrobiotics, it also turned many away.

Socially, Ohsawa was an affable and outgoing person. When traveling by train he would engage fellow passengers in conversation and usually try to interest them in macrobiotics. When guests visited his home or school, it was he rather than the shy and retiring Lima who would meet, greet and make them feel at home.

In dealing with patients in a medical consultation, though, Ohsawa could be very direct and harsh. His diagnoses were swift and incisive and followed by advice, often undiplomatic in the extreme. "Monsieur, you are a human toilet" was one appraisal of which he was fond of during his later years. "Your whole body is sick. Eat Diet Number Seven for ten days. No tea or drinking of any kind!" he would tell another. The purpose here apparently was to shock the patient into a constructive course of action. For some the approach worked. For others it did not.

In the more intimate and longer relations with his disciples, Ohsawa tended to be yet more harsh. He was critical and severe both to his students at the Maison Igno-ramus in Japan and to his European and American followers. At a summer camp on the East Coast in the early 1960s Ohsawa gave Cecile Levin some papers to type. It was a beautiful day and everyone at the camp went swimming. Cecile joined them, planning to do the typing when she came back refreshed. When she returned Ohsawa had taken the papers away. "When you have a job to do, do it first," he said coldly, "then play!" In lecture Ohsawa often posed questions to students and commented immediately on their answers. "Your thinking is totally dualistic and egocentric," he might say, or "You are a sentimental fool." On an essay that Cecile submitted to him, Ohsawa simply marked a large "X" in red pencil and wrote "You are a liar."

There are countless similar episodes, in Europe and Japan as well as in America. And it seemed that the closer one was to Ohsawa the harsher the treatment. Clim Yoshimi, who had been in Africa and then had gone to Europe at Ohsawa's request, was at a summer camp in France in 1959. Ohsawa discovered him eating in a res-taurant and, incensed, ordered him immediately away. Yoshimi, without money or a home, made his way to Belgium and managed to get a job with the Lima Company. About the same time, René, Ohsawa's son by the Armenian woman, had become known to Ohsawa. He attended a summer camp but happened to get bitten by a snake. When he proved unable to follow Ohsawa's dietary prescription exactly, Ohsawa banished him from the camp and virtually disowned him.

While some of Ohsawa's followers by great effort and discipline avoided his censure, it was almost impossible to get a compliment or word of recognition from "le Professeur", as he was called in France. Ohsawa sometimes gave his intimate disciples difficult tasks to do for him, perhaps with an educational purpose in mind. For example, one day he sent Yoshimi to the bank to withdraw money but failed to give him a bankbook or other document. After much difficulty Yoshimi managed to bring home the money. Another time, upon seeing a cartoon short in a Paris cinema Ohsawa asked Mme. Rivière to obtain a copy of the script. After weeks of searching she finally located it and trying it with a silver ribbon, presented it proudly to Ohsawa. In both cases, Ohsawa uttered no word of thanks. If he ever did commend or compliment someone, it was cause for anxiety, since a harsh attack probably was soon to follow!

To an outside observer Ohsawa might seem a cruel, arbitrary and ungrateful tyrant. Yet these patterns were part of a conscious method of education, of personal training for his followers. Ohsawa wanted to make them strong, independent, resourceful. He outlined his method in the "Seven Principles of Macrobiotic Educa-tion."

1. Let them discover the Order of the Universe.
2. Don't teach. Let them discover for themselves.
3. Test them severely through question and response.
4. Never give a compliment. Give them only shame so they will discover the depth of their ignorance.
5. Make them live in poverty, so they don't become one who sells their time

or who abandons "justice" in the face of difficulty.

6. Don't give time for reflection. Make them answer immediately so that their judgment becomes rapid.
7. Make them work hard physically to create a hard body which will stand up to obstacles and difficulties.

The following transcript gives some idea of Ohsawa in action. It records a class with a group of newcomers to macrobiotics in Paris in the early 1960s.

A student: You have written, "If one has a strong will..." But what should one do if he doesn't have this will?

GO: Eat rice mechanically. Chew one hundred times per mouthful and wait.
S: But I don't like to eat rice.
GO: That means that you don't have any hunger.
S: No, I have hunger. I am dying from hunger.
GO: Then die!
S: Then don't I have a right to live?
GO: You have the right to be free.

* * *

S: Often when I read your books or hear you in lecture I am shocked.
GO: If you let someone or something shock you it means you have a problem.

* * *

S: When you say that we are all fools and liars I think that you don't like us Westerners.
GO: (laughing) I have come to tell you all my secrets, and you say that I don't like you.

* * *

S: Your books are full of contradictions, sometimes from one page to the next. I get completely lost.
GO: You don't know how to read. You have no eyeglasses.
S: Yes, I have eyeglasses.
GO: You have to read with the spectacles of Yin and Yang. The contradictions are complementary. You should not read my books, but chew them.

* * *

S: Why is Macrobiotics so difficult?
GO: The bigger the front, the bigger the back!
S: How did you discover macrobiotics?

GO: (laughing) I have discovered nothing at all. I have merely uncovered something that already existed.

S: Is macrobiotics the only truth?

GO: Macrobiotics is the synthesis of all wisdom.

*   *   *

S: Can a person come to understand everything?

GO: The finite.

S: Does one have to be a wise man or an initiate?

GO: No, if his brain is not too poisoned he will receive everything through intuition.

S: What is the difference between the finite and the infinite?

GO: The finite will never be able to understand the infinite.

*   *   *

S: You say that macrobiotics means the great and long life. Do all macrobiotics die at an old age?

GO: What matters is not the length of life, but the quality.

*   *   *

S: Are you never angry?

GO: Oh yes. With my wife, but she accepts it. (Lima laughs.)

*   *   *

S: Although all illnesses are different you recommend for each the same diet.

GO: Only the symptoms are different. They all have the same origin: a false understanding of the Order of the Universe. Feed yourself in harmony with the Order of the Universe and you will cure all your diseases.

*   *   *

S: What must one do after the ten-day rice cure?

GO: Study the Unique Principle.

S: How long does one need to become macrobiotic?

GO: Two years, if you eat carefully according to the Order of the Universe.

S: Is that Buddhism?

GO: Yes. Everything is part of the Infinite.

S: How long does the study of the Unique Principle take?

GO: A lifetime.

S: What happens if one gives up macrobiotics?

GO: Try it.

S: What would happen to me?

GO: You would become more unhappy than before.

S: I eat properly but I don't find that my judgment is improved. I don't eat anything else, but my back aches as before.

GO: Do you cook?

S: No, I don't have everything that one needs. Besides, I have no wife. I eat here (at the center) every day and in the evening I usually eat bread.

GO: You should cook everything you eat. You should not be dependent on others.

*   *   *

S: What difference is there between the ten-day rice cure and fasting?

GO: The ten-day rice diet can be observed as a half-fast.

S: When is the best time to do the rice cure?

GO: Whenever you want. Just watch nature. When nature fasts you may also.

S: Does nature fast then?

GO: Be observant. You must find it out yourself.

*   *   *

S: When someone asks you a question, why do you always reply: "Find out for yourself!"

GO: If I give you the answer, you will never discover for yourself.

*   *   *

S: I eat rice, but I always want something else. I often binge. Does that mean that I don't use enough will?

GO: Be strict with yourself and understanding with others. For everything one must pay, if not today, then tomorrow. Be careful!

S: When someone speaks badly to you, you never answer. Why don't you tell him that he is wrong?

GO: You love your friends, but you should love your enemies also. Through them you learn most.

S: If a murderer or a thief sits next to you, then you must accept him?

GO: You must accept and love all men.

S: Why do you always say, "Be strict!" But we have seen you drink beer and eat fruit.

GO: Because it is fun!

*   *   *

S: Why don't you ask for money ever?

GO: I don't do anything for you at all. Everything that I do, I do for myself.

S: Why do you smoke?

GO: (lifting his head) Answer for your self!

Various students present several arguments:

    Because you like it.

    Because you are too Yin and tobacco makes you Yang.

    Because you want to contradict those who say tobacco is harmful.

GO: Because I am not a saint!

*   *   *

S: Professor Ohsawa, can you tell me what I should do to stop suffering with my rheumatism? I have been operated on nine times with no improvement. Should I have a new operation?

GO: (Looking at both sides of her hands and at the fingernails. She is an old woman with furs and jewelry.) It is not necessary.

S: But Professor Ohsawa, I ask for a diagnosis. I will pay you well.

GO: It is not necessary. You should not be cured. Please go.

*   *   *

S: If during my present life I don't achieve the seventh level and, for example, die on the fourth level, am I lost?

GO: You will continue your path in the next life.

S: How many lives must man experience to achieve this?

GO: Please try!

*   *   *

S: What do you recommend for menopause?

GO: There is no problem at all. Please follow my advice. Everything is in my books.

S: And what about white secretions?

GO: If you have white secretions, then your whole family is unhappy. Follow my directions.

S: Should children also eat in this way?

GO: Children can eat instinctively until the age of 12. If a girl between 7 and 12 eats too much fruit, though, she will have painful menstruation.

S: Is a child also responsible for his sickness?

GO: No, until 16 years the mother has the responsibility.

S: You have said that a sickness is first in the mind and then in the body. What about a baby, then, who is sick?

GO: You should think about that.

*   *   *

S: Can Yangization be dangerous?

GO: If you eat 50 grams of salt at once it will kill you immediately. If you eat no salt, then you die slowly. Don't be afraid of salt. If you eat too much you will automatically eat and drink accordingly.

S: You often say that "love of one's neighbor" is not good and one should be an egotist. All religions, though, say to love one's neighbor.

GO: If you are sick you cannot help anyone else.

S: Even if I am sick I can tell someone: Eat rice for ten days and you will be cured.

GO: It is easy to heal a sickness, but to heal a sick person is difficult. The person must be cured. That is the greatest difficulty. When one is truly cured then he is cured forever.

S: I don't understand that. Your answer is not clear.

GO: Your judging ability is covered.

S: What should I do to uncover it?

GO: Number Seven for ten days.

*   *   *

S: How many sicknesses have you healed?

GO: I have healed thousands of sicknesses, but if I could cure one sick person in each country I would be very happy.

S: You say that macrobiotics means the grand life, and the joy of life, but on the contrary, since I came here to eat I am sad. I can't eat other things, and I can't read. I have lost my friends, split up my family, left my wife, lost my hair, do poorly at my job. I am overwhelmed with problems.

GO: Very good. The greater the difficulty, the greater the joy.

*   *   *

A nurse: You have said that salt is the universal panacea and sesame salt is the best medication. The doctors are against salt though, and I believe them. Since I have been taking much salt I have been having severe kidney pains.

GO: Severe? (He laughs in surprise) Excellent. You have experimented. You should now answer.

N: But I am asking you.

GO: You have not understood. You have not thought according to Yin and Yang. Everything depends on your power of judgment. Look deeper!

N: I would like to do that, but how?

GO: Are the kidneys and salt Yin or Yang?

N: Salt is Yang.

GO: Why?

N: I do not know.

GO: If you answer salt is Yang and you do not know why, then you are a parrot. (The nurse blushes, stands up and leaves without a word.) She confesses her incurable disease. How sad!

*   *   *

S: Salt and the kidneys are both Yang—Yang repels Yang, that means you get pains when you eat salt.

GO: If you want that.

S: I don't understand. Why should one eat salt if the salt in the sesame salt is repelled by the kidneys?

GO: You must find out for yourself.

S: Oh please, Mr. Ohsawa, we will never understand salt if you don't help us.

GO: It is not salt that cures you. It is the blood. If you eat too Yin, then your blood becomes too Yin because your food produces blood. And if you eat too Yang your blood becomes too Yang. If you eat balanced food then your blood will become balanced and every sickness will disappear.

S: Are there times when you should eat no salt?

GO: That depends on many things. You can't divide Yin and Yang. Study!

S: You say a child should eat according to instinct, but if you test that, the child eats chocolate and candies.

GO: You are a dualist. A great misfortune.

S: If macrobiotics doesn't bring me happiness, what is the problem?

GO: Your low level of judgment.

S: I would like to understand everything but it is difficult.

GO: With the Unique Principle you will be given everything!

*   *   *

One must ask what, in the face of this pedagogy, prompted so many to remain devoted students of Ohsawa. The answer, which I heard again and again from close followers, is that Ohsawa's criticisms, rebukes and flashes of anger actually came out of a deep love and respect for the person. Ohsawa's aim was not to demean or to hurt, but to promote the development of the character and level of judgment. "No matter how harsh he was with me," a woman recalls, "I always felt that he absolutely loved and cared for me." "He could seem to be very cruel at times," another remembers, "but I never met a man so full of love and warm-heartedness. He was always totally concerned for the well-being of those around him."

Of course Ohsawa did not totally conceal this affection for his students and his confidence in their ability to evolve into "free" human beings. His constant refrain was an exuberant "Sautez! Sautez!" ("Jump! Jump!"—á la Flip). Jump into the world of freedom and health which is man's natural birthright! This deep and personal concern was shown most concretely perhaps at the table. Ohsawa would have Lima prepare special dishes for particular persons. Then he would serve each individually according to the student's condition and needs. As a father might serve his children he gave a bit of fish here, an extra portion of vegetable there. Even to this day some of Ohsawa's long-time followers, especially in Japan, refer to him as "Papa" and to Lima as "Mama."

Ohsawa aspired, of course, to a much broader appeal. He wanted to make macrobiotics a mass social, and even political, movement. Each of the various roles Ohsawa assumed—businessman, physician, scientist, philosopher, writer, social reformer, political activist, cultural broker, alchemist—had as its ultimate purpose the spread of the Unique Principle and macrobiotics. This was Ohsawa's consuming passion. He depicts himself as a frenzied street-corner salesman, trying to get the attention of the passing crowds. He tried every trick and ploy. In each epoch he presented his basic views in terms of the cultural and intellectual fashion of the day—Shinto and Japanese nationalism in the late 1930s, American and democratic values in the late 1940s, Zen Buddhism ten years later. In the process Ohsawa gave up a normal family and personal life. He dedicated all his time, energy and resources. He worked day and night for years. The concept of a day off or a vacation was foreign to him. He amassed no wealth, putting everything immediately back into his public efforts—magazines, books, lectures. He achieved little status. In Japan, where membership in a significant group and position in the status hierarchy are the basis of personal identity, he was a virtual nobody. In Europe and the United States his following was small and somewhat outside the social mainstream. Yet in spite of this lifelong effort and sacrifice Ohsawa came not even close to his vision of a large macrobiotic movement.

The reasons for this are complex, but certainly one factor was Ohsawa himself. However committed he was to a broad-based movement he had little patience with the organization and administration this would require. He admits to being a poor organizer. Ohsawa admits too to being intimidated by large groups of people. Thus while he enjoyed dealing with audiences of twenty or thirty or sixty, with more people present he was not at his best. His forte was inspiring individuals and small groups, firing them with his own enthusiasm and dreams. He did this with many, bringing into the macrobiotic movement, in Japan and elsewhere, men and women who would devote their lives to it. But there was always, at least during Ohsawa's lifetime, a fairly small critical mass beyond which his following did not grow.

On the ideological level Ohsawa formulated a comprehensive view of the origin, structure and operation of the universe. This included a view of the nature and destiny of man, and importantly, a practical means for man to realize that destiny. Thus far we have mentioned this Weltanschauung piecemeal in the course of our narrative. Since it is essential to understanding the macrobiotic movement after Ohsawa as well as Ohsawa himself, it deserves a systematic treatment.

The overriding concept in Ohsawa's world view is what he calls "the ocean of infinity." He uses many other terms, including "infinite expansion," "cosmic life energy," "the world of the spirit," "endless freedom, eternal happiness, perfect justice." It is identical with that absolute reality to which various cultures have given names like God, Allah, Yahweh, Brahman and Buddha. All refer to that undifferentiated Oneness, eternal, infinite, beyond space and time, without light or shadow, growth or decay. It is changeless, formless, silent.

The creation of the finite world begins with the intersection of streams of expanding energy within this infinite Oneness. As currents of water come together to create a whirlpool, the two streams result in a contracting vortex of energy. The spiral is three-dimensional, having depth as well as breadth. It is logarithmic, its speed increasing geometrically as it goes toward the center.

This contracting vortex is the Yang principle. When the inwardly spiralling energy reaches the center point it begins to go outward. Expanding, opposite energy is created. Thus within the infinite Oneness, two finite poles are created: Yin and

Yang, centripetality and centrifugality. From their interaction is born the rest of the relative, phenomenal world. This creation does not occur only once. It has been going on endlessly in the past, is going on now and will go on forever in the future. Ohsawa called the realm of Yin and Yang, "the sixth heaven," or the world of "bipolarity."

The next realm, "the fifth heaven," is somewhat more contracted. It is the world of space, time and energy, and within it appear light, radiation and electromagnetic energy.

Fig. 1 The Order of the Universe. (Showing the seven levels of the evolution of the logarithmic spiral of the infinite universe.)

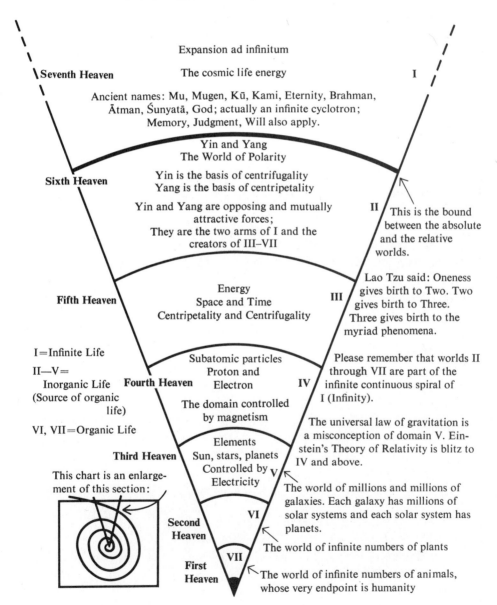

Expansion ad infinitum

The cosmic life energy

Seventh Heaven ... I

Ancient names: Mu, Mugen, Kū, Kami, Eternity, Brahman, Ātman, Śunyatā, God; actually an infinite cyclotron; Memory, Judgment, Will also apply.

Yin and Yang
The World of Polarity

Sixth Heaven

Yin is the basis of centrifugality
Yang is the basis of centripetality

Yin and Yang are opposing and mutually attractive forces;
They are the two arms of I and the creators of III–VII

II — This is the bound between the absolute and the relative worlds.

Fifth Heaven

Energy
Space and Time
Centripetality and Centrifugality

III — Lao Tzu said: Oneness gives birth to Two. Two gives birth to Three. Three gives birth to the myriad phenomena.

I = Infinite Life

II—V =
  Inorganic Life
  (Source of organic life)

VI, VII = Organic Life

Fourth Heaven

Subatomic particles
Proton and Electron

The domain controlled by magnetism

IV — Please remember that worlds II through VII are part of the infinite continuous spiral of I (Infinity).

The universal law of gravitation is a misconception of domain V. Einstein's Theory of Relativity is blitz to IV and above.

Third Heaven

Elements
Sun, stars, planets
Controlled by Electricity

V — The world of millions and millions of galaxies. Each galaxy has millions of solar systems and each solar system has planets.

This chart is an enlargement of this section:

Second Heaven

VI — The world of infinite numbers of plants

First Heaven

VII — The world of infinite numbers of animals, whose very endpoint is humanity

156

"The fourth heaven" is that of the pre-atomic particles, the electrons, neutrons, and protons which are the building blocks of the atom. It is controlled by the force of magnetism.

The next level, that of the chemical elements, is the first stage of the visible, material world, and is controlled by electricity. Within it appears the world of inanimate nature, including the sun and stars, and the earth with its atmosphere, water and soil. There are infinite galaxies in this realm, each with countless stars, and our sun with its solar system is just one of these.

From this inorganic world emerges the organic world of "the second heaven." This is the vegetable kingdom of living and dying plants.

"The first," or in terms of time, "the final," heaven is that of animated life, which arises out of, and is nourished by, the plant world. Humankind is the last development within this animal realm and is the culmination and perfection of the vast spiral of creation. In man the pure "Spirit of Infinity" has been materialized into finite form.

For Ohsawa then, the uncreated "Seventh Heaven" or Infinity creates and embraces everything. The finite world is a vast three-dimensional spiral within this "endless ocean." Each of its six levels is created by the one previous and creates the one following. For example, the vegetable kingdom emerges from the mineral and in turn nourishes the animal. The whole forms a continuous, interrelated spiral. All energy, life and matter within this spiral of existence come from Infinity, is always related to it, and eventually returns to that source.

In the relative world everything occurs according to specific laws which are intrinsic to the structure of the universe. All phenomena come into being, function and disappear (actually are transformed into something else) according to the laws of Yin and Yang, the twin cosmic energies. In 1932 Ohsawa for the first time described these systematically in the twelve "theorems" of "Le Principe Unique." He used other names for this at other times, including "the Order of the Universe," "the law of change," and "the magic spectacles."

In *Zen Macrobiotics* (1961) Ohsawa lists them as follows:[1]

1. Yin and Yang are the twin poles of the infinite pure expansion.
2. Yin and Yang are produced infinitely and continuously from the infinite pure expansion itself.
3. Yin is centrifugal. Yang is centripetal. Centrifugality produces expansion, lightness (in mass), cold and dark. Centripetality produces constriction, density, light and heat.
4. Yin attracts Yang. Yang attracts Yin.
5. All things and all phenomena are composed of Yin and Yang in different proportions.
6. All things and phenomena are constantly changing their Yin and Yang components. Everything is restless and in flux.
7. There is nothing completely Yin or Yang. All is relative.
8. There is nothing neutral. There is always an excess of Yin or Yang.
9. The affinity or force of attraction between things is proportional to the difference of Yin and Yang between them. There is a strong attraction be-

tween extreme Yin and Yang, a smaller attraction between what is slightly Yin or Yang.

10. Yin repels Yin. Yang repels Yang.
11. At the extreme, Yin produces (becomes) Yang, and Yang produces (becomes) Yin.
12. All physical phenomena are Yang at the center and Yin at the periphery.

To assist in the classification of things and phenomena (including, of course, foods) according to Yin and Yang, Ohsawa gives the following chart:[2]

	Yin	Yang
temperature:	hot	cold
direction:	ascent	descent
weight:	light	heavy
activity:	quiet	active
texture:	soft	hard
form:	long	short
light (color):	dark	bright
liquid:	wet	dry
structure:	hollow	dense
color:	violet—indigo—green—blue—yellow—orange—red	

After his initial presentation of the theorems in 1932, Ohsawa supplemented them with the Seven Axioms of "The Order of the Universe."[3]

1. Everything comes from the differentiation of one Infinity.
2. Everything changes.
3. All antagonisms are complementary.
4. There is nothing identical in the universe.
5. What has a front has a back.
6. The bigger the front, the bigger the back.
7. What has a beginning has an end.

According to Ohsawa's schema, man, as the culmination of the spiral of life, is the point at which the finite returns to the Infinite. Man is born into the relative world with a physical body and an individual self or "ego." As such he grows, matures, declines and dies. But besides this "petit moi" or "little ego," man has a "grand Moi," a "large" or "cosmic" self. This is the absolute Oneness, Infinity, the origin of all that exists. Man, Ohsawa insists, is the endless universe itself. Man ultimately is God, possessing eternity, infinity, and absolute joy within himself. The goal and destiny of each person, then, is the rediscovery of that Infinite Self. This is not something that occurs after death. It can be realized here and now, on earth, while in human physical form. In perfect physical, emotional and psychological health and in the constant spiritual awareness of the divine Oneness, a person can realize his identity with the Absolute. This, in fact, is the natural birthright of all human beings.

This state of absolute health and harmony is possible not only for the individual, but also for the groups which are comprised of individuals. A family, community, nation and potentially all of humanity can manifest that divinity if the individual members have realized it.

To this grand vision of human destiny Ohsawa adds the Tao of Shoku-Yō, or "macrobiotics," "the great art of life." This is a practical way of life based on the Order of the Universe. It is a means for anyone, at any time, without esoteric skills or knowledge, to enter "the Kingdom of God."

Ohsawa never tired of repeating that "Food is the basis of life. Without food there is no life. If the food is correct, then the life will be correct."[4] The first and essential steps on the path to health and harmony must concern the choice, preparation and consumption of food.

Health results from the proper balance of Yin and Yang elements in the food and thus in the human being. To secure this balance one should eat those foods which grow naturally and plentifully in one's immediate environment. Nature in its orderliness is providing at man's doorstep those foods which will allow him to live happily and healthily in that particular area. He need merely take what is proffered. In most temperate areas of the world cereal grains are the most abundant food crop and provide a good balance of Yin and Yang factors. Supplemental foods include beans and local vegetables, fruits, seeds and nuts (usually prepared with salt, and on occasion poultry, fish and eggs. Tropical fruits, refined foods such as white sugar and white flour, chemicalized foods, all very Yin, should be avoided. They debilitate, cause illness and make one passive and sentimental. Cow's milk is a food for young calves, not human beings. Its use violates the natural order and makes man dull and insensitive. Red meat, except in very cold climates, is too Yang. It too causes illness. It makes man aggressive and materialistic and in excess, cruel, violent and exploitative. In judging the Yin or Yang quality of foods within an environment one can use the indications of the Yin/Yang chart. A vegetable such as the carrot—red, compacted, dry—is more Yang than spinach—green, expanded, watery.

The choosing of foods in harmony with the natural environment and thus balanced in terms of Yin and Yang is the foundation of good health—physical, mental and spiritual. Improper selection is the first step to disease and misfortune.

Wise preparation is also important. By using Yin factors (such as water or spices), and Yang factors (fire, salt, time) the cook creates a meal suited to those who eat it. Cooking is "the art of life itself," it is putting "the Order of the Universe on the dinner table." Good cooking can restore the balance of Yin and Yang and thus cure any disease. It can nurture health and open the doors of Heaven. Poor cooking, even of well-chosen food, leads to sickness, disorder and unhappiness.

The manner of eating is also important. Food is sacred, a gift of life itself from the universe. To eat, then, is a sacrament. It must be done gratefully and carefully. Each mouthful should be reverently chewed. Thorough mastication is essential to both curing disease and to developing total health.

According to Ohsawa the choice, preparation and manner of eating of food comprise the keys to physical, emotional, and psychological well-being. They lead as well to a spiritual oneness with Infinity. The person balanced and healthy in body and mind will, as a matter of course, become attuned to nature and to the entire universe.

The Way of Eating is just one application of the Order of the Universe however. Every aspect of human life, individual and collective, can and should be organized according to it, Ohsawa says. Most important after food patterns are ways of thinking. One who would achieve his birthright of total health must keep in mind his place at the end of the spiral of creation. He is an infinitesimal point in the immensity of the universe. All the other levels of existence including infinity itself have combined to create him, and moment to moment they sustain and nourish him. He is constantly receiving the marvelous gift of life from every quarter. Thus man must be constantly aware of his smallness, insignificance and weakness. He must be filled with gratitude for everything which he receives—from nature, parents, society and ancestors.

Also, man has come into existence because of his great capacity to take, consume and transmute everything, including food, light, air and water. Ironically, his spiritual development depends on his ability to give away, to divest himself of as much as possible. Thus man must always be on guard against his *musaboru kokoro* [貪る心], his "heart of greed," which leads him into overeating and other types of selfishness. And he must cultivate the trait of generosity. He should be always giving gifts, material ones, but also spiritual ones: love, knowledge of the Order of the Universe, and faith in its justice.

Finally he must realize that everything that happens to him is his own doing. If he is sick or unhappy, he places no blame elsewhere. He makes no excuse, but rather takes full responsibility and endeavors to change himself. Thus humility, gratitude, modest appetite, generosity, and a sense of responsibility are necessary supplements to the Way of Eating. And by developing these traits the individual makes a simple and prudent diet easier to follow.

Ohsawa applied the Unique Principle to other areas of life—to child-rearing, education, male-female relationships, agriculture, economics, social structure and politics. The Unique Principle, the *Law of Yin and Yang*, was for him a "universal compass" which could guide man in all his activities and help him in all his researches.

Thus Ohsawa's "ideology" includes both a philosophy and a practice. As he often said, philosophy without practice is useless. Practice without philosophy is dangerous. In sum, this ideology is a positive and joyous and optimistic one. Explicit within it are a number of simple but powerful assumptions:

- The universe is orderly and predictable, operating according to definite laws.
- The universe and its order are comprehensible to man.
- The human birthright is health, joy and freedom.
- The universe is perfectly just. Man receives what he deserves. There are no accidents, no arbitrary twists of fate.
- Man is thus free to claim his birthright by living according to the Order of the Universe, or to renounce it. (Ohsawa often quoted the Greek philosopher Epictetus who said, "Everyone is happy—if not, it is his own fault.")
- If man does make himself sick or unhappy he can cure himself (of anything) or

extricate himself (from anything) by carefully adhering to the laws of nature. In other words, there is no incurable disease. In fact, the greatest sickness may be a prelude to the greatest health.

- The purpose of human life is enjoyment and amusement. Ohsawa revised the Zen dictum, "He who does not work shall not eat" to "He who does not play shall not eat."[5]
- Ultimately all oppositions and conflicts and dualities in the universe, between man and God, man and nature, good and evil, spirit and matter ultimately can be harmonized. All proceed from the same absolute source and are merely different aspects of the same reality.

Ohsawa repudiates then the philosophies of determinism, fatalism, pessimism and nihilism. Man is free, responsible and in control of his destiny. Health and happiness are within his reach. The universe, of which he is an intrinsic part, is of infinite value.

Ohsawa hoped to make a universal ideology, one that applied to all men everywhere. Yet inevitably his thought was influenced by his cultural background. Even the twelve theorems of the law of change, depending on Yin-Yang terminology and positing an impersonal Absolute, rather than a personal deity, demonstrate this. And in his applications of this universal law, in diet, in morality and mental attitude, in child-rearing practices, in education, and family relationships, Ohsawa's Japanese heritage is evident. The diet he usually recommended, even to Europeans and Americans, was a Japanese one based on brown rice, miso soup, and Japanese vegetables, condiments and cooking methods. The virtues and habits of mind to which he gave priority—gratitude, humility, deference—are clearly out of his Japanese, Confucian-influenced background. His emphasis on strict, spartan and undemonstrative child-rearing practices are peculiar to his samurai heritage. And his understanding of male-female relationships carries the same cultural imprint. While much of the core of Ohsawa's teachings may aspire to universality, much of the periphery must be understood as culturally determined.

The portrait of Ohsawa which emerges is of a complex, even contradictory, human being. He was both maudlin and heartless, loving and cruel, disciplined and self-indulgent, brilliantly insightful and intellectually sloppy. He had a dream of a world culture, yet remained firmly rooted in his own Japanese tradition. Ohsawa was a man who for forty years taught about health with a cigarette in his hand.

Of course, paradox is an inevitable part of any human being, as of any phenomena. What has a front has a back. But the polar oppositions within Ohsawa were extreme and he went back and forth between them with unusual quickness. Michio Kushi recalls, echoing the testimony of many long-time associates of Ohsawa, "He had so many personalities, so many faces. One moment he looked and acted like a gangster, then the next he would look and act like a saint. You never knew what to expect."

In spite (or perhaps because) of this protean character Ohsawa accomplished much during his lifetime. Despite the mixture of strengths and weaknesses, virtues and vices, universal aspiration and cultural limitation, Ohsawa left a substantial legacy:

- He took the ancient philosophy of Yin and Yang and presented it in a clear and explicit manner accessible to modern man.
- He interpreted the Shoku-Yō teachings in terms of this Unique Principle.
- He applied this to other fields—chemistry, biology, physics, history and religion.
- He established a movement in Japan based on this philosophy and practice which, though small, has remained active and vital.
- He brought this to the West and against great obstacles established a movement there which has continued.
- He helped introduce many aspects of traditional Japanese culture to the West including acupuncture, herbal medicine, flower arrangement, and the martial arts.
- He installed devoted students in various parts of the world so that macrobiotics has continued to grow after his death. In effect, Ohsawa, through his thought and activities, created the macrobiotic movement as it exists in the world today.

Everyone, at least within the movement, would agree that Ohsawa's legacy is a valuable and positive one. But in it, as in his personality, there are ambiguous elements. There are teachings still widespread in the movement which are at best of dubious value. Most involve issues in which Ohsawa tried to state as a universal truth what was particular to him or to Japanese culture.

For example, Japan is a rice-eating culture. It is also a culture in which, because of a largely vegetarian tradition, much salt has been used. Ohsawa, as a Japanese of course, preferred rice as a grain. And as a constitutionally weak person he found that large quantities of salt in his diet helped him remain healthy and strong. Thus he recommended a rice diet with plenty of salt as the basic macrobiotic regimen. Even during Ohsawa's lifetime this often proved difficult or dangerous, especially for Western people.

Also, by the time Ohsawa was teaching in Europe and America he was well over sixty years old. He was a bit weary of teaching about food. As is perhaps natural for an older person, he was usually content with a simple diet. So he often recommended Diet Number Seven, grains or even rice only, which was the most simple regimen. Again for many people, especially Westerners, this proved unwise.

Ohsawa enjoyed tobacco. When cigarette smoking was attacked by the medical establishment in America, he conveniently developed a theory to show that it is not only harmless, but actually beneficial. It is no accident perhaps that even today many macrobiotic people, including a good percentage of its leaders, smoke.

Ohsawa's prescriptions for child-rearing also, coming from his own samurai background, are not always applicable to people outside that tradition. Dipping an infant into a cold mountain stream, letting it cry when it is hungry, giving it a minimum of affection and physical contact may have worked for the Japanese warrior class in the pre-modern period, but these practices have to be carefully reviewed today by people in the West.

In his teaching Ohsawa sought to arouse a sense of guilt, shame and ignorance in his students. Again this comes out of a distinctly Japanese milieu. When Ohsawa was a young man it was still common for an office manager to cuff an adult employee on the side of the head when he made a mistake, and to rebuke him sharply and

162

publicly. This too, while appropriate perhaps to Japan does not necessarily work well in the West. People with an adequate supply of guilt already can simply become demoralized and depressed if reminded of their weaknesses. I met one man who had known Ohsawa in the early 1960s. Ohsawa told him that his body was "a mess" and that before he did anything he must cure his kidneys. When I asked this man how it was to be macrobiotic for twenty-five years, he smiled sadly and said "I haven't been able to cure my kidneys yet!"

These are minor, if real, aspects of Ohsawa's legacy. They are insignificant compared to the grand scope of his teaching and activity. They are insignificant even when compared to the legacy Ohsawa left in his own memory.

Ohsawa was a man who lived as he taught others to live. Life is a great drama, he said. We should write and act out as thrilling a scenario as we can manage. And this he did, as a young Bohemian on the Parisian Left Bank, as a crusader trying to deflect Japan from its rendezvous with disaster, as a tortured prisoner in an underground cell, as a courageous missionary setting out on an endless world journey, and as a pitiful mass of sores lying half-dead in an African hut. "Live as a free man!" Ohsawa counseled his students. "Play. Do exactly as you want to do and become loved by all humanity." And play Ohsawa did. He never took a vacation, but he was always on vacation. He was always doing what he wanted, what he considered of greatest importance—the spread of the Unique Principle, the secret of "Open Sesame," the key to the Kingdom of God.

And during his life Ohsawa seems to have entered that same kingdom. To those who met him or knew him well he had the charisma and radiance of a man of enlightenment and peace. Finsterlin recalls that his voice and whole manner reflected the wisdom and justice of the universe. He communicated trust and faith not so much by what he said but by what he was. Kushi remembers him as a man who could swing from branch to branch in the tree of life like a playful child. From the emotional level of judgment he could go quickly and easily to the intellectual and then to the sensory. Ohsawa had achieved the freedom, flexibility and joy of a man who has attained the seventh level of judgment, that of union with the infinite spirit.

---

[1] A copy of the list, as well as the following transcript were both available through the kindness of Ms. Magda van Baelan, a student of Ohsawa who now lives in Toulouse, France.

[2] It comes from Ohsawa's Book, *Uchū no Chitsujo* ("The Order of the Universe") originally published 1941, reprinted Nippon C.I., 1973. Chart appears on inside cover.

[3] Sakurazawa, Y., *Zen Macrobiotics*, Ignoramus Press, The Ohsawa Foundation, 1961, p. 113

[4] Ibid., p. 6

[5] Ibid., p. 111

10

After the Master:
Part One: America

The history of macrobiotics in America begins with the arrival late in 1949 in San Francisco of a young Japanese man on his way to New York City. Michio Kushi was twenty-three years old when, with the encouragement and support of Ohsawa, Norman Cousins, Professor Shigeru Nanbara and Rev. Toyohiko Kagawa, he first came to the United States. Once in New York Kushi enrolled in the graduate school of Columbia University as a student of international law, with the aim of studying world peace and with a rather more vague intent to spread macrobiotics and the teachings of Ohsawa.

Kushi was born in 1926 in the province of Wakayama, the same area from which Ohsawa's ancestors had come. He had grown up in Akita Province on the northwest coast of Japan's main island. His father was a professor of history at the university there. Too young to be drafted, Kushi entered Tokyo University and spent the war years studying politics and law. After the defeat of Japan he became especially interested in the issue of world peace. He heard of the World Federalist movement and, through it, of Ohsawa who at that time was running his Maison Ignoramus ("World Government Center") in Hiyoshi near Tokyo.

One evening in 1948 Kushi went to visit the M.I. As he arrived at the main entrance he took off his shoes, according to Japanese practice, before stepping onto the straw mats of the house interior. He placed his shoes neatly together, and noticing then that the other shoes were in disarray, he carefully lined them up in pairs. From the main room of the small house Ohsawa saw him doing this, and was impressed by the young man's fastidiousness. He ordered all his students out of the room and invited the newcomer in. They talked alone together for a while and Ohsawa, learning of Kushi's interest in world peace, posed a question. "Have you ever thought of the application of dialectical monism to diet, and its importance for world peace?" Kushi was dumbfounded. He did not understand the question, let alone have an answer.

Soon it was time for dinner, and the other students returned. Everyone was served the usual repast of miso soup, brown rice and takuan, or pickled radish. Even though rationing of food was still in effect, Kushi was not particularly impressed by the meal. When one of the M.I. students asked him, "It's delicious, isn't it?" he replied with unfaltering Japanese politeness. "Oh yes, it is very good." Kushi was likewise disappointed and mystified by the lecture which followed. He had expected a talk on international law and on peace through world government. Instead he heard what seemed a mish-mash of antiquated Yin-Yang thinking, with some nutritional theory thrown in. He left with no intention of returning.

A few weeks later Kushi received an invitation to pay another visit. Since there was not enough time to refuse by mail, and he had no access to a telephone, Kushi went in person to give his regrets. This time, however, something about the place, the "Sensei" and the other people, attracted him. Kushi began attending Ohsawa's lectures as a commuting student. He soon became a favorite of the strict and demanding Ohsawa. When Cousins visited in the summer of 1949 and there was an opportunity to go to the United States, Ohsawa encouraged this new star pupil to become the first missionary of the Unifying Principle and macrobiotics to the West. Kushi, in Ohsawa's eyes, had already completed the course. Shortly thereafter the young man set sail for San Francisco.

Kushi spent two years at Columbia, focusing on the issue of world peace. He recalls that he collected over sixty plans and propositions for utopian communities and for world governments, and carefully copied them over. Then he took them all down into a basement room in the University library to study carefully. The more he studied and read, the more he saw the simple wisdom of Ohsawa's teaching of biological revolution. Without a basic change in the biological and psychological makeup of humanity through a change in diet, there would be no lasting peace, he decided. It was to be some years, however, before Kushi would begin to teach actively.

During his first years in New York Kushi often wrote back to Ohsawa at the M.I. about his experiences in America. Ohsawa read these letters aloud at lectures, sharing them with his students. One of the young women there at the time was Tomoko Yokoyama [横山偕子]. She was very impressed by the elegant style and elevated tone of Kushi's letters. She resolved also to go to America to help with the work there for macrobiotics and for world government.

Miss Yokoyama was a native of Shimane province, and grew up in a small mountain village in that western part of Japan. Her family was Christian and she was brought up well-versed in the Old and New Testaments. An energetic and adventuresome soul, she was the tomboy of the village. She was the first there to ride a bicycle, and later became an accomplished gymnast. She attended college and became a teacher in a rural village school. She learned of Ohsawa through his writing and was struck especially by what he said about Christianity and food. She wrote him a letter of introduction and soon thereafter, giving up her job, arrived at Hiyoshi. She stayed almost two years, earning a reputation as the best salesperson of Ohsawa's newspaper, *Sekai Seifu*. She also earned the nickname of "Masakari" or "The Axe." One day Ohsawa was wrapping some books in a package and needed a knife to cut the string he was using. Tomoko was passing by and he asked her to bring something to cut the string. In a hurry at the time, she picked up the first available tool, which happened to be a small axe used for cutting firewood. After scolding her, Ohsawa christened Tomoko "Masakari," deeming it matched her fiercely determined and undemonstrative nature.

In 1951 "Masakari," also given the more gentle name of "Aveline," managed to get a ticket for passage to the United States. After visits to San Francisco and New York, she lived in Chicago for several months as a housemaid. Through this period she was poor enough, and devoted enough to her macrobiotic principles, that she lived mostly on Quaker Oats soaked in water or eaten dry. She then returned to New

York to settle. Kushi met her at the bus station and offered her, as a person sharing the same teacher and the same dream, the hospitality of his apartment. Soon the two were living as man and wife and began raising a family.

Late in 1952 Kushi, still active in the World Federalist movement, went to Europe for four months. He stayed first in London for two months, trying to contact and work with supporters of world government such as British M.P. Henry Osborne. After Aveline joined him he went to Paris for two months, and worked there with other students of Ohsawa, Augustine Kawano and Yasuyuki Ishii [石井保行] (Gavan). When the Kushis returned to New York they found there, newly arrived, another M.I. alumnus, Nobuo Aihara [相原信雄] (Herman). Aihara had first met Ohsawa in 1940. A student at Waseda University in Tokyo majoring in metallurgy, he had seen an advertisement for a seminar on "A Concept of World." It was hosted by Ohsawa but included various leading academics and intellectuals. Aihara attended and was most impressed by the man who spoke of Yin and Yang as an all-embracing philosophy that was applicable in everyday life.

Aihara tried to follow the Shoku-Yō diet while living at home. His family was unsympathetic, though, and cooking and eating by himself he used too much oil and salt. He became sick. His first marriage ended tragically a few years later with the suicide of his wife who was unable to tolerate the strict hierarchy of the family household. "My life was a mess," he remembers, "and I went to Ohsawa's school to find my direction. I was the worst student. I didn't do anything, no work. I just ate and slept and listened to Ohsawa's lectures. That is what always attracted me most—the philosophy—the broad thinking of macrobiotics."

The intelligent and unassuming Aihara regained his strength. Anxious to be out on his own, he left the M.I. and in 1952 headed for the United States. He had only a tourist visa and small amount of money. His immediate interest was to study the manufacture of helicopters. He went to New York and tried to get a job with an aviation company there but his English was still too poor to get the position.

Kushi and Aihara decided to go into business together. They established first the R.H. Brothers (Resurrection of Humanity by Brothers) Trading Company to do importing and exporting with Japan. They hoped that this business would help them obtain visas for permanent residence. The company was not a success. Kushi and Aihara ordered four thousand woodblock prints from Japan, but the delivery was delayed by a dockworker's strike. Meanwhile, a competitor in Chicago had flooded the gift-shop market with similar imported prints. Their supply sat in piles in Kushi's apartment and finally the two had to sell them from shop to shop in New York. Also, they began to collect used nylon stockings for shipment to Japan. New ones were still unavailable there, and there was a great demand for old, but sound pairs. Kushi collected these in his midtown office and spent several months holding each pair of nylons up to a light, checking for runs and determining if they were worth sending.

In 1955 Herman invited a young woman at the M.I. named Chiiko Yokota [横田ちい子] (Cornellia) to come to New York. They had never met, had only corresponded while Herman was in the States. Cornellia arrived in October, 1955 and the two were married a few months later in a ceremony prepared and officiated by Kushi.

Next Kushi and Aihara established a Japanese gift shop called "Azuma," along with another student of Ohsawa, Noboru Satō [佐藤登] (Roman). This venture was successful. Kushi then cooperated with another partner in a similar shop called "Ginza." He also represented a Japanese textile firm and later became vice-president of Takashimaya, New York. Takashimaya is one of the oldest and largest department store chains in Japan, with origins in the Tokugawa Period (18th century). Kushi was put in charge of setting up a branch on Fifth Avenue near the New York Public Library.

In the summer of 1953, Aihara went to California. A supporter of world government and macrobiotics, George Hicks, had offered to reactivate a defunct tungsten mine to raise money for the movement. Aihara, with his background in metallurgy, went to help run the mine. However, union opposition made the project impractical. Aihara moved to Los Angeles and there received the first of the many deportation notices that were to haunt him for the next years.

By late 1959 Aihara was back in New York City, when Ohsawa made his initial visit. He arranged the three ten-day lecture series which Ohsawa gave in the first months of 1960 and made a first mimeographed edition of *Zen Macrobiotics* to distribute at the meetings. Then, because of continuing pressure from the Immigration Service, he went to Europe with Cornellia and his two small children. Aihara returned to New York early in 1961 to discover that he had been elected president of the newly formed "Ohsawa Foundation." Accepting it with characteristic humility, Aihara worked to organize the small but growing macrobiotic community in New York City.

In the spring of 1961 the confrontation between the U.S. and the U.S.S.R. over the Berlin wall occurred. When a group formed and, following Ohsawa's advice to find a fall-out free haven, went to California, Aihara was one of its leaders. With his family, he was in the automobile caravan as it drove across the country. The group averaged three hundred miles a day and stopped each night to camp and to dine on rice and miso soup cooked over kerosene stoves. And Aihara was one of the leaders when the group, once settled in their new home, decided to form a food company, Chico-San.

With the Aiharas' departure from New York and resettlement with their fellow "pioneers" in Chico, a second focus of macrobiotic activity in America was created. Until then New York, where both the Kushis and Aiharas lived, and where Ohsawa and Lima came to visit, was the sole center. For the next several years Chico and New York were the twin poles of the movement. When Ohsawa came to America he visited both, and gave lectures and summer camps on the West Coast as well as in the New York area.

In New York, meanwhile, another M.I. student, Alcan Yamaguchi, had arrived from Japan. Yamaguchi, after meeting Ohsawa in 1943, had soon been drafted into the Army and sent to Manchuria. At the war's end he was taken prisoner by the Russians and like thousands of other Japanese soldiers spent the next several years in a Soviet labor camp under very harsh conditions. He contracted tuberculosis and, already a slight and not very robust man, returned home in a much weakened condition. Hungry for truth and a spiritual path, he entered a Zen monastery for a time. Then he went to Ohsawa's school, drawn by both the comprehensive philosophy of Yin and Yang and by the dream of world peace which lay at the heart of Ohsawa's activities. As one of the better educated and more literate students at the M.I., Yamaguchi was active in the writing and editing of *Sekai Seifu*. Yamaguchi came to know one of the head cooks at the school, a tall, forceful girl named Darbin, who was to become his wife.

After Ohsawa's departure for India in 1953, Yamaguchi remained active in the movement in Japan until Ohsawa summoned him to New York in 1960. Soon after arriving, Yamaguchi established, with the help of Kushi and Aihara, a tiny restaurant (there were only about ten seats) in Greenwich Village called "Musubi." It was America's first public macrobiotic eating place. Another restaurant, on West 46th Street, was attempted before Yamaguchi returned to his wife and family in Japan in 1963.

About the same time, the macrobiotic movement in New York was strengthened by the arrival of Michel Abehsera, a French Moroccan Jew who had met Ohsawa in Paris. Abehsera, sophisticated and flamboyant, established with his brothers a successful macrobiotic restaurant in the city. The Abehsera brothers created a delicate and international style of macrobiotic cooking which Michel made available in cookbooks such as *Cooking For Life*, published in 1967.[1]

Activities were also stimulated by the involvement of New York journalist and writer, William Dufty. A veteran writer for the New York Post, and the author of the celebrated biography of jazz singer Billie Holliday, *Lady Sings the Blues*, he had met Ohsawa in Paris in August 1964. After having experienced a tremendous change, physically and mentally, through the diet (he lost 60 pounds and "about ten years of age" in two months), Dufty agreed to do an English version of *Zen Macrobiotics* that could be presented to the general public. The result was *You Are All Sanpaku*, published in 1965.[2] As early as 1963 Ohsawa had become fairly well known in New York through feature articles by Tom Wolfe in the New York Herald Tribune. His prediction of problems for President Kennedy (because of the upward turning "sanpaku" or "three-whites" condition of his eyes), followed of course by the Dallas assassination, received considerable notice. But Wolfe's articles and an all-night interview on WOR Radio's Long John Silver show focused on Ohsawa as some kind of Oriental "medicine man." Only with Dufty's book were Ohsawa and his teachings presented to the public in a clear, non-sensational manner.

Late in 1965 though, the FDA raid closed down the Ohsawa Foundation. A year later Ohsawa died. These two shocks ended most macrobiotic activity in the city. For several years, until Abehsera moved to Binghamton, N.Y., he continued teaching on a modest scale. And from the late '60s Shizuko Yamamoto [山本しず子], a shiatsu massage therapist, gave cooking classes in her apartment on a sporadic basis. But otherwise the New York macrobiotic community was moribund. Only in November, 1984 did a new, permanent macrobiotic center finally reestablish itself.

Meanwhile, Kushi was increasingly dissatisfied with New York, both as a place to raise a family and as a place to teach macrobiotics. In 1964 Aveline and the children went to live in Gay Head on Martha's Vineyard. Kushi remained in New York. The following year he chose Boston, the intellectual capital of America, as a place to settle and teach. Kushi, Aveline, and their then four children moved into a rented house on a side street north of Harvard Square in Cambridge. From that time Boston became the new focus of activities on the East Coast. Ohsawa visited in 1965, classes were held and a small group began to form. Kushi, no longer with Takashimaya, or otherwise employed, began teaching, and giving lectures and massages. To meet the growing need for macrobiotic foods, Aveline Kushi started ordering rice, miso, and other staples in bulk and selling them to friends and lecture guests out of her front hall closet.

In 1965 the Kushis rented a large house in Wellesley, an affluent suburb west of Boston. They planned to set up an "East West Foundation" where macrobiotics and various Japanese traditional arts would be taught. Very quickly, though, opposition from conservative neighbors forced them to move again, this time to Brookline. Despite the setback, the macrobiotic group continued to grow. A tiny basement storefront on Newbury Street in Boston was rented as a retail food outlet. Aveline, the prime mover of the project, thought of using the name of Samuel Butler's utopia. With twenty-three-year-old former actor Evan Root as manager, the Erewhon Trading Company was founded.

Although it had escaped the fate of the Ohsawa Foundation the Kushi operation struggled during those first years in Boston. The bad publicity which resulted from the Simon case continued to hang over the name of "macrobiotics." National media attention had labeled it as the "killer diet" which caused extreme malnutrition and various deficiency diseases. One of its leading opponents was right in the Kushis' backyard. At the Harvard Medical School, Dr. Frederick Stare, head of the Department of Nutrition, spoke and wrote widely about the macrobiotic diet as a serious public health hazard. Nevertheless, because of the determination of the Kushis and the support of their small group of friends, Boston became a stable center of macrobiotic activity. From 1966 it, rather than New York, was the focus of the movement on the East Coast. And from this time, the history of macrobiotics in America is really two stories. One concerns macrobiotics on the West Coast as it developed under the influence of the Aiharas and their associates. One concerns the Boston-based movement which grew and spread under the leadership of Michio and Aveline Kushi. While sharing the same philosophy, practice and general aims, these two streams, influenced by geography, culture and personality, followed somewhat different courses.

While the East Coast branch of the family was having its ups and downs, the Chico community was having its own struggles. The first task was to survive economically in a strange city. Chico-San soon had stocks of native brown rice, wheat, beans, and of miso, soy sauce, sea vegetables and other foods from Japan. A bakery was opened, turning out the famous and now happily extinct unleavened macrobiotic "doorstop" bread. This was sold on consignment at local stores. But there was little demand for it or for the other exotica. The good burghers of the Sacramento Valley scarcely knew what the foods were, let alone had any inclination to buy or eat them. The "pioneers" found their best customers to be themselves. Many had to take outside jobs in order to support themselves. Herman, for example, worked as a fruit picker in the local orchards

Nevertheless, an Ohsawa Foundation was formed and became particularly active in publishing. A monthly magazine called *Yin Yang* was founded. A new edition of

Zen Macrobiotics was prepared. An English version of *La Philosophie de la Medicine d'Extréme Orient* was published as *The Book of Judgment.* The "Shoku-Yō Human Life Reader" published in Japanese in 1938 appeared as *The Macrobiotic Guidebook for Living.* Aihara was instrumental in these projects but got help from many others, including Shane and Lou Oles and Belgium-born Jacques de Langre. In 1964 *Zen Cookery* was compiled by Cornellia and other women in Chico and became the first macrobiotic cookbook published in English. It presented the very salty cuisine favored by Ohsawa, and by the second edition in 1966 an insert warned that the salt recommended in its recipes should be cut in half. The first West Coast summer camp was held in 1962 and became an annual tradition.

In 1964 Aihara suggested to his partners at the Chico factory that they import a rice cake machine from Japan. The *senbei* [煎餅] (rice cake), a flat, round wafer of puffed rice about three inches across, is a favorite Japanese snack food. In New York, at the second "Musubi" restaurant, rice cakes were being made and were well-liked. Aihara felt that these, containing only rice and salt, might be popular in the macrobiotic and in the broader "health food" market in America. A machine was shipped to America by George Ohsawa. Soon the rice cakes (which to their detractors have the texture and romance of styrofoam) were being produced by a hand-operated press. Chico-San partner and eventual president Bob Kennedy automated and refined the machine. Soon several descendants of the original were turning out rice cakes for a growing market. Also in 1964 Junsei Yamazaki [山崎順成], a Japanese macrobiotic farmer, settled in Chico. He had come to the U.S. in 1963 and had first gone to New York. He had experimented with miso production there, setting up kegs in the basement of the Diamond Jim building on 46th Street under Yamaguchi and Kushi's "Genpei" restaurant. Moving to Chico, Yamazaki started making miso on a large scale to be marketed by the company. By 1967, with native miso and rice cakes, the company at last had a stable financial basis.

Acceptance of the diet by the general public was slow, however. For most Californians the food and the ambience were perhaps too exotic, spartan and Japanese. In one group though, macrobiotic thinking and practice, in some form at least, was widely adopted. In 1965–66, and then especially in the following year, the "hippie" subculture developed, centered in the Haight-Ashbury district of San Francisco. Composed of the young and disaffected it rejected the values and lifestyle of bourgeois America. It embraced various vague anarchies and forms of mysticism, including that provided by hallucinogenic drugs. Marijuana, long available in the American subculture, and the newer, more powerful agents like LSD-25 and mescaline, were staples of daily life. By word of mouth and by the widespread distribution of the yellow paperback version of *Zen Macrobiotics*, the diet and something of its philosophy were introduced into the Hippie movement. By the summer of 1967 when the public media and the midwestern runaways arrived in force, brown rice, miso soup and sea vegetables had become the basis of the typical Hippie larder. These foods could be bought readily, for example at Fred Rohe's "New Age Foods," one of the first of a new breed of natural foods stores. Several macrobiotic restaurants opened, and when "street kitchens" were set up to feed the homeless young people, it was usually with a macrobiotic style meal.

There were several reasons for this attraction to macrobiotics. For one thing it was exotic, distinctly non-American. On the culinary level it was a clear rejection of Middle America and the diet of meat, potatoes and ice cream which nourished it. And if the Hippies were doing anything, they were rejecting Middle America. Besides, it was Oriental, and thanks to Ohsawa's well-intended ploy, associated with Zen Buddhism. Ever since the alcoholic mysticism of the 1950s Beatniks, Zen had a special appeal for America's alternate culture. Then, as presented in *Zen Macrobiotics*, the diet promised a quick fix—perfect physical and mental health, plus some species of enlightenment—in the ten days of the Diet Seven rice cure. To a generation raised on TV dinners and fast food this was quite appealing. And it was cheap. Brown rice, beans and twig tea were and remain relatively inexpensive food staples. And in a subculture where much of the ready cash came from handouts or welfare, and much of it went for drugs, economy was an advantage.

Despite the appeal of the diet there was little deep understanding of it or the philosophy behind it. Many, probably most, combined a brown rice-based diet with the free use of drugs. They did not realize that from a macrobiotic perspective, hallucinogens and other chemical agents at the extreme Yin end of the spectrum are very unbalanced and dangerous. They weaken the internal organs and the entire nervous system. Vitality, especially sexual vitality, as well as motor coordination, memory and mental acuity are all impaired by their use.

Meanwhile, the Aiharas had moved to Carmichael, near Sacramento. In 1966, Lou Oles, who with his wife Shane had managed the revived Ohsawa Foundation, died, and Shane asked Herman to assist her. Herman began to travel to Los Angeles once a month to give lectures at the Foundation headquarters. He was also instrumental in the publishing of Ohsawa's books, which were selling well on the East Coast as well as the West. By 1969, however, dissension had developed over the role of Shane's new husband in the organization. Herman resigned. In 1970 the Ohsawa Foundation dissolved. Aihara, who had moved to San Francisco, established the George Ohsawa Macrobiotic Foundation as a new educational and publishing organization.

In Boston activities were on a modest level. After Ohsawa's death in April of 1966 the Kushis were in a state of deep reflection for several months. Kushi began giving lectures each Monday and Wednesday evening in a back room of the Arlington Street Church in Boston. These talks were supplemented by cooking classes with Aveline in Brookline. Between five and fifteen people usually gathered for Kushi's talks. Most of them were under thirty and many were regular attenders. Erewhon limped along on about $300 per week in retail sales. Root's main compensation was room and board at the Kushis'. Another student and boarder, Jim Ledbetter, recorded and transcribed some of Kushi's talks and published them in mimeographed form as the first issue of *The Order of the Universe* magazine. The whole macrobiotic community in Boston at the time did not exceed 100 people.

Then in the summer of 1967, almost as an East Coast counterpoint to San Francisco's "Summer of Love," the tempo of activity increased markedly. Scores of young people began to arrive from around the country, many of them directly from Haight-Ashbury. They were anxious to study and practice macrobiotics seriously, and had heard that Boston was its center and Kushi its main teacher. Attendance at the church lectures doubled, then tripled and continued to grow. They were moved out of the back room with its central wooden table surrounded by wooden chairs to a large lecture room with rows of folding metal chairs. The Kushi house began to overflow with family plus live-in students, and a large ex-boarding house on nearby University Road was rented. It was the first Boston "study house." Kushi began to give special lectures there for its residents, including talks "only for women." Business at Erewhon grew rapidly. Root turned its management over to others and with the Kushis looked for a restaurant site. One was found nearby on Newbury Street and early in 1968 *Sanae* [早苗] ("young rice plant") was opened as the first macrobiotic restaurant in Boston.

The next years were a kind of heyday for macrobiotics in Boston. A large, tightly knit community developed, creating and supporting a wide variety of activities. The network of study houses grew so that there were usually 100–150 people living in "study" situations directly or indirectly controlled by the Kushis. Erewhon moved to new quarters on the other side of Newbury Street. Under the astute and far-sighted direction of Californians Paul Hawken and Bill Tara it became a pioneer and trend setter in the whole natural foods industry. Food production and distribution were started in a large warehouse on Farnsworth Street in South Boston, and new retail outlets were opened. At some point, most all those who came to Boston to study macrobiotics earned their living at the company. In 1969 Tao Books moved into the former Erewhon storefront and began to sell and distribute macrobiotic literature. The Order of the Universe Publications continued to publish monthly reports on Kushi's teachings. In 1970 former New York journalist Ron Dobrin started the *East West Journal* as a monthly magazine for the general public. The following year a second restaurant, large and relatively elegant ("Sanae 2," eventually "The Seventh Inn") was opened just off the Boston Public Gardens. Also in 1972, the East West Foundation was organized as a non-profit educational organization to promote macrobiotic teachings. A permanent center was established in spacious and bright quarters in downtown Boston. Kushi continued to lecture regularly there to a large and stable audience. Meanwhile Aveline was teaching cooking, training young women who in turn became cooking teachers. Deeply interested in *Noh* [能] drama, the traditional dance theater of Japan, Aveline set up a Noh study center at the East West headquarters. The master of the Kita Noh school in Tokyo visited periodically, and Aveline and a number of students in the macrobiotic community studied with him.

There were, to be sure, difficulties as well. Tao Books went bankrupt in the mid-1970s and the Seventh Inn, while busy, was hobbled with a $2,000 a month basic rental expense and never really thrived. Erewhon Farms, a macrobiotic rural community near Keene, New Hampshire, struggled for several years and then dispersed. Some of these problems were due to the fact that those running the various businesses and organizations were young and inexperienced, if dedicated, amateurs. There was a somewhat naive faith that if one ate properly, lack of formal training and expertise would be outweighed by good sense and good intuition. This often did work out. Sometimes it did not. There were also some tensions as Erewhon became a large company operating in the broader marketplace. When the retail stores in Boston began to sell potatoes, tomatoes, dairy foods, honey and other items not strictly "macrobiotic" there was a heated controversy within the community. Some argued that Erewhon was compromising its values for business reasons. Others said that the company should meet the needs of a broad spectrum of customers but with the highest quality products. The latter group won the day. Despite these difficulties and tensions, it was a time of growth and accomplishment, and of optimism about the future.

Thus by the mid-1970s there was a stable and substantial macrobiotic community in Boston, with flourishing businesses and with thriving educational activities. Several factors were crucial in this development. Chief among them, perhaps, was the work of the Kushis. Throughout these years both Michio and Aveline worked with energy and dedication to promote macrobiotics. Each, functioning in a distinct sphere, was crucial in the birth and growth of the community.

Kushi emerged as a forceful and original interpreter of macrobiotics. Despite a lack of real fluency in English he presented the basic themes of Yin and Yang, the spiral of materialization, and the "Way of Eating" in a clear and convincing manner. Yet he made some important changes and additions. For one thing, he greatly liberalized the diet. Under Ohsawa the emphasis had been on Diet Number Seven observed for ten days, followed by a less strict regime, but one still based on rice, much salt and a minimum of liquid. It became clear to Kushi, particularly after his many contacts with alumni of the American drug scene, that a less spartan form of the diet was better suited to most Americans. Many young people who had taken drugs proved too weak physically to thrive on such a simple diet. At the same time they were drawn for psychological reasons to very strict and rigid patterns. It became clear too that even healthy people had a hard time thriving on such a regimen. Thus Kushi began to recommend a transitional period during which meat, dairy products and raw fruits were reduced in a gradual way that would allow the body to adjust slowly. And for the long term he began to advise what he called the "Standard Diet." In terms of percentages of different types of foods, this regime is an average of the various "levels" of the diet which Ohsawa taught. It consists roughly of fifty percent grains, ten percent soup, five to ten percent beans, twenty to thirty percent cooked vegetables, plus occasional fish and seafood, seeds and nuts, salad and fruits. He advised a drastic reduction in the amount of salt taken. In general, Kushi urged a flexible and free approach, counseling people to eat and drink more in accordance with their natural intuition than according to rigid rules. Under this influence the diet became more attractive and practical for a wide range of people. It even acquired a hedonistic aspect as the grand tradition of "the Boston dessert" was born and developed. Interest in creating natural "sweets and goodies" added such delights as apricot-tofu custard and carob-carrot cake to macrobiotic cuisine. On the West Coast at the same time, Herman and Cornellia and others were also broadening the diet and adapting it to the needs of Americans.

Also, Kushi greatly increased the body of macrobiotic thought. With insight and imagination he systematized and explained in detail topics over which Ohsawa had passed lightly. These subjects included macrobiotic medicine, diagnosis and physiognomy, the "five-energy transformations" theory of Chinese traditional thought, agriculture and the particulars of world government. Also, he dealt with many areas which had previously not been an explicit concern of macrobiotics: history of the cosmos, human prehistory, astronomy, UFOs, human auras, the structure of the spiritual world, meditation, and spiritual practice. This expansion of macrobiotic thought by Kushi is so extensive and has had such a marked impact on the movement as a whole that it will be treated at length in Chapter 13.

Kushi functioned not only as teacher and philosopher for the burgeoning macrobiotic community in Boston. He was also counselor, friend and father figure to the scores of young people who arrived from around the country and from other parts of the world. With a high and broad brow above dark owl-eye glasses, a perennial black three-piece suit, and a cigarette poised toward the heavens, Kushi was an impressive and mysterious figure. Yet he was also an approachable one, friendly, patient and even-tempered. Always willing to listen to any problem or question, general or personal, he was usually ready with some good, plausible advice. Unlike Ohsawa, Kushi seldom criticized his students, let alone berate or embarrass them in public or in private. His most frequent rejoinder to a suggestion, idea or answer was "Ah yes, very good!" or "Ah so, that's great." Kushi was quite aware of this characteristic and its importance. In a lecture once he observed, "Mr. Ohsawa's approach to teaching was very Yang, mine is very Yin. If I were like Mr. Ohsawa I would be sitting here tonight all by myself. Americans need a little gentler method." Yet this was a natural rather than a consciously chosen inclination. Even as a young man Kushi apparently was almost uncannily patient and unflappable. During the first part of his stay in America Kushi received a particularly abusive letter from Ohsawa. He lost his temper, tore up the letter and wrote Ohsawa an angry reply. Ohsawa returned: "I am so happy to learn that even you too can become angry." The letter had been a test! Those who worked and studied with Kushi in Boston had to learn to deal with various, often disconcerting traits. He preferred to work late into the night and to rise late in the morning. He tended to be late for appointments or to forget them entirely. His business decisions were often inscrutable as well as ill-fated. But his patience and kindness were unfailing.

Kushi pursued these roles of teacher, guide and confidante with utter dedication. Like Ohsawa, he committed his time and energy totally to his mission. He pursued and seemed to thrive on a demanding schedule of lectures, meetings and consultations. Almost a classic case study of the "workaholic," he took no days off and, while lavishing time and energy on his students and their projects, had little time for his own children. He took no vacations. Once several students impelled Kushi to drive with them to the coast of Maine. When they pulled up to a rocky beach, Kushi remained in the car smoking a cigarette while the others gambolled by the water. "So this is a vacation?" he observed quizzically when they returned. Kushi's chief recreation seemed to be regular forays to the local coffee shop.

Through these activities and qualities, Kushi attracted literally hundreds of people to Boston, earned their respect and loyalty, and inspired them to study macrobiotics and to work for it. Meanwhile Aveline, diminutive and retiring, was the hidden dynamo behind much of what went on in Boston. With a clear vision of the future, she was the source for many of the ideas for new projects and enterprises. Possessing a relentless determination, she was the guiding force behind the realization of these same ideas. In a pattern typical of Japanese marriages, she managed the financial and mundane side of things, leaving Michio to deal with cosmology, world peace and other ethereal issues. At the same time she was teacher and role model to scores of young American women, many of whom became teachers in their own right.

The other key factor in the development of Boston as a macrobiotic center, of course, were the people who came and studied and worked. They were a heterogenous group, coming from a variety of religious, ethnic and social backgrounds. The majority though were white, and from the middle and upper-middle class. A sizable proportion were Jewish. All shared some degree of disillusionment with life in Middle America. Each found in Boston something for which they were looking: a charismatic teacher, a reasonable and healthful diet, an integrated lifestyle, a supportive community, a new philosophy and view of life, a promise of spiritual development. Idealistic and inspired, they studied and practiced macrobiotics and they worked long and hard, often with little pay, for the Kushi enterprises. Some stayed only a few months. Some married and settled in Boston. Some lost their idealism. Some retained it. All, however, through their work and their commitment to the movement contributed to the development of the Boston community.

Once the community was established firmly in Boston (by the mid-1970s) its attention turned to wider horizons. The same factors for growth were there: Michio as an inspiring teacher; Aveline as a pragmatic mover; and a large group of dedicated associates, more mature if perhaps less starry-eyed than before. In the late '70s the Boston-based group became a focus of national and international macrobiotic activity.

In part this was done by making Boston into a major ongoing educational center. In 1975 the first residential summer program was held at Amherst College. Organized by the East West Foundation and featuring the Kushis as teachers, the camp attracted people from around the country and from Europe as well. It expanded steadily so that by 1980 over five hundred people gathered on the picturesque college campus. The focus of study and practice was macrobiotics, but there were also classes in Yoga, meditation, and various Japanese traditional arts. These week-long intensives gave those unable to spend a long period in Boston the opportunity to absorb much in a short time.

In 1977 the Kushi Institute was established in Brookline. The Kushis rented and renovated large quarters in a substantial brick building to house this ongoing school for macrobiotics. A three-level program was set up, with coordinated courses in "The Order of the Universe," macrobiotic cooking, medical diagnosis and treatment, and shiatsu massage. The first class of Level I students included about twenty-five individuals, many of them from Europe and South America. Most of the day-to-day administration and teaching was done by "senior friends," long-time American and European students of macrobiotics, with Michio and Aveline handling several major sessions each term. After going through growing pains and various adjustments, the Institute stabilized as a self-supporting institution with about 100 students a term enrolled in its full- and part-time programs. In 1981 it began a program of teacher certification. Institute graduates who wish to have official status as teachers and counselors in macrobiotics take written and practical examinations and then appear before a review board.

Also, educational and other activities began to radiate from Boston. In the early '70s Kushi had made lecture tours around the country, visiting New York, Philadelphia, Chicago, Los Angeles and other places. In the late '70s young men and women, trained in Boston, began to establish full-time centers in various cities. A number of "East West Centers" were set up, often in conjunction with a food store and food production facilities. Guest meals, lectures, cooking classes, medical consultations and massage services were some of the common elements in these centers. In the early stages of operation the Kushis might have visited for a weekend seminar to encourage activity, but otherwise the teaching and direction were in the hands of the founders and their supporters. Still, there were strong formal and informal ties to Boston. Local people often went to Boston to deepen their study and experience of macrobiotics. And most centers had representatives at the annual North American Macrobiotic Congress held each year in Boston. Often, simultaneously, a special Teacher's Seminar would be held by Kushi to update the studies of the teachers in the local centers. The result is a Boston-centered network of macrobiotic centers throughout North America.

Also, from 1975 the Kushis began to look abroad. In that year Michio made his first lecture trip to Europe. His seminar "The Principles and Practice of Oriental Medicine" held at the Tara Hotel in London was attended by about 500 people. In the following years he made several trips each year, helping to stimulate macrobiotic interest and activity in most of the countries of Europe including Belgium, the Netherlands, Germany, Italy, France, Portugal and Spain. Usually accompanied by Aveline, he taught philosophy and medicine while she taught cooking. The Kushis also visited Central and South America, Japan and Hong Kong. Through their efforts there was a strong upsurge of macrobiotic activity in most of these areas. Many people came to Boston to study and then returned home to teach. "East West Centers" were established in a variety of countries. While independent, these looked to Kushi and to Boston for guidance and support. The development in the various nations will be discussed in Chapter 12. Suffice it to say here that Boston became the focus of international macrobiotic activity.

While macrobiotics was spreading geographically from Boston, it was also spreading socially. That is, it was gaining a wider respectability and was being adopted by many older people and by others not associated with the youthful "counterculture." Several factors helped this process. One was the increasing acceptance by the medical community of the macrobiotic diet as nutritionally safe, and even as effective against illness. From early in his teaching career Kushi took every opportunity to present the case for macrobiotics to doctors and health professionals. He met often with individual physicians and appeared frequently before medical groups. These efforts began to bear fruit as early as 1972 when Dr. Frank Sachs and Dr. Edward Kass of Harvard Medical School did a study of the effect of macrobiotic eating on blood cholesterol levels. They found that a sampling of macrobiotic people in Boston had optimally low cholesterol levels and thus hypothetically would be less prone to heart disease. Still, progress was slow. By the mid-'70s, though, there was a small but committed group of physicians who practiced and supported macrobiotics. This group included Drs. Mark Hegsted, Keith Block, Robert Mendelsohn and Christiane Northrup. Even Dr. Stare, the movement's one-time nemesis, was enough convinced by Kushi's broad presentation of the diet to allow that macrobiotics could be a sound nutritional regime. The image of macrobiotics as the "killer diet" gradually disap-

176

peared from the medical community and thus largely from the popular press.

Another factor in the spread of macrobiotics in general society was the emphasis Kushi placed on the diet as a therapy as well as a prevention for serious diseases including heart disease and cancer. Over the past decade Kushi has devoted a good proportion of his time to personally giving dietary counsel to people with cancer and other serious maladies. He has accumulated many case histories of apparently miraculous cures and has helped publicize them. Meanwhile, in the various East West Centers around the country similar activities have been going on. Literally hundreds, even thousands, of individuals (and often their families as well) have gotten involved in macrobiotics because of a life-threatening disease. These people come from every social class, every racial and religious group. With each successful case, particularly with a well-publicized one, macrobiotics becomes more a part of the mainstream of American life. In 1976 Dr. Jean Kohler, a professor of music from Indiana managed to control his pancreatic cancer. Out of gratitude he wrote *Healing Miracles Through Macrobiotics*, a book published in 1977 which helped introduce macrobiotics to many typical Americans.[3]

Curiously, perhaps the single strongest impetus for the recognition of the diet as an effective therapy has been the personal testimony of a Philadelphia physician. In 1977, Dr. Anthony Sattilaro was driving home from the funeral of his father who had died of cancer. He himself had just been diagnosed as having cancer of the lymphatic system and was given no hope of surviving. Satillaro picked up two young men hitchhiking on the road. In the ensuing conversation, one of them, a cook at the Seventh Inn in Boston, blithely suggested that the doctor's cancer was no cause for concern, that it could be treated with a macrobiotic diet. Satillaro, Chief Administrator of the Methodist Hospital in Philadelphia, decided he had nothing to lose. He contacted Kushi and went to Boston for a consultation. Under the guidance of Philadelphia macrobiotic counselor Denny Waxman, he began a strict therapeutic form of the diet. At the same time, Sattilaro carefully monitored his condition through the medical facilities at the hospital. After a year all signs of the cancer had disappeared. Satillaro soon became a highly visible figure in the macrobiotic movement. He was featured at a conference on diet and cancer held at the Amherst camp in 1979 and toured through Europe with the Kushis later that year. In March 1980 and then again in March 1981 the *East West Journal* featured articles about his dramatic recovery. There were pieces in the *Reader's Digest*, *Life* magazine and the *Saturday Evening Post* as well. In 1982 Satillaro's story, written with former *Journal* editor Tom Monte, was published by Houghton Mifflin under the title *Recalled By Life*.[4] On a promotional tour the doctor appeared on radio and television around the country. Since that time Satillaro has parted from Kushi and the macrobiotic movement and explains his cure in terms of standard medical treatment and religious faith as well as diet. Nevertheless, his case had a tremendous impact. Many of the people now receiving consultations for cancer and other diseases originally heard of macrobiotics through him.

The spread of macrobiotics socially and geographically from its Boston base was also helped by the publication and distribution of writings by the Kushis. In 1977 the Tokyo-based firm Japan Publications, Inc. brought out a compilation of Michio's teachings called *The Book of Macrobiotics: The Universal Way to Health and Hap-*

piness. For the first time the full scope of Kushi's teachings were available in one volume and through ordinary book retailing channels. *The Book of Macrobiotics* has become perhaps the single most important book in macrobiotic literature, eclipsing even the works of Ohsawa. Several hundred thousand copies in English have been sold and it has been translated into German, French, Dutch, Danish, Portuguese, Spanish, Italian and Japanese. The following year the same publisher brought out Kushi's *Natural Healing Through Macrobiotics*. Since then a miso cookbook by Aveline and two very popular introductory cookbooks by Ed and Wendy Esko (long-time Kushi associates) have also appeared.

Thus the late '70s and early '80s were a time of continuing growth and expansion. Educational activities in Boston were given structure and stability. A network of centers developed around the country and around the world. The diet was increasingly accepted by the medical community as a healthful regimen, as a prevention against illness and to some degree as a potent therapy. More and more people of all ages and backgrounds became involved in the movement. Attractive and popular publications made information available to those practicing macrobiotics and to those liable to become interested. There was even some excitement generated by celebrity interest. Actress Gloria Swanson and Beatle John Lennon with wife Yoko Ono had been supporters and friends of the Kushis for a while already. Then TV actor Dirk Benedict adopted the diet, and appearing on the cover of the *East West Journal*, told of his cure through it. Singer John Denver also spoke publicly of its benefits and became a member of the Kushi Foundation Board of Trustees. Former Georgia Governor Lester Maddox and Ruth Stapleton Carter, sister of the former President, both came to Boston for dietary and health advice. While the testimony of the beautiful and the great did not, as some hoped, spread macrobiotics magically across the land, at least it generated some excitement within the movement and put macrobiotics in the public eye in a positive way.

There were shadows in this more recent period as well. The largest came from the thickening cloud of difficulties which hung over Erewhon. The company, as all Boston macrobiotic enterprises, was run by "inspired amateurs" who were answerable to the Kushis. From its inception through the mid-1970s it seemed that Erewhon could do no wrong, that it would expand indefinitely. However, problems developed. A costly move was made to a large facility in East Cambridge. Money was borrowed just when interest rates were high and going up. Increased competition in the natural foods industry tempered sales. A long and often bitter dispute with employees over unionization sapped the company's energy and cash resources. These and other factors led to a painful, steady decline. The Kushis held on to the bitter end, turning down both offers of investment partners and of prospective owners. Finally in the fall of 1981 Erewhon filed for bankruptcy under so-called "Chapter Eleven." A few months later the company was sold to outside interests and debts to creditors were settled on about eleven cents to the dollar. Long-time suppliers in this country and in Japan were hard hit.

Erewhon's demise, however traumatic for all concerned, came as something of a relief to the Boston community. The company's crisis had taken the time and energy of the Kushis and many others for months. Since then the Kushis have pursued their particular interests. Aveline's main concern was to find for a home the

Kushi Institute more grand than the clean but modest facilities in Brookline Village. A fund raising campaign for money to purchase the campus of a former Catholic college in Brookline fell short. In 1982 however a 600 acre estate, formerly a Franciscan monastery, was purchased. Located in Becket in the Berkshire mountains of Massachusetts, it is being prepared as a permanent home for the Institute and perhaps other organizations. There are plans to develop the site for farming, food production and community living. In 1983–84, Aveline also helped prepare a book on pregnancy and child care and wrote and illustrated a new cookbook.

Michio, meanwhile, has been dividing his time between lecture tours, book preparation and educational activity. He has reduced his travel to Europe, going there only for special seminars and for the general congresses. Instead he has been quite active in the Caribbean and in Central America, particularly in Costa Rica, and recently organized a conference of macrobiotic leaders from that area. It was held in Miami in December of 1984. In addition to a book of macrobiotic home remedies, prepared with Dr. Marc van Cauwenberghe, he is working on a volume about world peace in conjunction with author Alex Jack. Kushi also oversees the several organizations which make up the "Kushi conglomerate." The East West Foundation promotes and coordinates public education. The Kushi Foundation, which in turn includes the *East West Journal*, the Kushi Institute and Macrobiotics International, is a nonprofit organization supporting educational and research projects. Since October, 1983 Kushi has actively supported the International Macrobiotic Society of New York City. Organized by Mr. Kit Kitatani at United Nations headquarters, this group includes UN staff from many countries and now numbers about one-hundred-seventy-five members. In September, 1984 Kushi was elected president of the World Federation of Natural Alternative Medicine at the group's meeting in Madrid Spain.

Kushi still spends a substantial portion of his time in individual guidance. Though he tries to refer inquiries to other counselors, there is still at least a six month waiting list. He is also involved in several medical research projects. The macrobiotic diet is still not widely accepted as an effective therapy. There are many convincing case histories, some more dramatic than Satillaro's, and as in Kushi's book *Cancer and Heart Disease* (published in 1982), they have been made public. But as yet there are no systematic, documented scientific studies. Underway, however, are several projects which may make a more convincing case for macrobiotics.

Over the last few years the medical community has increasingly recognized the role of diet in certain types of cancer. Recommendations of the American Medical Association and the American Cancer Society sound as if they were taken directly from Kushi's own *Cancer Prevention Diet*. A doctor in Philadelphia, Vivien Newbold, is now doing a study to see if a macrobiotic diet can indeed cure cancer. Dr. Newbold's husband, a stock broker, was stricken by pancreatic cancer which through the diet is now in remission. She is collecting numerous case histories to see if there is indeed consistent evidence to support the diet.

Another major health problem today is AIDS—Acquired Immune Deficiency Syndrome, which leaves its victims, mostly male homosexuals, fatally vulnerable to even mild infections. While researchers in France and the United States have isolated the virus, according to macrobiotic theory susceptibility to this disease is caused by poor health founded on poor diet. Hence a sound diet should provide resistance to the ailment and perhaps a cure. Since 1983 a group of about 30 AIDS sufferers in New York City have been following a macrobiotic regimen. Their overall condition is carefully monitored, and each week samples of their blood are sent to Boston University's Medical School for analysis. So far indications are hopeful though not conclusive.

Over the past decade the Kushis have been greatly helped by their so-called "senior teachers." These are generally American men and women who became involved with macrobiotics and the Boston community ten or more years ago and have remained committed and active. Some of these have started their own centers. These include Denny Waxman in Philadelphia, Murray Snyder in Baltimore, Cecile Levin in Los Angeles, Michael Rossoff in Washington D.C., Bill Spear in Middletown, Connecticut, Bob Carr in Cleveland, Sandy Pukel in Miami, and Blake Gould in Burlington, Vermont. Some have remained in or near Boston where they teach at the Kushi Institute and also visit and lecture at smaller centers. These include John Mann, Steve Gagne, Ed Esko, Richard France, Lenny Jacobs and Myron Frump. A few, like the very popular lecturer Bill Tims, have left Boston (Tims lives in Fayetteville, Arkansas) and lecture in other parts of the country. Probably the most influential person in the Boston community besides the Kushis is Bill Tara, presently director of the Kushi Institute and of the East West Foundation. There are also of course senior teachers who are women. These, like Olivia Oredson, Carolyn Heidenry and Wendy Esko, are active as teachers of cooking as well as authors and administrators.

While through the 1970s and early '80s Boston was becoming larger and more organized and was extending its influence further, the Aiharas and others on the West Coast were continuing their work. Herman and Cornellia maintained a center in San Francisco from 1970–74. Then, concerned about the effect of city life on their children, they moved back to the Sacramento Valley. Not finding an appropriate place in Chico they settled first in Oroville, a small city about 30 minutes away. A study house named "Vega" was established to accommodate those who wished to study macrobiotics. At the same time, the Aiharas were trying to establish a macrobiotic community on some land which they had acquired in the nearby mountains. Various state regulations made this impossible, though, and the idea was abandoned. Herman and his family lived on the property for several years, however, and Herman commuted every day to Oroville to run the George Ohsawa Macrobiotic Foundation (GOMF) and to teach at Vega. It was a difficult and trying situation for everyone, especially for him and Cornellia. Finally in 1978 Herman sold the property and purchased a house in Oroville.

Through these years and despite the moves and difficulties, Herman and Cornellia continued their activities on behalf of macrobiotics. They instructed many generations of Vega residents in its theory and practice. Herman was especially busy with writing, translating and publishing. He kept up his monthly magazine throughout, and in addition wrote pamphlets on such issues as the dangers of milk and of vitamin C, and on the relation between cancer and food. He translated and published much material by Ohsawa that was previously unavailable. Cornellia meanwhile was busy cooking and training cooks. Her excellent cookbook *The Dō of Cooking*[5] added new dimensions to macrobiotic cuisine. She and Herman, like the Kushis, had discovered the importance of a broad and somewhat less salty version of the diet.

The Aiharas were especially busy during the summer. In most years they spent the early part of the vacation season "on tour." Packing children, pets, food, plus a student-helper or two into their van, they traveled back and forth across the country. Along the way they stopped at macrobiotic centers to give lectures and cooking classes. These trips were long and arduous but very important for the dissemination of macrobiotics throughout America. Also, every year the Aiharas organized a popular ten-day camp at French Meadows in the Sierra Mountains. The campsite is at about 7,000 feet elevation, an hour from the nearest town and half an hour from the nearest telephone. Participants sleep in tents or under the usually cloudless sky. They wash in the chill, clear river that runs directly behind the camping area. The food is cooked over open wood fires and eaten at picnic benches clustered into an outdoor "dining hall." Lectures are held in open-air classrooms, a canopy of stately spruce and fir providing respite from the sun. Listeners usually sit on the ground, though in recent years Herman has noted sadly an increase in the number of lawn chairs. In the evenings there are songs, stories and dances around a campfire. The pristine surroundings, the unpretentious accommodations, and the warm family feeling of the camp all reflect the character of the Aiharas. Usually about 150 adults and children gather, some of them regulars who have been coming for years.

Since 1978 the Aiharas have lived and worked in Oroville. Herman has continued teaching at Vega and elsewhere up and down the West Coast. He has also continued to write and publish. He has begun, of late, to reissue in attractive, updated editions, several of Ohsawa's standard works and is busy translating more. With the upsurge of interest in macrobiotics as a cure for cancer, the type of people coming to Vega has changed. The young "counterculture" seekers for a philosophy, a way of life, a teacher, a community still find their way there. Many stay for long periods to help out at GOMF. But, increasingly, seriously ill people of all age groups and areas of society come as well. The Aiharas recently began shorter, more intensive programs to meet the needs of this latter group.

Early in 1984 the Aiharas received a contribution which made possible the purchase of a new facility in Oroville. The new Vega, a former hospital, has been refurbished to accommodate the various activities "under one roof." The GOMF offices and stock and shipping rooms have moved in. Also a schedule of three-week residential programs has been established. Each month between twenty and thirty live-in students come to study and to live the macrobiotic way of life. Herman is very happy about this arrangement. "People learn by living, not just by sitting in a lecture room," he says. Activities at Vega have mushroomed, and as of early 1985 the Aiharas have over twenty associates working with them in various full time capacities at Vega and GOMF.

Of course the Aiharas have not been alone in promoting macrobiotics on the West Coast. Though many of the original Chico group fell away from active involvement new people appeared on the scene to help. In 1971 Noboru Muramoto [村本登], an associate of Ohsawa from Japan and an expert in medicinal herbs, arrived in California. Muramoto's popular book, *Healing Ourselves* was published in 1973 (by Michel Abehsera's Swan House Press)[6] and introduced many therapeutic uses of food. A student also of traditional Japanese food production, Muramoto now produces high quality sea salt, miso, umeboshi, and plum vinegar at his base of operations in southern California. In 1975 Cecile Levin returned from seven years of macrobiotic study in Japan and set up a center in Los Angeles. About the same time, Jacques de Langre gave up his photography business to teach and to publish books related to macrobiotics. Eventually he set up his Happiness Press in Magalia, also in the Chico area. De Langre has done much interesting research into the production of sea salt and naturally-leavened bread. Indonesian-born Roy Steevensz had a center in Los Angeles (now closed) and helped start activities in San Diego.

Still, Herman remains the universally respected and liked elder statesman of macrobiotics on the West Coast. It is tempting of course to compare him to Kushi. Kushi has on occasion characterized Herman as a "country saint" in contradistinction to himself as a "city devil." And there is an element of truth in this. While Kushi is urbane, sophisticated and ambitious, Aihara is modest, unassuming and self-effacing in the extreme. He dresses casually in jeans and a sports shirt, his thick white hair pressed under a baseball cap. On the rare occasions when he wears a suit it seems as if he has been pressured into doing so at gunpoint. He is soft-spoken and even a bit shy. "I am not such a good speaker," he says. "I prefer to listen and to learn rather than to talk." At his own summer camp he will schedule younger, less well-known teachers into prime spots and attend their talks, carefully taking notes. He seems equally at home scrubbing out pots or cutting firewood as he does addressing an audience of students. Yet his classes are extremely popular.

Herman's pace reflects this same rural simplicity. His devotion to his work is great. He works hard and studies late. Yet he is relaxed and easy going, and always seems to have time to help students and associates with even minor problems. "I try to do what I can," he admits, "and then I like to take it easy a bit. If we are always rushing around we never can be happy and peaceful." Herman enjoys walking with his good friend and pet, Jiro, a white dog, and watching the San Francisco '49ers professional football team. He claims full responsibility for their 1985 Superbowl victory.

Yet, for all this rusticity, Herman is an excellent lecturer and writer. He focuses on the basics of macrobiotics, on Yin and Yang and on their application to diet and other aspects of daily life. He can talk about metaphysics, but when he does so, it is apt to be in a personal and ironic tone. In the final lecture of his 1984 summer camp Herman spoke about the "Seventh Heaven." We all come from that realm and go back to it, he said, but as it is a little boring we do not stay long. The world as it is, full of divorce, war and other problems, is much more interesting and challenging! Herman is especially interested in personal and psychological issues, and often draws on his own life experience. One central theme is the achievement of contentment and peace of mind. "If we don't have inner peace," he observes, "everything else is worthless." Herman counsels his students to "be humble," to take full responsibility for their own lives and happiness, to be grateful for everything and never to complain. He seldom treats the esoteric topics and the broad social and political issues on which Kushi focuses. "I leave the creation of world peace to Michio," he jests.

Perhaps Herman's greatest forte is in his training of the students who work with him. He is deeply concerned with each and is accessible to them at all times. "All I really want to do," he says, "is to teach a few people to think and to help them remember who they really are." To this end Herman will often give even a newcomer full control over a project so that he will learn responsibility very quickly. Much of the teaching on this level is non-verbal. "Herman is a person of incredible understanding and compassion," observes one student. "He has learned so much from life and has become so wise and loving, that I learn just by being around him, even when he doesn't say a thing!"

Cornellia has many of the same characteristics. She seems eternally attired in kitchen garb, with an apron covering her clothes and a kerchief on her head. Despite a congenital heart problem she is remarkably hard-working, always bustling about. At summer camp she is the first up in the morning to light the cooking fires and the last to be scrubbing pots in the evening. Her cooking and cookbooks reflect the simple "country style" of Japanese-American macrobiotics. Far from fluent in English, she prefers, in teaching, to show, rather than explain. Often, to a cooking class student with many questions, Cornellia will remonstrate, "Just watch carefully what I do. That is where the answers are." Deeply dedicated to her husband and to macrobiotics, she has shared Herman's trials and triumphs in America for over thirty years. As a good Japanese wife, Cornellia defers to Herman and stands happily in his shadow. But to understand him and his accomplishments it is necessary to keep her in mind.

It is now twenty-five years since Ohsawa first presented macrobiotics to the public in his New York lectures of 1960. And it is almost as long since the movement spread to the West Coast. After a quarter century it is appropriate perhaps to ask, what has been the net result in North America of the work of the Kushis and Aiharas and of the many other teachers, promoters, and supporters of macrobiotics.

The most precise answer would be a quantitative one, and in some degree such an answer is possible. There are two major educational centers (Vega and the Kushi Institute) where, annually, a combined total of about 300 students pursue some period of full-time study. The *1984–85 Worldwide Macrobiotic Directory* of the Kushi Institute lists some 175 "Macrobiotic Centers, Friends and Businesses" in the United States and Canada. Thirty of the fifty states have listings, with Massachusetts, California, New York and Colorado having the greatest concentrations. Of these, about fifty are fully operative centers. There are also some 150 individuals listed as "Kushi Institute Certified Teachers and Counselors." Besides the *East West Journal* there are two monthly magazines, both more specifically macrobiotic: "*MacroMuse*"[7] in Washington, D.C. and "*Macrobiotics Today*"[8] from Oroville. There are a number of successful summer programs. The Mid-Atlantic Camp co-sponsored by the Philadelphia and Baltimore centers draws about 600 people each year. A week-long session held by the East West Foundation in Becket, Massachusetts in August 1984 brought together over 500 people.

The most direct and crucial question is, however, how many macrobiotic people are there in North America today? It is very difficult to answer. The centers do not enroll "members." Nor do they generally keep records of people who attend meetings and lectures, or who receive individual guidance. With its tap roots in the

Orient and its more immediate roots in the American "counterculture" the movement has been light both on organization and on statistics.

Besides, there is no explicit, generally accepted understanding of what it means to be "macrobiotic." Macrobiotics is many-faceted. It includes a diet, a system of medicine, a philosophy, a way of life, a community, and a broad social movement. Some people accept and are active in macrobiotics at all these levels. Some practice the diet and medicine and have little interest in the other aspects. Even regarding diet, the principal common factor, there are various interpretations. Some try to follow a strict regimen of brown rice and vegetables. For others, a macrobiotic diet includes daily fish, beer and fruit. To others it is grains and vegetables plus vitamin and mineral supplements. And for all, perhaps, the practice falls short of the ideal. There are teachers who promote a strict form of the diet and eat something wholly different themselves. The declaration "I am macrobiotic" has a wide variety of meanings.

Despite this ambiguity, though, and the lack of hard statistics, it is possible to hazard a guess. Some sanguine observers say there are now hundreds of thousands, even millions of macrobiotics in America. Kushi estimates there are three to five hundred thousand true macrobiotics in the country, and some two million semi-macrobiotics. This may be true if we use a very broad definition of the term. Some purists, in their eighth year of Diet Number Seven say that there are only two true macrobiotics, and one of them, Ohsawa, is dead. The truth probably lies somewhere in between.

Magazine distribution is perhaps the most accurate indicator. Each month about 4,000 copies of *MacroMuse* and about 2,000 copies of *Macrobiotics Today* are sent out. The circulation of the *East West Journal* is close to 80,000, with about half being sent to people who define themselves as "macrobiotic." If we allow for crossover, this means that there are at least 35,000 households which are macrobiotic. If we assume that there are committed households which receive no periodical, and that there is an average of three persons per household, the total comes to about 120,000 individuals.

This means that there are close to 100,000 adults who have chosen to practice macrobiotics to a significant degree. Among these, of course, there are countless levels of involvement and influence. For some, macrobiotics is a simple, reasonable diet which keeps them active and healthy. For some it is literally the difference between life and death. For some it is a way of looking at and understanding the world, as well as a way of eating and living. For all, perhaps, it has been the source of substantial benefit, physical, emotional, psychological or spiritual.

Yet the impact of macrobiotics on American society cannot be expressed solely in terms of the number of people who consciously practice it. Through the dissemination of its ideas and through the varied activities of its adherents, the macrobiotic movement has played an important role in several key developments in American society of the past two decades. Particularly through its place in the natural foods and the holistic health movements, it has influenced the lives of countless people who would never call themselves macrobiotic and who perhaps have never even heard the word.

In 1960 the typical, almost universal, American diet consisted of meat, eggs, dairy products, white breads and other products made from refined flour, potatoes, canned and frozen vegetables, tropical fruits and juices, coffee, soft drinks and sweets. This diet was generally approved by the medical and nutritional scientific establishment. Concern about meat eating (from an ethical or a health standpoint), about chemical additives, about white sugar and other refined foods, or about the poisons used in agriculture was virtually absent. Some religious groups such as the Seventh Day Adventists and the Mormons followed a mild food discipline. There were a few informed voices urging diet reform. J.I. Rodale in Pennsylvania and Dr. Carlton Fredericks Jr. in New York were among them, but they were only isolated voices of protest. There were a few "health food" stores in larger cities, but they tended to feature high-priced supplements and elixirs rather than whole foods. In general, anyone who was concerned about diet and its effect on health was liable to be consigned to the "lunatic fringe."

While the food attitudes and eating patterns of the past still pertain in much, indeed in most of the country, there have been substantial changes. Vegetarianism or some degree of it is a common phenomenon. Even among meat-eaters there is a marked trend toward poultry and fish in lieu of red meats. There is a substantial and growing awareness of the importance of whole foods. While once it was impossible to buy anything other than puffed-cotton white breads, now in almost every supermarket one can get whole-wheat breads, and even brown rice. There is widespread concern about chemicals in food and about the effects of white sugar. There is a small but growing market for organically produced grains, vegetables, meats and fruits. How Americans think about food and how they eat has changed radically in the past two decades.

A whole new economy has developed to accommodate this change. There are over ten thousand "natural foods" stores around the country, selling whole foods and fresh vegetables rather than pills and potions. There are vegetarian and natural foods restaurants in nearly every city and town. There are a score of major wholesale distributors and a host of manufacturers and processors to supply these stores and restaurants. At the base of the pyramid are the steadily growing number of farms practicing a self-sustaining, organic method of agriculture. These include huge, sophisticated operations raising cereals and legumes (such as that of the Lundberg brothers in California and of Frank Ford in Deaf Smith County, Texas), and modest vegetable gardens.

Many individuals and groups have contributed to these new eating patterns and to the "natural foods" industry. And among them the macrobiotic movement must be counted a chief influence. Long before it became fashionable or commonplace, Ohsawa, Kushi, Aihara and others were advocating a whole food, high-fiber diet and warning against white sugar and refined flour, additives, agricultural poisons and excess protein and animal fat. While their teachings directly affected those who took up macrobiotics, they also percolated throughout the society. For example, in 1977 a Committee on Nutrition was formed in the United States Senate under the chairmanship of George McGovern. Several physicians and health professionals who had been influenced by macrobiotics, chief among them Dr. Mark Hegsted, testified before the committee. Their opinions helped form the epoch-making findings of the group. In their report the committee recognized that:

1. Diet is an important factor in the nation's health.
2. The current American diet is a factor in many degenerative diseases.
3. Major changes in American dietary patterns are desirable.

The group then advised a reduction in the consumption of animal fats, refined foods, simple sugars and salt, and an increase in complex carbohydrates, vegetable fats, and roughage. In other words, it suggested less meat, dairy foods, white bread and sugar, and more whole grains, beans, fresh vegetables and fruits. These recommendations, in accord with macrobiotic thinking, have had a continuing impact on changing American food habits.

The imprint of macrobiotics on the natural foods industry has also been great. From the beginning of the industry's boom in the early 1970s, Erewhon was its signal pioneer and trendsetter. The company influenced all phases of the industry from agricultural production to retailing. One day in 1970 Paul Hawken was tending the then small Erewhon outlet. A customer asked how he knew for certain that a product labelled "organically grown" really was so. Hawken gave a hasty answer and realized later that he didn't really know for sure. The next day he was unloading a shipment of oats from a purportedly "organic" producer. Left by mistake on one bag was a label indicating that the oats originally had come from a regular commercial grower. Angry, disillusioned, and determined to correct the situation, Hawken began to travel to various suppliers to check their operations. Also, he began to encourage farmers to grow organically by purchasing crops before they were grown. Also, he began in-house production, adhering to uncompromised standards of quality. During the same period, the Erewhon retail outlets became the model for the many natural foods stores springing up over the country. Their decor—featuring natural wood surfaces, indirect lighting, wooden barrels offering foods in bulk—and their high standard of quality for all products, became the dominant influence in the industry.

In addition, many of the organic farms, food manufacturers, retail stores and restaurants were started by macrobiotic people, or by people directly influenced by macrobiotics. The soyfoods portion of the industry is a case in point. For centuries the soybean has been the "milk cow" of the Orient. High in protein, it is a staple food in the form of tofu [豆腐] (soy curd), miso [味噌] (fermented paste) and shoyu [醬油] (soy sauce) for the Chinese and Japanese people. Twenty years ago these foods were virtually unknown in America, found only in neighborhood shops of the Oriental minorities. Today, soy products have become a notable source of protein for the American public. Tofu, miso, shoyu, and more recently *tempeh* (a soybean "cheese" coming originally from Indonesia), are available almost everywhere, in supermarkets and groceries as well as natural foods stores. This development has been largely the result of activity in the macrobiotic community. Responding to the suggestions of Ohsawa, Kushi and Aihara, American young people learned about these foods, incorporated them into their diet and then made sure that there were adequate supplies of high quality versions. The import of traditional-style miso and *tamari* [溜] from Japan, the beginning of miso production in the United States, the establishment of tofu producers and distributors, were undertaken mainly by macrobiotic people. One of the key figures in these developments has been William Shurtleff, now director of the Soyfoods Center in Lafayette, California. Long connected with the macrobiotic movement, Shurtleff, with Akiko Aoyagi, has written a series of books on tofu, miso, tempeh and other Oriental foods. These books alone have had a major impact on America's eating habits. In *The Book of Miso* Shurtleff observes, " ... the macrobiotic community unquestionably played the leading role in introducing miso to the Western world."[9] The same could be said of tofu, shoyu, tempeh, and sea vegetables as well, of course, as brown rice. The macrobiotic food companies in Japan have also been instrumental. Since the late 1960s two macrobiotically-oriented companies have been the chief suppliers of high quality Japanese foods to North America, Europe and other parts of the world. They are Mitoku Co. Ltd of Tokyo, founded and managed by Akiyoshi Kazama [風間昭美], and Musō Shokuhin of Osaka run by the Okada family. Along with the smaller "Ohsawa Japan" company they have both supplied the international macrobiotic community with a variety of excellent natural products, and have helped introduce these foods to the general public around the world.

Over the past twenty-five years there has also been a significant change in attitudes about health and sickness and in the types of medical therapies available. Behind the general indifference to food quality was the idea that life-style (including diet) had little effect on one's health. Sickness was considered a result of chance infection or of unfortunate heredity. Its treatment was left to the medical profession, with its long, specialized training and its armory of medications and surgical techniques. In 1960 allopathic or symptomatic medicine reigned supreme in the United States. The idea that how one lives plays a role in sickness and health, and the concept that the person, once sick, plays an important role in his own cure, were virtually unknown. There were a few alternate therapies available. Osteopathic medicine, chiropractic, and fasting cures were practiced, but were not at all widespread.

Since then, of course, attitudes have changed radically for at least a sizable portion of the population. There is a widespread recognition of the role of diet in health, not only in maintaining vitality but in preventing major disease. Even establishment organizations like the AMA and the American Cancer Society attest to the role of diet in cancer, heart disease, and other illnesses. There is almost a universal appreciation (theoretical at least) of the benefits of exercise. And a variety of alternative therapies have flourished, including acupuncture, shiatsu, naturopathy and homeopathy.

Here again many factors are operating. Among them is the accumulation of scientific evidence to support ideas that from the macrobiotic perspective have long been obvious. But the persistent testimony of the macrobiotic movement over the years is also a factor. In *Zen Macrobiotics* (1960) Ohsawa presented the then near revolutionary idea that health and sickness are not a matter of chance. He said that each person creates his own illness and unhappiness by how he eats, lives, and thinks, and that he can cure his illness by changing his life style. For years, this basic message of macrobiotics has been proclaimed in every lecture and seminar, every book and article coming out of the movement. Roughly 100,000 Americans have been moved to adopt a macrobiotic diet and way of life. A far greater number have at least had their overall perspective changed. They have become more aware of their responsibility for their own health and perhaps are more open to alternate forms of medicine. While this impact is diffuse and impossible to gauge, it is certainly real.

In addition, the macrobiotic community has played an important role in the introduction and development of some of the alternative therapies. Kushi, though not professionally trained in acupuncture or shiatsu, practiced these techniques early in his career and taught them to several generations of students. Some macrobiotic people seeking deeper study went to Japan, China and England (specifically to Professor Donald Worsly's acupuncture school) and returned to practice. Through her large practice in New York City, her teaching and her excellent book, *Barefoot Shiatsu*,[10] Shizuko Yamamoto has been promoting shiatsu for the past twenty years. *Healing Ourselves*, by Noboru Muramoto has helped spread Japanese herbal remedies. In addition, many macrobiotic people have opted for careers in naturopathy, chiropractic, homeopathy and other areas of the holistic medical scene. And this is a two-way process. Many of the practitioners and clients of the alternate healing arts have gravitated towards the practice of macrobiotics.

The natural foods and the holistic health movements are two parts of the broader "counterculture" which has been developing over the past twenty years. There are various other groups within it. Each is dissatisfied with some aspect of the dominant culture and is trying to develop new patterns. The environmentalists focus on preserving the quality of the natural environment. The back-to-the-land people seek a simpler way of life, close to nature. The cooperative movements, sensing the limitations of economic life based on materialism and personal accumulation, seek new ways of producing, consuming and exchanging goods and services. The human potential movement, with its many variant seminars and programs, has emphasized a positive approach to human nature and to its evolution. Spiritual groups, many pursuing some Eastern practice or discipline, affirm the ultimate importance of spiritual development.

Between the macrobiotic movement and these groups the same process of cross-fertilization has taken place and continues. This is because of common values and aspirations. From the macrobiotic point of view the love and protection of nature, the return to a more natural life style, the pursuit of cooperation and quality in business, the development of untapped human potential and the concern with spiritual destiny are all important and necessary aspects of modern life. Thus many of the leaders and participants in these movements came originally from macrobiotics. Or if not, they often have incorporated macrobiotic practice and theory into their own work.

For example, between 1970 and 1984, Duncan and Susan Sim lived on and from the land at their Still Mountain Farm in British Columbia and shared their experience with many visitors and students. Robert and Cynthia Hargrove became important in the "est" movement and then began their very successful Boston-based "Relationships Seminar." Paul Hawken, after leaving Erewhon in 1975 became active in the Findhorn spiritual community in northern Scotland, and more recently with the publication of his book, *The Next Economy*, has become a guru of the forward-looking business community. Each of these people spent long periods in Boston as part of the macrobiotic community, and while they might not necessarily call themselves macrobiotic now, each would admit to its strong influence.

On the other hand, in the mid-'70s two of the most respected Indian gurus, Swami Satchidananda and Yogi Amrit Desai, recommended a macrobiotic-style diet for their students. And in the kitchen of nearly every rural homestead and commune in North America can be found brown rice, miso and gomashio.

Thus throughout American society and particularly within the "counterculture," macrobiotics, the Shoku-Yō of Ishizuka and Ohsawa, has had a substantial impact. It has helped change the way people think about food, about their health and about disease and medicine. It has contributed as well to a new consciousness of the natural environment, and of the psychological and spiritual potential of the human being. But the movement itself remains a small and peripheral one. Even compared to other groups of the counter-culture (T.M., est, Rajneeshis) it is modest in size and on the fringes of mainstream American culture. There are a number of reasons for this. They apply not only to the situation of macrobiotics in America, but also elsewhere in the West and to some degree in Japan.

One is that while macrobiotics promises much it also demands much. It offers a healthful, harmonious life-style based on an optimistic view of the world. But it requires for most a major change in ways of thinking and living. One has to take complete responsibility for one's health and well-being. One has to make certain sacrifices and to exercise self-discipline. Food habits and preferences are deeply ingrained. It is not so easy to give up a lifetime diet of hamburgers, french fries and ice cream in favor of brown rice and tofu. And there are social complications as well, in dealing with the reactions of family, friends and business associates. Even if one makes the commitment and the change, the benefits of the diet can be subtle and slow. Even when they are relatively quick and impressive they may not appear as intense as, for example, the impact of an est weekend seminar. The changes are physiological and basic, and thus perhaps more permanent, but still they are more gradual.

Another reason for the slow growth of macrobiotics has been its "amateur" quality. The great majority of people coming into the movement have been young and inexperienced. Those with education, training or experience did not necessarily use their particular expertise in their activities within macrobiotics. Hence macrobiotic educational and counseling activities, businesses, publications, and organizational work have been in the hands of enthusiastic and well-meaning people, who were, however, not professionals nor experts. This certainly has affected the successful presentation of macrobiotics to the general public. The lack of a strong organization to coordinate activities, to foster cooperation and to get the most from available resources has been another hindrance.

Also, patterns of dogmatic and narrow-minded thinking have been present within the movement. Though not universal, they have been widespread and clear enough to give macrobiotics a questionable image in the public mind. They are perhaps inevitable in any movement which like macrobiotics has a definite and integrated ideology, several strong voices of authority, and which has drawn largely from the disaffected and searching fringe elements of society. These tendencies go against the letter and the spirit of the teachings of Ohsawa, Kushi, Aihara, et al. Nevertheless, they are a part of the movement along with its more positive characteristics, and make it much less interesting and attractive to those outside. I list them here in full and humble recognition that I am no stranger to them myself. These habits of thought and actions include the following.

"Ohsawa (or Michio, or Herman . . .) said this, therefore it is true." This is simply an intellectual passivity, a blind dependence on authority. Because of it, one accepts as true things which one does not understand, which one has not experienced, and things for which there may be no evidence. For example, many people still accept Ohsawa's pronouncements regarding the harmlessness of smoking, while there is no evidence to support it and much to countermand it.

"We are right and everyone else is wrong, or at least seriously misguided." Intellectual arrogance is integral to dogmatic thinking, and macrobiotics has had its fair share of it. This has been true especially in regard to Western nutritional science and medicine. One of Ohsawa's persistent themes was the basic inadequacy of Western nutrition and medicine, and within the macrobiotic movement there has been a strong tendency to ignore or deride any idea or practice coming from these sources. Sometimes the results have been unfortunate. During the 1970s in Boston, London and elsewhere, some macrobiotic children were exhibiting bowleggedness and other symptoms of calcium deficiency. The orthodox belief was that the "standard" diet supplies adequate calcium in sea vegetables, green leafy vegetables, and beans. Therefore there could be no deficiency. In the end some of these children were diagnosed by the medical authorities as indeed suffering from calcium deficiency or from calcium metabolism problems (rickets), and were treated for it. The situation was complex. According to Kushi, some of the children were not actually on a macrobiotic diet. They may have been taking too much salt and flour products and not enough vegetables and other types of food. Probably they were not outside enough in the sunshine and thus were lacking vitamin D, which is essential for calcium utilization. Until the time of diagnosis and treatment, the attitude of parents and of others in the community was that they could handle the situation and that the doctors were unnecessarily alarmed.

"Food, food, and again I say food." Around 1969 one of the macrobiotic men in Boston went to a psychiatrist in order to avoid the draft. He was diagnosed as a "food obsessive." At the time we thought this quite a joke, but there was more than a little truth in the doctor's observation. The intense interest concerning food that exists in the macrobiotic movement probably has seldom been matched in human history. Food is sometimes seen as the sole controlling element in human life. Everything is explained in terms of it. People focus on it as the most important thing in their daily life. While there may be an element of validity in this attitude, it can be carried to an extreme. Thus one may hear comments like "I am depressed today and don't want to go to work. It's because I had two oranges yesterday," or the even more self-defeating, "I am eating an orange, therefore I will be depressed tomorrow." This concern with food detracts from the energy and attention given to other aspects of life: art, music, dance, athletics, relationships. Macrobiotics can easily nurture a one-dimensional view of life and a limited range of activities.

"Hello. You are sick and the sky is falling." While ideally macrobiotics is about health, in practice its focus often falls upon sickness, that of the individual and of society. Armed with the tools of Oriental diagnosis, macrobiotic people can become consumed with interest about their own physical condition and that of others, and the emphasis is likely to be on the negative. I once sat in on an upper level diagnosis class at the Kushi Institute. Individual students were asked to sit in front of the group and to speak briefly. Then their "condition" was analyzed. There were endless hypotheses about "bad kidneys," "weak intestines," etc. etc. During the two-hour-session not a single positive comment was made. The underlying assumption was that to evaluate someone was to perceive their illness.

Also, there has been a tendency to focus exclusively on what is wrong with American and Western society as a whole. Ever since Ohsawa's tirades against French culture in the late 1950s and his prophecies of nuclear doom a few years later, there has been a strong "Chicken Little, the sky is falling" theme in macrobiotic thinking. This may indeed be warranted. But there has been little recognition of the positive factors at work (other than macrobiotics) in society. When the jogging and physical fitness craze hit, many teachers dismissed it as "too Yangizing." When est appeared it was derided as "too sentimental." In its extreme (and fortunately rare manifestation) this attitude amounts to an approach which assumes, "if it's not from macrobiotics, it can't be good."

These attitudes—intellectual dependence and arrogance, obsessiveness and negativity and narrow-mindedness—are not universal or dominant. They co-exist with a freedom and independence of thought, an openness to new ideas and ways of living, with an optimistic and hopeful view of life. But they do exist to an extent within the macrobiotic movement and affect how it is perceived by those outside it.

Two other characteristics have inhibited the growth of macrobiotics in America. One is the inevitable gap between the "ideal" and the "real." Any group which bases itself on an idealized, ideological vision is vulnerable to this. And macrobiotics is no exception. One would expect the teachers and long-time macrobiotics to be eating the "Standard Diet," and to be paragons of health and vitality, free from sickness and personal problems. Some do eat a strict diet, but many do not. Smoking and coffee drinking are common, a fact which usually surprises and dismays newcomers. Most are fairly healthy but are apt to be thin and pale. As a group the macrobiotic community seems to have about the same rates of divorce and family breakdown as other segments of society. The utopia of enlightened individuals may be on its way but is slow in arriving. Of course, to claim to have the key to health and happiness is to set oneself up for at best only partial success.

The final, probably most critical, factor is the "Japanese" quality of the macrobiotic movement. In theory, macrobiotics is a universal ideology and set of principles which can be applied to any particular circumstances. In practice, however, it has largely retained the Japanese ambience given it by its first teachers. In America as elsewhere in the West, macrobiotics often appears to be a Japanese "cult." The cosmology of Yin and Yang dominates thought and conversation. The central foods of the diet, brown rice, miso, tamari, tofu, etc. are Japanese, as are the standard cooking methods and dishes. Macrobiotic therapies are based on Japanese home and herbal remedies. Social relations also tend to have a Japanese flavor. Male and female role stereotypes reflect traditional Oriental patterns (similar to, but even more clearly defined than Western patterns). The organizations are strongly, if implicitly hierarchic. There has been an assumed identity between "macrobiotic" and "traditional Japanese" culture. This tendency has been decreasing in the past several years, but it is still a strong characteristic.

For some people, this orientation may actually be attractive. For others, those interested in the purely medical application of the diet, it is a matter of indifference. They are interested in curing a serious or life-threatening disease and if they have to eat miso soup to do it, that is fine. But for most Americans, this Japanese character of macrobiotics makes it something foreign, inaccessible and perhaps threatening. Without a very strong motivating factor, like an illness, they are unlikely to be much drawn to it.

Macrobiotics arrived in America over twenty-five years ago. Since then its development and spread have been helped by a number of factors: a comprehensive, optimistic world view; promises of physical, mental and spiritual health; strong, charismatic leadership; and a dedicated and idealistic community. On the other hand, it has been hampered by a lack of organization and professionalism, by patterns of dogmatic thinking, by a failure to realize its own ideals and by a strong exotic quality. The future of the movement in America (and elsewhere) depends on how it cultivates the positive set of circumstances and deals successfully with the negative.

[1] Abehsera, Michel, *Cooking for Life*, Swan House, Binghamton, 1967
[2] Dufty, William, *You Are All Sanpaku*, University Books, New York, 1965
[3] Kohler, Jean, *Healing Miracles Through Macrobiotics*, Parker, West Nyack, N.Y., 1979
[4] Satillaro, Dr. Anthony (with Tom Monte). *Recalled By Life*, Houghton Mifflin, Boston, 1982
[5] Aihara, Cornellia, *The Do of Cooking*, George Ohsawa Macrobiotic Foundation, Oroville, CA, 1978
[6] Muramoto, Noboru, *Healing Ourselves*, Swan House, Binghamton, NY, 1977
[7] *MacroMuse* is available through Michael Rossoff, 11119 Rockville Pike, Suite 321, Rockville, MD 20852
[8] *Macrobiotics Today* is published monthly and is available through the George Ohsawa Macrobiotic Foundation, 1511 Robinson St. Oroville, CA 95965
[9] Shurtleff, Wm. and Aoyagi, Akiko, *The Book of Miso*, published by the Soyfoods Center, Box 234, Lafayette, CA 94549, 1981
[10] Yamamoto, Shizuko, *Barefoot Shiatsu*, Japan Publications, Tokyo, 1979

18. Toshi Kawaguchi.

19. Michi Ogawa.

20. Hiroshi Maruyama.

21. Kaoru Yoshimi.

22. Mme. Francoise Riviere.

23. Cecile Levin.

24. Dr. Kikuo Chishima.

25. Dr. Moriyasu Ushio.

26. Michio Kushi.

27.   Aveline Kushi.

28.   Michio and Aveline Kushi.

29. Herman Aihara.

30. Cornellia Aihara.

31.   Herman and Cornellia Aihara.

32.   Michio and Aveline Kushi, Herman and Cornellia Aihara, Shizuko Yamamoto.

200

33. William Dufty.

34. Bill Tara.

35. Aveline Kushi and Wendy Esko.

36. Alex Jack.

37. Dr. Marc van Cauwenberghe.

202

38. Edward Esko.

39. Murray Snyder.

40. Noboru Muramoto.

42. Jacques de Langre.

41. Yvette de Langre.

43. Jerome Carty.

44. Duncan Sim.

45. Lima Ohsawa.

205

46. Shūzo Okada.

47. Hideo Ohmori.

48.

First European Congress of Macrobiotics in London, November 1978.

49.

50. Family consultations in Lenk summer camp, Switzerland, July 1984.

51. (From left to right) Jan Lansloot, Peter Doggen, Rik Vermuyten, Georges Van Wesenbeeck.

52. Roland Keijser.

53. Mayli Lao Shun.

54. Tomio Kikuchi.

11.

After the Master:
Part Two: Japan

In December 1967 I went to Japan for the first time. I had been involved with the macrobiotic community in Boston for about a year, and went with a rather vague plan to continue my study of macrobiotics, and to experience Japanese culture. At that time the Boston community was small, but busy and growing, with the Kushis at its center and a host of energetic idealists active in the various businesses and projects. I expected to find a similar upbeat situation in Japan—it was, after all, the birthplace of the movement. Such did not prove to be the case.

I stayed first in Tokyo. It was over eighteen months since Ohsawa's death. Lima Ohsawa still lived in the small fifth floor apartment in a modern building called Star Heights. With her helper and companion Ellie Sugamoto she gave cooking classes there to groups of ten or fifteen, mostly older women. There was a macrobiotic "center" in a rented room in a high rise shopping mall nearby. Food staples, assorted brown rice crackers and several books on macrobiotics were on sale. A few classes were held there, including one on flower arranging. I went a few times and the teacher was kind and patient. She called me a "genius" for arranging a few flowers and branches in a not totally revolting way. There were occasional lectures in a cold and cramped Buddhist temple, with at most 30 or 40 people, again mostly older, in attendance. Despite the kindness and hospitality of all, there was a somber, dispirited air about the activities.

Somewhat surprised and dismayed at the time, I realized only much later that Lima and the other macrobiotic people in Tokyo (and elsewhere) were still in a state of shock from Ohsawa's death. Even though he had been abroad much in his last years, Ohsawa remained the incandescent focus of macrobiotics in Japan. He was the beloved father-figure, the "Papa." He was the tireless leader, who did everything from scrub the bathroom to write the articles for the magazine and give the lectures. He was the wise sage who, with the compass of Yin and Yang, could give the definitive answer to all questions and problems. And he was the respected and feared spiritual Master, the sensei, who guided the development of his students. Suddenly he had disappeared, and those who for years had depended on him were profoundly disoriented as well as deeply saddened.

After several months I went to Osaka, Japan's "second city," a commercial and business center. There, in a ramshackle Buddhist temple called Fukusenji, Shūzo Okada [岡田周三], a long-time associate of Ohsawa, had established a food company (*Musō Shokuhin* [無双食品] ("Unique Foods")) and a small macrobiotic center. In one alcove was a pile of cartons and bags containing various packaged and bulk food items, including rice, miso, soy sauce, beans, and so on. This was the retail outlet. Food processing (i.e., sorting out stones from trays of red beans) was done on the kitchen table by the young men and women who worked there. Deliveries were made by bicycle and mini-truck to retail and wholesale customers in the city. Okada, who had given up the family textile business, also was practicing macrobiotic medicine. A man about forty was staying at the temple, trying to cure cancer of the tongue. He ate twice a day, at each meal taking only a single bowl of *kayu* ("brown-rice cream") and a cup of bancha tea. The general ambience was somewhat more dynamic but the operation was still a small and struggling one.

Finally I settled in Kyoto, the ancient capital about twenty-five miles to the north, where I was to study at the national university. There was no macrobiotic center or store in that city of over one million people. The only substantial activity was a kindergarten on the far west side of the city in which macrobiotic food was served to children at lunch. Alcan Yamaguchi, back several years from America, lived with his family in a small house on the eastern mountains overlooking the city. I visited him regularly, and as the city shimmered brilliantly below, we talked and shared meals prepared by Darbin. Through Yamaguchi I met a single other university student, Eiji Kohso [高祖英二], who was also practicing macrobiotics.

Early in the summer of 1968 I attended a week-long summer camp organized by the Tokyo group. It was held at a Buddhist temple in the countryside and was attended by about 120 people, including Lima, Dr. Ushio and other teachers. Although there were children and young people and a smattering of men of various ages, many of the participants were women over fifty. Most of these I learned had been sick at one time, had been cured by a macrobiotic diet and were returning for an annual tune-up. The day began early with cleaning and physical exercises. There were lectures and cooking classes throughout the day. The talks focused on the Unique Principle, diet and medicine. A Mr. Hideo Ohmori [大森英櫻], who had for years been working successfully with macrobiotic diet therapy in a clinic near Tokyo, was present. He gave long, though interesting, talks on curing with food, on the crucial role of salt, and other subjects. As I recall, the meals, like most macrobiotic meals I received in Japan, consisted of brown rice, miso soup and well-cooked vegetables, and were, for me, very salty. The highlight of the week was the serving of a huge fresh watermelon which everyone enjoyed with great relish. Later that season I attended a similar session organized by the Osaka group. Okada and Yamaguchi were the featured teachers and the ambience and the type of people participating were about the same..

I returned to the United States in August, 1968 and did not visit Japan again until eight and a half years later, in February of 1977. Much had changed. Lima still lived in Star Heights but there was a new five-story center in the northwest part of the city, not far from her home. This was the headquarters of Nippon C.I. ("Centre Ignoramus") and of Intermac ("Macrobiotics International"). On the ground floor was a well-stocked and busy shop selling high quality food including organically grown rice and vegetables, as well as miso, tamari and whole grain breads. On the second floor was a large lecture and meeting room, and a shop selling macrobiotic books and tapes. On sale were new editions of Ohsawa's works, some of which had been out of print for 30 or 40 years. There was also a reprint of Ishizuka's "A Scientific Nutritional Theory of Long Life" available. On the third floor there was a large kitchen which Lima used for cooking classes several times a week. The building also contained editorial offices for the monthly magazine *Atarashiki Sekai e* [新しき世界へ] ("To the New World"). Printed on thick glossy paper, it contained excerpts from Ohsawa's letters, books and former magazines; long, beautifully photographed cooking articles by Lima; pieces on macrobiotic food and medicine; and news from around Japan and from abroad. Though those working and participating in the center still tended to be middle-aged, there were also men and women in their twenties and thirties.

In Osaka, as well, there were new quarters and expanded activities. On a side street in a busy section of the city was a similar ferro-concrete building of five stories. A large sign read "Sekai Seishoku Kyōkai" [世界正食協会] ("World Proper Food Cooperative"). A smaller one said "Musō Shokuhin." On the ground floor was a large retail shop with macrobiotic products, but also featuring Lima brand natural cosmetics, and a host of the semi- or not-quite-macrobiotic foods that fill the typical Japanese "health food" store. Above were lecture rooms and a large "teaching kitchen." Two floors were occupied by the main offices of Musō which had grown into a major producer and distributor of natural and macrobiotic foods, both in Japan and internationally. There were also editorial offices for a monthly magazine, and on the top floor, a clinic. Here Okada and others gave dietary consultations and practiced acupuncture and moxibustion.

There was even by this time a macrobiotic center in Kyoto. In the northeast part of the city, not far from the university, was a tiny storefront with an English sign "Kyoto Macrobiotic Center." This was more than a gesture of internationalist panache. Many of the customers were in fact foreigners. Run by Toshihiko Matsuda [松田敏彦], the shop, no larger than twelve feet by twelve feet, was piled high with bags of rice, boxes of noodles and kegs of miso and tamari. With Matsuda's help I discovered a restaurant in the city that served brown rice.

Since returning to the U.S. in August, 1978 I have made two more trips to Japan, each about one month long, in 1981 and in 1984. On the more recent, I toured the chief macrobiotic centers. In Tokyo the various activities at Nippon C.I. were going well. Lima, vital and elegant in her mid-eighties, continues to write and to teach. Students come from around Japan (and from around the world) to attend her cooking classes. The food company under the name "Ohsawa Japan" is thriving and has begun to export its high quality goods to the United States. Several groups now offer activities in English for the city's large foreign population and for English-speaking Japanese. "Macrobiotics Tokyo," directed by Phillip and Yukiko Janetta, longtime students of the Kushis, sponsors lectures, counseling, cooking classes and a newsletter. "Makro-Bios", headed by Tadashi and Noriko Ito offer similar activities, and there are English classes as well at the "Open Center" of Nippon C.I.

In Osaka the macrobiotic community had been set back by the death of Okada. It rallied, though, and formed a steering committee to promote activities in the area and to expand on the work done by the past president. Musō has become one of the largest natural foods companies in the country, riding the *shizen shoku boomu* ("natural food boom") that is now sweeping Japan. A fresh and revitalized magazine, *Konpa* 21 ("Compass for the 21st Century") is trying to reach a broader audience.

212

In Kyoto, Matsuda is alive and well, and somehow supporting six children and a wife with his shop. He has even squeezed a macrobiotic restaurant into a tatami room behind the store. There his brother Teruo, a master chef and for six years the head cook at a macrobiotic restaurant in Paris, prepares gourmet meals. Not far away, though, there is competition from a macrobiotic eating place in the Kyoto Holiday Inn!

I traveled as well to more out of the way places. In Wakayama Prefecture I visited a farm homestead established by Izumi Maruyama (丸山和泉], son of Dr. Hiroshi Maruyama, long-time associate of Ohsawa. Named "Shin Do Fu Ji" it is an attempt to realize, even in a highly technological and urbanized society, the ideal of "man and earth not two." In a tiny teacup valley high in the mountainous interior of the province, Maruyama has taken an abandoned farm and made it nearly self-sufficient. He raises his own rice and other grains, beans, vegetables and fruit, including ume plums for pickling.

In his early forties, Maruyama lives with his wife (a second, the first having fled the hardships of the life) and children and publishes a little newsletter each season called *Shin Do Fu Ji*. Maruyama seems to enjoy his life on the land for its own sake and as an inspiration for others. "My greatest pleasure is to feed my family and guests on the food I have raised on my own land, and picked with my own hands," he says.

In another part of Wakayama, in the city of Nachi Katsuura, not far from the birthplaces of Ohsawa and Kushi, I visited another center. Its roots go back to the time of Ohsawa and many of its members are of that older generation. But there is also a substantial younger group which has formed a smaller circle within the organization. Calling themselves "*Koku no Kai*" [穀の会] ("The Cereal-Grains Club") these people take the macrobiotic diet and way of life as basic, and try to combine it with other aspects of an alternate life-style, including communal living, organic farming, handicrafts, meditation, yoga and other spiritual practices.

In Kanagawa Prefecture, a young couple have a center where they teach macrobiotic diet and cooking as well as "Oki Yoga." This is a dynamic form of Yoga developed by Masahiro Oki [沖正弘], a one-time student of Ohsawa. Oki runs a large dōjō or training center in Mishima City, where a macrobiotic regime is observed. The couple seem to do very well with their combined macrobiotic and yogic practice and teaching. A sizable and active community has formed around their center.

These experiences and encounters reflect the history of macrobiotics in Japan since 1966. Immediately after Ohsawa's death there was a period of stagnation, even paralysis, when the focus was on the mere survival of the movement. Then slowly, with the persistent efforts of Lima, Ushio, Ohmori and others in Tokyo, and of Okada, Maruyama, Yamaguchi and their associates in Osaka, the two principal centers of the movement were strengthened and stablilized. In each, a strong business foundation was established. Educational and publishing activities expanded and began to attract new people, including young ones. Many of these were interested in macrobiotics not merely as a dietary cure for disease, but as part of a broader way of life. Many incorporated it into related activities such as agriculture, yoga and the martial arts. Meanwhile, around the country, macrobiotic activities increased. Old centers revived, new ones appeared. A 1984 issue of "*Atarashiki Sekai e*" lists some 160 affiliated centers and food shops throughout the country.

As in America it is difficult to estimate the number of macrobiotic people in Japan. Here too there is the problem of definition. What indeed distinguishes a macrobiotic person? Is it the eating of brown rice, the acceptance of the Yin-Yang cosmology, membership in the Nippon Centre Ignoramus? The combined circulation of the macrobiotic magazines is less than 10,000. So while there are estimates of hundreds of thousands, a realistic and conservative figure would be around 30,000.

Here again, though, the impact of the movement is greater than its numbers indicate. It has helped greatly to make the public aware of dangers in the present diet. In 1953 Japan was shocked by the "Morinaga Incident." The Morinaga Milk Company was using arsenic in the production of dried milk, and a batch became lethally contaminated. One hundred and eighty-six infants died of poisoning. A furor arose and the company passed the incident off as a freak occurrence. Ohsawa contacted his long time associate Keishi Amano, a biologist then working in the research laboratory of the National Fisheries Ministry. He urged Amano to write a book exposing the company and the dangers inherent in its processing techniques. The scientist did so, and later published other books on the dangers of food processing and of chemical additives. These included *Doku no Goshiki* [毒の五色] ("The Five Colors of Poison")[1] and *Osoroshii Shokumotsu, Osorubeki Shokuhin* [恐ろしい食物・恐るべき食品] ("Horrible Foods, Frightening Foods").[2] To the present time Amano has remained a strong voice warning Japan about its adulterated food products.

Dr. Hiroshi Maruyama, until his retirement in the late 1970s, was Professor of Nutrition at Osaka University. He too has been an outspoken and influential critic of contemporary manufactured foods. His book *Shokuhin Kōgai Ron* [食品公害論], ("A Theory of Pollution in Food"), published in 1974, also did much to increase public awareness.[3] Amano, Maruyama and other macrobiotic teachers have been among the few authorities speaking out on the dangers of agricultural chemicals and food additives. Recently, public attention to these problems has helped create a "natural foods boom."

Through its foods businesses the macrobiotic movement has helped establish an alternative food economy in Japan. Musō is one of the three largest natural foods companies in Japan, and Ohsawa Japan, while smaller and catering to the macrobiotic market, is also influential. Mitoku, though solely an exporter at this time, is a dynamic and growing company. These firms have deeply affected the growing and production of foods within the "natural foods" network. They have actively encouraged farmers to use organic methods to cultivate rice, beans, tea, pickling-plums and other basic macrobiotic items. They have encouraged food processors who use traditional methods of producing such staples as miso, shoyu, umeboshi, tofu, and vinegar. In many cases they have helped revive lapsed and nearly forgotten methods.

In addition, many of the people active in organic agriculture and in the manufacture of natural foods come from the macrobiotic community. An example is in the natural salt industry. The Japanese salt supply is controlled by a government monop-

214

oly which imports and distributes highly refined Mexican sea salt. It is technically illegal to produce or market salt except on a very small scale. Two companies, both founded and run by macrobiotic people, have begun to make and to distribute, where possible, a better salt. To the refined Mexican salt they add *nigari*, a sea water concentrate, to replenish the important trace minerals. This *amashio* or "sweet salt" currently accounts for about 2 percent (6,000 tons) of the annual consumption of edible salt. Macrobiotic people are active at the retailing end of the industry as well. Musō itself has developed a franchise system of about eighty "Musō Health Shops" which make available macrobiotic and near-macrobiotic quality foods.

As in America, the macrobiotic community has had an impact on the broader alternative medical movement. Many acupuncturists, shiatsu practitioners and experts in palm-healing etc. were introduced to holistic medicine through macrobiotics. And many established practitioners have adopted aspects of macrobiotic practice to supplement their own techniques. The other dimensions of the "counterculture" in Japan are not nearly so developed. Nevertheless, among back-to-the-land people and spiritual communities one is likely to find macrobiotic people or at least signs of macrobiotic influence in diet.

Thus, in the past twenty years, after surviving the trauma of Ohsawa's death, the movement has established a solid and growing, if still modest, base. It has influenced several important areas of life in Japan. Yet it is still by no means widely known nor a major force in Japanese life. Ohsawa, his career, and the terms *genmai seishoku* [玄米正食] ("brown-rice-proper-diet") and *makurobiotikku* all are unfamiliar to the general public. The impact of the macrobiotic movement on the lives of the 120 million Japanese citizens is small. Naturally, the questions arise. Why is the prophet still without honor in his own land? Why, in the culture which for centuries nurtured a macrobiotic tradition and in which this tradition re-emerged in the modern period, has macrobiotics failed to flourish?

One obvious factor is the absence for the past twenty years of a single powerful spokesman and leader. In Japan, social and religious movements often are founded as much on a charismatic individual as on a set of teachings. The founder or leader is the focus of the group. He attracts, holds and inspires people as much by what he is as by what he teaches. Ohsawa had a measure of this kind of personal charisma. Since his passing, however, no similar figure has emerged within Japanese macrobiotics. There are numerous capable and dedicated teachers, but none with the power to attract and motivate large numbers of people. And without a strong central figure the movement has been diffuse. While on good terms, the Tokyo and Osaka groups operate independently, as do scores of smaller centers around the country. The benefits of large-scale cooperation have been lost.

The main reason, though, has been Japan's continuing love affair with Western culture. This began, of course, a century ago and, after the nationalist interlude of the 1930–45 period, resumed with a vengeance after the war. Ohsawa struggled against it in the last two decades of his life and his followers have had to do the same since then. The Japanese seem to be irresistibly drawn to what is modern, Western, and, particularly, American. With remarkable energy and thoroughness they have continued to import, adopt, adapt and usually improve every fashion and trend coming out of America and, to a slightly lesser degree, out of western Europe. In science, technology, medicine, fashion, music, in fact in nearly every domain of life they have followed the lead of the West. In many areas, particularly industry and business, they have surpassed their mentors and become leaders and innovators. The result is a high technology, consumer-oriented, secular society. The focal point of Japanese life is no longer the Buddhist temple or the Shinto shrine, it is the modern department store. Here one finds the nation's current vision of paradise—an endless glittering array of modern consumer goods. Of course native and traditional products, arts and crafts, values and way of life have not totally been discarded. Even in the department stores one may still buy a kimono or a beautifully crafted ceramic bowl for the tea ceremony. And in the appeal of the popular "new religions" is evident some religious concern. But these have been at best subtle undertones in Japanese culture.

Within this context, macrobiotic diet, medicine and philosophy seem out of date and out of place. For example, Japanese nutritional science is still largely committed to the high-protein and vitamin orientation which it inherited long ago from the West. Its recommendations, plus the drift of popular taste, have continued to change Japanese food habits. Rice, miso soup and other traditional foods are still eaten, though often in an instant and highly processed form. But, especially for the young, the diet consists increasingly of hamburgers (MacDonald's, needless to say, is very popular), potatoes, milk, cheese and ice cream, soft drinks and candy. To them, a macrobiotic meal of thick miso soup, brown rice, and fried burdock may seem as exotic, incomprehensible and unappealing as it might to a Kansas high school cheerleader. Few young people have ever eaten brown rice, and many do not even know what it is. Once I asked my junior college English class what they thought of a "brown rice diet." In the ensuing conversation it became clear that most of the girls did not know what brown rice is, that they thought it grew from a different seed than white rice. That the macrobiotic movement has tended to emphasize a narrow and Yang form of the diet, featuring brown rice, salty soup and vegetables, with little salad or fruits, has not helped. For the younger generation in Japan, raised on a Westernized diet, such foods may be biologically inappropriate as well as unappealing in taste. Like their American and European counterparts, they may require a gentle transition to a more liberal form of the diet. For the older generation, spartan meals of brown rice and vegetables carry memories of poverty and war. Before World War II, unpolished rice was the food of those too poor to afford white rice. During the conflict, brown rice, usually poorly and tastelessly prepared, was everyone's main food.

Macrobiotic medicine has a similarly disadvantaged position in Japanese society. Western allopathic medicine is very strong. Its doctors have the highest income and status of any group in the country. A standard medical degree is the passport to a life of prestige, wealth and ease. There is, to be sure, an alternative medical system consisting of acupuncturists, herbalists and shiatsu practitioners. Of these, the acupuncturists are particularly well-organized and well-respected. They have three years of full-time training and must pass a national licensing exam. Still their status and income does not match that of the medical doctors. The national health insurance covers only "modern" therapies and medicaments. At the bottom of this hierarchy is macrobiotic medicine, something like a fringe of the fringe, a court of last resort. The typical Japanese with a health problem will go first to a medical doctor. Failing to find relief he may go to an acupuncturist or herbalist. Then he may even try a faith healer or one of the religious groups which focus on healing. One of these is named simply *Gan ga naoru Kyō* [癌が愈る教] ("The Religion That Cures Cancer"). Finally, in desperation, he may end up at a macrobiotic counselor learning about brown rice and the importance of chewing.

Despite these various hurdles a good number of sick people do resort to macrobiotics. Many, however, even if they are obviously helped by it, do not continue the diet nor remain active in the movement. Because they have come to it in a medical crisis they tend to regard it as a crisis therapy to be put aside when the illness is gone. In 1978 I was sitting in a coffee shop near Kyoto University discussing my research with a Japanese friend. A well-dressed woman with gray hair was sitting across the table and, overhearing our conversation, interrupted to say that she had known Ohsawa some years before. She had been seriously ill and when all else failed had met him and received dietary advice. Her cure was rapid and total. I asked her if she still observed a macrobiotic diet or had any contact with the local center. A bit shamefacedly she glanced down at her cup of coffee and apple pastry and answered "no" to both questions. Soon after regaining her health she had resumed her former eating habits. There are many such people who have been cured once or several times by a therapeutic form of the macrobiotic diet.

Within Japan's modern, scientific, and secular milieu, macrobiotic philosophy also seems a bit out of place. Ohsawa tried, and his successors in Japan have continued the effort, to make the Yin-Yang cosmology into an up-to-date, scientifically respectable system. Nevertheless, to most Japanese, especially to the youth, its basic terms and approach seem *"furukusai,"* antiquated, musty, irrelevant. And, to a decidedly secular and materialistic society, themes such as the "spiritual destiny of man" and the "Tao of Food" have scant appeal. The minority with a real religious interest are more likely to be drawn to the "new religions." These offer religious systems based on familiar Buddhist and Shinto traditions; rites of worship and devotion; varied artistic, athletic and medical facilities; and a well-developed system of community support. The yet smaller minority wishing to pursue rigorously some Tao or spiritual path will go to a living teacher of an established discipline such as judō or kadō. Ohsawa and the macrobiotic literature promise, through proper diet, liberation from the ego and from the material world into the bliss and peace of the egoless, spiritual state. But, as a Tao, macrobiotics lacks a long and convincing tradition. More crucially, it lacks a living master. The *sensei-deshi* [先生—弟子] ("master-disciple") relationship implicit in a Tao requires a living teacher as an immediate inspiration and guide. Among the macrobiotic teachers in Japan today, few would claim this role.

Thus, over the past decades in Japan, macrobiotics has had little popular appeal. As a diet, medicine, philosophy and way of life it has been out of step with the dominant culture. And its offerings to those seeking alternatives have been limited. What Japan has wanted, macrobiotics did not have to give. And what macrobiotics has had to give, Japan has had little interest in. Yet another circumstance has inhibited the spread of macrobiotics in Japan. That is the special nature of social life.

Let us assume that Mr. Tanaka, suffering from stomach ulcers, has come upon macrobiotics. Faced with a major operation he decides to try a therapeutic diet. He convinces his wife to cook brown rice and vegetables for him. He is soon cured and is absolutely convinced that this way of eating is the basis of life and long health.

Tanaka also studies macrobiotic philosophy and becomes deeply interested in Ohsawa's Yin-Yang theories. He learns of the work of Nippon C.I. and other macrobiotic organizations and sees them as important for the welfare of Japan. There is, nevertheless, a good chance that Tanaka will not pursue his involvement with macrobiotics.

Japan is a society of groups, rather than of individuals. The harmony and welfare of the whole is more important than that of any part of it. The family is the primary social group. Tanaka's enthusiasm for macrobiotics may threaten the unity of the family. His wife may object to the long trips to buy food. His children may be afraid of being ridiculed or ostracized in school. His elderly parents may find the brown rice unpalatable and difficult to chew. Under medical duress, Tanaka might ask that a separate meal be cooked or that everyone temporarily share his regimen. Over the long term, though, he will more likely give in to the majority wish. The general sharing of a common diet, even one he does not prefer, is better than undermining the harmony of the household.

At Tanaka's office there would be additional pressures. Like most large firms, his company has a cafeteria, and he eats there daily with his co-workers. For Tanaka to eat separately or to bring his own food would create a subtle fissure in his relationship with the group. Also, he is expected to socialize and drink several evenings a week with his clients. Much important business is transacted at such times. If, for dietary reasons, Tanaka could not take part he would be hurt professionally as well as socially.

A more subtle social pressure, of which Tanaka himself might not be aware, also could prevent his involvement with macrobiotics. Japan is not only a society of groups, but of hierarchically arranged groups. Each company, university, golf club and religious group has a specific social status. Depending on wealth and tradition, some are high, some are low. And the place in society of a person and his family depends on the status of the groups with which he is associated. While the macrobiotic groups are entirely respectable, their status is not particularly high. This goes back in part to Ohsawa, who was an outsider and a renegade in relation to the high prestige groups in Japan: the academics, scientists and physicans. The movement now includes many distinguished people but not yet enough to change this basic image. Also, it is not very rich. It has not had the money to build a magnificent headquarters such as those belonging to many of the "new religions." If Tanaka were a very status-conscious person he might hesitate in getting too involved with the macrobiotic group.

There are, of course, many versions of Tanaka's case. There is the housewife who wants to follow a macrobiotic diet but whose husband and children have no interest. There is the college student living at home whose parents do not share his passion for unpolished rice. There is the ambitious young "salary-man" who has decided to focus on advancing his career. It is not surprising that there are many "ideological macrobiotics" in Japan. These are people who believe in the diet, accept its philosophy, and may attend an occasional lecture. But they seldom eat macrobiotic food and do not take an active role in any of the organizations. It is also not surprising that the macrobiotic movement consists largely of single people living alone, and of entire families in their full three or four generational span.

Since 1966 (as before) the macrobiotic movement in Japan has encountered obstacles, both obvious and subtle. That it has survived and thrived as much as it has is a tribute to the energy and commitment of its leaders and supporters, and to the relevance of its teachings, even in a hostile or indifferent environment. Though it still lacks a charismatic leader and massive popular support, it has today an array of resources. They include:

- many older teachers with long experience in macrobiotic cooking, medicine and philosophy;
- a growing number of younger teachers and supporters;
- well-established publishing activities;
- strong businesses engaged in the growing, manufacture, wholesaling and retailing of macrobiotic-quality foods;
- interlocking relations with the holistic health and the organic agricultural movement, as well as other parts of Japan's fledgling counterculture; and
- the stimulation and support of macrobiotic people from the West now living in Japan.

At present, the tide of Japanese popular culture still seems to be moving in a direction opposite to that of macrobiotics. But there are signs that this is changing. Japan, after a long period of looking outward for inspiration and direction may now be turning within, looking to its own traditions and cultural genius. In part, it may be following the lead of America and western Europe in re-examining the assumptions of modern life, and searching for a simpler and more integrated style of life. Whatever the reasons, Japan, a decade or so after the West, is beginning to develop a broad-based counterculture and to incorporate elements of it into the mainstream way of life.

This means that there will be more and more people in Japan looking for things that, until recently, were not in great demand. Among them are:

- a simple, practical and healthful diet;
- a holistic approach to the prevention and cure of disease;
- a way of understanding the universe that is insightful and free of superstition and cant; and
- a vision of the spiritual destiny of humankind.

Theoretically, the macrobiotic movement in Japan has something to offer relevant to each of these points. Whether it will be able to marshal its resources and to speak compellingly to the coming era remains to be seen.

---

[1] Amano, Keishi, *Goshiki no Doku* ("The Five Colors of Poison"), (Shin-Seikatsu Kyōkai, 1953)
[2] ———, *Osorubeki Shokumotsu*, ("Horrible Foods, Frightening Foods") (Chikuma Shobō, Tokyo, 1956)
[3] Maruyama, Hiroshi, *Shokuhin Kōgai Ron* ("A Theory of Pollution in Food") (Iryō Tosho Shuppan-sha, Tokyo, 1974)

12

After the Master:
Part Three:
Europe and Elsewhere

In 1966 macrobiotics in Europe was a very small but vital movement. In Paris and in Brussels there were substantial groups, each supporting food shops, restaurants and publishing activities. In St. Martin-Latem, near Ghent, the Lima Company had developed into a thriving producer and distributor of macrobiotic food. In Sweden, Germany, Holland, and Italy there were smaller centers of interest and activity. All this was held together by Ohsawa's charismatic authority. His sudden death was a tremendous blow to the movement.

There were, however, others qualified to lead and to teach. They included several Japanese disciples of Ohsawa—Clim Yoshimi who had settled in Belgium, and Eb Nakamura and Augustine Kawano who were in Germany. Among them also were long-time European associates such as Mme. Rivière and René Levy in France, a Dr. Meganck in Belgium, and Ilse Clausnitzer in Sweden. Though shocked and demoralized, these and other leaders kept up their activities after Ohsawa's passing. Meetings, lectures, summer camps, magazine and book publishing, food shops and restaurants were continued.

There was little if any growth, however. The teachings were much the same—the Unique Principle, the brown-rice-diet,—but without "le Maitre" the impact was not the same. Few new people, even from among the young, who in America were flocking to macrobiotics, entered the movement. In France, differences in opinion and personality which had begun to surface while Ohsawa was alive grew more intense. A major split developed in the Paris community. Smaller centers in other countries limped along or closed down. In the years following Ohsawa's death macrobiotics in Europe was at best "on hold."

In the late '60s and early '70s there was an influx of young Americans into Europe. Many had been involved in the drug culture and the peace movement or other early aspects of the counterculture. Many had some experience and understanding of macrobiotics as it was developed in the States under Aihara's and Kushi's influence. Little substantial activity developed, however. It was mostly a diffusion of new ideas. In 1972 Bill Tara, who had worked with the Kushis in Boston and Los Angeles, went to London and decided to stay on. Though at first active mainly in the food business, he began to lecture regularly. In 1975 he helped arrange a seminar for Kushi in London. Kushi went to London and also visited the continent. With this visit began a new era of macrobiotics in Europe.

Between 1976 and 1980 Kushi, often accompanied by his wife Aveline, visited Europe two or even three times a year, staying a month or more each time, and giving lectures, seminars, and consultations. He visited nearly every country in western Europe, some of them many times. Kushi taught a more liberal form of the diet and emphasized the importance of transition periods. He explained diagnosis, physiognomy, and macrobiotic medicine. He spoke inspiringly about agriculture and ecology, about individual spiritual development, and about macrobiotics and world peace. As had happened in America, Kushi's personal qualities and his teaching attracted many people, especially among the young. One group of about twenty-five people was so impressed that they followed him around from country to country. Convinced that Kushi was an extra-terrestrial, they did not wish to miss one precious word! Others, no less inspired, decided to commit themselves to macrobiotics. Many went to Boston or London (where Kushi Institutes had been established) to get a firm grounding in macrobiotic theory and practice, and then returned to set up activities and centers in their own countries.

Thus, by the early 1980s there was a large and growing network of macrobiotic groups. In the summer of 1981 an all-European conference was held in Innsbruck, Austria. Over seven hundred people gathered to study with the Kushis and with various teachers from around the continent. There was simultaneous translation into five languages. In 1982 a European Macrobiotic Association was formed. A permanent secretariat was established in Antwerp and annual congresses began to be held. In the summer of 1984 an international summer camp was held in Lenk, Switzerland and drew over 500 people from around Europe. Plans were made to set up a central Kushi Institute in Bern to provide advanced studies for all of Europe.

While this new, Kushi-inspired movement was developing, the long-established leaders in Europe continued their activities. Riviere, Levy, Yoshimi, Nakamura and others kept working as they had for many years past. There was little cooperation between the two groups, however. As a result there are now two distinct macrobiotic communities in Europe. One is quite small, made up mostly of older people, and focuses on Ohsawa and his teachings. The other is large and expanding, is dominated by people under forty, and looks mainly to Kushi. There is little or no animosity between the two. They have many cordial social, business, and intellectual contacts, and they tend to see themselves as part of a larger whole. Yet there is not the mutual support and pooling of resources one would expect from two groups that have so much in common.

Besides this general history of macrobiotics in Europe after 1966, there are various national ones. Each country, each center, has its own story with its cast of characters and sequence of events. To cover these in detail would take a volume in itself. The brief accounts which follow give only highlights. Through oversight or because of limitations of space I have failed to mention, or mentioned only in passing, many people who have worked hard and made substantial contributions. My apologies to them.

Great Britain: Great Britain is one of the few European countries which had little or no macrobiotic activity during the Ohsawa years. The first signs of life were in the late 1960s when Greg and Craig Sams began to promote macrobiotics in

London. Of Anglo-American parentage they had learned of the movement while in the States. The brothers started a food company, Harmony Foods, and opened a small restaurant in the Portobello Road section of London. While there was little formal teaching done, macrobiotic literature and food were made available. The warmest reception was in the emerging counterculture. Many young people involved with radical politics, rock music, or with various fringe social and religious groups saw macrobiotics as a viable dietary expression of their views. There was, as in America, some misunderstanding of the diet, and proponents of the brown rice and marijuana regimen were not unknown.

In 1970 Bill Tara, then a manager of Erewhon, passed through on a longer trip eastward and gave several talks. Two years later he returned to look into the possibility of opening an Erewhon operation somewhere in Europe. When the plan fell through Tara decided to stay on and began to manage Ceres, the Sams brothers' food shop. Well-spoken, and with experience teaching macrobiotics in Boston, Chicago, and Los Angeles, Tara started to hold public meetings and talks at his home. In 1974, working with Peter Bradford, a Britisher just returned from a period of study in Boston, Tara set up Sunwheel Foods. This was a macrobiotic food company modeled after Erewhon. It dealt in macrobiotic staples including imported specialty items from Japan. Also, it produced and distributed more generally popular items like peanut butter and granola. That same year Tara, Bradford and others organized the Self Health Center to promote macrobiotics and other holistic and spiritually-oriented teachings.

By 1976 the group which had grown up around the Center felt ready for a major expansion. They organized the Community Health Foundation and rented a large, five-story Victorian school in East London. A restaurant and bookshop were opened on the ground floor. The first Kushi Institute, earlier than even the Boston school, was established on the upper level. The core curriculum, which Tara had worked out with the Kushis during one of their visits, included macrobiotic philosophy, cooking and medicine, plus Oriental diagnosis and massage. Extra space was rented out to groups with similar views and aims. The CHF was among the first self-supporting centers of macrobiotic activity. It served as a model for macrobiotic groups in other European countries including Holland, Belgium and Switzerland.

In 1975 Tara had helped arrange Kushi's first European tour. As interest developed on the continent Tara traveled widely and lectured in Belgium, Holland, Germany, and Scandinavia. Also, many aspiring teachers and leaders went from other countries to the Kushi Institute in London. Thus Tara and the London center played a major role in the development of macrobiotics throughout Europe.

Meanwhile, smaller centers began to open up around Britain. In 1978, for example, Michael Burns, an Irishman who had studied in Boston, went to Edinburgh to start activities. London, however, remained the basis of the movement. Perhaps the first macrobiotic nursery school in the West was opened in the yard behind the CHF building on Old Street.

In 1981 Tara returned to the United States to become director of the Kushi Institute of Boston. Denny Waxman, head of the Philadelphia East West Center, went to London to run the CHF and the Kushi Institute. He stayed two years. Since then the operations have been run by Kenyan-born Britisher Jon Sandifer and others.

222

Belgium: In 1966 Brussels was a major focus of macrobiotic activity. With a study group, magazine, and restaurants, and with a support community that included many academics and professionals, it was second only to Paris as a center. Despite the loss of Ohsawa, the group there has continued to function over the years. A number of individuals have been important in this. Clim Yoshimi, though living near Ghent and working in Paris, was a consistent supporter. Until his death in 1975, Dr. Meganck was active lecturing and applying macrobiotics in his medical practice. In 1969 Roland Yasuhara [安原ローラン] arrived from Japan. He had been Ohsawa's personal secretary in Tokyo during the early 1960s. Yasuhara joined forces with Josianne Bagno, who had worked for Ohsawa in the same role during his European sojourns. The two eventually married and still work to continue educational and publishing activities. While no permanent center exists, this group, which looks mainly to Ohsawa and his teachings, does support a restaurant and other modest activities. Yoshimi, who now lives full time in Ghent, has a small center.

Meanwhile, Flemish-speaking Antwerp has developed as a center of the "second wave" of macrobiotics. In 1970 Marc van Cauwenberghe, a young doctor from Ghent, became involved in macrobiotics through Dr. Meganck. After some study with the Brussels group he went to Boston to study with Kushi. Returning to Belgium he began to practice macrobiotic medicine and to lecture in Antwerp and Ghent. By the mid-'70s other young men, including Rik Vermuyten and George von Wessenbeck, had become committed to the movement. They attended Kushi's lectures around Europe. They invited him to give seminars in Antwerp. Some went to Boston or to London to study further and then returned to Belgium. By the late '70s various activities had developed in Antwerp including a food store, book shop, and extensive publishing ventures. An attractive magazine, *Netelblad* ("Thistle Leaf"), was appearing monthly. Since 1981, there has been a Kushi Institute with a summer intensive as well as year-round study. Antwerp is the home of the secretariat of the European Macrobiotic Association and has hosted the annual congress.

Meanwhile, in St. Martin-Latem, the Lima Company has continued to supply food to the macrobiotic, and to the broader natural foods community throughout Europe. Still owned and operated by the Gevaert family, it is widely recognized as a pioneer in the natural foods movement and an upholder of the highest standards in food quality. Recently it has opened a branch operation in southern France where it is encouraging growers to produce organic cereals and other crops.

Holland: The roots of macrobiotics in Holland go back to the Ohsawa period. In the early '60s a young jazz musician named Mike Leusch discovered Ohsawa and the diet. He attended the 1965 summer camp in Port Manech. Returning to Amsterdam, he founded a small restaurant where the food and the ambience reflected the salty and spartan "Zen Macrobiotic" ethos. This attracted many people from the Bohemian and musical community in the Dutch capital, and Leusch dreamed of having a macrobiotic jazz club facing on one of the city's canals. This was never realized but Leusch did introduce many young people to macrobiotics before withdrawing from an active role in the mid-'70s.

Two of these were Adelbert and Wieke Nelissen, a young, energetic couple. They founded a food wholesale and retail company called Manna which, despite some ups and downs, is now one of the largest natural foods companies in the country. They are also active in teaching and publishing translations of macrobiotic books. An Ost-West Zentrum was established in Amsterdam, housing a restaurant, administration offices, consultation rooms, and areas for practice of the martial arts. Since 1980 there has been a Kushi Institute there as well, which has offered a macrobiotic program in German as well as in Dutch.

In 1980 Tomas Nelissen, Adelbert's brother, returned from several years in Japan. He had studied natural agriculture there with Masanobu Fukuoka. Tomas has since set up a farm, a food company, and a small macrobiotic study center in the countryside. Also, in the past several years graduates of the various Kushi Institutes in London and Boston, as well as in Amsterdam, have set up numerous centers in the smaller cities and towns of Holland.

France: At the time of Ohsawa's death, Paris was his favorite city and France his second homeland. Despite his frequent criticisms, Ohsawa loved the French people and their culture, and they loved him in return. In Paris and around the country he had many loyal followers who regarded him with a mixture of affection, reverence, and fear.

While some disappeared from macrobiotics with the loss of Ohsawa's inspirational presence, many continued their activities. In Paris Mme. Tartiere kept open her Maison Ignoramus as a source of macrobiotic information. With a quite different approach, Mme. Rivière operated, as she still does today, the *Institut Tenryu*. It includes a food shop and restaurant, both dedicated to the memory of Ohsawa. With the help of Yoshimi as translator, Riviere published many of Ohsawa's writings. She gave weekly cooking classes, which have continued until the present time. Several macrobiotic restaurants, including the Bol en Bois continued to serve the public. Outside Paris, flamboyant former actor René Levy went on teaching, writing, and giving medical advice. He established and successfully ran several macrobiotic clinics around the country.

Despite the dedicated work of these and others, macrobiotics in France did not prosper. The strict and narrow version of the diet taught by Ohsawa in his last years attracted few, even among the young. Macrobiotics played little role in the alternative culture in France as it developed in the late '60s and early '70s.

Kushi's first visit in 1976 began what promised to be a major change. With skilled linguist Mateo Margarinos (who also accompanied him to Spain and Portugal) translating for him, Kushi lectured to receptive audiences in Paris and elsewhere. On subsequent visits as many as 700 people attended his talks and seminars. Many were young people, some of whom subsequently went to Boston to study. While among the old guard there were objections to Kushi's liberalizing the diet and to his giving away "too many secrets" (i.e., advanced diagnostic techniques and spiritual teachings), it seemed as if new life were coming into the tired body of French macrobiotics.

This renaissance, though, was short-lived. In the late '70s the movement suffered a major setback. Roger Ikor, a professor at the Sorbonne and a prize-winning novelist, began a bitter attack on macrobiotics. Ikor's son, a man in his early twenties, apparently had been having physical and psychological problems and had stayed for a while at Levy's residential clinic. Some time later he committed suicide. The elder Ikor wrote a book, *J'accuse Forte* ("I Strongly Accuse"), in which he attacked the macrobiotic movement as a sect based on superstition and fallacy, and which leads young people astray. He analyzed Ohsawa's writings, criticizing statements such as "I can cure any incurable disease in ten days," as ridiculous and self-contradictory. Ikor threatened to bring Levy and others to court. While no suit was ever filed, Ikor and his attacks received wide attention in the press and media. Macrobiotics was presented to the public eye as the "killer diet." Both the activities of the veteran teachers and the growing momentum of the newer group were severely damaged. Most educational activities stopped and the *Yin Yang* monthly magazine ceased publication.

As of late 1984, however, there are again signs of an awakening. Levy's clinic in the southwest corner of the country seems to be doing quite well. In nearby Toulouse, Gerard Cazals has established a small center including a restaurant. In Paris there are educational activities at the restaurant-center Le Grain Sauvage. Also, Kushi has begun to visit Paris again, and his work with cancer patients has received much attention. *Le Linie Bleu* ("The Blue Line") which is an association of people fighting cancer, wants to promote macrobiotics in France. There are plans to open a permanent center in Paris in 1985.

Germany: Despite Ohsawa's and Lima's pleasant sojourn in the Black Forest Inn of the Finsterlins, and the presence of two of his students, Augustine Kawano and Eb Nakamura, there was little macrobiotic activity in Germany during Ohsawa's lifetime. After his death, and even in recent years, macrobiotic activities in Germany have been minimal. Nakamura has a mail-order business in Düsseldorf, selling macrobiotic books and food. He publishes a newsletter but does little public teaching. Kawano also is in business and has spent much energy in formulating and elaborating his own version of the Unique Principle.

Even the influence of Kushi and American-based macrobiotics has had little impact as yet. Since the mid-'70s, several centers in Munich and elsewhere began but had a brief life. Thus, there has been very little macrobiotic education going on in Germany. Those wishing to study have had to go to Boston or London or to German language intensive programs held in Amsterdam. In the early '80s, American Steve Acuff and his Danish wife Karen (both trained primarily through the London center) developed a small group in Hamburg. Though the Acuffs have moved to Sweden, this center has continued under local leadership. It now runs a food shop, a small restaurant and offers classes in cooking, massage, yoga and related topics. Acuff and Mario Binetti of Bern, Switzerland do occasional seminars in German cities. But as two of the very few German speaking macrobiotic teachers they are in great demand elsewhere. Late in 1984 Jan van Toorn, a Dutchman long a leader in South American macrobiotics, returned to Europe with the intent of starting activities in Germany. In general, though, macrobiotics there has lagged far behind the movement in neighboring countries.

There is one group which prefers the macrobiotics of an earlier era. In West Berlin, 30-year-old Til Dietrich von Rentzow and a small coterie cherish the teachings of Ohsawa. Publishing a small magazine, von Rentzow decries the recent emphasis on physical health and on appealing to the general public. The real aim of macrobiotics, he asserts, is spiritual and esoteric. Well-spoken and always elegantly dressed, von Rentzow occasionally makes dramatic appearances at European congresses and seminars to remind his colleagues of the Ohsawa tradition.

Switzerland: There has been little macrobiotic activity in Switzerland until quite recently. In the '60s, as a result of Ohsawa's work in neighboring France, there were a few macrobiotic people in French-speaking Geneva. But only in the late '70s did organized activities begin. A young man named Paul Simon sponsored several summer camps in Gstaad. These were attended by the Kushis and attracted people from all over Europe. In 1980 Pierre Pesch, a Frenchman who had studied at the Kushi Institute in Boston, settled in Geneva and began to teach macrobiotics and to gather a small community. About the same time Mario Binetti, a native of the German speaking part of the country, returned from the United States where he had been studying "special education." He and his Texas-born wife Marlise studied at the Kushi Institute in London and then established a center in the capital city of Bern. This soon included a restaurant, food store, and educational facilities. In the summer of 1984 the Bern group organized a successful all-European summer camp at Lenk, high in the picturesque Alps. This event promises to become an annual tradition. Since a German language Kushi Institute and an international advanced study course will be sited in Bern from 1985, Switzerland promises to become a focus of international macrobiotic activity.

Austria: Here too, there seems to have been little or no activity during or immediately after the Ohsawa years. To date, the influence of the Kushi brand of macrobiotics also has been small, though in the late '70s some Austrian young people did study in Boston. The primary stimulus for macrobiotics in Austria has come through the work of Yugoslav Zea Lao Shun and his Austrian wife Mayli Lao Shun. Although the couple knew of Kushi, and even visited Boston, they developed their own expression of macrobiotics. While sharing basic teachings, they emphasized meditation and other explicitly Taoist spiritual practices. In 1977 Zea and Mayli established the "East West Foundation" in Wiener Neustadt, about an hour south of Vienna. They attracted a devoted group of disciples, many of whom went annually with them to China or Japan for intensive spiritual training in a temple environment. Although Zea died in an auto crash in 1982, the group has held together under Mayli's strong leadership. According to Eric Ess, the Foundation's chairman of 1984, the group sponsors "macrobiotic meetings, lectures, and cooking classes, meditation seminars in Austria and abroad, seminars for Do-In, Tai-Ch'i Chuan, shiatsu massage, polarity work and other physical and mental trainings." The group publishes a magazine as well as books on macrobiotic philosophy, medicine and cooking. There is a small branch group in Graze.

Portugal: Ohsawa's own travels did not take him to the Iberian peninsula or to Portugal. In around 1968, however, a Portuguese man returned from France where he had learned about Ohsawa and macrobiotics. He opened a small restaurant in Lisbon and began serving meals of the Ohsawa style consisting of pressure-cooked brown rice and a small amount of salty vegetables A clientele developed and a food cooperative was organized. Several years later this was taken over by Jacinto Vieira, a man who had been cured of a serious illness by the diet. Vieira was a skilled businessman, and under his direction the organization, Unimave, (United Macrobiotic Vegetarian Association) thrived. Large-scale direct importation of Japanese macrobiotic foods was begun. More food shops and restaurants opened in Lisbon and in other cities.

By the time Kushi first came to Portugal in 1976 to give seminars, the macrobiotic movement had a firm foundation. It had a broad and good reputation among the general public and was favorably presented in the media. Three to four hundred people would gather for Kushi's talks and there was often radio, television, and press coverage. With this new stimulus the movement expanded further. There are now thirteen macrobiotic restaurants in Lisbon alone. There are centers in other cities such as Porto, and for several years macrobiotic diet programs have been set up in some prisons.

Recently some problems have developed, however. Unimave, as an open cooperative with a membership fee of about 75 cents, has grown to about 7,000 members. Of these, only about ten percent have a clear idea of what macrobiotics is and have a strong commitment to it. Since its directors are elected, the early macrobiotic leaders have been replaced by people with little knowledge and/or commitment to the movement. Direction and policies have changed. Foods containing sugar, eggs, and yeast are being sold as macrobiotic foods. Dietary consultants are recommending various idiosyncratic diets and calling them "macrobiotic" regimens. There is no clear idea of what a macrobiotic diet is and what it means to be macrobiotic. The movement is in some disarray.

Consequently, Chico Varatojo, a graduate of the Kushi Institute in Boston and the ranking macrobiotic teacher in Portugal, is no longer active in Unimave. Wanting to create a clear and consistent image of macrobiotics, he has concentrated recently on educational activities. He lectures often throughout the country, and in the summer of 1984 conducted an intensive study course in the countryside. In October of that year a Kushi Institute Level I session was established in Lisbon. With his wife, Eugenia Varatojo, has been preparing a macrobiotic cookbook in Portuguese. He also hopes to publish introductory materials.

According to Varatojo, some of the difficulties arise from the poor state of the national economy. Because of the low exchange rate of the currency, it is prohibitively expensive to import Japanese macrobiotic foods. It is also very costly to bring in foreign teachers and to acquire copyright and translation privileges for books in other languages. Of course these factors will make the Portuguese more independent and strong and will prove a benefit in the long run. And there are clear advantages for the movement in the country. The typical Portuguese diet consisting of grains, fish, vegetables and fruit, with very little meat and sugar, is not unlike the basic macrobiotic diet. Thus the people quickly feel at home with the regimen. Also, the pace of life is slow and the mentality of the people straightforward. They are able to comprehend the macrobiotic philosophy and way of life very easily. Varatojo is optimistic that with adequate educational activity the movement can regain its direction and momentum.

Spain: The situation in Portugal's neighbor is somewhat similar. In the '60s and early '70s there was some Ohsawa-inspired activity, mostly in Barcelona. Roland Yasuhara took some time from his work in Brussels to run a restaurant there. And in the mid-'70s, Jan van Toorn, prior to going to South America worked with Spanish associates in promoting macrobiotics in Malaga. They began with a direct sales approach, setting up pushcarts in the streets, selling rice and miso, and explaining macrobiotics to whomever would listen.

It was after Kushi's seminars in Barcelona and Madrid in the late '70s that substantial interest developed. There was little followup education, however, and some of the activities were based on a partial or personal understanding of macrobiotics. A number of naturopathic and holistic doctors quickly adopted the macrobiotic label and began to prescribe and teach in a manner not consistent with usual macrobiotic practice. Much confusion resulted, and the government and the medical establishment began to step in. In the fall of 1984, Kushi visited Madrid and arranged to have a Kushi Institute established in that city. It is hoped that this and other educational activities will provide a strong and consistent base for the movement.

Italy: The first macrobiotic centers in Italy date from Ohsawa's time or soon afterward. All these, including the one in Rome (which catered to a rich, fashionable, mystical element of the early "counterculture," according to one eyewitness), have since disappeared. In the mid- and late '70s a new set of centers emerged. There are now major groups in Genoa, Turin and Florence and smaller ones in about forty other cities and towns. The Florence center occupies a downtown building dating from the 16th century and used formerly as a left-wing student commune. It is administered by Ferro Ledvinka, who is also senior teacher at the Kushi Institute of Florence founded in 1983. The center has a large food shop and restaurant and lists over 600 active members. In the fall of 1984 Florence hosted the annual European Congress, the first time it has been held outside of northern Europe.

Sweden: Although Sweden lies a bit north of the more beaten paths of western and central Europe, the macrobiotic movement there has had a long and interesting history. Roland Keijser has been active for many years and very kindly wrote the following "short history" expressly for this book. In it Sweden appears as a case study of European macrobiotics that is typical in many ways, but also has its unique features. We gratefully include it here.

> In June 1962 Georges Ohsawa visited Sweden and gave a very well attended lecture at "Medborgarhuset," a big lecture hall in central Stockholm. At that time vegetarianism was already rather popular and also well organized in Sweden. Among the listeners, curious about the "new prophet," were many long-time followers of various raw food and salt-free regimens. Their most powerful "guru" was the late, well-known Scandinavian dietary philosopher, Are Waerland. Ohsawa's teaching, with its emphasis on grains, salt and cooking, naturally stirred up some very strong emotions among the stoic Swedes.
>
> While everybody admired the economic simplicity and artistic sensitivity of

Japanese macrobiotic cooking, as demonstrated in October the same year by "sister" Toshi Kawaguchi, just a few seemed to grasp the depth of Ohsawa's Unique Principle, or appreciate his somewhat "primitive" and "unscientific" way of expression. Generally speaking, the Oriental ambience and way of thinking was very alien to most Nordic people at that time. Nevertheless, in the early '60s, a macrobiotic society was formed under the leadership of the late Ilse Clausnitzer and others.

For several years a rather harsh debate on macrobiotics was going on with the Swedish vegetarian movement. The result of this "battle of the sects" was that "Ohsawa-ism" was more or less condemned as heresy. At the same time the term "true macrobiotics" was reserved for a non-Oriental, more Germanic tradition largely based on the romantic nature philosophy of the early 19th century and on modern nutritional science. Among the hot topics of the day in Swedish vegetarian magazines was the question whether it was correct to call Ohsawa a "Professor," a title that has a much more specific meaning in Swedish than in French.

From then on, the young Swedish Macrobiotic Society (*Sveriges Makrobiotiska Sallskap*) had to continue almost completely on its own, without any support from the rather well-established Swedish vegetarian movement. This original conflict can still be felt more than twenty years later, and you might say that macrobiotics in Sweden always has been something like the "black sheep" of the broader Swedish health food movement.

Ilse Clausnitzer was a very hard worker. She translated some of Ohsawa's writings into Swedish, wrote her own books, edited a small macrobiotic magazine, gave lectures, consultations and cooking classes. Herself a professional chemist, she tried to give macrobiotics a stronger scientific base. Although Miss Clausnitzer wanted to develop a more Scandinavian style of macrobiotics, the Japanese influence remained very strong and gave macrobiotics a certain exotic flavor. Thanks to the enthusiasm of the early Ohsawa followers, several new food items were introduced in the Swedish natural foods market during the 1960s. Brown rice, sea salt, soy sauce, miso, sea vegetables, *bancha*, *tekka* [鉄火], have been available staple foods in Sweden ever since these pioneering years. Most of these foods were imported from Lima Products in Belgium.

At this time the ideological inspiration came largely from European macrobiotic friends in France, Germany, Switzerland, Holland and Belgium. To most Swedes in the early '60s, Japan was a rather unknown place and America, "the land of Coca Cola," was not at all the place you looked to for ideas on natural living and wholesome food.

However, in the late '60s a new wave of macrobiotics swept Scandinavia and Sweden. Young American hippies, political refugees and other adventurers, some of them students of Michio Kushi entered the country. For some years, macrobiotics became popular in certain intellectual, artistic, and political circles, and in the young "counterculture" in general. Several farming communes were started in the beginning of the '70s, and in the big cities macrobiotic-inspired restaurants began as well.

The connection between the older Ohsawa followers and these younger macrobiotic activists was not strong, however. Among other things, there was a certain "generation gap," involving different life-styles as well as different versions of the diet. While the former group remained active, but rather small and somewhat esoteric in its exclusion from the broad Swedish natural foods movement, the latter expanded and collapsed in a few years. After Ilse Clausnitzer's death in the mid-'70s, macrobiotics was ripe for a new direction.

While the Swedish Macrobiotic Society survived mainly in Stockholm, the work was also carried on by independent individuals, families and small groups here and there in all of Scandinavia. During the second half of the '70s the macrobiotic movement, as a whole, seemed to pass through a revival in a variety of places in Europe and Scandinavia. At this time Michio Kushi started to make his popular European tours, and some of the young Swedish macrobiotic friends went to Holland, France, Italy and England to get new inspiration. This was also the time when several "new age" teachings started to enter Sweden, and the rebellious generation of the late '60s generally began to take more interest in their own health of body and mind.

In these years macrobiotic friends from both the "Ohsawa tradition" (Yang), and the "hippie-tradition" (Yin), started to meet and together practice a more balanced "middle way" of macrobiotics. Several new centers were established; internationally prominent teachers began to visit Sweden more frequently; direct import of Japanese macrobiotic foods was arranged; experiments with small-scale native macrobiotic food processing was initiated; the two magazines, *Fröet* and *Tugga Själv*, found their present forms; many seminars and classes were arranged throughout the country; more active Scandinavian cooperation was developing; and in 1979 the first big macrobiotic summer camp in Sweden was realized.

During the '80s this work has continued with somewhat fluctuating, but over-all undiminished, strength. In the last few years many Swedes and Scandinavians have also visited Boston, London and Amsterdam for more intensive Kushi Institute studies. Today you will find more imported Japanese products of high quality than ever in Swedish health food shops. At the same time Scandinavia's first tofu factory, located outside Sotckholm, is doing quite well and is now also producing some miso and tempeh. Some new crops, like daikon and Hokkaido pumpkin, are being cultivated here and there; several friends are foraging their own wild dandelion and burdock roots; and the harvesting of indigenous sea vegetables is increasing.

A still-small macrobiotic movement in Sweden is today slowly reaching out a bit more to the general public, and also gaining some sympathy from the medical establishment. Its members are grateful for all the support and inspiration from the Japanese/American segment of the movement over the last decade. In 1984, though, the trend seems to be away from the centralization and institutionalization that has become a vital part of the New England style of macrobiotics which is internationally dominant. The need to find Scandinavian and European spiritual roots and to develop a more locally grounded way of life and eating are frequently-heard themes.

This orientation gives Swedish macrobiotics a somewhat ambiguous character. On the one hand it may lead to confusion and difficulties in communication with foreign friends and organizations. On the other it creates varied activities and viewpoints. The central scene is constantly changing and shifting focus. This is perhaps a balance to the early history of macrobiotics in Sweden and to the conformist and centralized nature of Swedish society as a whole. At the same time, the group tries to keep in mind the international and universal aspects of macrobiotics. Eagerly it looks ahead to the next chapter of the movement."

Roland Keijser, and Steve and Karen Acuff now settled in Ulricehamn, are actively teaching in Sweden today.

Denmark: Denmark's first major contact with macrobiotics seems to date from the late '60s and to have resulted from the influx of American "counterculture" young people. One of these was Barbara Berger. At first active mainly in the anti-war movement, Barbara learned of macrobiotics through Dufty's book *You Are All Sanpaku*, and soon became very active in it. She wrote several books and cookbooks and with her husband, Tue Geersten, and founded an East West Center in Copenhagen. Unlike most other young teachers of their generation, the Geerstens chose not to go to Boston or London to study. Their teaching developed out of contact with Ohsawa's and Kushi's books and their own study and experience. While as of 1984 the Center is still operating, it has had difficulties and is in a transition period. Tue Geersten is busy mainly with consultations and Barbara has ceased active participation.

Elsewhere in Scandinavia there are recently established centers in Oslo, Norway and Helsinki, Finland.

Frontiers Old and New: Outside North America, Japan, and western Europe, there are macrobiotic centers in most parts of the world. In some places the groups are old, large, and well-established. In others, they may consist only of a few interested people. There are also many countries in which macrobiotics is as yet unknown.

In Brazil the macrobiotic movement is extremely well-developed. This is due primarily to the work of Tomio Kikuchi [菊池富美雄], a Japanese disciple of Ohsawa who went to Brazil nearly three decades ago with the express purpose of spreading macrobiotics. Kikuchi has a large and prosperous center in Sao Paolo as well as a beautiful farm and school in the nearby countryside. In the city there are nearly a score of macrobiotic restaurants, where hundreds of people eat daily. While Kikuchi has sponsored a visit and seminar by Kushi, he has expressed disapproval of the more liberal forms of the diet as practiced in America and elsewhere. His own approach seems to be according to the more strict Ohsawa tradition. There is another large macrobiotic community in Rio de Janeiro, directed by a Mr. Zanata and smaller groups scattered throughout the country. There are various ethnic groups in Brazil, and the macrobiotic movement draws from them all, including from the one-million-member community of Japanese descent.

There is also a macrobiotic movement in the Spanish speaking section of the continent. Its primary focus is in Uruguay, and though not as old as that in Brazil, it is large and growing. It began around 1973 with the work of Enrique Kersevich, who remains active today. It was greatly bolstered by the arrival in the late '70s of Jan van Toorn and Mauricio Waroquiers. The personal sagas of van Toorn and

Waroquiers give a sense of the varied ways in which people have gotten involved in the macrobiotic movement.

Van Toorn, born in Holland, traveled all over the world as a young man. He was moved by the desire for a truth which would make life meaningful and understandable. Disappointed in this search, he finally married and settled down, learning the family meat business. Then, he went off to Uruguay to establish his own meat export firm. He met Kersevich and was given a copy of the first issue of *The Order of the Universe* magazine which had been published back in 1967. Before he had read ten pages he knew that he had found what he was looking for. Immediately he resolved to get rid of his business interests and to devote himself to macrobiotics. He rushed home, exultantly informing his wife that he at last had "found it." At first she thought he had struck oil in the back yard. She then listened patiently as van Toorn explained that they must get rid of all the food in the house and start a totally new way of life. Van Toorn agreed in time to a more gradual approach but otherwise threw himself totally into the movement. He went to Boston to meet Kushi and to unconditionally offer his services. Then he went to Malaga, Spain to introduce macrobiotics. When it seemed, with Kushi's successful seminars, that macrobiotics was going to develop there, he opted for a new frontier. Teaming with Spaniard Robert Mariani, he moved with his family back to Uruguay and settled in Montevideo.

Waroquiers, an Argentine by birth, was living on the coast of Spain near Barcelona in the mid-'70s. One night someone left a book in the bar which Waroquiers owned. It was a copy of William Dufty's *You Are All Sanpaku*. Waroquiers stayed up all night reading it, and the next morning went out to buy some brown rice. Anxious to find out more about Ohsawa and macrobiotics he went to Paris and visited one of the centers mentioned in the book. A young man there informed him that Ohsawa had died in a car crash! Waroquiers decided to go back to South America. He went to Uruguay, where he met Kersevich and van Toorn, and became actively involved in the movement. He now lives on a farm in Maldonado, where he grows burdock, lotus root and other vegetables and is busy translating and publishing macrobiotic literature.

Through the efforts of Kersevich, van Toorn, Mariani, Waroquiers and others the movement in Uruguay has prospered. The Macrobiotic Association has almost 500 active members, and among Montevideo's one million citizens there are about 6,000 people eating macrobiotically. Of these, many are lawyers, doctors and other members of the small, but influential, professional and middle class. There are three busy restaurants and over 500 places in Montevideo alone where macrobiotic staples can be purchased. Lectures and cooking classes are held at the center and there are weekly cooking classes presented on television. Macrobiotics is well known and has a very favorable public image.

These gains have not been made easily. The standard Uruguayan diet consists of about two pounds of meat per day per person, much cheese and milk, and very little grains or vegetables. Not surprisingly, many people come to macrobiotics because of health problems. Also, there is a very strong meat lobby in Uruguay. Several years ago the macrobiotic group began to distribute pamphlets focusing on the dangers of meat eating, especially in relation to cancer. Soon it was attacked

232

by the Ministry of Health. The center was ordered closed and was fined for misleading the public. The group filed a countersuit, challenging the government's claim and questioning its support of the meat industry. To back its claims, the group gathered a tremendous amount of data (much of it from the government publications and files), and won the case.

Thus Uruguay is, for the moment, the center of macrobiotics in Spanish-speaking South America. According to both Waroquiers and van Toorn, however, a greater potential center lies across the mouth of the La Plata River in Buenos Aires, Argentina. There are over 800 natural foods stores in the city and much interest in macrobiotics. There is as yet no full-time teacher and no permanent center.

Further north, in the Caribbean basin, there is also some macrobiotic activity. Venezuela has several small groups. There is a strong center in Trinidad and on Jamaica can be found one of the very few macrobiotic resort hotels, "Lady Diane's By the Sea." There are also macrobiotic people in Costa Rica, where the Kushis have visited and taught several times. Erstwhile promises of active government support of macrobiotics there have, because of political changes, failed to materialize.

In the South Pacific, both Australia and New Zealand have centers. That in Sydney was founded about ten years ago by Americans Dan and Marcea Weber. The couple had studied in Boston in the early '70s, then spent a few years in London. They went to Japan to study at the Oki Yoga Dōjō and continued on to Australia. There is also a group in Melbourne, under Don and Ann Lazzaro. More recently, a young English couple, graduates of the London K.I., have begun activities in New Zealand.

The macrobiotic group in Viet Nam goes back nearly thirty years. Since the Communist takeover of the south, however, there has been little communication with other parts of the world macrobiotic community. At least until the early '70s, there were centers in Saigon and Hue. And in Hong Kong, where Austrian leader Mayli Lao Shun has a second base of operations, there is a macrobiotic center.

The centers in the Middle East and Africa tend to be small and very recent. Both in Israel and Lebanon there was interest and activities in the late '70s, but permanent centers have emerged only in the last five years. In 1981 Sherman Goldman, former editor of the *East West Journal*, arrived in Jerusalem and did much to create a stable community. In the same period Lebanese young people, many of whom studied in Boston or London, have established ongoing activities. Greek physician Dr. John Kiprianou, after a period in Boston, established a center on the island of Rhodes in 1980. In the fall of 1984 Jon Sandifer, director of the London K.I., responded to invitations from groups in South Africa and Kenya and did extended seminars in both Johannesburg and Nairobi.

As of early 1985 there is no appreciable macrobiotic activity in the countries of Eastern Europe. In Poland, East Germany and Czechoslovakia there are small groups of interested people. It is difficult for them to get either information or macrobiotic foods. The totalitarian governments are suspicious about macrobiotics, as they are of any foreign ideology or movement. Macrobiotic books, magazines and teachers have a hard time finding their way in. Also, since the state-run food economy is oriented to meat and dairy products, grains, beans and vegetables are in short supply. There are rumours of breakthroughs, however, Supposedly, some of Kushi's writings are being translated into Russian, and a macrobiotic hotel may be opening on the Yugoslavian coast. As yet, though, macrobiotics is virtually unknown within the sphere of Soviet-dominated communist countries.

There are many other blank spaces on the world map of macrobiotics. They include mainland China, India, almost all of Africa, the Arab nations, Iran, hapless Afghanistan, and most of Spanish-speaking South and Central America.

13.

The Gospel According to Kushi

Michio Kushi is not, of course, the only interpreter of macrobiotics at the present time. There are a number of other teachers who, with their own emphasis and contributions, have developed their particular version of Ohsawa's message. They include Ohsawa's direct students such as Aihara, Yoshimi, Kikuchi, Ohmori, Yamaguchi, and Levy. They include also second generation teachers such as Tara, Tims, and Jerome Canty (active in Colorado and on the West Coast). Kushi's thought, however, is particularly wide-ranging, dealing in depth with topics from galactic history to sexual practices. Also, it has been very influential. Most of the teachers and leaders in the growing network of Kushi Institutes and East West Centers around the world have studied with Kushi. And through them, and through this network most people coming into macrobiotics are introduced to Kushi's teaching. His thought, then, represents a *de facto* orthodoxy in contemporary macrobiotics. Not everyone in the movement endorses it, of course. Some of the other first generation teachers like Kikuchi and Levy express severe reservations. But to understand the situation of macrobiotics in the world today and its possible development in the future, an overview of Kushi's thought is essential.

In developing his presentation of macrobiotics Kushi has taken much from Ohsawa, often verbatim. He has tapped various other sources ancient and modern, Eastern and Western. And he has drawn much from his own experience, research and inspiration. The result is a comprehensive and integrated system of thought, dealing with most areas of human inquiry and activity. It is a vision which has attracted and inspired many thousands of people.

The foundation of Kushi's world view is the Unique Principle, the law of Yin and Yang. In the first pages of *The Book of Macrobiotics* he observes that everything is changing, the universe is in constant flux. Kushi then lists Ohsawa's seven axioms and twelve laws, citing them as a key to understanding this ceaseless process of change. He observes too that the logarithmic spiral is the universal structure in which the law of opposites is manifested. In all phenomena, from a hydrogen atom to a seashell, from the ocean currents to the solar system and the Milky Way galaxy, the laws of change and the spirallic pattern are evident.

Another key element is the importance of food in human life. "We are what we eat," Kushi says simply. Food is the primary factor not only in a person's physical condition, but also in his emotional, psychological and spiritual state. Whether one is healthy or sick, happy or sad, at home in the universe or alienated from it depends mainly on daily food. Eating patterns in accordance with the natural order result in well-being and long life. A diet which violates the Order of the Universe results in sickness and disorder.

Kushi has analyzed in some detail the role of food in human illness. In *The Book of Macrobiotics* he lists the disorders of the various parts and systems of the body and their cause.[1] For each an excess of Yin or Yang foods, or an excess of both is the root of the problem. Yin, or expansive foods, include sugar, tropical fruits and fruit juices, coffee, alcohol, milk and yogurt, honey, drugs, vegetables of the night-shade family (tomatoes, potatoes, eggplant) and chemicalized products. They are responsible for a variety of illnesses including allergies, diabetes, arthritis, ulcers, epilepsy, varicose veins and many types of cancer including leukemia. Yang, or contractive, foods include meat, eggs, cheese, salt, overcooked, baked or burned foods. In excess they lead to premature graying, appendicitis, menstrual disorders, and some cancers including that of the liver, rectum, and duodenum. Excess of both Yin and Yang foods results in such disorders as warts and moles, arteriosclerosis, pancreatic and bone cancers, gallstones, cataracts, kidney stones and hemorrhoids.

Since emotional and mental condition are based on physiological condition, psychological disorders also are rooted in an unbalanced diet. According to Kushi there are two types of progressive mental disorder. One is caused by an excess of Yin foods. Its seven stages include:

1. general mental fatigue shown in complaining and loss of clarity in thought and behavior;
2. melancholy, and loss of ambition, self-confidence and memory;
3. irritability, fear, depression and defensiveness;
4. chronic suspicion and skepticism;
5. discrimination and prejudice based on an inferiority complex;
6. chaotic thought and behavior, schizophrenic symptoms; and finally,
7. Yin arrogance, meaning a total inability to adapt to the environment—thus leading to a retreat to a world of delusion.[2]

The other type of mental imbalance, resulting from an excess of Yang foods, also has seven stages. They are:

1. general mental fatigue, including frequent changes of mind;
2. rigidity and stubbornness, and petty attention to trivial matters;
3. excitability, short temper, constant discontent and an offensive attitude;
4. conceptualizing one's delusions in various "isms";
5. discrimination and prejudice based on a superiority complex;
6. dogmatic thinking and paranoia; and finally,
7. Yang arrogance, including total inability to accept others and forcing one's own opinions and standards on them.[3]

An excess of both Yin and Yang leads to a mixture and alternation of these two types of symptoms.

Even nightmares come from food. Dreams of violence, murder, monsters and bloodshed come from overconsumption of beef, pork and other meats. Dreams of fires, earthquakes, wars and other disruptions result from alcohol, hot spices and aromatic herbs, and too much baked and burnt food. Excessive eating of tree fruits bring dreams of falling from high places, while excess animal protein and fat cause nighttime visions of sexual indulgence.[4]

To prevent or to cure these various conditions one must eat a diet balanced in Yin and Yang elements. Kushi's "Standard Diet" is a grain-based regimen in which at least fifty percent of daily food is cooked whole cereals. In particular he recommends brown rice, the "queen of grains," as an ideally balanced food. Uniquely potent in the curing of disease, it promotes the harmonious development of the physical, intellectual and spiritual aspects of the person. Kushi recommends the other grains as well—wheat, barley, corn, etc.—but says that they may promote a more physically or intellectually oriented condition. Every grain should, if possible, be eaten in its whole, unbroken form. Using broken or milled grains as a principal food (as bread or noodles for example) may cause mucus deposits, retard recovery from illness and lead to dualistic thinking. Kushi advises a "Diet Number Seven" all-rice or all-grain diet only under special circumstances and only for a short time. He does not recommend it for sick people, and thinks of it more as a "rice fast." It is for healthy persons who want to clear their mental and spiritual faculties.

The rest of the "Standard Diet" includes miso- or tamari-based soups, beans, soy products such as tofu and tempeh, beans, and cooked vegetables. Depending on the person's condition it may also include fish, pressed and raw salad, cooked fruit, local and seasonal fresh fruit, roasted seeds and nuts, and the more Yin vegetables such as asparagus, spinach and beets. The usual beverages are grain and dandelion "coffees," non-aromatic herbal tea and "three-year" bancha twig tea.[5]

This diet, however, is not meant as a rigid regimen, but only as a broad guideline which must be adjusted to the individual case. The sex, age, health history and type of activity, as well as climate and season of year must all be considered. So, while in theory there is a "Standard Diet," there are as many variations as there are people practicing it. A laborer in northern Canada, for example, would need a broader, generally more Yang diet. He might eat more fish, and even some poultry and wild game. He would use the more Yang grains like buckwheat and would be able to take rather large quantities. A housewife in Alabama who had eaten much animal food in the past would eat a more Yin version: lighter grains, less salt, lightly cooked vegetables, and more fruit. Also, Kushi urges people, once they have established their health, to eat according to their natural inclinations rather than adhere to strict concepts of what is "good" and "bad." The wisdom of the body is often greater than that of the mind.

Kushi maintains that the macrobiotic diet thus interpreted provides all necessary nutrients. Quite aware that it has been criticized as deficient in calories, proteins, and various minerals and vitamins, he has strived to show that it is indeed sufficient. The generally recommended daily caloric intake is from 2,000–3,000 calories for an adult. It is very hard to get this amount eating only whole grains and vegetables.

Kushi argues that these figures are unnecessarily high and observes that the longest lived peoples in the world, hard-working peasants in Russia and Ecuador, take far fewer. He says that protein "requirements" are also inflated and points out that current research indicates that excess protein (and fat) in the American diet may be a cause of degenerative disease. Although there have been some problems in the macro-biotic community with calcium, and vitamins A, C, and B_{12}, Kushi, often referring to nutritional tables, is adamant that with proper care there should be no difficulties.[6] He actively encourages scientific research on such issues, and is helping support a study on "Vitamin B_{12} nutritional status in the macrobiotic community."

Kushi does warn, though, that early in a person's practice of the diet there may be reactions as the body discharges accumulated toxins and adjusts to the new regime. These may include fatigue, aches and pains, fever, chills, excessive sweating and urination, skin discharges and body odors, diarrhea or constipation, loss of sexual desire, cessation of menstruation, and mental irritability. While unpleasant and disconcerting, these are only indications that the body is cleansing itself.[7] They are temporary, and can be slowed down and moderated by a less strict form of the diet. Often, for those not seriously ill, Kushi advises a "transition" diet in which extreme Yin and Yang foods such as sweets, tropical fruits, eggs and meat are gradually reduced and eliminated and more balanced staples are made the basis of daily eating.

To help counselors diagnose and prescribe for their patients and to help everyone judge their own condition, Kushi has introduced and developed traditional methods of Oriental medical diagnosis within macrobiotic teaching. In particular he has used the "Five Element" theory of the *Yellow Emperor's Classic of Internal Medicine*. According to this system, dysfunctions in certain organs are reflected in specific external symptoms and types of behavior. Organs and symptoms are classified according to the five "elements" or, as Kushi has interpreted it, five "transformations of energy": wood, soil, fire, air, and water. A dysfunction in a certain organ is reflected in specific outward signs and behavioral patterns. For example, a person with yellowish skin and a short temper has a troubled liver. Pallid complexion and a dour, worrisome personality indicate that the lungs and large intestines are in poor condition. A florid face and an excitable, loud personality mean that the heart and small intestines are especially weak.

Kushi also uses and teaches other methods of diagnosis, including Oriental pulse diagnosis (which discriminates as many as nine pulses on each wrist) and palmistry. Drawing on traditional sources, including Nanboku, and on his own observations, he has refined physiognomy as a diagnostic tool. Thus every line, wrinkle, mole, discoloration and peculiarity of structure and movement is a clue to past diet, to the condition of the internal organs and to the present state of emotion, mind and spirit. A person with deep, dark circles under the eyes has tired kidneys, probably from an excess of extreme Yin such as sugar and coffee. Accordingly, they are inclined to depression, negativity and a fearful attitude.[8]

This refinement of diagnosis has been accompanied by a refinement in dietary recommendations. According to the five-energy theory the various grains, vegetables and other foods are related to specific organs and functions and can be used to strengthen and stimulate them. Wheat, for example, along with the liver and gall bladder, is dominated by the "extreme Yin" or "wood" energy (which Kushi calls "upward" or "tree-nature" energy). It is especially helpful for people with trouble in those organs. In the same way beans, characterized by "water" or the extreme Yang ("floating") phase of the energy transformation, are good for the kidneys.

Kushi's experience with counseling literally thousands of sick people has enabled him to make further refinements in dietary prescription. He has found that lightly cooked leafy green vegetables are very effective, almost necessary, in the treatment of many forms of cancer and that pumpkin and squash and other "sweet" vegetables are helpful in treating hypoglycemia and diabetes.

While stressing good diet as the basis of any cure, Kushi recognizes the effectiveness of other holistic therapies. In particular he has incorporated acupuncture, shiatsu massage, Do-In, and palm healing into macrobiotic teaching. Each is based on the idea that the human body is energized by a form of electro-magnetic energy called ki. Constantly entering the body from the atmosphere and from the earth this ki flows along certain pathways. These "meridians" channel the energy along the arms, legs and trunk of the body and through the various internal organs. When an organ becomes weak or overstimulated, the harmonious flow of energy is disrupted. In acupuncture, needles inserted in the skin bring the body back into Yin/Yang balance and stimulate the curative function of the weak organ. In shiatsu this is done by a trained masseur and in Do-In by oneself. In palm healing the balanced and powerful ki of a person in good health is transmitted directly through the light touch of the palm on the affected area.

Kushi also utilizes, as part of macrobiotic medicine, various external treatments. These can be used to meet emergency situations or to hasten improvement of a condition. For example, a tofu plaster applied directly to a swollen or inflamed area can help restore it to normal. A plaster of *taro* [タロ芋], or mountain potato, is often used in conjunction with hot ginger compresses for certain cases. Their combination draws out toxins and reduces tumors. Drops of pure sesame oil applied to the eyes will drive out excess fluids and help myopia and other eye problems. Most of these are traditional Oriental remedies or were developed by Ohsawa and other early Shoku-Yō doctors.

To those wishing to regain or retain their health Kushi offers additional advice:

- Avoid synthetic clothing, especially next to the skin, since it interferes with the easy and harmonious flow of natural energy through the body.
- Exercise in the sunshine and fresh air every day. Walk on the earth in bare feet whenever possible.
- Rub the body with a dry towel vigorously at least once a day to stimulate circulation.
- Use only cosmetics and body care products that are natural and organic. Everything that touches the body is absorbed to some degree, and synthetic chemicals can be very harmful.
- Keep one's house and immediate environment clean and orderly.[9]

However, for Kushi macrobiotics is not merely a diet buttressed by arcane diagnostic techniques, natural therapies and various hints for health. It is a total way of life, including specific ways of thinking and acting. To those who wish to become truly healthy in mind and spirit as well as body, Kushi advises the cultivation of certain mental attitudes and types of behavior.

Above all one must nurture a sense of gratitude, respect, love and generosity towards all objects, creatures, human beings, and to the universe itself. Kushi advises the following five daily "self reflections":

    I.   *Biological:* Did I eat properly and chew well today?
    II.   *Social:* Did I think of my elders, parents and ancestors today with love and respect?
    III.   *Psychological:* Did I happily greet everyone I met?
    IV.   *Ideological:* Did I marvel at the wonders of nature today?
    V.   *Comprehensive:* Did I thank everyone and appreciate everything I experienced today?[10]

Kushi particularly emphasizes the importance of gratitude and respect towards parents and ancestors. He advises that one should above all be concerned about the health and happiness of one's mother and father. He often counsels the use of a small home shrine where offerings can be made, in the traditional Oriental fashion, of rice, salt and tea, and where prayers can be said for the welfare of the departed. Our lives on earth can be influenced strongly by the state of our dead ancestors, he maintains.

The cultivation of a selfless and generous mind is also important. Human beings assume physical form and ego by the accumulation and consumption of energy and vibration, of food, and of material things. Usually we make ourselves sick by over-consumption. To become healthy we must take less and give away more. Thus one of Kushi's consistent themes is "Give away what you have—distribute, share!" Learning to give small gifts for the joy of giving is an important part of life. A friendly smile or a word of appreciation or concern can be more valuable. But the greatest sharing is of our happiness and of the "Order of the Universe" which gives it to us. So, to all students of macrobiotics, Kushi has advised: Teach macrobiotics, the Order of the Universe and the Way of Eating. There is no greater gift. Give, give, give. The more you give the more you will have. The more people you make happy, the happier you will be.

Kushi also teaches more specifically "spiritual" disciplines. He says that the surest way to develop awareness of the spiritual world and a sense of oneness with it is a diet of simple food in small amounts. An occasional rice fast or total fast will help accomplish this. One's entire body contracts, or Yangizes, and is able to pick up the Yin vibrations of the spiritual world. Meditation, chanting and visualizations can also help, though they do not involve any supernatural or mystical agency. For example, in clearing the mind and chanting *AUM* one stimulates the various organ systems, slows and regulates the breathing, and calms the nervous system. With the body thus quieted but energized, the brain can better receive the vibrations of the invisible realms and of infinity itself.

Kushi's version of the "macrobiotic way of life" includes specific ideas about the distinct natures of men and women and about the way they should interact. Man is more dominated by the centripetal, Yang energy of the heavens spiralling down from above. Thus he is inherently active, restless, sexually aggressive, and given to adventure and enterprise. By nature, he tends to seek a vocation in the world and is drawn to practical, technical pursuits and to more ideological and philosophical ones. Woman, dominated by the centrifugal, Yin, energy of the earth spiralling up and then out into the heavens is by nature more calm, aesthetic and sensitive. Her inherent vocation is the creation and the nurturing of new life, and she does so by bearing, feeding and educating her children. In providing a peaceful home and refuge for her husband and by choosing and preparing his food, she makes his life in the world possible and also subtly controls its direction. In effect, she (or any person who cooks) is the hidden director of life, controlling the destiny of family and of society.[11]

For Kushi, the state of marriage is natural for the healthy adult. Man and Woman, Yang and Yin, are inevitably attracted to each other, seeking harmony and balance. Marriage is the union between the two and involves a sharing on various levels. It includes, of course, a sharing of food. Husband and wife should eat the meals prepared by the wife, with minor modifications made for their individual conditions. According to Kushi, poor quality food and radically differing diets are the main cause of contemporary divorce. Marriage is a physical sharing in terms of space and also in sexual relations. In sex the cosmic energies of Yin and Yang are combined. New life is created and the partners enjoy the wholeness and balance of infinite oneness. Husband and wife should also share their finances, their friends and families, emotions and ideas but also, most importantly, their "dream." They should have a common vision of life and what they wish to accomplish in it. Thus in marriage man and woman are able to realize their true nature and to seek their destiny together.

This traditionalist viewpoint has affected Kushi's position on related social issues. Not surprisingly, he has not been an avid supporter of feminism. A woman who finds it necessary to go into "man's battlefield" will lose her true femininity and her destiny as a woman. Such impulses come from a Yang imbalance resulting from overconsumption of meat, eggs and other animal foods. Also, often in the face of fierce opposition, Kushi has maintained that homosexuality is a loss of natural balance and not just a matter of preference. From his biological point of view male homosexuality is stimulated by an excess of Yin factors in the diet such as fruits, sugar, honey, dairy products and oily foods. Lesbianism is an extreme imbalance caused by excess Yang from animal foods. Both conditions, he maintains, are reversible. A person eating a balanced macrobiotic diet gradually will develop more heterosexual desire. Although refusing to compromise in theory, Kushi has in practice been sympathetic to the situation of homosexuals. He has been very active in applying macrobiotic diet to the AIDS epidemic.

Kushi has also been a consistent opponent of birth control and abortion, on practical and health as well as on moral and spiritual grounds. All techniques of birth control interfere to some degree with the natural exchange of energies between man and woman. Many, like the pill and the IUD, are physically and emotionally harmful. All reflect the limited mentality of persons who do not want to take responsibility for their own actions. Abortion shows a similar attitude. Besides, it has major and long term ill effects. Kushi says that women who have had abortions are more susceptible to certain illnesses, including cancer. Also, the unhappy spirit of an aborted infant may hover around the reluctant mother for months or years.

Thus, for Kushi, macrobiotic life normally includes marriage and family and the joyful acceptance of the attendant responsibilities as well as pleasures. Family life, combined with proper diet, health practices, mental attitudes, ethical patterns and spiritual activities comprise a path to total well-being. Using Ohsawa's version as a base, Kushi describes the seven conditions of health as follows:

1. Never be tired. Be able to respond with physical energy and mental vitality to every job and challenge.
2. Have good appetite—for food, sex, activity, knowledge, work, experience, health and freedom. Never consume to satiation and always give away immediately what has been taken or learned.
3. Have good sleep, and awake rested after a short but deep sleep without dreams. A healthy person sees only "true dreams," accurate visions of what has been or will be.
4. Have good memory of names and numbers, of past experiences and scenes but also of our spiritual origin and destiny.
5. Never be angry. Anger is a symptom of deep physical and mental illness. The angry person has forgotten that he and his enemy are part of an infinite oneness. Anger comes from fear and a sense of inadequacy. The healthy person greets all circumstances with a smile and treats an enemy with love, changing him into a friend.
6. Be alert and joyful. The healthy person is clear in expressing himself, orderly in behavior, swift in action and response. He radiates optimism, joy and humor in everything he says and does.
7. Have endless appreciation—of the gift of life and of the Order of the Universe, which gives us everything we need for our enjoyment and development. We should be especially thankful for difficulties and sickness which help us evolve and grow.[12]

Also, the macrobiotic path helps one achieve higher and higher levels of judgment, or consciousness. One retains, in fact develops, mechanical, sensory and emotional "judgment" but also embraces higher, more subtle domains as well. On the fourth or intellectual stage one is concerned with reason and truth. On the social level one seeks what is functional and suitable for the common good. On the sixth or ideological, one strives through religions and doctrines to realize justice and righteousness. And on the seventh or supreme level one achieves universal and eternal consciousness, endless gratitude and all-embracing unconditional acceptance. One is eternally happy and free.

This awakening of perfect freedom and love, this enlightenment, is the ultimate goal of macrobiotics. As Kushi writes:

"Macrobiotics is the practicing of the Order of the Universe in our daily life .... It shall guide all of us toward health and happiness, freedom and justice in this everlasting, living, Infinite Universe .... It shall enable all of us to entertain ourselves in endless play as present inhabitants of this small planet earth."[13]

Some will realize this perfectly in their present lifetime. Some will make progress towards it. For Kushi, who teaches the ideas of karma and reincarnation, all will continue their journey after death. He teaches that at death the "plasma body" (made up of a person's vibrations, energy and consciousness) separates from the physical body. It returns to the invisible spiritual realm where its level of consciousness at death determines its progress. The "soul" of the person who has achieved supreme judgment is ready to retrace the evolution by which it had become man, going back through the realms of vibration, energy, Yin and Yang and, ultimately, Infinity. If the person was at a lower level of judgment at death and thus is still attached to some aspect of the finite world (for example, to sensual pleasure, to sentiment, to some religious concept), the soul must live for a while in the spirit world and then incarnate as man again.

Regarding the concept of hell, Kushi says:

> There are many interesting stories about hell, but they are all illusion. There is no need at all to be afraid. There is no punishment or hell in the plasmic world, only self-imposed struggles and tests. The best thing is to maintain your health and positive mind during life and when death comes to die, giving thanks to the whole universe and thinking of the happiness of many people. If you pass away in this state you will be very happy in the next life. No problems!

And ultimately, according to Kushi, all return to the perfect freedom and bliss of the Infinite, having enjoyed fully their playful romp in the finite realm.

For Kushi, then, part of the gospel or "good news" of macrobiotics is that through it the individual may enjoy physical, emotional, mental and spiritual health and may achieve enlightenment in this lifetime, and in any case will be well prepared for the next stage of the journey. While this personal dimension is important, it is not the only one. Macrobiotics includes as well a path and a promise for humanity as a whole. One of Kushi's main themes is world peace and the place of macrobiotics in it. His views on the origin and evolution of humanity, on ancient and recent history, and on the current global crisis are a background for this theme.

About four billion years ago the earth was a cloud of whirling gases. Within it simple organic molecules, carbohydrates and proteins, viruses and bacteria began to form. Then as the entire mass continued to contract, a central solid core formed, covered by water and surrounded by gases. Within this mineral-rich water the evolution of life continued, with primitive sea moss and sea vegetables and then invertebrate and vertebrate animals appearing. This process took about 2.8 million years. As the water subsided and land masses appeared, plants and animals continued to evolve, moving into the land-air environment. At each stage a more complex form of vegetable life appeared first. Becoming food for the still-simple animal forms, it affected their evolution to the next stage. For example, newly evolved land mosses were the food through which sea vertebrates developed into amphibians. Land development in the plant world has gone through ancient plants (now mostly extinct), to fruits, and most recently to herbaceous plants including cereal grains. The parallel evolution in the animal world has been from reptiles and birds (including the now extinct dinosaurs), to the mammals, apes, and finally mankind, which

244

appeared about 20 million years ago. At the same time, the solar system had just entered the winter phase of its 200-million-year orbit around the center of the galaxy. The cooling trend in the earth's climate resulted in the emergence of hardy grasses with compact fruit-seeds. Through eating these cereal grains humanity evolved to more or less its present form.[14]

When humankind first emerged it ate raw, uncooked grains as its basic food. The general climatic cooling gradually made this more difficult. Then a sudden axis shift caused the equatorial centers of habitation to become very cool, even frigid. In order to survive, humankind developed the use of fire in food preparation. The development toward an upright physical posture and the increase of human intelligence, both of which had been stimulated by raw cereal eating, quickly advanced. With cooking came the development of human civilization.

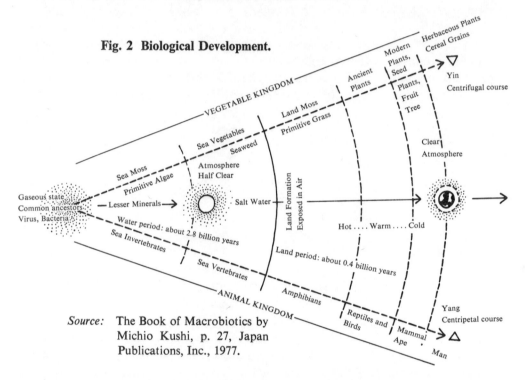

Fig. 2 Biological Development.

Source: The Book of Macrobiotics by Michio Kushi, p. 27, Japan Publications, Inc., 1977.

In the prehistoric period high levels of technical and spiritual achievement were attained. According to Kushi, some was due to influence from extra-terrestrials. As the planet Venus gradually moved closer to the sun it became unfit for human habitation. Immigration to the newly habitable neighboring planet (Earth) occurred. Also, there were visits from intelligent beings from other parts of the galaxy who came to guide, to teach and to intermarry with earthly humans. Over the millenia as many as twenty civilizations rose and fell. Understanding the laws of Yin and Yang, they were able to control the energies of nature and to use the great powers of the human mind. Kushi maintains that the pyramids and other ancient megaliths were built to attract and direct cosmic energies. Telepathic communication over great distances and telekinesis, the movement of physical bodies by thought, were commonplace practices. Since they understood the role of food in human life, the ancients were able to establish peaceful and long-lived global communities. The most recent "world scientific and spiritual community" is represented in the story of the lost continents of Atlantis and Lemuria. About 12,000 years ago this civilization was destroyed by catastrophic floods resulting from another partial shift in the earth's axis.[15]

For the most part, the wisdom of this civilization, its cosmology of complementary dualism, its understanding of food, was lost. Some of it survived, however, and some was gradually rediscovered. The various cosmic symbols of the ancient religions, Zoroastrianism, Judaism, Buddhism, and Christianity, and the assorted dietary rules in each, show that bits of the prior teachings were retained or regained. The most significant rediscovery of the cosmic laws was by the Chinese emperor Fou Hi who lived around 4,500 B.C. He recognized that from a common Oneness emerge the two complementary forces Yin and Yang and that all phenomena result from them. Fou Hi used a straight line to signify the Yang or masculine force and a broken line to signify the Yin or feminine force, and began to study the various possibilities of their interaction.

Despite the re-emergence of the prehistoric cosmology, a stable and harmonious world community did not again arise. This is because the earth has been passing through a particular phase in a historical cycle of 25,800 years. As the planet revolves around the sun its axis wobbles so that the North Pole points to different spots in the heavens. Actually, the earth's axis describes a circle, returning about every 26,000 years to perfect alignment with Polaris, the North Star. According to the position of its axis, the earth receives different types and amounts of celestial influence in the form of energy and vibrations, from the constellations and from the entire galaxy itself. This changes how human beings think and behave, making them individually and collectively more or less active, emotional, intellectual and spiritual. The past 12,000 years has been "The Time of Struggle" within this cycle. Humanity has become more and more materialistic, egocentric and concerned with power. This tendency is reflected in the "spiral of history." The creation and concentration of material wealth, the control and exploitation of nature, conflict and violence in a fragmented world have all been increasing at a logarithmic pace. Soon this process will move into its second and opposite phase, "The Time of Paradise." Under different celestial influences humanity will become more spiritual and more concerned with harmony and cooperation.[16]

Until recently, memory of the "Order of the Universe" and the "Way of Eating" was preserved in the Far East. Japan, because of its geographical and cultural isolation and its rice-based diet, preserved much of the wisdom and civilization of the distant past. Now, however, it is lost even there and all humanity lacks a compass with which to orient itself in the universe and with which to create a way of life. The result is worldwide biological and social degeneration, which Kushi calls the "biological flood of Noah."

This modern crisis of humanity is one of Kushi's central themes. Everywhere and at every level of society, he observes, conflict, chaos and suffering characterize human life. Physical illness is almost universal. Birth defects, retardation, cancer, degenerative diseases and mental illness are all at epidemic proportions. High levels of juvenile delinquency, drug addiction and divorce show that family life and society itself are disintegrating. Violence and crime permeate community and national life as war and threats of war dominate international relations. Even if humankind does not destroy itself through nuclear war, within fifty years it will degenerate into some kind of abnormal species. The development of artificial limbs and organs and of artificially-conceived and gestated human life are part of this macabre process of reverse evolution. Humanity seems to be sliding inevitably toward an Armageddon of destruction, either a sudden or a slow-motion version. For the many, whose physical and mental condition constitutes a "living hell," it has already arrived.

Although celestial and cosmic influences are playing a role, the primary immediate cause, according to Kushi, is bad food. Improper diet, out of harmony with the natural environment, leads to the physical, emotional, and mental illness of the individual. Since families, groups, and societies are aggregates of individuals, these reflect the sickness and disorder that exist on the personal level. Epidemic disease, family decay, crime and violence, injustice, exploitation, social and political upheaval all are rooted in the biological imbalance, caused by diet, of individual men, women and children.

Thus for Kushi the remedy for all the ills rampant in the world must be based on biological regeneration through diet, i.e., on macrobiotics. This is the life-saving compass which will lead humankind out of the present crisis into a New Era. This is the means by which universal health and harmony will be realized. Macrobiotics is the path to "One Peaceful World."

Kushi maintains that a global community without conflict will come about when:

- each individual is free of mental and physical disorder;
- each individual is free of all nightmares and illusions;
- each individual recognizes all other human beings as brothers and sisters in spite of differences in race, nationality, tradition, culture and ideology.

In other words, it will be realized when all humanity is eating and living according to the Order of the Universe.

This is possible. It is, in fact, inevitable. But it will take about 2,000 years to be realized. In the coming decades and centuries the number of macrobiotic people will steadily increase. Gradually, spontaneously, disease, violence, crime, war, prejudice, mental illness and environmental pollution will decrease. The medical, police, judicial, defense and insurance systems, all based on individual and general illness and fear, will wither and disappear. Meanwhile, in the macrobiotic centers around the world a new type of government, local and international, will be taking shape. Its primary function will be to educate and to serve rather than to control or exploit. It will include the usual (Yang) type of political and social leader, aggressive and socially oriented, but also reflective (Yin) types whose natural inclinations are more intellectual and spiritual. Kushi observes that in traditional cultures prophets, monks and hermits often played an important, though frequently hidden, role in the management of affairs.

As a public health service, macrobiotic centers will educate the general public to proper health care through diet and lifestyle. They will provide facilities for the care of the mentally and physically handicapped. Eventually, since "all crimes are the manifestation of physical and mental illness," they will take charge of criminals and rehabilitate them through proper diet and mental education.[17]

They will establish schools for children and promote education whereby the various levels of human judgment are all developed. Thus their schooling will include:[18]

- basic techniques to maintain and develop health and to cure oneself if sick;
- practical arts such as gardening, cooking, sewing, carpentry and repair;
- methods of intellectual communication and artistic expression;
- a spirit of respect and gratitude to parents, elders and to all ancestors;
- the laws of Yin and Yang and their operation in the world of nature and in all phenomena;
- detailed study of biology, psychology, astronomy, cosmology and spiritual science; and
- encouragement to discover one's personal destiny and to pursue it as fully as possible.

Such education will, according to Kushi, enable all to realize their destiny as happy, healthy, and free persons. Each will live in the awareness that all persons and phenomena are part of the "family" of the universe, and that harmony, love and respect are essential for the happiness of all. Each will discover his true origin and the way to realize his spiritual destiny.

The centers also will be very active in agriculture, an area crucial to the health of each person and thus to the entire community.[19] They will promote local agriculture on the principle that the main food supply of all areas should come from within a two- to four-hundred mile radius. They will encourage "organic" farming techniques without chemical fertilizers, herbicides and pesticides. And they will urge the return as quickly as possible to natural agriculture.

According to Kushi, during the previous world spiritual community a minimalist farming technique was practiced. Archaeological remains indicate that up to 10,000 years ago there were no plows, scythes and other agricultural implements in use. This does not mean that farming did not exist. Rather, it means that a form of cultivation which respected natural processes and which produced food crops conducive to health and vigor was practiced. It is to this "natural agriculture" that mankind must return to. Citing the work of Masanobu Fukuoka [福岡正信], a Japanese farmer who has re-discovered natural agriculture, Kushi says its principles include:

a. *Non-weeding*. This may include replacement of large weeds with smaller, softer ones such as clover.
b. *Non-tilling*. Tilling will be done naturally by the weeds.
c. *Non-fertilization*. Soil replenishment comes from dead weeds and from the unused portion of harvested plants, returned to the land.
d. *Non-spraying*. Insects and worms are attracted to areas where one plant is cultivated. Mixed plants and non-weeding will deter pests.

e. *Non-seeding*. Particularly for vegetables crops, ten to twenty percent should not be harvested. They should be allowed to reseed the field for the coming year.

f. *Non-pruning*. Trimming trees produces a symmetrical form but this is unnatural, as are the products of the trees.

Since the quality of food determines the quality of life, agriculture is crucial to the regeneration of humanity. A return to natural agriculture, Kushi claims, would greatly accelerate recovery from physical, mental and spiritual disorders. Rapid progress in human evolution would take place, with the development on a broad scale of the powers of telepathy, foreknowledge and extra-sensory perception. "Natural agriculture is the gate opening into the garden of paradise, which was lost before our written history began," he writes.

As seeds of the new world government, the macrobiotic centers will also promote a radical reappraisal of the assumptions of the current economy.[20] Presently, it is generally assumed that:

1. It is necessary to work to survive.
2. Wealth lies in the consumption and possession of materials.
3. Capital consists of financial wealth or of machinery and equipment.
4. Energy must be mined from the limited resources of the earth.

In the next era the economy will be based on a different set of principles:

1. The concept and practice of "work" is an unnecessary and imprisoning delusion. The real purpose of life is "play," free and spontaneous amusement leading to artistic, intellectual, social and spiritual development.
2. Technological production methods should be made more simple and natural so that neither humanity nor the environment are adversely affected.
3. Capital is the physical and mental and spiritual health of the individual persons in the world as well as the natural forces and phenomena of the earth's environment.
4. Energy should be taken primarily from the forces which have created and which fill and move the natural environment: solar power, electromagnetic energy and other cosmic waves and rays.

Through the work of the macrobiotic communities and centers, the movement will spread and its influence will be felt in many critical areas of life. The life of individuals, families, communities, nations and of the planet will be slowly but profoundly transformed. Sometime during the transition period, perhaps very shortly, a great catastrophe, man-made or natural, will occur. If so, macrobiotic people will be the best prepared, physically and mentally, to survive.

In any case, eventually the way of life according to the Order of the Universe will spread over all the world. Past political and national boundaries, usually arbitrary in origin, will vanish. Ecological units, bound together by a common natural environment, will arise. People will be able to move freely between them without passports

and visas even as birds fly freely from one place to another. On the local and international levels government will serve and educate the people. An era of unmarred
peace and plenty will begin. Favored by celestial influence it will endure for 10,000
years.

Thus, for Kushi, macrobiotics is the key to individual health and spiritual development. It is also the necessary basis for a global utopia already taking shape within
the macrobiotic movement. This vision of macrobiotics is not universally applauded,
of course. There are critics both within and without the movement. Some say that it
is too simplistic, that the forces for good and evil in the individual and global human
body cannot be explained only or primarily in terms of food. Some say that it is too
fanciful and esoteric, that the theories about galactic cycles, ancient civilization and
astrological influence are theories only. Some say that it is too grandiose and full of
self-importance.

Nevertheless, Kushi's presentation of macrobiotics has been a compelling and
inspiring one for many people within the movement and on its fringes. In the many
centers and groups around the world its influence is certainly dominant at the
present time. Some of the inspirational quality of Kushi and his thought is evident
from his following "Daily Dedication for One Peaceful World."

Daily Dedication for One Peaceful World:

- When we eat, let us reflect that we have come from food which has come from
nature by the order of the infinite universe, and let us be grateful for all that we
have been given.

- When we meet people, let us see them as brothers and sisters and remember that
we have all come from the infinite universe through our parents and ancestors,
and let us pray as One with all of humanity for universal love and peace on earth.

- When we see the sun and moon, the sky and stars, mountains and rivers, seas
and forests, fields and valleys, birds and animals, and all the wonders of nature,
let us remember that we have come with them all from the infinite universe.
Let us be thankful for our environment on earth, and live in harmony with all
that surrounds us.

- When we see farms and villages, towns and cities, arts and cultures, societies
and civilizations, and all the works of man, let us recall that our creativity has
come from the infinite universe and has passed from generation to generation
and spread over the entire earth. Let us be grateful for our birth on this planet
with intelligence and wisdom, and let us vow with all to realize endlessly our
eternal dream of One Peaceful World through health, freedom, love, and justice.

- Having come from, being within, and going towards infinity,
may our endless dream be eternally realized upon this earth,
may our unconditional dedication perpetually serve for the creation of love and
peace,
and

may our heartfelt thankfulness be devoted universally to every object, person and being.

---

[1] Kushi, Michio, *The Book of Macrobiotics: The Universal Way of Health and Happiness*, Japan Publications, Tokyo, 1977, p. 115 ff.

[2] Ibid., p. 136

[3] Ibid., p. 84 (ca.)

[4] Ibid., p. 135

[5] Ibid., p. 49 ff

[6] Ibid., p. 67 ff, p. 172 ff

[7] Ibid., p. 125 ff

[8] Ibid., p. 134, p. 144 et. al.

[9] Ibid., p. 77

[10] Ibid., p. 164

[11] Ibid., p. 86 ff

[12] Ibid., p. 104 ff

[13] Ibid., p. 29

[14] Ibid., p. 25 ff.

[15] Kushi, Michio, *The Era of Humanity: Visions of a New World*, East West Journal, Brookline, Mass. 1980, p. 97 ff.

[16] Ibid., p. 111

[17] ——, *The Book of Macrobiotics*, p. 153

[18] ——, *The Era of Humanity: Vision of a New World*, p. 85 ff

[19] Ibid., p. 113 ff.
Kushi seems indebted here to the work of Masanobu Fukuoka, pioneer of the "natural agriculture movement" in Japan. Fukuoka's book "*The One-Straw Revolution* was published in 1979 by The Rodale Press, Emmaus, PA.

[20] ——, *The Book of Macrobiotics*, p. 156 ff.

14.
Macrobiotics in Western Culture

The tradition of macrobiotics we have been following has its roots in ancient China. It was present in 17th century Japan in the work of Ekken Kaibara and was rediscovered at the dawn of Japan's modern era by Sagen Ishizuka. Since then it has been continued and elaborated on by Ohsawa, Kushi and others. Throughout its history certain basic ideas have been present, explicitly or implicitly. They concern the nature of the universe, the nature and destiny of man, and the relation of food to human physical and spiritual health.

According to the macrobiotic Weltanschauung, the universe is an undifferentiated Oneness, infinite and eternal. By polarizing into opposite and complementary energies, Yin and Yang, this Oneness creates within itself all beings and phenomena according to specific laws. All things, then, have a common origin and substance. As interrelated parts of the cosmic whole they are constantly changing into each other and will ultimately return to Oneness. Man is the perfect manifestation of the Absolute in the finite. In him, the created world becomes aware of its infinite origin and nature. Man is "infinity itself," and the goal of human life is the realization of this. Food is a crucial factor in man's life. His physical, emotional, psychological and spiritual well-being are deeply influenced by it. As a general principle, man should eat according to the natural order. Specifically, this means he should rely on cereal grains as a staple food, with local vegetable foods as supplements.

From a philosophical perspective macrobiotics is a dialectical monism. It affirms the unity of all phenomena in the universe, yet observes that all creation, destruction and change occur through the interaction of opposite energies. It affirms, too, the complementary nature of all opposites. Man and the absolute, man and nature, matter and spirit, life and death, time and eternity and all other apparently exclusive pairs, actually comprise an indivisible whole and are constantly changing one into the other.

From a religious point of view, macrobiotics is a mystical pantheism. Everything that exists is holy, shares in the divine essence. And man, originating in infinity, makes his way through many lifetimes back to it. In blissful union with all that exists and with the Oneness that contains all, man realizes his destiny.

The macrobiotic attitude toward food reflects both this pantheism and this dialectical monism. Food is sacred, both in and of itself as a product of nature, and as bearer of the gift of life to man. And while as plant or animal substance it seems separate from man, in becoming food it becomes man. Thus the type and quality of food determines the quality of human life. On food depend health or sickness, happiness and unhappiness, enlightenment or alienation.

Elements of this general world view can be found in most of the Oriental cultures and in many of the traditional and "primitive" cultures. Though with different vocabularies, emphases and perspectives it is evident in the *Upanishads* of India, in the *Tao Te Ching*, in the religion and way of life of the American Indians and of the Australian aborigines. In Western culture, however, dominated by the Judaeo-Christian tradition and more recently by science, it is much less evident.

In the religion and philosophy of the West a more dualistic tendency seems to pertain. According to the Genesis story God creates nature and man but remains distinct from them. There is an "ontological gulf," a chasm of being, between God and man. This can be overcome only through God's revealing His will in revelation and later through the incarnation in Christ. But even after the alienation between God and man has been overcome by Christ's suffering, God remains God and man, man. As Dante describes in the *Divina Commedia* ("The Divine Comedy"), man may hope to eternally enjoy a vision of the glory of God, but he does not become God. Creator and creature remain separate.

This underlying dualism is evident in other relations as well. Man, though a part of nature, is somehow apart from it. As the divinely ordained pain of childbirth, the need to labor and perspire, and the antagonism with the serpent indicate, man is not totally at home in the natural world. At the same time he has dominion over it and is free to do with it what he wants. Also, just as there is a principle of good operating in the world, there is also a principle of evil, independent and irreconcilable. The Satan who had led Adam and Eve astray in the Garden of Eden, later battles Christ for the world and for the soul of man. With St. Paul the separation and antagonism between body and spirit became very clear. The idea that the body must be deprived or mortified for the spirit to develop became an important element of the Christian tradition. Accordingly, salvation was thought of as a state, necessarily after death, when the spirit is free of the prison of the body. These uncompromising oppositions of man and God, man and nature, good and evil, heaven and earth, have pervaded Western culture to the present day.

Since the 17th century science has deeply influenced how Western man understands the universe. At that time the work of Isaac Newton, René Descartes and Francis Bacon combined to produce a vision of the universe as a huge machine. Like a human-made machine it consists of many interacting, solid parts, which move by force and motion transmitted directly through contact or over distance as in gravity. Only those phenomena with mass and dimension are real, and hence worthy of study. And to study something is to reduce it to its smallest part, to measure, quantify and analyze.

The scientific perspective heightened the dualistic tendency in Western thought. The Absolute, or God, if such a reality were thought to exist at all, was considered "out there" and in the past. It had created the world, wound it up like a clock and disappeared from the scene with no ongoing relation to nature or to man. The split between man and nature widened as well. The world around was something to be objectified, studied, deprived of its secrets and used for man's purposes. Man's body and mind as well were viewed as virtually unconnected. According to Descartes, the two functioned independently with only a tenuous relation in the pineal gland. Also, in focusing on smaller and smaller segments of the material world, science diverted attention from and denied or ignored man's spirit and its destiny.

Thus the macrobiotic world view seems quite different from the mainstream of Western religious, philosophical and scientific thought. And macrobiotic ideas about food and health seem similarly out of place. Western nutrition and medicine is dominated by ideas generally contrary to those of macrobiotics. For fifty years, conventional nutritional science has emphasized the importance of balancing the four food groups: meat, dairy, grains and vegetables, and fruits. Except for warning against deficiency diseases it has little recognized any role of food in disease. Neither has it looked to diet as a means of curing illness. Meanwhile, Western allopathic medicine has been dominated by the germ theory of disease and the use of radical medications and surgical techniques. The net result is that the typical medical student will take one course, if any, on nutrition in four years of schooling. And the idea that diet affects behavior, way of thinking, and spiritual development is foreign to most Western intellectuals.

This overview, however, while generally true, is somewhat misleading. From ancient times to the present, the Western philosophical and religious tradition has harbored within it, as a kind of "minority voice," ideas similar to those of macrobiotics. Though expressed in different terms, dialectical monism and mystical pantheism have been present throughout. At certain points they were very influential. And in the food and medical history of the West there have been beliefs and practices very close to those of macrobiotics. In fact, until the modern era they have played a prominent role. Again, the particulars of theory and practice are different but the basic orientation is the same.

Ancient Greece, of course, has been a source of much of Western culture. And in the legacy of some of its leading philosophers, religious thinkers and physicians there are views basically consonant with aspects of macrobiotics. Thales, considered the "father of philosophy," was born in about 650 B.C. in the city of Miletus. Since none of his writings survive we know little of the specifics of his thought. He did assert, though, that there is a primal world stuff (water) from which everything is created. This is constantly changing, transforming itself into the myriad phenomena and creatures of the world. All that exists, every object and being, is a momentary permutation of the universal substance.

In the thought of Anaximander, a pupil of Thales, a clear dialectical quality is added to this rather vague monism. Anaximander calls the source of the universe "the Boundless" or "the Indefinite Something." It is infinite without time or space and is filled with countless souls or gods. The earth and the rest of the physical universe began when within "the Boundless" a part began to revolve like a vortex or spiralling eddy. Heat and fire rose and swirled around, enclosing a cold, moist center. The four elements—fire, water, earth and air—became distinct, and from their interaction the earth and heavens were created. The earth is shaped like a drum and is located in the center of this vortex, spinning with it. In all natural phenomena there is a succession of alternating opposites, in which one or another of the four elements dominate.

The cosmology of Heraclitus also comes close to that of macrobiotics. Born in

540, B.C. in the city of Ephesus, Heraclitus held that fire is the primal world stuff, of which all things are a transformation. Change is the basic characteristic of the universe. Heraclitus expressed this idea in the aphorism, "You cannot step into the same river twice." But all change occurs according to a fixed, predictable law which can be understood by man. This is the principle of alternation in which things change to their opposite. Fire changes to water, water to earth, earth to air and finally water back to fire. All oppositions and distinctions are ultimately illusory. "To God, all things are fair and good," Heraclitus observed, "but men hold some things right and wrong." The world stuff, though not a god in a personified sense, is divine. Thus, all that exists is also divine.

In the same era, the mathematician and philosopher Pythagoras was teaching a similar dialectical monism. The universe consists ultimately of what he calls "the Boundless," or "Unlimited Breath," a dark, boundless void. Within in it arise points of fire, which he calls "the Limit." The opposition of these two realities is reflected in eight other contrasting pairs which they produce. These pairs include one and many, male and female, resting and moving, right and left. From their interaction comes the world of nature in which all things, including man, bear the mark of their double origin.

Pythagoras, who is said to have traveled throughout the known world as a young man, introduced several new ideas to the Hellenic world. They concern the nature and destiny of man and the role of food in human behavior and spiritual development. According to Pythagoras, man consists of a soul and a body. Each human soul goes through a process of evolution in which it lives in many bodies in successive lives. In this evolution it becomes increasingly spiritual and pure, free of the weight and passions of the physical body. When finally perfected, the soul, after death, escapes from the cycle of rebirth.

Pythagoras taught that a vegetarian diet is essential to the evolution of the human soul. Meat and animal food excite the physical passions and strengthen ties to the material realm. A vegetable diet produces a calm and pure mental and spiritual state. The religious brotherhood which gathered around Pythagoras in Croton in southern Italy followed a life of strict discipline. This included abstention from all animal food and a simple diet of grains, vegetables and fruits.

The Orphic mystery cults of the time held similar beliefs. Based on the myth of Orpheus (the young man who descends to Hades to rescue his dead wife Eurydice and manages to return) and accepting the theory of transmigration of souls, these groups, too, aimed at release from the cycle of death and rebirth. To them human nature includes a divine and a worldly element. To evolve toward spiritual freedom man must cultivate the one and suppress the latter. Accordingly, the Orphics abstained from all animal food, wore white garments and avoided contact with death.

It is possible that these Pythagorean and Orphic ideas arose spontaneously from the Hellenic genius. It is possible too that they came from the East, perhaps India. Ideas such as reincarnation and the liberation of the soul had been part of the Indian world view for centuries. And the effect of food on human health, personality, behavior and spirituality was well understood. By the 7th century, one expression of it was in the Sankhya philosophy, formulated by Kapila. According to this, there are three types of energy or *gunas: sattvas*, *rajas*, and *tamas*. These are interwoven in all phenomena, including men and food. Sattvas is the guna of purity, balance and light; rajas that of heat, activity, and movement; and tamas that of stagnation and dissolution. Foods in which sattvas dominates include cereal grains, legumes, fruits, vegetables and milk. Rajasic foods include meat, fish, eggs, onions, garlic and hot spices. Tamasic foods are fermented or spoiled products. Thus a person who eats rajasic foods will become worldly, passionate, aggressive, concerned with power and wealth. One who eats tamasic foods will be weak, lazy and dissolute. One who wishes to become calm, clearheaded, generous and spiritual will eat sattvic foods alone. Hence, from ancient times, in India vegetarianism was almost universal and anyone who wished to develop spiritually followed a strict and simple diet. Did Pythagoras travel as far as India and pick up there his ideas about food as well as about reincarnation? Perhaps, but in any case these ideas were present and influential in the Greek cradle of Western civilization.

Also, in the medicine of ancient Greece there are intimations of macrobiotic views on food and health. Hippocrates, "the Father of Medicine," lived from 460 to about 350 B.C. He is credited with taking medicine out of the realm of superstition and magic. He made it into a science, based on observation and analysis. According to Hippocrates (or at least to the writings attributed to him) medicine is basically the art of adjusting diet to cure an illness. He asserts that in the distant past men had eaten wild foods raw and had suffered greatly because of this. Then they learned to choose foods appropriate to their nature and to prepare them properly. They hulled and ground wheat to make bread, and from barley made cakes. By various cooking methods they learned to make "intense" foods "moderate," and thus conducive to health, growth and strength rather than to illness.[1]

According to Hippocrates, the primary cause of illness is food which is "extreme," that is, having too strong a bitter, salty, acid or other quality. The basis of treatment must be mild foods such as bread and grain cakes. The art of the physician consists mainly in knowing which and how much of these nourishing, balancing foods should be fed to the patient, and how they should be prepared. To do this he must understand the four "humors"—hot, cold, dry and moist—which characterize foods, persons and illnesses. For example, a patient with a weakened "cold," condition will recover with "hot" foods such as bread, boiled flesh and wine. If fed "cold" foods such as porridge, wheat, raw meat and water, he will weaken and die.

From this basis Hippocrates developed a medical system which included purgatives and medicines as well as dietary recommendations. But he always emphasized the importance of letting an illness "be," of "letting nature run its course." In many instances, he said, the best treatment is no treatment, i.e., fasting or a very simple diet. Hippocrates stressed that if the physician "wishes to perform his duties (he) should strive to know what man is in relation to his articles of food and drink, and to his other occupations, and what are the effect of each . . . ."[2]

Ancient Hebrew culture was, like that of the Greeks, a major souce of Western civilization. While it had a basically theistic and dualistic world view, it also had a highly developed awareness of food and its importance in human life. In the book of Genesis the two great epochs of human life, that before and that after the Fall, are characterized by two different diets. In chapter 1, verse 29 Yahweh tells Adam and Eve: "Behold I have given you every plant yielding seed which is upon the face of all the earth, and every tree with seed in its fruit; you shall have them for food."[3] But after the Fall, the expulsion from paradise and the Flood, Yahweh tells Noah (in 9:1): "The fear of you shall be upon every beast of the earth and upon every bird of the air, upon everything that creeps on the ground and all the fish of the sea; into your hands they are delivered. Everything that lives shall be food for you; and as I gave you the green plants I give you everything."[4]

Later, the Mosaic Law established many rules concerning food. Certain foods (pork, shellfish, carrion) and certain combinations of foods (for example, milk and meat) were prohibited. Preparation procedures, such as the swift and painless slaughter of animals by the piercing of the carotid artery, were prescribed. These injunctions were not arbitrary. They were based on a consciousness of the importance of food quality in human health and perhaps on an awareness of its effect on human behavior and thought.

Though the ancient Hebrews were not vegetarian, they knew the special benefits of a grain diet. There is even an interesting example of "Diet Number Seven" recorded in the Old Testament. In the first chapter of the *Book of Daniel* is told a story of the Babylonian captivity. King Nebuchadnezzar summoned ten Hebrew youths to his court to be trained as royal pages. One of them, Daniel, chose not to eat the rich food and drink of the King's table. When the stewards said that he would weaken without it, Daniel suggested an experiment. "Test (us) for ten days. Let us be given pulses (cereal grains) to eat and water to drink. Then let our appearance and the appearance of the youths who eat of the king's rich food be observed . . . ." As the text records, the steward "tested them for ten days. At the end of ten days it was seen that they were better in appearance and fatter in flesh than all the youths who ate the king's rich food. So the steward took away their rich food and wine . . . and gave them pulses."[5]

In the 2nd and 1st centuries B.C. there arose within Israel a group known as the Essenes. They were ascetics who withdrew to the desert to live simple communal lives of worship and prayer. According to the Roman historian Josephus (1st cent. A.D.), the Essenes lived on a strict bread and vegetable diet. They began each day with prayers, worked for several hours, then took a cold bath. After donning fresh clothes they entered the dining hall, a place of special sanctity, for the morning meal. Josephus describes the scene as follows:

> When they are quietly seated, the baker serves out the loaves of bread in due order, and the cook serves only one bowlful of each dish to each man.
>
> Before the meal the priest says a prayer and no one is permitted to taste the food before the prayer; and after they have eaten the meal he recites another prayer. At the beginning and end they bless God as the Giver of Life.
>
> Afterward they lay aside the garments which they have worn for the meal, since they are sacred garments, and apply themselves again to work until the evening.
>
> Then they return and take their dinner in the same manner and if guests are passing through they sit at the table. No shouting or disturbance ever defiles the houses. They allow each other to speak in turn.
>
> To those outside, the silence of the men inside seems a great mystery; but the

cause of it is their invariable sobriety and the fact that they are satisfied and no more!

I think it is because of the simplicity of their way of life and their regularity that they live long, so that most of them reach the age of more than a hundred years.[6]

Some scholars, including Edmund Bordeau Szekely, maintain that Jesus lived in such an Essene community before he began his public ministry at the age of thirty. According to Szekely, Jesus presented Essene beliefs and practices in his teaching. Though expurgated from the four canonical gospels these are preserved in *The Essene Gospel of John*. This is an ancient Aramaic text discovered in the last half century and translated by Szekely. If the document is indeed genuine, Jesus and the Essenes, in their general world view and in their dietary practice, had much in common with macrobiotics.

In the gospel Jesus speaks of man and of all other creatures as created by the union of "the spirit of the divine Father (Heaven)" and "the spirit of the divine Mother (Earth)." Every plant, tree, bird and animal, as well as every human being, is a child of the "divine parents" and bears within it "the law of life." Man need only live according to this "law of life" in order to be healthy and to see "the light of the heavenly Father."[7]

A good part of this discipline, as recorded in the Essene gospel, concerns the choice and preparation of food and the proper way to eat it. Jesus says: "From the coming of the month of Jiar, eat barley; from the month of Sivan eat wheat, the most perfect among all seed bearing herbs. And let your daily bread be made of wheat, that the Lord may take care of your bodies." He gives directions for making the bread. The whole kernels are soaked in water and then allowed to germinate. Then they are crushed, formed into a loaf and baked on a rock in the hot desert sun.

Jesus continues with suggestions for the manner of eating:

> Eat not as the heathen do, who stuff themselves in haste, defiling their bodies with all manner of abominations.
>
> For the power of God's angels enters into you with the living food which the Lord gives you from his royal table. And when you eat, have above you the angel of air, and below you the angel of water. Breathe long and deeply at all your meals, that the angel of air may bless your repasts. And chew well your food with your teeth, that it become water, and that the angel of water turn it into blood in your body. And eat slowly, as it were a prayer you make to the Lord. For I tell you truly, the power of God enters into you if you eat after this manner at his table. But Satan turns into a steaming bog the body of him upon whom the angels of air and water do not descend at his repasts. And the Lord suffers him no longer at his table. For the table of the Lord is an altar, and he who eats at the table of God is in a temple. For I tell you truly, the body of the Sons of Man is turned into a temple, and their inwards into an altar, if they do the commandments of God. Wherefore, put naught upon the altar of

the Lord when your spirit is vexed, neither think upon any one with anger in the temple of God. And enter only into the Lord's sanctuary when you feel in yourselves the call of his angels, for all that you eat in sorrow, or in anger, or without desire, becomes a poison in your body. For the breath of Satan defiles all these. Place with joy your offerings upon the altar of your body, and let all evil thoughts depart from you when you receive into your body the power of God from his table. And never sit at the table of God before he calls you by the angel of appetite.

Rejoice, therefore, always with God's angels at their royal table, for this is pleasing to the heart of the Lord. And your life will be long upon the earth, for the most precious of God's servants will serve you all your days: the angel of joy.

Jesus makes clear that the motive behind the avoidance of meat is not only moral, but also physical and spiritual.

He who kills his brother, from him will the Earthly Mother turn away, and will pluck from her quickening breasts. And he will be shunned by her angels, and Satan will have his dwelling in his body. And the flesh of slain beasts in his body will become his own tomb. For I tell you truly, he who kills kills himself, and whosoever eats the flesh of slain beasts, eats of the body of death. For in his blood every drop of their blood turns to poison; in his breath their breath to stink; in his flesh their flesh to boils; in his bones their bones to chalk. And their death will become his death. For the wages of sin is death. Kill not, neither eat the flesh of your innocent prey, lest you become the slaves of Satan. For that is the path of suffering, and it leads to death. But do the will of God, that His angels may serve you on the way to life.

In the Gospel, Jesus leads a group of the sick and suffering through a cleansing fast, supplemented by enemas. This purification, he says, is necessary to the birth of spiritual vision, as well as to physical health.

Follow first only the laws of your Earthly Mother, of which I have told you. And when her angels shall have cleansed and renewed your bodies and strengthened your eyes, you will be able to bear the light of our heavenly Father. When you gaze upon the brightness of the noonday sun with unflinching eyes, you can then look upon the blinding light of your Heavenly Father, which is a thousand times brighter than the brightness of a thousand suns. But how should you look upon the blinding light of your heavenly Father, when you cannot even bear the shining of the blazing sun. Believe me, the sun is like the flame of a candle beside the sun of truth of the Heavenly Father.[8]

Even in the New Testament gospels there are signs that Jesus might have held a monistic and dialectical world view. In Luke 17 he says that the Kingdom of God is "in the midst of men." Elsewhere he tells his followers that the Kingdom is "within you." And the Beatitudes (Matthew 5 and Luke 6) are a perfect application of the law of alternation of opposites:

> Blessed are the poor in spirit, for theirs is the kingdom of heaven.
> Blessed are those who mourn for they shall be comforted.
> Blessed are the meek for they shall inherit the earth.
> Blessed are you poor for yours is the kingdom of God.
> Blessed are you that hunger now, for you shall be satisfied.
> Blessed are you that weep now, for you shall laugh.[9]

All things contain the seed of paradox. Everything changes into its opposite.

The Gospel of Thomas is a collection of 114 *logia* or "sayings of Jesus" which was discovered in 1945 in a ruined tomb near Nag Hamadi in Upper Egypt. It includes the following passages:

> Jesus said to them: "If they say to you: 'From where have you originated?', say to them 'We have come from the Light where the Light has originated through itself.'
>
> "If they say to you: 'Who are you?' say 'We are His sons and we are the elect of the living Father.'
>
> "If they ask you, 'What is the sign of your Father in you,' say to them 'It is a movement and a rest! You have come here from the kingdom and will return to it'.[10]

Later, in answer to the question, "When will the Kingdom come?" Jesus says, "It will not come by expectation; they will not say: 'See here,' or 'See there.' But the Kingdom of the Father is spread out upon the earth and men do not see it."[11] Here again, the dialectical nature of reality, the closeness and even identity of man and God, and the sacred quality of all that exists, are expressed.

Though the Essene gospel and the Nag Hamadi text may reflect doctrines and practices taught by Jesus and retained by peripheral groups early in Christian history, the orthodoxy established by the Church was quite different. While Christ had bridged the chasm between man and God, there were still two distinct realms, one divine and one natural and human. And of any awareness of the role of food in spiritual life only the faintest traces remained. Abstention from meat on certain days or during certain periods as in the pre-Easter Lenten time, was observed. Also, the Christian monastic tradition began as a strictly vegetarian way of life. St. Benedict of Nursia (c. 480–c. 543) established the first community of monks and wrote the book of rules which still governs much of the communal ascetic life in the Christian world. He said that bread should be the basic food of the monks and that no meat should be eaten. Benedict's rules on diet seem to have come mainly from a desire for austerity and morality, rather than from an understanding of the effect of food on mental and spiritual growth. Yet even today a few orders, such as the Trappists (the Cistercians of the Strict Observance), still observe a vegetarian regimen.

It is interesting that almost a millenium later, from one of these presumably vegetarian monks should arise a monistic and mystical expression of Christianity. Johannes (Meister) Eckhart (1260–1328) was a German Dominican friar. He was a learned man, well schooled in the Bible and Christian doctrine, but also a humble one, who preached and ministered to his Saxon parishioners. Though a loyal son of the Church, Eckhart had personal spiritual experiences which caused him to overstep the bounds of orthodoxy. He discovered within himself a kernel of divine being, a bit of God. This impressed him with the ultimate unity of the divine and the human. For Eckhart, God had said, "Let us make man in our own image," and indeed he had. "God and I; we are one," exulted the German monk.[12]

Also, Eckhart proposed a new concept of God. The divine reality which he found within himself was not the God of history, the deity of the Judaeo-Christian tradition who intrudes into human events, talks to Adam, Moses and the prophets, fights with the Hebrews against their enemies, and then takes on the form of man in Jesus Christ. Eckhart spoke of the "God behind God," from whom the deity of the Bible had emerged. About this "God behind God" nothing can be expressed in words. Containing within itself all qualities, including opposite and contradictory ones, it is totally ineffable. According to Eckhart one can only experience this reality by stripping off superficial, individual identity and seeking a simplicity and purity of life. And when one discovers this Godhead within one's soul there is no need for the mediation of the sacraments. There is no need for the kneeling and bowing of formal worship. Man and God are one. Not surprisingly, Eckhart was accused of heresy and after his death many of his teachings were condemned by the Church.

Around the same time in Europe, Hippocratic ideas about food and health were enjoying a renaissance. With the decline of classical civilization and the onset of the Dark Ages (6th–11th century) they seem to have disappeared. However, Arabic scholars and physicians had preserved the Hippocratic tradition and developed it further. During the 10th and 11th centuries they transmitted it to Christian doctors and students at a medical college in Salerno, Italy. A basically dietetic medicine flourished there and from the 11th century began to spread through Europe. Crusader knights returning from the Holy Land stopped in Salerno to recover, and in returning home introduced the system to the lands west and north. According to one historian, the High Middle Ages were the "heyday" of medical nutrition.[13]

This approach to diet and medicine is based on an elaborated version of the four Hippocratic "humors." Each humor is contained in a particular bodily fluid and gives rise to a particular physical and personality type. Blood is dominant in the "sanguine" or eagerly optimistic person; bile in the "choleric" or excitable person; phlegm in the easygoing, lethargic ("phlegmatic") type; and black bile in the sad, contemplative, "melancholic type." Every food, each type of meat, fish, fowl, grain, vegetable, fruit and spice, has a distinct effect on the humors, and thus on the physical and mental condition of the person. The effect might be good or bad, immediate or delayed, obvious or hidden, but it is inevitable and real.

Thus to the typical European of the medieval period, food played a very important role in health, mood and behavior. The study of these particular effects, and the use of discretion in eating and drinking, was considered the responsibility of every intelligent citizen. In each country books like the German *Garten der Gesundheit* ("Garden of Health") were available. These discuss the effect on the humors of the various kinds of food, and list specific dietetic cures for everything from arthritis to sexual apathy. For the unlettered there were folk rhymes which preserved and spread this practical wisdom. The saying, "An apple a day keeps the doctor away," goes back to a verse on medical hygiene which came out of Salerno at this time.

Moses Maimonides was a Jewish scholar and physician who lived in Spain during the 12th century. He was a typical and prominent practitioner of this type of medicine. Maimonides said that any disease that could not be treated with diet should not be treated at all. One of his medical treatises is titled *On Asthma*, and gives exhaustive dietetic recommendations to relieve the illness and also to promote sexual vitality. The first seven (of thirteen) chapters concern diet and specifically list forbidden and recommended foods, give detailed recipes, and prescribe the number of meals per day and the amount of food to be eaten. The basis of the therapeutic diet is two kinds of bread, one made from finely ground rye flour mixed with salt, well-kneaded and baked. The other is made of unsifted whole wheat flour, half ground. Besides these, Maimonides recommends lean fish and meats, and certain vegetables such as beets, asparagus, fennel and parsley. To be avoided are flour puddings and pastries, especially those with honey or sugar, beans, nuts (gas-producing), heavy meats, aged cheese, moist or watery vegetables, and most fruits. The ideal light meal for the asthmatic chest is chicken soup flavored with vinegar, lemon juice and mint.[14]

This approach dominated through most of Europe until the 16th century. It has not, of course, disappeared even today. The descendants of Maimonides the world over, in New York, Tel Aviv and Paris still drink chicken soup as a trusted panacea. And in other cultures, much has survived in folk wisdom. Over the last fifty years, medical doctors in the Anthroposophical movement have developed a system of medicine according to indications given by Rudolph Steiner. It is based on the four humors, on the effects of certain foods and homeopathic preparations, and on the role of psychic and spiritual factors. The Hippocratic approach and its various descendants cannot be described as "macrobiotic." Still, there are many points of similarity with the macrobiotic outlook: the emphasis on and interest in food; the concern to create harmony and balance; the idea that health is the natural condition of man; the assumption that food affects character and behavior as well as health; and the belief that the recovery of health usually requires simple and natural, rather than extreme and exotic measures.

During the 17th and 18th centuries the scientific and mechanistic world views were very influential throughout the West. In the late 18th and early 19th centuries, however, there appeared in philosophy, and in diet and medicine as well, ideas that had much in common with macrobiotics. While definitely a minority view, they provided an important counterpoint to the ethos of the age.

George Friedrich Wilhelm Hegel was born in Stuttgart Germany in 1770, and by the time of his death in 1831 was regarded as the leading philosopher of his day. Hegel's thought is not easy to understand. His vocabulary is often original, his sentences convoluted and long, his reasoning obscure and his concepts complex. Even the devoted student will at many points wonder not only what Hegel meant, but whether Hegel himself knew what he meant. But beneath the complexity and obscurity, the mind-numbing explanations of the "Absolute Idea," of "essence, existence and change," is a vision of the world much like that of Ohsawa's.

Hegel's starting point is the "Absolute Mind," which contains the "Absolute Idea." In order to become aware of itself and the Absolute Idea, the Absolute Mind manifests itself as "Absolute Spirit." As such it creates nature, man and history. It does so by a dialectical process involving thesis, antithesis, and synthesis. According to Hegel, all phenomena are created by the interaction between contradictory factors (thesis and anti-thesis). Each is a synthesis that is more complex and evolved than either of the prior factors. This process pertains in all domains including physical-chemical and organic worlds. There, the human body is the perfection of the possibilities of living nature. It is the physical organ that allows the Absolute Spirit to become a self-conscious soul.

This dialectical movement toward perfection is also occurring in human history, in the development of social and political forms, and in human culture, in the evolution of art, religion and philosophy. In history, the interaction of the principles of freedom and order, of the individual and the community, have culminated in the polity of the German Enlightenment. In this social and political system, the self-directed and free individual voluntarily subjects himself to the objective freedom of a social organization based on reason and morality. In art, the fantastic symbolism and mystery of the "Oriental," and the poised, serene balance of the "Classic," have been interwoven to produce the soaring, mystical, yet meditative mood of the "Gothic." In religion this evolution through dialectic has led to Christianity, and in philosophy (not surprisingly) to Idealism, i.e., Hegelianism. Thus, in human culture and history, the Absolute has manifested and become increasingly aware of itself. Yet the process continues. In and through man God discovers what He is and can become.

Thus in Hegelianism we encounter, though expressed in different terms, by now familiar concepts. Nature, man and history are all manifestations of an absolute, spiritual reality. With that Absolute they form an interrelated whole. All change, transformation and evolution occur through the interaction of opposing energies and phenomena. And humanity, on an individual and a corporate level, moves toward an ever fuller consciousness of identity with the Absolute.

The great lyric poet and dramatist Johann Wolfgang von Goethe (1749–1833) is known as "the Shakespeare of Germany." Yet he was also a philosopher who saw all things as manifestations of a single cosmic Self which assumes myriad, constantly changing forms and identities. As he writes in his poem, *Parabasis:*

> Years ago with joy abounding
> Eagerly the spirit sought
> To discover, to experience
> Nature living as it wrought.
> And it is the One Eternal
> Self-revealing manifold;
> Small is great and great is small,
> Each in its distinctive mold.
> Ever changing, still remaining . . . .[15]

Goethe was also a man of science. He carefully observed and studied the world of animals and plants. Yet he sought not to reduce nature to material parts mechanically interacting, but to discern the spirit operating within it. In true science one cannot simply dissect, analyze and name, Goethe maintained. In *Faust* he writes:

> He who would study organic existence,
> First drives out the soul with rigid persistence
> Then the parts in his hand he may hold and class
> But the spiritual link is lost alas.[16]

His own researches led Goethe to conclude that in nature the spirit operates through alternating, opposing forces of expansion and contraction. In two didactic poems, "The Metamorphosis of Plants," and "The Metamorphosis of Animals," he explains how all germination, growth, maturation and cessation of life take place according to this complementary pulse. As a plant grows, the contractive energies of the earth form its roots, while the expansive force of the heavens send its branches and leaves out and upwards.

For Goethe, man is part of nature and of the cosmic whole. He too is created, and lives and dies according to the universal pattern. He yearns for the unifying Spirit. Like others of the Romantic movement, Goethe saw in nature a door to the divine. Not only by observation and study of the natural world, but by close contact with it, by immersion in its harmonious beauties, man intuits and experiences the peace of the cosmic Spirit.

In 1796 a young German doctor, who was to become Goethe's personal physician, wrote a book called *Makrobiotik oder die Kunst das menschliche Leben zu Verlängern* ("Macrobiotics, or the Art of Prolonging Human Life"). Christolph Wilhelm von Hufeland was establishing, he wrote, an art distinct from usual medical practice, which seeks only to cure specific diseases at a certain moment. "Die Makrobiotik" aims at lengthening life by considering the whole life of the individual.

Von Hufeland had studied the accumulated medical wisdom of the day, including Hippocrates and the Salerno school. Also, he made an exhaustive study of individuals and people who were unusually long lived. With this basis he presents a theory of longevity, explaining the factors which hinder or promote it. The key to a long and healthy life, he asserts, is the proper cultivation of "*die Lebenskraft*" or "Life Force." This is the active force underlying the universe. It creates, maintains, moves and renews all phenomena, of both the organic and of the inorganic worlds. It is especially present in light, heat, air and water. Man absorbs the Life Force through these elements and through the foods which are created by them. To live long one must do those things which preserve and renew the Life Force, and avoid those which dissipate it.

Among the factors which shorten life, von Hufeland lists a weak physical condition, an overindulged childhood, excess sexual activity, breathing impure air in a large city, too high or too low a level of activity, an unhappy or angry disposition, and a chronic fear of death. Among the factors lengthening life are a strong physical constitution (that is, a well-balanced physique with no weak points, and especially a good digestive system and set of teeth); physical activity (especially hard work out of doors); a happy marriage; sound (but not excessive) sleep; fresh air and sunshine; a life in the country, including the cultivation of a garden; travel to foreign lands (including the enjoyment of local foods—in moderation); cleanliness of the skin through cold water baths, bathing in the sea, and the use of loose, comfortable clothing; a satisfied and peaceful state of mind; a love of nature; a leisurely pace of life; a disposition that is optimistic, cheerful and loving, and free of fear, anger and jealousy; and a moderate use of doctors and medications in the event of sickness.

Both in shortening and prolonging life, diet plays an important role, according to von Hufeland. The person destined for an untimely end eats and drinks to excess. He takes much alcohol, which dissipates the Life Force. He eats much meat which makes one violent, cruel, passionate and overactive. Also, he takes spices, coffee, chocolate, cheese and various foods rich in fat and sugar, all of which afflict the body, overstimulating it or upsetting digestion.

He who will be blessed with a healthy longevity eats meat, but in small quantity, relying more on the "flour vegetables" or grains, including rice, wheat, rye, barley, oats, lentils and beans, and potatoes and root vegetables. He eats these cooked since they are easier to digest in that state. He eats slowly, chewing his food very well, and does not read or study while at table. He dines at regular intervals and not in between, and eats until he is not quite full. He avoids eating just before going to bed, but takes a brief rest following each meal. He does not smoke or take beverages during the mealtime.

In discussing illness, von Hufeland makes clear that prevention is far better than cure, and that proper diet and life-style prevent many sicknesses. In case of distress one should not go immediately to the doctor. Overuse of medications and extreme medical procedures is a major cause of shortened life. Rather, through rest, simple diet and home remedies, one should try to balance the humors. Among the items for a home dispensary von Hufeland recommends barley groats, cream and oil, linseed, mustard, horseradish, wine, brandy, and herbal teas such as camomile, elderberry and peppermint. Properly used these suffice for most ailments. In case of serious illness fasting is often the best treatment. If a medical doctor is called in, no remedy should ever be used without a clear reason. The ideal physician understands the individual condition of the patient and the best way to harmonize it. He has little interest in money, being concerned primarily with the health and happiness of his patients.

The correspondences regarding diet, manner of eating, life-style and medicine, between von Hufeland's Makrobiotik and the later movement which borrowed the term are, of course, striking. And there are more profound parallels as well. For von Hufeland, as for Ohsawa, a long, happy and healthy life is the human birthright, which can be realized if one lives in an intelligent and natural way. Nature is a loving and charitable mother who embraces and rewards all those who sincerely seek her. This human life is part of a development to yet higher levels of existence, and it is meant to be lived in strength, confidence, and friendship, and with love for all humanity. It is possible that Ohsawa never heard of von Hufeland nor of "Die Makrobiotik." But it is fitting and propitious that he happened to choose that term.

In England at around the same time, a new consciousness about food was appearing, mainly in the form of vegetarianism. It came both from an awakening of

Christian conscience and from a rediscovery of the Pythagorean tradition. In the mid-18th century, John Wesley (1703–1791), the founder of Methodism, advocated vegetarianism on moral grounds. In 1809 the first vegetarian association was formed as part of a Christian fellowship. That same year Dr. William Lambe wrote a pamphlet claiming that a meatless diet combined with distilled water could cure certain tumors and cancerous ulcers. Two years later, John Frank Newton published "A Return to Nature," a pamphlet citing the physical and mental benefits of a meatless diet and tracing the history of vegetarianism back to the *Book of Genesis*.

Soon Percy Bysshe Shelley (1792–1822) and other leading lights of the Romantic movement were converting to a "Pythagorean diet," as it was called. Believing meat the great corrupter of humanity, they had mental and spiritual, as well as physical, aims. In his pamphlet, "A Vindication of Natural Diet," Shelley writes: "I hold that the depravity of the physical and moral nature of man originated in his unnatural habits of life. The Fall of Man in the garden of Eden through Adam and Eve's eating of the forbidden fruit is allegorical proof that disease and crime have flowed from unnatural diet."[17]

This movement led to the founding of the British Vegetarian Society in London in 1847. Its aim was to promote abstention from meat, primarily for ethical and moral reasons. Although vegetarianism grew and became a substantial factor in British life it seems not to have developed the idea of food as a key factor in human life. Even George Bernard Shaw, the most famous advocate of a vegetarian diet in Britain, said that he was motivated only by moral considerations. He denied that a meatless regime has any particular physical or mental effects or benefits. Except for the exclusion of flesh foods, he was omnivorous, eating eggs and often consuming sugar by the spoonful. He did, however, cantankerous soul that he was, live to 93 years of age!

Meanwhile, the French in their usual inimitable and elegant manner were clarifying what they had known and practiced for centuries, that food is the basic element in human life. Jean Anthelme Brillat-Savarin was born in 1755 in the town of Belley in provincial France. A lawyer, magistrate and public official, he led an eventful life, experiencing with his country the Revolution, the Reign of Terror, the rise and fall of Napoleon. At one point he fled for his life to New York City and lived there for two years teaching French.

Savarin returned to France to an undisturbed old age. In 1825, a collection of his meditations on food, entitled *The Physiology of Taste*, was published. In it he is concerned mostly with the sensory and aesthetic enjoyment to be found in fine food. Only the most imaginative interpreter could correlate his recommendations for various dishes of game and fowl, for coffee, sugar, and chocolate (including a three-page-recipe on the "Official Method of Preparing Chocolate") with the macrobiotic diet or way of life. Yet, though Brillat-Savarin described and pursued the luxurious life of the gourmet, his point of departure is quite similar. He prefaces his book with a list of aphorisms, "the eternal foundation of (his) science."

I.   The world is nothing without life and all that lives takes nourishment.
II. Animals feed; man eats: only the man of intellect knows how to eat.
III. The fate of nations depends on the way they eat.

IV. Tell me what you eat and I will tell you what you are.[18]

Meanwhile, across the Atlantic, philosophers in New England were developing a new way of looking at the world. Transcendentalism emerged in the 1830s within an elite circle of writers and intellectuals. It was influenced by German Idealism (including that of Hegel), British and German Romanticism, and also by Oriental religion and philosophy. At the time, the *Upanishads*, the *Bhagavad-Gita*, the *Tao Te Ching* and other classic texts of the East were first becoming available in translation. Reacting against the dominant rationalism, materialism and scientism of the day, Transcendentalism asserted that there is a reality beyond the visible and material world, and that man's origin and destiny lie there. Its three leading figures were the philosopher and essayist Ralph Waldo Emerson, the famous recluse Henry David Thoreau, and the brash, wandering poet of Brooklyn, Walt Whitman.

Emerson, in essays such as "The Oversoul" and "On Nature," presents the basic ideas of Transcendentalism. The Oversoul is the Supreme Being, which like Brahman of Upanishadic thought contains all within it and is beyond description and limitation. From it emanates nature and man. The natural world, as a whole and in all its parts, is a perfect expression of the Oversoul. And each phenomenon, as a microcosm reflecting the macrocosm, bears the mark of the supreme Spirit. And this, as Emerson writes in "The American Scholar," is:

> That great principle of Undulation . . . that shows itself in the inspiring and the expiring of breath; in desire and satiety, in the ebb and flow of the sea; in day and night; in heat and cold; and is yet more deeply ingrained in every atom and every fluid, is known to us under the name of Polarity. These 'fits of easy transmission and reflection,' as Newton called them, are the law of nature because they are the law of the Spirit.[19]

The human soul, in particular, is a replica of the Oversoul, and seeks to return to its source. It can do so by looking outward to the world of nature. By careful observation of the natural world, and by close contact with it, one can experience the Divine Spirit. "When in nature," Emerson writes, "the currents of universal being circulate through me. I am part and parcel of God."[20] One can also look within. Again, in "The American Scholar" Emerson declares: "In yourself is the law of all nature, . . . in yourself slumbers the whole of Reason (the Spirit)."[21] To experience the divine in nature and within himself, man must use his intuition, his ability to perceive and know directly, rather than his rational faculty. Reason and empirical science, rather than revealing truth, obscure the whole in which Truth lies.

The practical import of these ideas for Emerson was an inspiring one. The individual possesses a soul which is part of the Oversoul and thus is bound to all other beings and things. He is able to know everything and to do anything. Form an idea of your life, Emerson counsels exultingly, and realize it. "Hitch your wagon to a star. It is for you to know all. It is for you to dare all."

Thoreau, fourteen years younger than Emerson, has been called the chief "practitioner" of Transcendentalism. In 1845 he resolved to try in practice the principles of Emerson's essay "On Self-Reliance." In Concord, near Boston, he built a ten-by-fifteen-foot cabin on the shores of Walden Pond, and lived there in near isolation for over two years. He worked only so much as necessary to provide the necessities of life, and devoted his time to the observation of nature, to study, and to the cultivation of his spirit. In the account of his experiences published as *Walden* in 1854, Thoreau elaborates four basic ideas.[22]

- Man, by nature free, has been enslaved by himself.
- The way to freedom is through self-reliance and a life simplified and free of luxurious necessities.
- Health and happiness are best achieved by living closely with nature.
- Truth is to be valued, more than love, fame or wealth.

In Walt Whitman's life and in his magnum opus, *Leaves of Grass*, the tenets of Transcendentalism are expressed flamboyantly and poetically. Whitman affirms the soul's identity with all other souls, all other beings. He revels in man's freedom, in the beauty of nature and in the importance of nature to man. "Now I see," he writes, "the secret of making the best person. It is to grow in the open air, and to eat and sleep with the earth."[23]

It is not surprising that Ohsawa saw these men as kindred spirits, who saw the world as he did and who tried to live with the same ardor, simplicity and joy. He often cited them in his own writings and recommended their works to anyone who wanted to understand macrobiotics more deeply. When Ohsawa visited Boston in 1965 he made a pilgrimage to Walden Pond. Bowing his head and bringing his palms together in salutation and respect, he uttered, "Thank you, Thoreau, thank you."

Until the early 19th century there was in America little special awareness of food. The popular wisdom was that all food was essentially equal. It didn't matter what one ate, so long as one ate enough to sustain growth and activity. At the time the typical diet included large quantities of meat and game, animal fats and alcohol, with very few vegetables and fruits. Bread was a staple but the whole grain wheat and corn used previously began to be replaced by refined white flour. One early instance of concern about diet and health is in the life of Benjamin Franklin (1709–90). As a young man Franklin, inspired by a British temperance tract, lived on a vegetarian diet for several years. While a sporadic vegetarian thereafter, Franklin remained conscious of the relation between food and health. In the aphorisms of his *Poor Richard's Almanac* he broadcast throughout colonial America such ideas as:

- "He that lives carnally (eats meat) won't live eternally."
- "To lengthen thy life, lessen thy meals."
- "A full belly is the mother of all evils."
- "Cheese and salt meat should be sparingly eaten."
- "Against disease the strongest fence is the defensive virtue, abstinence."[24]

In 1809, Rev. William Metcalfe arrived from England and settled in Philadelphia. A convert to vegetarianism, he began to preach abstention from meat and alcohol. In 1830 Metcalfe made an important convert in the Rev. Sylvester Graham, a Pres-

268

byterian minister who was already an active prohibitionist. Graham incorporated
new elements into his temperance lectures, including sexual restraint and cold baths,
as well as vegetarianism, and soon became a leading spokesman of the movement.
He advised against eating meat, especially pork, but also warned against shellfish,
eggs, milk and honey. Man is by nature a vegetarian, Graham taught. If he eats too
much animal food, he becomes easily angered, aggressive and sexually overactive.
Seasoning such as pepper and mustard also are overstimulating and may lead to
insanity.

Graham looked upon whole grain bread as the essential food of man. He strongly
opposed white flour, saying that all foods, including grains, should be eaten in their
complete form, as they come from God. Although he knew nothing of the nutrients
lost in the milling process, and only suspected the laxative effect of bran, Graham
was quite adamant on this point. His name became associated with the unbleached,
unrefined flour which he recommended. Graham also encouraged the eating of fresh
fruit, which at the time was considered very dangerous. His teachings, spread through
the "Graham Journal of Health and Longevity," were widely accepted. "Graham
Hotels" were founded to accommodate the faithful and their food preferences.

An important associate of Graham was the Massachusetts physician William
Alcott. He wrote a major defense of vegetarianism citing physical, moral and economic advantages and giving both the Essenes and the Pythagoreans as examples of
its benefits. In 1843 Alcott, his notable cousin Bronson Alcott (father of Louisa May,
author of *Little Women*) and other New Englanders (many of them Transcendental-
ists) founded Fruitlands, a utopian community based on vegetarian principles. They
wore cotton clothes only, tilled the soil by hand, took cold baths, and raised rye,
oats, corn, beans, potatoes and other vegetables. A dispute on family organization
closed it within a year, however.

Emerson and Thoreau were part of the group influenced by Graham. The following passage from Walden reflects this.

I learned from my two years' experience that it would cost incredibly little
trouble to obtain one's necessary food, even in this latitude; that a man may
use as simple a diet as the animals, and yet retain health and strength . . . . Even
the little variety which I used was a yielding to the demands of appetite, and
not of health. Yet men have come to such a pass that they frequently starve,
not for want of necessaries, but for want of luxuries . . . . Bread I at first made
of pure Indian meal and salt, genuine hoecakes, which I baked before my fire
out of doors on a shingle or the end of a stick of timber sawed off in building
my house; but it was wont to get smoked and to have a piny flavor. I tried
flour also; but have at last found a mixture of rye and Indian meal most convenient and agreeable. In cold weather it was no little amusement to bake
several small loaves of this in succession, tending and turning them as carefully
as an Egyptian his hatching eggs. They were a real cereal fruit which I ripened,
and they had to my senses a fragrance like that of other noble fruits, which
I kept in as long as possible by wrapping them in cloths. I made a study of the
ancient and indispensable art of bread making, consulting such authorities as
offered, going back to the primitive days and first invention of the unleavened

kind, when from the wildness of nuts and meats men first reached the mildness and refinement of this diet .... Every New Englander might easily raise all his own breadstuffs in this land of rye and Indian corn, and not depend on distant and fluctuating markets for them. Yet so far are we from simplicity and independence that, in Concord, fresh and sweet meal is rarely sold in the shops, and hominy and corn in a still coarser form are hardly used by any. For the most part the farmer gives to his cattle and hogs the grain of his own producing, and buys flour, which is at least no more wholesome, at a greater cost, at the store.[25]

Sister Ellen Harmon White, founder of the Seventh Day Adventist movement, was also affected by Graham's message. White had been a follower of William Miller, who had predicted the end of the world and the Second Coming of Christ for October 22, 1844. When the day passed uneventfully Miller and his followers were a bit disappointed. Most deserted the movement but Sister White regrouped the remnant and settled it in Battle Creek, Michigan. After 1863 she began to introduce teachings about food and health. To the idea that Christ is coming again to establish heaven on earth, White added the view that the human body is the temple of God, and any abuse of it is a violation of the Deity. She taught the avoidance of tobacco, alcohol and meat and various other dietary principles to promote health. These included:

- Eat plain food prepared in the simplest manner (Graham bread, fresh vegetables and fruits, and plain water).
- Discard rich pastries. Fruit is a better dessert.
- Eat slowly and moderately. Overeating leads to headache, indigestion and cholic, and aggravates various diseases.
- Food should correspond to climate.
- Increase physical exercise.

In 1867 the Adventists established the Western Health Reform Institute in Battle Creek, and used therapies there based on diet, exercise, baths and the breathing of fresh air. Ten years later John Harvey Kellogg, an Adventist with a medical degree, was made director. He changed the name to Battle Creek Sanatorium and used it as his base of operation for 67 years. The basic diet Kellogg instituted was grain-based. Breakfast, for example, consisted of boiled rice, wheatmeal or oatmeal porridge, and milk toast. In addition, Kellogg and his brother William experimented with various grains to make ready-to-eat cereals. Their development of corn flakes, wheat flakes and granola did much to bring whole grains back into the American diet again. That the company they founded has become a giant manufacturer of products made with refined grains and white sugar is an ironic footnote. The Seventh Day Adventist movement has continued, however, and most of its adherents still observe some form of vegetarian diet.

Thus in America as well as in Europe there have been movements which aimed at a return to a more natural and healthful diet. And besides those here described there have been groups in central Europe, Scandinavia, and elsewhere (that associated with Dr. Bircher-Benner of Switzerland, for example), which have likewise advocated dietary reform. Citing the connection between food and physical and mental health, they too have promoted the use of fresh, whole, organically produced foods, and the avoidance of meat and refined, adulterated and chemicalized foods. Thus, certain macrobiotic ideas and practices have been present in the West, especially in the last 100 years, and have played a significant if minor role in the history of diet and health.

Besides in these various explicit food and health movements, macrobiotics has been present in another domain. On the simplest level, macrobiotics is "eating the foods of one's environment," which in most temperate areas means eating a whole grain diet, supplemented by vegetables, fruits and animal products. And through most of Western history, the majority of the population were peasants living on the land. Producing most or all of their own food, they have eaten more or less in this manner. Until 50 or 100 years ago (and even today in some isolated areas), a *de facto* "semi-macrobiotic" diet has been the daily fare of most people in the West.

In central and western Europe, in Scandinavia, around the Mediterranean and in North America the traditional diet has been based on whole cereals. Oatmeal porridge, whole wheat and rye breads, spaghetti and pastas, and occasionally, as in Italy and Spain, brown rice, have been the staple foods, with beans and vegetables as supplements. Meat, game, and dairy foods were used in small quantities, and imported delicacies such as sugar, chocolate and spices were unknown to the masses. Only the nobility and the high clergy (to whom much of the credit for Europe's tumultuous past may be given) were able to eat these foods daily. Even just eighty years ago in Germany, for example, most people lived on rye bread, lentils, kale, turnips, and good dark beer. Even in a cheese and milk country such as Denmark, dairy foods were not common until the last century. Before then grains were the dominant crop and food. Large dairy herds were developed only when cheap grain from eastern Europe and North America upset the grain market. The diet of the early settlers in America was similar. The East Coast Indians, from whom they learned their food economy, were agriculturalists. Their basic foods were corn, beans, and squash, game and wild plants. Only with the opening of the western cattle range lands and the building of the east-west railroads did the American diet shift toward its animal food emphasis.

From a strict macrobiotic standard these traditional diets were not always ideal. There was often an excess of meat and other animal foods, such as eggs, cheese and milk. There may have been insufficient use of fresh vegetables and fruits. Cooking methods may not have balanced Yin and Yang elements in as exact a manner as desirable. And when imported and refined foods—white flour, white sugar, coffee, tea, etc.—became available and affordable they were quickly incorporated into the daily regimen. Still, in a broad sense these eating patterns were "macrobiotic." And they had little in common with what is now considered a "normal" diet: hamburgers, potatoes, orange juice, ice cream and coca cola. Macrobiotics is often labeled a "fad." From a historical point of view, however, the typical diet of today, not macrobiotics, is really a fad.

In the 20th century, the grain-based, ecological eating of the past has all but disappeared from Europe and America. Its role in the health of the individual and of society was little appreciated and it has been set aside for what is over-spiced, unnaturally sweet, exotic, convenient, refined then "enriched," attractively packaged, and well-advertised. Here and there a remnant of the old way persists, as in the flatbreads of Scandinavia and the black pumpernickel of Germany. A combination of nostalgia, good intuition and perhaps the impact of the natural foods movement have allowed them to survive. For the most part, though, this traditional aspect of Western diet is all but gone from the mainstream culture.

Ironically, however, at perhaps their lowest ebb the value of these traditional foods is being discovered by science. And in effect, Western scientific research is in the process of formulating a "macrobiotic" theory of diet and health. This is being done by the accumulation of historical, anthropological and nutritional research.

For example, about twenty years ago Gene Matlock, a student of early Mexican and Central American history, published the results of his work.[26] In the 16th century, when Spanish conquistadores invaded Mexico, they were struck by the health, beauty and longevity of the Mayan Indians who lived there. Many lived to 100 or 120 years of age without losing their teeth, hair, or vitality. The Spaniards searched for a "Fountain of Youth" within the herbal medicine of the Indians. The Mayans themselves understood that the source of their health and well-being lay in their diet, and especially in their principal food, corn. According to the *Popul Vuh*, the Mayan mythological record, the first human beings were fashioned from corn by the gods. Corn was still their divine nourishing mother. They believed it made them strong and immune from disease. They held that to eat corn was to become intelligent, sensitive, creative and ultimately divine. To abandon corn was to become savage, diseased and ignorant. The Mayans fed their infants and children a 100 percent corn diet until the age of ten. Adults ate a diet of 60–100 percent corn. When they became ill they always returned to a pure corn regimen. Matlock discovered that a similar diet and philosophy characterized other Indians of the Americas, including the Hopis.

Early in this century a dentist named Weston Price did a study of dietary patterns and health among various peoples, including inhabitants of the Scottish islands. Among the islanders who had retained the traditional diet of oat products and seafood, there was a high level of health and virtually no tooth decay. On islands where modern foods such as white bread, marmalades, chocolate and candies were present, the level of health was markedly lower. Tuberculosis was endemic, as were tooth decay and tooth loss. The results of this study were born out by more general observations all over Europe. Where traditional eating patterns endured the people were healthy and robust. Where they had given way to modern, refined foods, the populace had degenerated, and suffered from poor physical development, low resistance to disease, and dental problems.

In the late 1940s a remarkable people were discovered by Western travelers in a remote valley of northwest Pakistan. Known as the Hunza, they were extremely healthy and long-lived and were virtually free of cancer and degenerative disease. Men and women in their 90s were still active and vigorous. The Hunza, their diet and life-style, became an object of study.

One research project was carried out by Dr. Robert MacCarrison, Director of the Hindu Institute of Nutrition. To a group of 1,000 healthy mice he gave the diet of

272

the Hunzas. This consisted of whole grain chapati or flatbread, soybeans, raw carrots, raw cabbage and raw milk. To an equally sound group of 2,000 mice he gave the standard Indian diet of white rice, beans, and vegetables cooked with spices. After 27 months he performed autopsies and compared the groups. The mice fed on the Hunza diet were in excellent condition. Those fed on the Indian diet were sick, afflicted with weak vision, tumors, dental caries, stunted growth, loss of hair, and ailments of the skin, heart, kidneys, stomach and intestines. Then MacCarrison put 1,000 mice on an English diet of white bread, margarine, tea with sugar, cooked vegetables, canned meat, rolls and jelly. This group became physically sick, and suffered atrophy of the nervous system as well. They became aggressive and vicious, attacking each other.[27]

A more recent study was a cross-cultural comparison involving the Hunza and two other relatively isolated groups known for their health and longevity. These were the Vilcabamba Indians of the Ecuadorean mountains and the Georgian mountain folk of the Russian Caucasus. The researchers examined the diet and life-style of each, looking for common factors. These included a pollution free environment, good water, stable social life, vigorous but not exhausting outdoor labor, and a generally stress free life. Also, dietary patterns, while differing in particular ingredients, were basically similar. In each, whole cereal grains were the staple food, supplemented by beans, local vegetables, and fruits in season. Meat, dairy and other animal foods were used but in very small quantities. Total protein, fat and calorie intake was very low. Refined foods such as white flour and sugar, and all processed, chemicalized products, were virtually unknown. By necessity, the people ate only moderate amounts and during some seasons had to observe a near fast. They were practicing, in effect, near perfect *de facto* macrobiotics.

During the past ten or fifteen years medical and nutritional scientists, impressed perhaps by such general studies, have focused increasingly on the role of food in human health and disease. The role of excess protein and animals fats, of refined sugars, and of chemical additives in cancer and various degenerative diseases has been established. The importance of the full and balanced nutrition, including minerals and fiber, available in whole grains, beans, fresh vegetables and fruits has been recognized. The impact of white sugar and chemical additives on emotional and behavioral disturbances has been suggested. While the research continues, those who follow it closely already are drawing conclusions. Recent pronouncements of the A.M.A. and the cancer and heart societies increasingly reflect opinions about diet that are in accord with macrobiotics.

An outstanding example of how this research is being synthesized and put into practice is in the work of Nathan Pritikin in the United States. An independent researcher, Pritikin correlated available experimental data and designed a diet to arrest and to reverse various kinds of degenerative disease. He established an institute staffed by medical personnel to test and to apply his method. Excellent results with various conditions, including heart disease, diabetes and ulcers, have been obtained. The "Pritikin Diet" is low in fats, proteins and simple sugars and high in complex carbohydrates and fiber. In practice it is a regimen which features whole grains, including brown rice, lightly cooked vegetables, fruits and salads. A small amount of lean meat is permitted, but dairy food, all oils, and salt are minimized. The net result is a macrobiotic regime, specially tailored, perhaps, to Americans who have eaten excessive meat, fats and salt.

Thus, Western scientists, using the tools of observation, quantification, analysis and generalization, seem to be discovering or rediscovering essentially macrobiotic ideas about diet, health and behavior. The same process is occurring on the philosophical and cosmological level as well.

Until early in the 20th century, the view of the universe as a great machine made up of countless and separate objects dominated in Western science. Since then, research into the nature of the atom and of the particles which comprise it, into the nature of light, and into electromagnetism (issuing in the quantum theory) has shown that such a model is problematic. According to Fritjof Capra, author of two pioneering books on modern physics, recent research indicates that the universe must be seen as "one indivisible, dynamic whole, whose parts are all interrelated and are part of a cosmic process."

Also, it is increasingly clear that a Taoist style of Yin-Yang thinking is very helpful in interpreting phenomena in this type of world. The electron, for example, has a Yin and a Yang aspect, sometimes functioning as a wave, sometimes as a particle. Light has a double life as well, acting both as a wave and a ray. To describe the reality one must use both concepts and see them as complementary, not mutually exclusive. Capra asserts that this dialectical way of thinking which sees opposites as forming a harmonious whole applies to all physical, organic and human phenomena. This "systems view of life" and the notion of complementarity which underlies it are not as yet widespread. But Capra, who is a leading spokesman of the "counterculture" as well as of the "new physics" believes that they will come to dominate Western science, philosophy and ways of life.[28]

Thus, from the birth of Western civilization in ancient Greece and Israel until the present time, macrobiotic ideas about the world, about man, about food and health have been present in the West. The world view, the medical theory and the dietary practice brought by Ohsawa to Europe and America seem alien and exotic. But in fact they were not. They are, and remain today, an intrinsic part of the Western cultural tradition, one perhaps whose day is yet to come.

[1] Hippocrates, *Hippocratic Writings*, Great Books of the Western World Vol. 10, Encyclopedia Brittanica, Chicago, London, Toronto pp. 1–7

[2] Ibid., p. 7

[3] *The New Oxford Annotated Bible* (RSV) Oxford University Press, New York, 1977 Genesis 1: 29 (p. 3)

[4] Ibid., Genesis 9: 2–3

[5] Ibid., Daniel 1: 12–16

[6] Josephus *The Essene* as recorded in Szekely, Edmund Bordeaux *The Essenes Observed by Josephus and his Contemporaries*, International Biogenic Society, Cartago, Costa Rica

[7] *Essene Gospel of John*, Szekeley, E.B. (translator) International Biogenic Society, Cartago, Costa Rica

[8] Ibid., *passim.*

[9] *Oxford Annotated Bible*, Matt. 5: 1 ff. Luke 6: 20 ff.

[10] *The Gospel According to Thomas* (Coptic Text Established and Translated) E.J. Brill, Leiden, Harper and Row, New York and Evanston, p. 29.

[11] Ibid.,

274

[12] Eckhart, Meister, *Meister Eckhart: A Modern Translation* (trans. by Raymond Blakney), Harper and Brothers, Publishers, New York, 1941 This collection of sermons of Eckhart is the primary source for understanding his thought.

[13] Cosman, Madeleine P. "A Feast for Aesculapius: Historical Dicts for Asthma and Sexual Pleasure" Annual Review of Nutrition, 1983 p. 1

[14] Ibid.,

[15] Goethe, J.W. von, *Gedichte* (*Werke*, III, 84) as cited in Cassirer, Ernst, *Rousseau, Kant, Goethe: Two Essays*, Princeton University Press, Princeton, NJ. 1970, p. 93

[16] Goethe, *Faust*, Modern Library, New York, p. 66 as cited in Cassirer, Ibid., p. 69

[17] As cited in Barkas, Janet, *The Vegetable Passion*, Charles Scribner's Sons, New York, 1975, p. 82

[18] Brillat-Savarin, Jean Anthelme, *The Philosopher in the Kitchen*, Penguin Books, Ltd., Harmondsworth, Middlesex, England, 1970, p. 13 ff.

[19] Emerson, R. W., "The American Scholar"

[20] Emerson, R. W., "On Nature"

[21] Emerson, R. W., "The American Scholar"

[22] Koster, Donald N., *Transcendentalism in America*, Twayne Publishers, Boston, 1975, p. 52

[23] Koster, Ibid., p. 61

[24] Franklin, B. as cited in Barkas, J. *The Vegetable Passion*, p. 135

[25] Thoreau, Henry David, *Walden*, p.

[26] Matlock, Gene, Article in "Today's Health" magazine, 1963

[27] As cited by Morishita, Keiichi, in "Yin Yang" magazine, 1968, Paris

[28] Capra, Fritjof, *The Turning Point*, Simon and Schuster, New York, 1982, p. 78

15.

Prospects for the Future

Macrobiotics, or at least macrobiotic ideas, attitudes and practices, have been present in the East and in the West since ancient times. In the modern period, an explicit, organized movement began less than a century ago in Japan. Thirty years ago this was still only a tiny group in that remote island nation. It has grown since then to an international, though modest, movement with followings in America, Europe, South America, the South Pacific and elsewhere. Growth continues to be steady, if not explosive.

The eventual fate of macrobiotics is a secret of the future. It may become, as Kushi predicts, the basis of a world community. It may stabilize as a movement involving a substantial though a minority portion of the world's population. Or it may disappear as a distinct movement entirely, its ideas and practices taken over by more dynamic groups. In any case, the ability of the macrobiotic movement to mature and to develop, to adapt to new circumstances will determine its future role in human history.

At the end of Chapter 10 we discussed several factors which have inhibited the growth of macrobiotics. The focus was on the situation in America in the years from 1966–1984. The points made, though, are relevant wherever a macrobiotic community exists, and they pertain to the future as well as to the past. Among the factors mentioned were: a lack of professionalism and organization; the presence of dogmatic and narrow-minded attitudes: and a distinct Japanese "exoticism." These elements strongly affect the quality of life within the movement and its ability to appeal to those outside it. If macrobiotics is to play a significant role in the development of humanity in the coming years, let alone in the next decades and centuries, it must consciously and honestly confront each of these issues.

Amateurism within the movement is much less apparent now than it was even a few years ago. People active in macrobiotics have gained maturity and experience with the years (as one would hope). Also, there are more older, established people entering (often from medical motives). The form and content of macrobiotic education is being improved and standardized. Standard levels of competence are being required of teachers, counselors and cooks. Thus the various activities and businesses are much more smoothly and professionally run than previously, and continue to improve.

The resistance to organization (or at least to good, efficient, organization) also seems to be disappearing. The network of Kushi Institutes and East West Foundations in America and around the world is growing. In periodic regional congresses clear patterns of association and cooperation are being established. There are plans for a Macrobiotics International which will tie the world movement together. Some patient work needs to be done to incorporate the activities and outlooks of other teachers such as Aihara, Kikuchi, Yasuhara, Levy and Yamaguchi into these programs initiated by Kushi. But a strong basic foundation is being laid.

These developments will greatly assist the development of macrobiotics, providing certain dangers are avoided. One is the confusion of professionalism with "commercialism." At present, medical consultations provide income for many leaders and teachers. The average fee for a one-hour session is about $125, though it ranges from zero to $300. Macrobiotic advice is liable to become the privilege of the well-to-do. Commercialism also threatens to sow the seeds of dissension. Recently a teacher based in Boston gave a weekend seminar in a nearby city, and gave several medical consultations there also. Soon he was reprimanded by local counselors for invading their "turf."

With organization, of course, come a variety of crucial issues. They include:

- Who controls the organization and on what basis of authority? Is it a democracy, monarchy, oligarchy?
- What are the standards in belief and practice for membership. What, in effect, does it mean to be "macrobiotic?"
- At what point, if any, does one cease to be macrobiotic and become liable to be de-frocked, so to speak. One long-time senior teacher already has, very quietly, been relieved of his certification.

These are all important and difficult questions. But they must be clearly and openly addressed. Macrobiotics International may well benefit from a constitutional convention.

Dogmatism, intellectual arrogance, obsessive and narrowminded thinking are still present within macrobiotics as perhaps they always will be. However, as the movement as a whole and the individuals within it mature these signs of intellectual and emotional adolescence should diminish. And there are already indications that such is the case.

Ohsawa, Kushi, and other senior teachers of macrobiotics still are respected as wise and insightful men who have discovered and shared important truths. Yet there is also a clear and spreading awareness that:

- Their teachings are not infallible.
- Their ideas must be tested and critically evaluated.
- When these ideas do not correspond to experience or evidence they should be discarded or revised.
- In effect, everyone must practice *non credo*, a basic but oft-forgotten principle of macrobiotics.

Along with this awareness is the growing sense that macrobiotics does not have all the answers, that there is still much to learn. This applies even to basic dietetic practices. Many people, while accepting the macrobiotic approach to nutrition, are concerned about still unresolved issues. Is there enough vitamin B_{12} in the diet? Is there enough calcium? And if so can a person raised on a meat and dairy food diet absorb and utilize it? Etc., etc. And in their search for answers people are looking more to the scientific method. They are realizing that observation, quantification and analysis are valid and important ways to understand the world, that science and intuition are complementary rather than antagonistic.

A recognition of the importance of food and a deep concern about it as a factor in human life lie at the heart of macrobiotics. There is, though, a growing consciousness that the food man eats is only one type of nourishment. Art, music, ideas, emotions and social relationships are also "food" and play a crucial role in human health and well-being. People are realizing that care and energy must be spent on all of these types of food if one is to become truly healthy; that in its meaning of "great life" macrobiotics involves a well-rounded, not a food-obsessed, way of living.

Again, none of these ideas are new. They have long been part of the macrobiotic teachings. Nevertheless, their rediscovery and re-emphasis is important to the survival of the movement, and also its growth. To the extent that they displace dogmatic, rigid and narrow habits of mind, the prospects for macrobiotics in the future will improve.

The most interesting and perhaps the most important development in the macrobiotic movement concerns its relation to Japanese culture. A reassessment of the Japanese ambience in macrobiotics has begun, and its results will affect greatly the future of the movement.

After originating in late 19th century Japan, modern macrobiotics has been elaborated and disseminated by Japanese teachers—first Ohsawa, then a generation of his direct disciples. Thus the movement had from its beginning a strong Japanese character which it retained even when transplanted to the West. Its philosophy has been expressed in the Japanese/Oriental terms of Yin and Yang. Its cuisine has been dominated by Japanese foods and cooking methods, so much so that for many both within and without the movement, macrobiotics has meant brown rice, miso soup and azuki beans. Its medicine has been based on traditional Japanese therapies and remedies. Macrobiotic education often has included instruction in Japanese arts and crafts, in the martial arts, and in Japanese religious beliefs and practices. Even patterns of male-female relations and of general social interaction have been markedly influenced by Japanese models. This is all understandable. Ohsawa, Kushi, Aihara, Kikuchi, et al. have drawn on the ideas and practices most familiar to them. And for many Westerners disaffected with modern culture the elegance, subtlety and beauty of traditional Japanese life has had a very strong appeal.

The basic truths of macrobiotics, however, are universal. They are not tied to any particular culture. Simply stated, they include the following.

- The natural birthright of man is health, freedom and happiness.
- The realization of that birthright is entirely the responsibility of the individual. There are no accidents nor blind decrees of fate. Man's sickness or health, sorrow or joy, alienation or well-being all depend on how he lives.
- One of the key factors in human life is food. It plays a direct, significant, if often

overlooked, role in human health. It can prevent and cure disease. It affects emotional, mental and spiritual, as well as physical, life.

- An optimal diet is an ecological one, based on the natural environment and climate, and on the history and circumstances of the individual. In most cases this is a diet based on whole grains supplemented by local, seasonal, vegetable foods.

- The universe is a harmonious and dynamic whole in which all oppositions are complementary. Humankind is an integral and important part of this whole, and human life has ultimate meaning and value.

These ideas are applicable anywhere. According to the natural and cultural environment, however, they will be expressed and practiced in slightly different ways. The culture of traditional Japan (in its highest manifestations) is one such expression. But there is no unique and necessary connection between it and the basic truths of macrobiotics. In fact, according to the principle of shin do fu ji ("Man and environment are one"), there can and should be various native expressions of macrobiotic philosophy, diet, medicine, etc. That macrobiotics developed and kept a Japanese ambience, is an accident of history.

For the most part, people within the macrobiotic movement have accepted this "Japanese macrobiotics" as its valid and standard form. Recently, however, in America, Europe and elsewhere there has arisen a questioning of, and dissatisfaction with this "Japanese-ness." While holding to the central tenets of the macrobiotic world view and practice, people are beginning to explore their own traditions and cultural genius. They want to re-examine the religion and philosophy of their native culture. They want to draw on their own heritage, on its staple foods, cuisine, medicine, arts and crafts, patterns of social interaction, and spiritual practice. They want, in effect, to create a form of macrobiotics that is in harmony with their natural, cultural and historical circumstances.[1]

What will result from this foment remains to be seen. In Europe, for example, traditional staple grains such as oats, barley and rye may replace rice as the foundation of the macrobiotic cuisine. Native fermented foods such as sourdough bread, sauerkraut, and kvass (an East-European drink of lightly fermented cereals) may replace or supplement miso and tamari. In philosophy, Christian (or pre-Christian) symbols and concepts may be used to express a world view. Native herbal medicine, traditional patterns of family life, of community organization, and of religious observance may be revived. Of course this need not and will not mean that all Japanese elements, from Yin-Yang terminology to chopsticks, will disappear. Some will be set aside to be sure, but others will be retained, synthesized perhaps with native ideas and practices.

This process of "acculturation," of adapting macrobiotics to different cultures, is just beginning. Very likely, and perhaps inevitably, it will continue. If so, in each country or cultural area a different expression of macrobiotics will emerge. While based on common, universal principles, each will be distinct in particulars of theory and practice. To a degree, the homogeneity which now binds the international community together will be lost. But the movement as a whole will be strengthened. Within each nation macrobiotics may prove a more satisfying way of life for those already involved. And it will be better able to attract and benefit people from the mainstream of the population. Now the typical Danish housewife or Uruguayan laborer, who has no serious illness to motivate them, is not likely to be attracted to a Japanese style of macrobiotics. But they might be interested in a diet of native and traditional foods, and in a generally familiar way of life that offers them and their family health and well-being.[2]

There are, then, several important trends in macrobiotics at the present time. Professionalism is increasing and the organization of the movement is developing. There is an emotional and intellectual maturing and an evolution beyond earlier dogmatic and narrow-minded modes of thought. And there is an impulse to adapt macrobiotics to suit the past traditions and present needs of people in the various countries of the world. Should these several processes continue, macrobiotics will survive. Probably it will grow and flourish. Perhaps it will play, in the individual and collective destiny of humanity, that grand and benevolent role to which it aspires.

---

[1] Perhaps the earliest occurrence of this is Michel Abehsera. About a decade ago, after years as a disciple of Ohsawa and as a leader of the macrobiotic community in New York and Binghamton, Abehsera returned to his own Jewish heritage and became a Hasidim. He now lives in Brooklyn, New York as a member of the orthodox community there.

[2] Japan is a special case of course. Part of the difficulty for the Japanese community is that macrobiotics already is "too Japanese," particularly for the present generation. The Japanese people, as ever, are drawn to what is new, foreign, and Western (especially American). The key to developing macrobiotics in Japan may lie in making it less familiar and traditional, rather than more so. The greatest boon might be the arrival of a teacher from America or Europe, who introduces macrobiotics as a Western philosophy and diet. *Soylami* (tempeh based "salami"), *mock pizza* (made with tofu-cheese and carrot sauce), *amazake* (sweet rice) ice cream and other delights current in Boston and London probably would sweep the nation.

Bibliography

Works in English

Aihara, Herman, *Learning from Salmon and Other Essays*, George Ohsawa Macrobiotic Foundation, Oroville, CA., 1980.

Anesaki, Masaharu, *Nichiren, Buddhist Prophet*, Harvard University Press, Cambridge, Mass., 1949.

Aston, W. G. (Translator), *The Nihongi*, The Japan Society, London, 1896.

Barkas, Janet, *The Vegetable Passion: A History of the Vegetarian State of Mind*, Charles Scribner's Sons, New York, 1975.

Brillat-Savarin, Jean Anthelme, *The Philosopher in the Kitchen*, Penguin Books Ltd., Harmondsworth, Middlesex England, 1970.

Brown, Delmer, *Nationalism in Japan*, University of California Press, Berkeley and Los Angeles, 1955.

Capra, Fritjof, *The Turning Point: Science, Society and the Rising Culture*, Simon and Schuster, New York, 1982.

Carrel, Alexis, *Man the Unknown*, Harper and Brothers., New York and London, 1935.

Cassirer, Ernst, *Rousseau, Kant, Goethe: Two Essays*, Princeton University Press, Princeton, New Jersey, 1970.

de Bary, Wm. Theodore, *Sources of Chinese Tradition*, Columbia University Press, New York and London, 1964, Volumes I and II.

———, *Sources of Japanese Tradition*, Columbia University Press, New York and London, 1958, Volumes I and II.

Earhart, H. Byron, *Japanese Religion: Unity and Diversity*, Dickenson Publishing Co., Inc., Belmont, California, 1969.

———, *Religion in the Japanese Experience: Sources and Interpretations*, Dickenson Publishing Co. Inc., Encino and Belmont, California, 1974.

Eckhart, Meister, *Meister Eckhart: A Modern Translation* (translated by Raymond Blakney), Harper and Brothers, New York, 1941.

Eliot, Sir Charles, *Japanese Buddhism*, Routledge & Kegan Paul Ltd., London; Barnes and Noble, Inc., New York, 1969.

Engi-Shiki, Procedures of the Engi Era, Sophia University, Tokyo, Japan, 1970.

Fairbank, John K., E. O. Reischauer and Albert M. Craig, *East Asia: The Great Tradition* (Volume 1), *East Asia: The Modern Transformation* (Volume 2), Houghton Mifflin Co., Boston, 1965.

Fuller, A. G. and McMurrin, Sterling, *A History of Philosophy*, Holt, Rinehart and Winston, New York, 1964.

Gauntlett, John, *Kokutai no Hongi (Basic Principles of the National Polity)*, Harvard University Press, Cambridge, Massachusetts, 1949, Edited with an Introduction by Robert King Hall.

Hippocrates, *Hippocratic Writings*, Great Books of the Western World Vol. 10, Encyclopedia Brittanica, Chicago, London, Toronto, 1952.

Ienaga, Saburō, *The Pacific War*, The Pantheon Asia Library, Pantheon Books, New York, 1978.

Kaibara, Ekken, *Yōjōkun: Japanese Secrets of Good Health*, Tokuma Shoten Publishing Co., Tokyo, 1974.

Koster, Donald N., *Transcendentalism in America*, Twayne Publishers, Boston, 1975.

Kushi, Michio, *The Book of Macrobiotics*, Japan Publications, Tokyo, 1977.

———, *The Book of Dō-In*, Japan Publications, Tokyo, 1979.

———, *How to See Your Health: The Book of Oriental Diagnosis*, Japan Publications, Tokyo, 1980.

———, *Natural Healing Through Macrobiotics*, Japan Publications, Tokyo, 1979.

———, *The Era of Humanity: Visions of a New World*, (edited by Sherman Goldman), East West Journal, Inc., 1980.

———. *The Cancer Prevention Diet*, (edited by Alex Jack), St. Martin's Press, New York, 1982.

———, "Order of the Universe Magazine" 1969–1983, Order of the Universe Publications, 17 Station St. Brookline, Mass.

Lao Tzu, *The Way of Lao Tzu*, The Library of Liberal Arts, The Bobbs-Merrill Company Inc., Indianapolis, New York, 1963, Wing-Tsit Chan (Translator).

Lu, Henry C., Ph. D., *A Complete Translation of The Yellow Emperor's Classic of Internal Medicine and the Difficult Classic*, Academy of Oriental Heritage, Vancouver B.C., 1978.

Matson, Wallace, *A History of Philosophy*, American Book Company, 1968.

Miller, Saul, *Food for Thought: A New Look at Food and Behavior*, Prentice Hall Inc., Englewood Cliffs, New Jersey, 1979.

Najita, Tetsuo, *Japan*, Prentice Hall Inc, Englewood Cliffs, New Jersey, 1974.

———, Irwin Scheiner (Editors), *Japanese Thought in the Tokugawa Period*, The University of Chicago Press, Chicago, London, 1978.

Nakane, Chie, *Japanese Society*, University of California Press, Berkeley and Los Angeles, 1972.

Nitobe, Inazo, *Bushido: The Soul of Japan*, Kenkyusha, Tokyo, 1935.

Norbeck, Edward, *Religion and Society in Modern Japan*, Rice University Press, Houston, Texas, 1970.

Northrop, F. S. C., *The Meeting of East and West*, The MacMillan Co., New York, 1960.

Offner, Clark B. and Henry van Strachen, *Modern Japanese Religions*, Twayne Publishers Inc., New York, 1963.

Okakura, Kakuzo, *The Book of Tea*, Dover Publications Inc., New York, 1964.

———, *The Ideals of the East with Special Reference to the Art of Japan*, John Murray, Albemarle St., London, 1904, Second Edition.

Pelzel, John C., "Human Nature in the Japanese Myths," T. S. Lebra and Wm. P. Lebra (Editors), *Japanese Culture and Behavior*, An East-West Center Book, The University Press of Hawaii, Honolulu, 1974.

Philippi, Donald L., *Norito: A New Translation of the Ancient Japanese Ritual Prayers*, The Institute for Japanese Culture & Classics, Kokugakuin University, Tokyo, 1959.

Rabbitt, James A., "Rice in the Cultural Life of the Japanese," Transactions of the Asiatic Society in Japan, December 1940.

Sugimoto, Etsuko, *Daughter of the Samurai*, Doubleday, Garden City, New York, 1934.

Suzuki, D. T., *Zen Buddhism and its Influence on Japanese Culture*, Eastern Buddhist Society, Otani Buddhist College, Kyoto, 1938.

Thomas, The Gospel According to (Coptic Text Established and Annotated) E. J. Brill, Leiden, Harper and Row, New York and Evanston, 1959.

Thompson, Laurence G., *Chinese Religion: An Introduction*, Dickenson Publishing Company Inc., Belmont, California, 1969.

Thoreau, Henry David, *Walden*

Veith, Ilza, *The Yellow Emperor's Classic of Internal Medicine*, University of California Press, Berkeley, Los Angeles, London, 1972.

von Hufeland, Christolph Wilhelm, *Makrobiotik, Die Kunst das Menschliche Leben zu Verlängern*, Matthes und Seitz Verlag, München, 1978.

Wilhelm, Richard, Carl Baynes, *The I Ching or Book of Changes*, Bollingen Series XIX, Princeton University Press, 1970.

Yui-en, *Tannishō (A Tract Deploring Heresies of Faith)*, Higashi Honganji, Kyoto, 1961.

Works by George Ohsawa

Atarashii Eiyōgaku [新しい栄養学]
  (*The New Science of Nutrition*), Musō Genri Kōkyūjo, Ohtsu City, 1942.
Baikin no Kuni Tanken [バイキンの国探検]
  (*Exploration of the Land of Bacteria*), Musō Genri Kōkyūjo, Ohtsu City, 1943.
Biological Transmutation: Natural Alchemy, with Louis Kervran, George Ohsawa Macrobiotic Foundation, First Ed. 1971, 1976.
Byōki o Naosu Jutsu, [病気を治す術]
  (*The Technique of Curing Disease*), Nippon C.I., Tokyo, 1956.
Cancer and the Philosophy of the Far East, Swan House Publishing Co., Binghamton, New York, 1971.
Carrel's Ningen Kaisetsu [カレル「人間」解説]
  (*Carrel's "Mankind" An Explanation* [*Commentary*]), Tokyo P.U. Center, 1947.
Chūō Afrika Ōdanki, with Lima Ohsawa, [中央アフリカ横断記]
  (*A Record of a Crossing of Equatorial Africa*), original date of publication: 1958; reprinted Nippon C.I., Tokyo, 1976.
Clara Schumann [クララ シューマン]
  Konpa Shuppan Sha, Tokyo, 1948.
Eien no Kodomo [永遠の子供]
  (*Eternal Children*), Musō Genri Kenkyūjo, 1944.
Eien no Shōnen: Benjamin Franklin no Isshō ni yotte [永遠の少年・ベンジャシンフランクリンの一生によって]
  (*The Eternal Youth: The Life of Benjamin Franklin*), original date of publication: 1952; reprinted Nippon C.I., Tokyo, 1976.
Eien no Shōnen・Tsuzuki: Gandhi no Shōnen Jidai [永遠の少年・続: ガンジイの少年時代]
  (*The Eternal Youth・Continued: Gandhi's Youth*), original date of publication: 1954; reprinted Nippon C.I., Tokyo, 1977.
Furippu Monogatari Kaisetsu [フリップ物語解説]
  (*The Story of Flip: An Explanation*) Konpa Shuppan Sha, Chiyoda-Ku, Tokyo, 1949.
Haku Shoku Jinshu o Teki to Shite: Nihon wa Tatakawaneba Naranu Riyū [白色人種を敵として日本はたたかわねばならぬ理由]
  (*With the White Race as Enemy: Why Japan Must Fight*), original date of publication: 1932; reissued as *Nihon o Horobosu Mono wa Tare Da* cf. p. 455
Heihō Nanasho no Shin Kenkyū [兵法七書の新研究]
  (*A New Study of the Seven Articles on Military Strategy*), original date of publication: December 1943; reprinted Nippon C.I., Tokyo, 1976.
Heiwa to Jiyū no Genri [平和と自由の原理]
  (*The Principle of Peace and Freedom*), original date of publication: 1949; reprinted Nippon C.I. , Tokyo, 1973.
Hitotsu no Hōkoku: Aru Byōin ni okeru Jikken no Hōkoku [一つの報告―ある病院における実験の報告]
  (*A Single Report: A Report of a Hospital Experiment*), original date of publication: July 1941; reprinted Nippon C.I., Tokyo, 1976.
Ishi Kyōiku Gojūnen no Jikken Hōkoku [「意志」教育五十年の実験報告]
  (*A Report on Fifty Years Experience in the Education of the Will*), Nippon C.I., Tokyo, 1966.
Ishizuka Sagen [石塚左玄]
  Original date of publication: 1928; reprinted Nippon C.I., Tokyo, 1974.
Jack et Mitie en Occident ou deux "non-civilisés" dans la jungle dité "civilisation," Librarie J. Vrin, Paris, 1971.
Katei Shokuryō Tokuhon [家庭食療読本]

(*A Guide to Household Food Cures*), Shoku-Yō Kai, Tokyo, 1937.

Kenkō Gakuen [健康学園]
(*School for Health*), Musō Genri Kōkyūjo, Ohtsu City, 1941.

Kenkō no Nana Dai Jōken: Seigi ni Tsuite [健康の七大条件・正義について]
(*The Seven Great Conditions of Health: Concerning Justice*), original date of publication: March 1962; reprinted Nippon C.I., Tokyo, 1977.

Kenkō Sensen no Dai Issen ni Tachite [健康戦線の第一線に立ちて]
(*Standing on the Front Line of the Health War*), Musō Genri Kōkyūjo, Ohtsu City, June 1941.

Kenkō Techō [健康手帖]
(*Health Notebook*), Shoku-Yō Kai, Tokyo, 1939.

Kōkaijō: Kennedy oyobi Khrushchev Ryōshi ni Atau [公開状―ケネディ及フルシチョフ両氏に与う]
(*A Public Proposal Presented to Kennedy & Khrushchev*), Foundation Ohsawa, Paris, New York, Tokyo, November 1962.

Kome no Chishiki, Takikata Tabekata [米の知識，炊き方，食べ方]
(*The Consciousness of Rice, and the Art of its Cooking and Eating*), Dai Nippon Hōrei Shuppan, Tokyo, June 1940.

Konpa Bunko #4 [コンパ文庫#4]
(*Konpa Magazine, Collection* #4 [*January-July* 1948]), Nippon C.I., Tokyo, 1960.

Konpa Bunko #5 [コンパ文庫#5]
(*Konpa Magazine, Collection* #5 [*April* 1947–*December* 1947]), Nippon C.I., Tokyo, 1960.

Konpa Bunko #6 [コンパ文庫#6]
(*Konpa Magazine, Collection* #6 [*September* 1948–*May* 1949]), Nippon C.I., Tokyo, 1960.

Kōseishō no Shidō Genri to Konpon Musō Genri [厚生省の指導原理と根本無双原理]
(*The Guiding Principles of the Dept. of Welfare and the Fundamental Unique Principle*), publisher unavailable; probably Shoku-Yō Kai, Tokyo, 1939.

L'Acupuncture et la Médicine d'Extrême Orient, Original date of publication: 1934; reprinted Librairie Philosophique, J. Vrin, Paris, 1973.

Le Cancer et la Philosophie d'Extrême Orient, La Librairie Ohsawa, Paris, 1964.

Le Compas International, "Open Letters," Sekai Seifu Kyōkai, Yokohama, No. 27: November 4, 1951, No. 33: March 3, 1952, No. 34: March 21, 1952, No. 41: May 25, 1953, No. 42: March 29, 1953, No. 44: October 5, 1953.

Le Livre des Fleurs, Vrin, Paris, original date of publication: 1931; new edition 1972.

Le Livre du Judo: Commentaire sur le Principes des écoles de "Do," Centre Ignoramus de Paris, 26 Rue Lamartine, Paris 75009, 1952.

Le Principe Unique de la Philosophie et de la Science d'Extrême Orient, Librarie Philosophique, J. Vrin, original edition 1931, 1978.

Manshūkoku no Kōsei undō [満洲国の厚生運動]
(*The Public Welfare Movement in Manchuria*), Shoku-Yō Kai, Tokyo, April 1940.

Manshū Shoku-Yō Tokuhon [満洲食養読本]
(*A Shoku-Yō Guidebook for Manchuria*), Atago Insatsu, October 1939.

Mahō no Megane [魔法のメガネ]
(*The Magic Spectacles*), original date of publication: December 1940; reprinted Nippon C.I., Tokyo, 1976.

Mikaijin no Seishin to Nihon Seishin [未開人の精神と日本精神]
(*The Spirit of "Primitive Man" and the Japanese Spirit*), Musō Genri Kenkyūjo, Ohtsu City, 1943.

Musō Genri: Eki—Jitsuyō Benshōhō [無双原理―易・実用弁証法]
(*The Unique Principle・Eki—A Practical Dialectical Method*), original date of publication: March 1936; reprinted Nippon C.I., Tokyo, 1976.

Naze Nihon wa Yabureta ka [ナゼ日本は敗れたか]
(*Why Was Japan Defeated?*), Musō Genri Kenkyūjo, Ohtsu City, September 1947.

Nihon o horobosu mono wa tare da [日本を亡ぼすものはたれだ]

(*Who are Those Who Destroy Japan?*), Nihon Shuppan Haikyū Kabushiki Kaisha, Tokyo, 1941.

Nihon Seishin no Seirigaku [日本精神の生理学] with Nishibata Manabu
(*The Physiology of the Japanese Spirit*), Nihon Shoku-Yō Kenkyūjo, Tokyo, 1929.

Ningen Kakumei no Sho [人間革命の書]
(*A Book of the Human Revolution*), original date of publication: January 1948; reprinted Nippon C.I., Tokyo, 1976.

Ningen no Chitsujo [人間の秩序]
(*The Order of Humanity*), original date of publication: March 1941; reprinted Nippon C.I., Tokyo, 1976.

Ningen no Eiyōgaku oyobi Igaku [人間の栄養学及医学]
(*Human Nutritional Science and Medicine*), Dai Nihon Hōrei Shuppan, Tokyo, 1939.

Pasteur no Saiban [パストゥールの審判]
(*Pasteur on Trial*), Musō Genri Kenkyūjo, Ohtsu City, June 1943.

P. U. Chūgoku Yonsennen Shi [PU 中国四千年史]
(*P. U. Four Thousand Year History of China According to the Unique Principle*), Musō Genri Kenkyūjo, 1943. (Privately published; not for public sale)

P. U. Keizai Genron: Yume to Jōnetsu no Sekai [PU 経済原論・夢と情熱の世界]
(*A Theory of Economics According to the Unique Principle: the World of Dreams and Passion*), Musō Genri Kenkyūjo, June 1944. (Privately published; not for public sale.)

Saigo ni soshite Eien ni Katsu mono [最後にそして永遠に勝つ者]
(*The Last and thus the Eternal Winner*), Musō Genri Kenkyūjo, Ohtsu City, 1943. (Privately published.)

Satō no Doku to Nikushoku no Gai [砂糖の毒と肉食の害]
(*The Poison of Sugar and the Harm of Eating Meat*), Dai Nihon Hōrei Shuppan, December 1939.

Seimei Genshō to Kankyō [生命現象と環境]
(*Phenomena of Life and the Environment*), original date of publication: 1942; reprinted Nippon C.I., Tokyo, 1975.

Seitai ni Yoru Genshi Tenkan [生体による原子転換]
(*Atomic Transmutation in Living Bodies*), Nippon C.I., Tokyo, 1964.

Seiyō Igaku no Botsuraku [西洋医学の没落] (*The Collapse of Western Medicine*)
Translation of *Les Ideés Medicales* by Dr. René Aranji, Senshin Sha, Tokyo, 1934.

Sekai Kōkyū Heiwa An [世界恒久平和案]
(*A Proposal for Lasting World Peace*), Nippon C.I., Tokyo, 1966.

Sekai Musen Musha Ryokō [世界無銭武者旅行]
(*The World Journey of the Penniless Samurai*), Institut de Philosophie et Medicine d'Extrême Orient, Paris, July 1957; reissued by Nippon C.I., Tokyo, 1976.

Sen Nihyaku Nen Mae no Jiyūjin—Dengyō Daishi [千二百年前の自由人・伝教大師]
(*A Free Man of 1,200 Years Ago—Dengyō Daishi*), original date of publication: June 1959; reissued Nippon C.I., 1976.

Sensō ni Katsu Shokumotsu [戦争に勝つ食物]
(*Foods for Victory in War*), Dai Nihon Horei Shuppan, Tokyo, August 1940.

Shin Shoku-Yō Ryō Hō: Shoku ni yoru Kenkō to Jiyū [新食養療法・食による健康と自由]
(*New Shoku-Yō Treatments: Health and Happiness through Food*), original date of publication: March 1939; reprinted Nippon C.I., Tokyo, 1977.

Shin do Fu Ji no Gensoku [身土不二の原則]
(*The Principle of "Man-Nature-Not-Two"*), published as part of *Seimei Genshō to Kankyō*, February 1936.

Shizen Igaku: Shokumotsu Ryōhō Sōran [自然医学—食物療法総覧]
(*Natural Medicine: An Overview of Food Treatments*), original date of publication: July 1938; reprinted Nippon C.I., Tokyo, 1976.

Shinzen Igaku to shite no Shintō: Norito no Seirigaku [自然医学としての神道—祝詞の生理学]
(*Shinto as a Natural Medicine: the Physiology of the Norito*), Shoku-Yō Kai, Tokyo, 1936.

Shizen Kagaku no Saigo, Atarashii Sekai Kan no Tanjō [自然科学の最後，新しい世界観の誕生]

(*The Termination of Natural Science, The Birth of a New Weltanschauung*), original date of publication: December 1941; reprinted Nippon C.I., Tokyo, 1976.

Shokumotsu ni yoru Kenkō to Kōfuku [食物による健康と幸福]
  (*Health and Happiness through Food*), Shoku-Yō Kai, Tokyo, March 1939.

Shokumotsu no Ronri [食物の倫理]
  (*The Ethics of Food*), Nihon Shoku-Yō Kenkyūjo, Ohtsu City, November 1940.

Shokumotsu to Jinsei: Shin Seikatsu Undō no Shishin [食物と人生—真生活運動の指針]
  (*Food and Human Life: A Guide for the "True Life" Movement*), original date of publication: July 1943; reprinted Nippon C.I., Tokyo, 1976.

Shoku-Yō Jinsei Tokuhon: Hito no Isshō no Sekkei [食養人生読本・人の一生の設計]
  (*The Shoku-Yō Guidebook for Living: A Plan for a Human Lifetime*), original date of publication: October 1938; reprinted Nippon C.I., Tokyo, 1976.

Shoku-Yō Kōgi Roku [食養講義録]
  (*The Shoku-Yō Lectures*), original date of publication: 1928; reprinted Nippon C.I., Tokyo, 1977.

Shoku-Yō Sensen [食養戦線]
  (*The Shoku-Yō Battle Line*), Shoku-Yō Kai, Tokyo, 1938.

Shōnen Shōjo Kenkō Gakuen [少年少女健康学園]
  (*The Boy's and Girl's School for Health*), Musō Genri Kōkyūjō, Ohtsu City, 1940.

Tadashii Shokumotsu ni tsuite [正しい食物について]
  (*Concerning Proper Food*), original date of publication: December 1941; reprinted Nippon C.I., Tokyo, 1976.

The Book of Judgment: The Philosophy of Oriental Medicine, Volume II, Ignoramus Press, The Ohsawa Foundation, Los Angeles, 1966.

Tōkyō Kenkō Gakuen no Kiroku [東京健康学園の記録]
  (*Report on the Tokyo "School for Health"*), Nippon C.I., Tokyo, 1965.

Tōyō Igaku no Tetsugaku [東洋医学の哲学]
  (*The Philosophy of Oriental Medicine*), original date of publication: January 1956; reprinted Nippon C.I., Tokyo, 1973.

Two Great Indians in Japan: Sri Rash Behari Bose and Netaji Subhas Chandra Bose, Sri K. C. Das Kusa Publications, Calcutta, 8 August 1954.

Uchū no Chitsujo [宇宙の秩序]
  (*The Order of the Universe*), original date of publication: March 1941; reprinted Nippon C.I., Tokyo, 1973.

Unagi no Musō Genri [ウナギの無双原理]
  (*The Unique Principle of the Eel*), Musō Genri Kōkyūjo, 1941.

Zen Macrobiotics, The Ohsawa Foundation, Los Angeles, 1965.

Works in Japanese by Authors other than Ohsawa ━━━━━

Georges Ohsawa Album, Nippon C.I. Kyōkai, Tokyo, 1976.

Ishiko Fukashi, *Wakaki Hi no Sakurazawa Yukikazu Shi* [石河浚　若き日の桜沢如一氏],
  (*Sakurazawa Yukikazu in his Younger Years*), privately published memoir, October 1971, available through M. Hashimoto, Nippon C.I. Kyōkai, 11–5 Ōyama-chō, Shibuya, Tokyo [日本 C.I. 協会，東京都渋谷区大山町11–5]

Ishizuka Sagen, *Kagakuteki Shoku-Yō Chōjuron* [石塚左玄，化学的食養長寿論]
  (*A Chemical-Nutritional Theory of Long Life*), date of original publication: 1897; reissued by Nippon C.I., Tokyo, 1975.

———, *Shokumotsu Yōjōhō: Ichimei Kagakuteki Shoku-Yō Taishinron* [食物養生法，一名化学的食養体心論]
  (*A Method of Nourishing Life Through Food: A Unique Chemical Food Nourishment Theory of Body and Mind*), date of original publication: 1899, Ishizuka Shokuryōjo; reissued by Nippon C.I., 1974.

Maeda Koichirō, *Chiseigakuteki Kokka no Kōbō* [前田虎一郎，地政学的国家の興亡]
(*The Rise and Fall of Nations According to Geopolitics*), Nihon Shuppan Haikyū, January 1943.
Matsumoto Ichirō, *Shokuseikatsu no Kakumeiji: Sakurazawa Yukikazu no Shisō to Shōgai* [松本一郎，食生活の革命児・桜沢如一の思想と生涯]
(*The Food Life Revolutionary: The Life and Thought of Sakurazawa Yukikazu*), Chisan Shuppan, Tokyo, 1976.
Nakayama Tadanao, *Kanpō Igaku no Shin Kenkyū* [中山忠直，漢法医学の新研究]
(*New Researches in Chinese Medicine*), Hōbunkan, Tokyo, 1927.
Shoku-Yō Kai Shōshi [食養会小史]
(*A Short History of the Shoku-Yō Kai*), Shoku-Yō Kai, April 1937.
Taira Hidemichi and Mizuno Nanboku, *Kansō Jutsu no Hiden* [平秀道・水野南北，観相術の秘伝]
(*The Secret Teachings of Visual Diagnosis*), Chisan Shuppan, Tokyo, 1977.

Index

Abehsera, Michel, 167
abortion, 241
Acuff, Karen, 224
Acuff, Steve, 224
AIDS, 178
Aihara, Cornellia, 132, 144, 165, 179, 180, 182
Aihara, Herman, 78, 132, 133, 165, 169, 170, 179–181
Ainu, 41
Alcott, William, 268
AMA, 186
Amano, Keishi, 91, 213
American Cancer Society, 186
Amherst College, 174
Amsterdam, 222
Anaximander, 253
Anthroposophical Society, 129
Antwerp, 222
Aoyagi, Akiko, 186
Aranji, René, 60
Atarashiki Sekai e, 211, 213
Atlantis, 245
Atomic Age and the Philosophy of the Far East, The, 135
Atomic Transmutation in the Living Body, 134
Aurobindo, Sri, 123
Auroville, 123
Austria, 225
Ayurveda, 123

Bagno, Josianne, 222
Beatitudes, 259
Becket, 178
Belgium 222
Benedict, Dirk, 177
Berger, Barbara, 230
Bern, 225
Binetti, Mario, 225
Binetti, Marlise, 225

birth control, 243
Block, Keith, 175
Blut und Boden, 76
Book of Changes, The, 15
Book of Daniel, The, 256
Book of Flowers, The, 58
Book of Judgment, The, 169
Book of Macrobiotics, The, 176, 235, 236
Boston, 9, 10, 168, 170–175, 231
Bradford, Peter, 221
Brillat-Savarin, Jean Anthelme, 265
Brookline, 168, 174
Brussels, 219, 222
Buddhism, 27, 122
Buenos Aires, 232
Burns, Michael, 221
Butler, Samuel, 116

Calcutta, 120
cancer, 176, 180, 186
Cancer and the Philosophy of the Far East, 136
Capra, Fritjof, 273
Carr, Bob, 179
Carrel, Alexis, 77
Cazals, Gerard, 224
Chaitarangya, 121, 123
ch'i, 25
Chico, 125, 133
Chico-San, 166, 168
Chico-San Company, 133
China, 54, 56, 96
Chishima, Kikuo, 136
Christianity, 58, 114, 115
Claushitzer, Ilse, 219, 228
Community Health Foundation, 221
Confucianism, 15
Copenhagen, 230
Costa Rica, 232

Cousins, Norman, 107, 109, 164

Darré, Walther, 76
Denmark, 230
Denver, John, 177
diagnosis, 238
Diet Number Seven, 132, 133, 161, 172, 183, 256
Diet Seven rice cure, 170
Dobrin, Ron, 171
Dornach, 129
Dufty, William, 167, 231

East West Centers, 11, 175
East West Foundation, 11, 168, 171, 174, 178
East West Journal, 11, 171, 176, 178, 182, 183
Eckhart, Johannes (Meister), 260
Eguchi, Toshihiro, 68
Eliséev, 59
Emerson, 268
Engi Shiki, 72, 73
Erewhon, 10, 116, 129, 130, 170, 171, 177, 185
Erewhon Farms, 171
Erewhon Trading Company, 168
Esko, Ed, 179
Esko, Wendy, 177, 179
Ess, Eric, 225
Essenes, 256
Essene Gospel of John, The, 257
Ethics of Food, The, 95
European Macrobiotic Association, 220

Federal Food and Drug Administration (FDA), 137
feminism, 241

290

Finsterlin, Helmut, 129
Five-Element, 25
"Five Element" theory, 238
Five-Energy, 25, 26
five "transformations of
    energy", 238
Florence, 227
Forty-Seven Rōnin, 63
Fou Hi, 54, 56, 245
4,000 Year History of China
    According to the Unique
    Principle, The, 96
France, 128, 223
Franklin, Benjamin, 267
French Meadows, 180
Fukuoka, Masanobu, 223

Gagne, Steve, 179
Gandhi, Mahatma, 119
Geersten, Tue, 230
Germany, 75, 76, 92, 128,
    224
George Ohsawa Macrobiotic
    Foundation (GOMF), 179,
    180
Gevaert, Edgar, 131
Goethe, Johann Wolfgang,
    262, 263
Goldman, Sherman, 232
Gospel of Thomas, The, 259
Gould, Blake, 179
Graham, Sylvester, 267, 268
Great Britain, 220

Hargrove, Cynthia, 187
Hargrove, Robert, 187
Hawken, Paul, 171, 185, 187
Heart Sutra, The, 57
Hegel, George Friedrich
    Wilhelm, 261
Hegelianism, 262
Hegstad, Mark, 175, 184
hell, 243
Henaf, Nevan, 134
Heraclitus, 253
Hicks, George, 166
hippie subculture, 169
Hippocrates, 255
Hitler, Adolf, 75, 76
Hiyoshi, 107
Holland, 222
homosexuality, 241
Hunza, 271

I Ching, 15, 40
Ikor, Roger, 223

India, 54, 56, 114, 121, 122
infinite expansion, 154
Innsbruck, 220
Institute Tenryu, 131, 134,
    223
Intermac, 210
Ishii, Yasuyuki, 165
Ishizuka, Sagen, 15, 25, 42–
    45, 47, 55
Italy, 227

Jack, Alex, 178
Jack and Mitie, The, 130
Jack and Mitie in the Jungle
    Called Civilization, 129
Jamaica, 232
Japan, 15, 21, 23–25, 30, 33,
    39–42, 44, 45, 47, 54, 56,
    63, 70, 76, 93, 94, 97,
    101–105, 245
Japan Publications, Inc., 176
Jesus, 114, 115, 257, 258
Jews, 74–76, 113
Josephus, 256
judō, 47

ka-dō, 47, 58
Kaibara, Ekken, 12, 15, 27,
    44, 71
Kanō, Jigorō, 115
Kass, Edward, 175
Kawaguchi, Toshi, 67, 89,
    228
Kawano, Augustine, 165, 219,
    224
Keijser, Roland, 227
Kellogg, John Harvey, 269
Kennedy, Bob, 133, 169
Kenya, 123
Kersevich, Enrique, 230, 231
Kervran, Louis, 133
Ki, 17, 22
Kikuchi, Tomio, 230
Kiprianou, John, 232
Kitatani, Kit, 178
Kobayashi, Ruizō, 106
Kobe, 39, 40
Kohler, Jean, 176
Kohso, Eiji, 210
Kojiki, 41
Koku no Kai, 212
Kushi, Aveline, 109, 128, 132,
    143, 164, 173, 174, 178,
    219
Kushi Foundation, The, 178
Kushi Institute, 11, 174, 178,

182, 190, 220, 221, 223,
    225
Kushi, Michio, 9, 13, 109,
    132, 133, 142, 160, 163–
    165, 170, 172, 173, 176,
    178, 219, 223, 226, 235
Kyoto, 37, 38, 210, 212
Kyoto Macrobiotic Center,
    211

L'Acupuncture et la Medicine
    Chinoise, 63
Lady Diane's By the Sea,
    232
Lambarené, 125
Lambe, William, 265
Langre, Jacques, 181
Lazzaro, Ann, 232
Lazzaro, Don, 232
Le Principe Unique, 59
Le Principe Unique de la Phi-
    losophie et de la Science
    d'Extrême Orient, 54
Leaves of Grass, 267
Ledbetter, Jim, 170
Ledvinka, Ferro, 227
Lemuria, 245
Lenk, Switzerland, 220, 225
Lennon, John, 177
Leusch, Mike, 222
Levin, Cecile, 135, 142, 147,
    181
Levy-Bruhl, René, 59, 97
Levy, René, 139, 145, 219,
    223, 224
Levy, Riviére, 219
Lima Company, 219
Lima food company, 132
Lisbon, 225
London, 219, 221
Long Island, 133
Lundberg brothers, 184

MacCarrison, Robert, 271
Magic Spectacles, The, 91
Macrobiotics, 169, 183, 186–
    191, 239, 242, 243
Macrobiotic Guidebook For
    Living, The, 78, 169
Macrobiotics International,
    179
Macrobiotics Today, 182, 183
Macrobiotics Tokyo, 211
MacroMuse, 182, 183
Maimonides, Moses, 261
Maison Ignoramus, 106–109,

119, 121, 123, 163, 223
Man, The Unknown, 77
Manchuria, 60, 65, 66, 71, 72, 100
Mann, John, 179
Manyoshū, 40, 45
Margarinos, Mateo, 223
marriage, 242
Martin, George, 116
Maruyama, Hiroshi, 67, 89, 101, 119, 123, 212, 213
Maruyama, Izumi, 212
Matlock, Gene, 271
Matsuda, Mitsuhiro, 138
Matsuda, Toshihiko, 211
Mayan Indians, 271
McGovern, George, 184
meditation, 240
Meeting of East and West, The, 111, 112
Meganck, 219, 222
Mendelsohn, Robert, 175
mental disorder, 236
Mitoku Co. Ltd of Tokyo, 186, 213
Mizuno, Nanboku, 26, 238
Monte, Tom, 176
Montevideo, 231
Morant, Soulie, 63
Morinaga Incident, 213
Morishita, Keiichi, 135
Mosaic Law, 256
Muramoto, Noboru, 180, 187
Musō Shokuhin, 186, 209, 211, 213
Musubi, 89, 167

Nachi Katsuura, 212
Nairobi, 123
Nakamura, Eb, 219
Nakayama, Tadanao, 62, 63, 75
National Socialists, 75
natural agriculture, 247, 248
Nazis, 76
Nazism, 75
Nei Ching, 15
Nelissen, Adelbert, 222
Nelissen, Tomas, 223
neo-Confucian, 44
Netelblad, 222
New Inquiry into the Seven Articles on War, A, 97
New Science of Nutrition, The, 93
New York, 132, 137, 164–167

Newbold, Vivien, 178
Newton, John Frank, 265
nightmares, 236
Nihon Shoki, 41
Nihongi, 73
Nippon C.I., 210
Nippon-shugi, 41, 42, 44, 45, 60–62, 65
Nishihata, Manabu, 44
North America Macrobiotic Congress, 175
norito, 73
Northrop, F.S.C., 111
Northrup, Christiane, 175
Notebook for Health, 70

Ogawa, Michi, 67, 89
Ohmori, Hideo, 210
Ohsawa, Chūichi, 104, 115
Ohsawa Foundation, 137, 166, 167
Ohsawa, George, 10, 11, 13, 15, 34, 166, 209, 214
Ohsawa Japan, 186, 211, 213
Ohsawa, Lima, 68, 94, 99, 101, 104, 106, 110, 122, 124, 125, 127, 137, 138, 209, 210
Ohtsu, 91, 92
Okada, Shūzo, 209–211
O'Keeffe, Georgia, 114
Oki, Masahiro, 212
Oles, Lou, 170
Oles, Shane, 170
One Peaceful World, 249
Onna Daigaku, 16
Ono, Yoko, 177
Open Letter to Kennedy and Khrushchev, 136
Order of the Universe, The, 156, 159, 170, 231
Oredson, Olivia, 179
Oroville, 179, 180
Orphic mystery cults, 254
Osaka, 31, 209

Paris, 51, 52, 63, 64, 128, 131, 219, 223
Pasteur, Louis, 24
Paul, Irma, 137
Pesch, Pierre, 225
Physiology of the Japanese Spirit, 43
Portugal, 225
Price, Weston, 271
primitive, 98

Pritikin, Nathan, 272
Proposal for a Human Revolution, 105
Proposal for Lasting World Peace, A, 137
Protocols of the Elders of Zion, The, 74
Pythagoras, 254

Rhodes, 232
rice, 22–26, 32, 44, 67, 73, 90, 105, 161
Rio de Janeiro, 230
Riviere, Francoise, 134, 139, 147
Rohe, Fred, 169
Rolland, Romain, 59, 99
Root, Evan, 168, 171
Rossoff, Michael, 179

Saichō, 122
Sakamoto, Hajime, 66
Sakurazawa, Magotaro, 37
Sakurazawa, Setsuko, 37, 38
Salerno, 260
Sana, 107
Sanae, 171
Sandifer, Jon, 221, 232
Sankhya philosophy, 254
Sams, Craig, 220
Sams, Greg, 220
Sao Paolo, 230
Sarogi, 121
Sattilaro, Anthony, 176
Sachs, Frank, 175
Schumann, Clara, 113, 114
Schweitzer, Albert, 107, 116, 124, 125, 127
Sekai Seifu, 107, 108, 164, 167
Sekai Seishoku Kyōkai, 211
Seven Axioms of "The Order of the Universe", 157
seven conditions of health, 242
Seven Levels of Judgment, 126
Seventh Day Adventists, 184, 269
Seventh Inn, The, 171
Shaw, George Bernard, 265
Shelley, Percy Bysshe, 265
shin-do-fu-ji, 44, 72, 76
Shinran, 40, 57, 100
Shinto, 58, 65, 72–74, 94, 97, 103, 104

292

Shinto as a Natural Medicine, 72
Shoku-Yō, 32, 33, 37, 39, 42–44, 46–48, 51, 52, 58, 66, 69, 70, 72–74, 76, 78, 93
Shoku-Yō Kai, 31, 40, 42–44, 66–68, 70, 80, 89, 92
Shoku-Yō Lectures, The, 43, 47
Shoku-Yō Human Life Reader, The, 78
Shoku-Yō Shimbun, 31
Shun, Mayli Lao, 225
Shun, Zea Lao, 225
Shurtleff, William, 186
Sim, Duncan, 187
Sim, Susan, 187
Simon, Ann, 137
Simon, Paul, 225
Sister White, Ellen Harmon, 269
Snyder, Murray, 179
sodium (Na) and potassium (K), 28–32
Southampton, 133
Spain, 227
Spear, Bill, 179
Spirit of the Primitive Man and the Japanese Spirit, The, 60, 97
Spiritual Olympics, 137
St. Benedict of Nursia, 259
St. Martin-Laten, 131, 222
Standard Diet, 172, 237
Standing on the First Line of the Health War, 92
Stare, Frederick, 168
Ste. Marie-sur-Mer, 132
Steevensz, Roy, 181
Steiner, Rudolph, 129, 261
Stockholm, 229
Story of Flip, The, 113
Sugamoto, Fujiko, 123, 132, 209
Swanson, Gloria, 177
Sweden, 227
Swedish Macrobiotic Society, 228, 229
Switzerland, 225

Tai-Kyoku, 56, 57
Tamura, Toshio, 72, 100
Tannishō, 40, 57, 59
Tao, 47

Tao Books, 171
Tao Te Ching, 15, 16
Taoist, 15
Tara, Bill, 171, 179, 219, 221
Tartiere, 223
Thales, 253
Thoreau, Henry David, 266, 268
Tims, Bill, 179
Tokyo, 42, 43, 133, 138, 209, 211
Transcendentalism, 266, 267
transmutation of elements, 134
Trappists, 259
twelve "theorems" of "Le Principe Unique", 156

Unimave, 226
Unique Principle, 58, 105, 109, 126, 159
Uruguay, 230, 232
Ushio, Moriyasu, 138, 210

Varatojo, Chico, 226
van Cauwenberghe, Marc, 178, 222
van Toorn, Jan, 224, 227, 231
Vega, 179, 180, 182
Vermuyten, Rik, 222
Vieira, Jacinto, 226
Viet Nam, 41, 136
von Hufeland, Christolph Wilhelm, 107, 263, 264
von Liebig, Justus, 24
von Rentzow, Til Dietrich, 224
von Wessenbeck, George, 222

Wakayama, 163
Waroquiers, Mauricio, 231
Waxman, Denny, 176, 179, 221
Wesley, John, 265
Western civilization, 46
Western medicine, 24, 52, 253
Western science, 46, 52, 61, 77
Whitman, Walt, 116, 266
Who are Those Who are Destroying Japan, 92
Why Was Japan Defeated, 105

Wiener Neustadt, 225
With the White Race as Opponent: Why Japan Must Fight, 61
Woman Worker's College, 106
world federalism, 106, 107
World Federalist, 115
World Federalist movement, 106, 163
World Federation of Natural Alternative Medicine, 178

Yamaguchi, Alcan, 166, 210
Yamaguchi, Takuzō, 90
Yamamoto, Shizuko, 167, 187
Yamato-Damashii, 23, 28, 40, 42, 45, 52, 59, 60, 62, 93, 103
Yamazaki, Junsei, 169
Yasuhara, Roland, 222
Yellow Emperor's Classic, 25
Yellow Emperor's Classic of Internal Medicine, The, 15, 238
Yin and Yang, 16, 28, 40, 48, 54–56, 70, 73, 79, 91, 96, 97, 105, 110–113, 120, 128, 132, 135, 154, 156–158, 190, 216, 235, 251
Yōjōkun, 12, 16, 26
Yokohama, 106, 107
Yokohama Worker's College, 106
Yokota, Chiiko (Cornellia), 165
Yokoyama, Tomoko, 164
Yoshimi, Kaoru, 123, 132, 138, 147, 219, 222, 223
You Are All Sanpaku, 167

Zen, 133
Zen Buddhism, 58, 170
Zen Cookery, 169
Zen Macrobiotics, 132, 133, 142, 146, 166, 167, 169, 170, 186
Zionism, 76
Zionist, 75
Zionist movement, 74
Zanata, 230